✠

# ENRICHING
# WORSHIP

✠

Books by A. J. WILLIAM MYERS

THE OLD TESTAMENT IN THE SUNDAY SCHOOL (1912)

TEACHING VALUES OF THE OLD TESTAMENT (1918)

CHRISTIAN LIFE IN THE COMMUNITY (1919)

WHAT IS RELIGIOUS EDUCATION? (1925)
*Translated into Portuguese*

EDUCATIONAL EVANGELISM (1925)

TEACHING RELIGION (1928)

CHRISTIAN EDUCATION IN THE LOCAL CHURCH (1929)

TEACHERS OF RELIGION (1932)

TEACHING RELIGION CREATIVELY (1932)
*Translated into Japanese and Chinese*

HORACE BUSHNELL, AND RELIGIOUS EDUCATION (1937)

RELIGION FOR TODAY (1941)

ENRICHING WORSHIP (1949)


and in collaboration

THE LONDON SURVEY (1913)

RURAL SURVEY (1914)

THE COUNTRY CHURCH AS IT IS (1930)

LIVING STONE (1936)

ADVENTURING WITH KWO YING (1937)

# ENRICHING
# WORSHIP

COMPILED AND EDITED BY

## A. J. WILLIAM MYERS

## HARPER & BROTHERS
PUBLISHERS: NEW YORK

ENRICHING WORSHIP

COPYRIGHT, 1949, BY HARPER & BROTHERS

PRINTED IN THE UNITED STATES OF AMERICA

Special acknowledgment is made to the following, who have granted permission for the reprinting of copyrighted material from the books and periodicals listed below (see also pp. 391-393):

ABINGDON-COKESBURY PRESS for "Christ and History's Voices" from *The Christ of the Indian Road* by E. Stanley Jones, copyright, 1925, by E. Stanley Jones; "Paul's Work" from *Pioneers of the Primitive Church* by Floyd V. Filson, copyright, 1940, by Floyd V. Filson; "Resurrection" (from "Eternal Spring") from *Hilltop Verses and Prayers* by Ralph Spaulding Cushman, copyright, 1945, by Whitmore & Stone.

ADVANCE for "A Dieu! and Au Revoir" by John Oxenham, copyright, 1940, by Advance.

APPLETON-CENTURY-CROFTS for "Faith Is Better than Doubt and Love Is Better than Hate" from *Life and Letters of Sir Wilfred Laurier* by Oscar Douglas Skelton, copyright, 1921, by Appleton-Century-Crofts; and John L. Balderston for "Heaven or Hell" from *A Morality Play for the Leisured Class* by John L. Balderston, copyright, 1920, by Harper & Brothers, 1924, by Appleton-Century-Crofts.

ASSOCIATION PRESS for "More Light and Truth" from *Prayers for Times Like These* by S. Ralph Harlow, copyright, 1942, by Association Press; "The Cross As Symbol," "God's Emerging Plan," "The Living God," "A Prayer," and "Sensitiveness to God" from *Religion for Today* by A. J. William Myers, copyright, 1941, by Association Press.

AUGSBURG PUBLISHING HOUSE for "The Burma Road" from *West China and the Burma Road* by H. D. Friberg, copyright, 1941, by Augsburg Publishing House.

THE BEACON PRESS for "O Church of God, Divided" by Marion Franklin Ham from *Hymns of the Spirit*, copyright, 1932, by The Beacon Press, Inc.

THE BETHANY PRESS for "A Children's Litany of Praise" from the Litany in *Living Stone* by A. J. William Myers and Alma N. Schilling, copyright, 1936, by The Bethany Press; and Lulu Snyder Hamilton for "After Moving into a New House," "For Our Automobile," "On Easter Morning," and "On the Wedding Anniversary" from *God Lives in Homes* by Lulu Snyder Hamilton, copyright, 1942, by The Bethany Press.

THE BOBBS-MERRILL COMPANY, Edmund H. Eitel, Miss Lesley Payne and Mrs. Elizabeth Eitel Miesse for "Away" and "Ike Walton's Prayer" from *Afterwhiles* by James Whitcomb Riley; "Song of the New Year" by James Whitcomb Riley from *Biographical Edition of the Complete Works of James Whitcomb Riley*, copyright, 1912, by The Bobbs-Merrill Company, renewal, 1940, by Edmund H. Eitel, Lesley Payne and Elizabeth Eitel Miesse.

COLUMBIA UNIVERSITY PRESS for the quotations regarding the Psalms from *The Literature of the Old Testament* by Julius A. Bewer, copyright, 1922, 1933, by Columbia University Press.

CENTRAL CONFERENCE OF AMERICAN RABBIS for the following anonymous passages from *Union Prayerbook*, copyright, 1940, by Central Conference of American Rabbis: "Author of Life and Death," "Everliving God," "Fountain of All Good," "The Lord Reigns," "Our Guardian" and "The Triumph of Truth."

THOMAS CURTIS CLARK for "God Give Me Joy" from *God's Dreams* by Thomas Curtis Clark, copyright, 1943, by Thomas Curtis Clark.

[ v ]

[ viii ]

✠

DEDICATED
TO
ALL DIRECTORS OF RELIGIOUS EDUCATION
AND OTHER RELIGIOUS LEADERS
WHO ARE TRYING TO MAKE WORSHIP
ENRICHING AND VITAL IN THE
LIVES OF THE PEOPLE

✠

# CONTENTS

# Introduction

THE COMPILER was for twenty-five years head of the Department of Education in the Hartford Seminary Foundation, Hartford, Connecticut. During that time he worked with students who were ministers, missionaries and directors of religious education or candidates for these professions. He worked with them not only in classes but in churches and religious and social agencies of all kinds. These religious leaders are almost always eager to find varied worship materials but they do not always know just where to find them and seldom have a satisfactory library nor the time to search through a number of books for just what suits their purpose. One result is that worship programs tend to lack variety and to become stereotyped. Prepared worship programs are very valuable but if depended on too much may even hinder the development of leadership and the stimulus to creative worship.

There is great need for a collection of materials culled from scores of sources, varied in form and content, and available between the covers of one book. Such a treasury allows the wise scribe "to bring forth out of his treasure" what best suits the present need and yet to use his own ideas creatively. The leaders are, in this way, able to prepare enriched services for their group.

The materials here presented are not just another collection brought together for sale. The compiler has been collecting worship materials for over twenty years. These have been sifted again and again with the aim (however successfully attained) to retain only what is good literature, in keeping with scientific knowledge, and rich in Christian content. The highly sentimental has been ruled out but not sentiment growing out of actual experience.

The aim also has been to include only what is ethical. Prayers and other writings that implore God to bless us and our family and our cause regardless of character are scarcely Christian and those that beg God to care for the sick and feed the hungry and take the Gospel to the ends of the earth and to do all the work that should be done by our own will and sacrifice are not in accordance with the idea of God which Jesus taught. God is ever doing all that love can do. The Father "worketh even up to now" in history, in the human heart and in nature. It is for us to do our part, to get into the yoke with him that his will may be done on earth as it is in heaven.

The volume is made up of five books or sections:

I. Poetry. This is, naturally, the largest section and is greatly varied.

II. The Psalms for Christian Worship. All the passages in the Psalms that are in keeping with the teaching of Jesus and suitable for Christian worship are here assembled for the first time.

III. *Prose*. It is more difficult to find appropriate short prose passages than it is to find poems, but a fairly wide variety is presented.

IV. *Prayers*. A considerable proportion of the quoted prayers have been slightly altered in keeping with the above principles and the situations confronting worshiping groups today.

V. *Aphorisms*. Worship services are sometimes made memorable by a brief, pithy saying which highlights the essential point of the message.

The compiler found his wife's "Commonplace Book" a mine of choice selections, and in sifting the vast amount of material he depended much on her fine taste and sense of literary and religious values.

His deep gratitude is expressed to a long succession of students and co-workers, especially to those who, along with librarians and stenographers helped him in research and contributed their own discoveries.

A. J. W. M.

January 15, 1949

✠

# ENRICHING

# WORSHIP

✠

# BOOK I
# POETRY

•

## *A Dieu! and Au Revoir!*

As you love me, let there be
No mourning when I go—
No tearful eyes,
No hopeless sighs,
No woe—nor even sadness!
Indeed I would not have you sad,
For I myself shall be full glad,
With the high triumphant gladness
Of a soul made free
Of God's sweet liberty.
—No windows darkened;
For my own
Will be flung wide, as ne'er before,
To catch the radiant inpour
Of Love that shall in full atone
For all the ills that I have done;
And the good things left undone;
—No voices hushed;
My own, full-flushed
With an immortal hope will rise
In ecstasies of new-born bliss
And joyful melodies.
Rather of your sweet courtesy
Rejoice with me
At my soul's loosing from captivity.
Wish me "Bon voyage!"
As you do a friend
Whose joyous visit finds its happy end.
And bid me both "à Dieu!"
And "au revoir!"
Since, though I come no more,
I shall be waiting there to greet you,
At His Door.
And, as the feet of The Bearers tread
The ways I trod,
Think not of me as dead,
But rather—
"Happy, thrice happy, he whose course is sped!
He has gone home—to God,
His Father!"                    —*John Oxenham*

[ 1 ]

## Abou Ben Adhem

ABOU BEN ADHEM (may his tribe increase!)
Awoke one night from a deep dream of peace,
And saw within the moonlight in his room,
Making it rich and like a lily in bloom,
An angel writing in a book of gold;
Exceeding peace had made Ben Adhem bold,
And to the presence in the room he said,
"What writest thou?" The vision raised its head,
And, with a look made of all sweet accord,
Answered, "The names of those who love the Lord."
"And is mine one?" said Abou. "Nay, not so,"
Replied the angel. Abou spoke more low,
But cheerily still, and said, "I pray thee, then,
Write me as one that loves his fellow-men."
The angel wrote, and vanished. The next night
It came again, with a great wakening light,
And showed the names whom love of God had blessed—
And, lo! Ben Adhem's name led all the rest!

—*James Henry Leigh Hunt*


## The After-Death Experience
## of an Unelected Child

AN UNELECTED infant sighed out its little breath,
And wandered thro' the darkness, along the shores of death
Until the gates of heaven, agleam with pearls, it spied,
And ran to them, and clung there, and would not be denied,
Tho' still from earth rose murmurings, "You cannot enter in;
Depart into Gehenna, you child of wrath and sin."

At last the gates were opened; a man with features mild
Stooped down and raised the weeping and unelected child.
Immortal light thrilled softly down the avenue of bliss,
And on the infant's forehead the spirit placed a kiss.
"Who are you, thus to hallow my unelected brow?"
"Dear child, my name was Calvin, but I see things better now."

—*Anonymous*


## The All-Great Is the All-Loving Too

THE very God! think Abib; dost thou think?
So, the All-Great, were the All-Loving too—
So, through the thunder comes a human voice
Saying, "O heart I made, a heart beats here!
Face, my hands fashioned, see it in myself!

[ 2 ]

Thou hast no power nor may'st conceive of mine,
But love I gave thee, with myself to love,
And thou must love me who have died for thee!"
The madman saith He said so: it is strange.[1]
—*Robert Browning*


## All's Well!

Is THE pathway dark and dreary?
   God's in his heaven!
Are you broken, heart-sick, weary?
   God's in his heaven!
Dreariest roads shall have an ending,
Broken hearts are for God's mending.
     All's well! All's well!
       All's . . . well!

Are life's threads all sorely tangled?
   God's in his heaven!
Are the sweet chords strained and jangled?
   God's in his heaven!
Tangled threads are for Love's fingers,
Trembling chords make heaven's sweet singers.
     All's well! All's well!
       All's . . . well!

Is the burden past your bearing?
   God's in his heaven!
Hopeless?—Friendless?—No one caring?
   God's in his heaven!
Burdens shared are light to carry,
Love shall come though long He tarry.
     All's well! All's well!
       All's . . . well!

Is the light for ever failing?
   God's in his heaven!
Is the faint heart ever quailing?
   God's in his heaven!
God's strong arms are all around you,
In the dark he sought and found you.
     All's well! All's well!
       All's . . . well!
         —*John Oxenham*

[1] An epistle containing the strange medical experience of Karshish, the Arab physician.

## All Shrines Are One

I've traveled far in many lands,
    The open road I've trod;
And through the devious ways of men
    I've searched with them for God.

The Ancients found Him in their groves,
    The Wise Men saw the Star.
God comes to some in paths of peace,
    To some in flaming war.

Before the Buddha some men bow;
    Some love the Nazarene.
The mystic feels a presence near,
    Although no form is seen.

On desert sands the vision comes,
    As men turn toward the East,
And while some fasting see His face,
    Some find Him at the feast.

In temple, mosque, cathedral dim,
    Through vigil, chant, and prayer,
Wherever man cries out to God
    The living God is there.

Wherever man has fought for right,
    Where man for man has died;
Beside him stands, could we but see,
    One that was crucified.

Alone I have communed with Him
    Beneath a starlit sky,
And I have touched His garment hem
    Where crowds go thronging by.

And this is clear in all my search,
    As clear as noonday sun;
The name and form are nought to God,
    To him all shrines are one.
            —*Hinton White*

## All the World's a Stage

        ALL the world's a stage,
And all the men and women merely players;
They have their exits and their entrances;
And one man in his time plays many parts,

[ 4 ]

His acts being seven ages. At first the infant,
Mewling and puking in the nurse's arms;
Then the whining school-boy, with his satchel
And shining morning face, creeping like snail
Unwillingly to school. And then the lover,
Sighing like furnace, with a woeful ballad
Made to his mistress' eyebrow. Then a soldier,
Full of strange oaths, and bearded like the pard,
Jealous in honour, sudden and quick in quarrel,
Seeking the bubble reputation
Even in the cannon's mouth. And then the justice,
In fair round belly with good capon lin'd,
With eyes severe and beard of formal cut,
Full of wise saws and modern instances;
And so he plays his part. The sixth stage shifts
Into the lean and slipper'd pantaloon,
With spectacles on nose and pouch on side;
His youthful hose, well sav'd, a world too wide
For his shrunk shank; and his big manly voice,
Turning again toward childish treble, pipes
And whistles in his sound. Last scene of all,
That ends this strange eventful history,
Is second childishness and mere oblivion;
Sans teeth, sans eyes, sans taste, sans everything.
—*William Shakespeare*
(As You Like It)


## And Cheaper, Too!

"You may have what you like," the warden said,
　"Plank steak, caviar, champagne—
The State provides it, you know," he explained.
'Twas not the Law but the man who spoke,
For the hand on the shoulder, the kindly voice
　Were expressions of a friend.

The prisoner's face was drawn and white.
　"Thank you,—thank the State," he replied.
"But now it's too late,"—with a wistful look—
"Had I had a meal and a friendly word
When there was nothing but black despair
　The deed had never been done."

And he spoke a word like a surgeon's knife
　That cuts to Society's heart—
"A meal and a friend are not much to ask
When life has something to gain." Then with

[ 5 ]

A wan smile "Tell the State—tell the Church—
That a friend and a meal would be cheaper, too,
Than to-morrow's electric chair!"
—A. J. William Myers

## And God Was There

LOOK, God, I have never spoken to you,
But now I want to say, "How do you do?"
You see, God, they told me you didn't exist,
And, like a fool, I believed all this.

Last night from a shell hole I saw your sky—
I figured right then they had told me a lie.
Had I taken time to see things you made,
I'd have known they weren't calling a spade a spade.

I wonder, God, if you'd shake my hand;
Somehow, I feel that you will understand,
Funny I had to come to this hellish place
Before I had time to see your face.

Well, I guess there isn't much more to say,
But I'm sure glad, God, I met you today.
I guess the "zero hour" will soon be here,
But I'm not afraid since I know you're near.

The signal! Well, God, I'll have to go;
I like you lots, this I want you to know.

Look, now, this will be a horrible fight—
Who knows, I may come to your house tonight.

Though I wasn't friendly to you before,
I wonder, God, if you'd wait at your door.
Look, I'm crying! Me! Shedding tears—
I wish I had known you these many years.

Well, I have to go now, God. Goodbye!
Strange, since I met you, I'm not afraid to die.[1]
—Anonymous

## Any Wife to Any Husband—Any Husband to Any Wife

How do I love thee? Let me count the ways.
I love thee to the depth and breadth and height
My soul can reach, when feeling out of sight

[1] Found on a soldier killed in action in Italy, 1944.

[ 6 ]

For the ends of Being and ideal Grace.
I love thee to the level of every day's
Most quiet need, by sun and candlelight.
I love thee freely, as men strive for Right;
I love thee purely, as they turn from Praise.
I love thee with the passion put to use
In my old griefs, and with my childhood's faith.
I love thee with a love I seemed to lose
With my lost saints—I love thee with the breath,
Smiles, tears, of all my life!—and, if God choose,
I shall but love thee better after death.

[And the universal longing is to be *told* of love]

Say over again and yet once over again
That thou dost love me. . . .
Cry, "Speak once more, thou lovest!" Who can fear
Too many stars, though each in heaven shall roll,
Too many flowers, though each shall crown the year?
Say thou dost love me, love me, love me—toll
The silver iterance!—only minding, Dear,
To love me also in silence with thy soul.
                              —*Elizabeth Barrett Browning*
                              (Sonnets from the Portuguese)


## April

THE April winds are magical
And thrill our tuneful frames;
The garden walks are passional
To bachelors and dames.
The hedge is gemmed with diamonds,
The air with Cupids full,
The cobweb clues of Rosamond
Guide lovers to the pool.
Each dimple in the water,
Each leaf that shades the rock
Can cozen, pique and flatter,
Can parley and provoke . . .
The south winds are quick-witted,
The schools are sad and slow,
The masters quite omitted
The lore we care to know.
                    —*Ralph Waldo Emerson*


## The Arrow and the Song

I SHOT an arrow into the air,
It fell to earth, I knew not where;

[ 7 ]

For, so swiftly it flew, the sight
Could not follow it in its flight.

I breathed a song into the air,
It fell to earth, I knew not where;
For who has sight so keen and strong,
That it can follow the flight of song?

Long, long afterward, in an oak
I found the arrow, still unbroke;
And the song, from beginning to end,
I found again in the heart of a friend.
—Henry Wadsworth Longfellow

## Aspiration

THESE are the gifts I ask of thee,
                    Spirit serene—
Strength for the daily task;
Courage to face the road;
Good cheer to help me bear the traveler's load;
And for the hours of rest that come between.
An inward joy in all things heard and seen.
These are the sins I fain would have thee take away—
Malice and cold disdain;
Hot anger, sullen hate;
Scorn of the lowly, envy of the great;
And discontent that casts a shadow gray
On all the brightness of a common day.
—Henry van Dyke

## At the Gate of the Year

AND I said to the man who stood at the gate of the year:
"Give me a light that I may tread safely
into the unknown!"
And he replied: "Go out into the darkness
and put your hand into the Hand of God.
That shall be to thee better than light
and safer than a known way."
—M. Louise Haskins

## Autumne

THEN came the Autumne, all in yellow clad,
As though he joyed in his plenteous store,
Laden with fruits that made him laugh, full glad
That he had banisht hunger, which to-fore
Had by the belly oft him pinched sore.

Upon his head a wreath, that was enrold
With eares of corne[1] of every sort, he bore:
And in his hand a sickle he did holde,
To reape the ripened fruits the which the earth
        had yold.

—*Edmund Spenser*
(The Faerie Queen, Book VII, Canto VII)

## Away

I CANNOT say, and I will not say
That he is dead. He is just away.

With a cheery smile, and a wave of the hand,
He has wandered into an unknown land,

And left us dreaming how very fair
It needs must be since he lingers there.

And you—O you, who the wildest yearn
For the old-time step and the glad return—

Think of him faring on, as dear
In the love of there as the love of here;

. . . . . .

Think of him still as the same, I say:
He is not dead—he is just away!

—*James Whitcomb Riley*

## Back of the Loaf

BACK of the loaf is the snowy flour
    And back of the flour is the mill,
Back of the mill is the wheat and the shower,
    The sun—and the Father's will.

Amen.
—*Maltbie Davenport Babcock*

## Bankrupt

ONE midnight, deep in starlight still
I dreamt that I received this bill:
N_____M_____in account with life:
5,000 breathless dawns all new
5,000 flowers fresh with dew;

_____
[1] Wheat and other cereals.

[ 9 ]

5,000 sunsets wrapped in gold;
1,000,000 snowflakes served ice-cold;
100 music-haunted dreams
Of moon-drenched roads and hurrying streams;
Of prophesying winds and trees;
Of silent stars and browsing bees;
One June night in fragrant wood;
One friend I loved and understood.
I wondered when I waked that day
How in the world I ever could pay!
—*Anonymous*

## Battle Clouds Shall Scatter

WHAT of the night, O watchman? Turn to the east thine eyes
And say is there any token of the dawning in the skies?
Or do the shadows linger; thy lips are they sad and dumb
With never a word of gladness that the tarrying morn is come?
Then answered the patient watchman from the mountain's lonely height
To the waiting souls in the valley: I can see the breaking light;
There's a glow on the far horizon that is growing more wide and clear
And soon shall the sun be flinging his splendours both far and near.
What of the night, O watchman, rises to thee our cry;
Thou, O God our Father, dost make to our hearts reply.
Over the earth's wild warfare comes not a time more fair;
Swords into ploughshares beaten, peace throned everywhere?
Wait, said the heavenly Watchman, let not thy spirit quail;
Strife shall not be eternal, harmony shall prevail.
Battle clouds all shall scatter, hatred shall be outcast;
Love's ever-broadening glory break on the world at last.
—*An anthem arranged by J. W. Thompson*

## Battle-Hymn of the Republic

MINE eyes have seen the glory of the coming of the Lord;
He is trampling out the vintage where the grapes of wrath are stored;
He hath loosed the fateful lightning of His terrible swift sword;
His truth is marching on.

I have seen Him in the watch-fires of a hundred circling camps;
They have builded Him an altar in the evening dews and damps;
I can read His righteous sentence by the dim and flaring lamps;
His day is marching on.

I have read a fiery gospel, writ in burnished rows of steel:
"As ye deal with my contemners, so with you my grace shall deal;
Let the Hero, born of woman, crush the serpent with his heel,
Since God is marching on."

He has sounded forth the trumpet that shall never call retreat;
He is sifting out the hearts of men before His judgment-seat:
Oh, be swift, my soul, to answer Him! be jubilant, my feet!
     Our God is marching on.

In the beauty of the lilies Christ was born across the sea,
With a glory in His bosom that transfigures you and me:
As He died to make men holy, let us die to make men free,
     While God is marching on.
         *—Julia Ward Howe*

## Be Then No More by a Storm Dismayed

THAT cause can neither be lost nor stayed
Which takes the course of what God has made;
And is not trusting in walls and towers
But slowly growing from seeds to flowers.

Each noble service that men have wrought
Was first conceived as a fruitful thought;
Each worthy cause with a future glorious
By quietly growing becomes victorious.

Thereby itself like a tree it shows:
That high it reaches, as deep it grows;
And when the storms are its branches shaking
It deeper root in the soil is taking.

Be then no more by a storm dismayed,
For by it the full grown seeds are laid
And though the tree by its might it shatters,
What, then, if thousands of seeds it scatters!
      *—Christian Ostergaard*
      (Danish Folk Song)

## Beauty Everywhere

THE night is beautiful,
So the faces of my people;
The stars are beautiful,
So the eyes of my people;
Beautiful also the sun,
Beautiful also are the souls of my people.
I will not be grieved that other men do not know me,
I will be grieved that I do not know other men.
        *—Anonymous*
      (From the Chinese)

LET praise devote thy work, and skill employ
Thy whole mind, and thy heart be lost in joy.
Well-doing bringeth pride, this constant thought
Humility, that thy best done is nought.
Man doeth nothing well, be it great or small,
Save to praise God; but that hath saved all:
For God requires no more than thou hast done,
And takes thy work to bless it for his own. . . .

Gird on thy sword, O men, thy strength endue,
In fair desire thine earth-born joy renew.
Live thou thy life beneath the making sun
Till Beauty, Truth, and Love in thee are one. . . .

Thy work with beauty crown, thy life with love;
Thy mind with truth uplift to God above:
For whom all is, from whom was all begun,
In whom all Beauty, Truth and Love are one.

—*Robert Bridges*

## Belief in God's Plan

GIVE me, O God, to sing that thought!
Give me—give him or her I love, this quenchless faith
In Thy ensemble. Whatever else withhold, withhold not from us,
Belief in plan of Thee enclosed in Time and Space;
Health, peace, salvation universal.

Is it a dream?
Nay, but the lack of it the dream,
And, failing it, life's lord and wealth a dream,
And all the world a dream.

—*Walt Whitman*

## Benediction

THE sun be warm and kind
To you,
The darkest night, some star
Shine through.
The dullest morn
A radiance brew.
And when dusk comes—
God's hand
To you.

—*Eleanor Powers*

[ 12 ]

## The Better Prayer

I THANK Thee, Lord, for strength of arm
To win my bread,
And that, beyond my need is meat
For friend unfed:
I thank Thee much for bread to live,
I thank Thee more for bread to give.

I thank Thee for my quiet home,
'Mid cold and storm,
And that, beyond my need, is room
For friend forlorn:
I thank Thee much for place to rest,
But more for shelter for my guest.

I thank Thee, Lord, for lavish love
On me bestowed,
Enough to share with loveless folk
To ease their load:
Thy love to me I ill could spare,
Yet dearer is Thy love I share.
                              —*Robert Davis*

## Between Midnight and Morning

You that have faith to look with fearless eyes
    Beyond the tragedy of a world at strife,
And trust that out of night and death shall rise
    The dawn of ampler life;
Rejoice, whatever anguish rend your heart,
    That God has given you, for a priceless dower,
To live in these great times and have your part
    In Freedom's crowning hour;
That you may tell your sons who see the light
    High in the heaven their heritage to take—
"I saw the powers of darkness put to flight!
    I saw the morning break!"
                              —*Owen Seaman*

## The Birds Praise Thee

THOU hearest the nightingale begin the song of spring;
The lark, sitting upon his earthy bed, just as the morn
Appears, listens silent; then, springing from the waving corn-field, loud
He leads the choir of day: trill—trill—trill—trill—
Mounting upon the wings of light into the great expanse,
Re-echoing against the lovely blue and shining heavenly shell
His little throat labours with inspiration; every feather

[ 13 ]

On throat, and breast, and wing, vibrate with the effluence divine,
All nature listens to him silent; and the awful Sun
Stands still upon the mountains, looking on this little bird
With eyes of soft humility, and wonder, love, and awe.
Then loud, from their green covert, all the birds begin their song—
The thrush, the linnet and the goldfinch, robin and the wren,
Awake the Sun from his sweet reverie upon the mountains;
The nightingale again essays his song, and through the day
And through the night warbles luxuriant; every bird of song
Attending his loud harmony with admiration and love.
—*William Blake*

## Blessing of the Road

MAY the hills lie low,
May the sloughs fill up,
In thy way

May all evil sleep,
May all good awake,
In thy way.
—*Anonymous; recovered by Kenneth MacLeod*
(Old Gaelic Rune)

## Break, Break, Break

BREAK, break, break,
On thy cold grey stones, O Sea!
And I would that my tongue could utter
The thoughts that arise in me.

O, well for the fisherman's boy,
That he shouts with his sister at play!
O, well for the sailor lad,
That he sings in his boat on the bay!

And the stately ships go on
To their haven under the hill;
But O, for the touch of a vanish'd hand,
And the sound of a voice that is still!

Break, break, break,
At the foot of thy crags, O Sea!
But the tender grace of a day that is dead
Will never come back to me.
—*Alfred Tennyson*

[ 14 ]

## The Breath of Heaven

WESTWARD I chanced to look, ere yet the night
  Fell on a day of clouds, to note what sign,
  If any, on the horizon night outshine,
Of a fair morrow; and there met my sight
Astonished a long line of silver light
  Off in whose soundless aery depths divine
  Peeped the faint stars, and drew these eyes of mine
Far hence, as native to some orb more bright.

So sometimes come to the tired spirit of man
  Glimpses of rest and home; and for a space
  He feels the breath of heaven upon his face,
  Glad earnest of the glory yet to be,
When Light and Love shall compass earth's round space
  Even as the waters fill the hollow sea.
                                    —*Thomas LePage*


## Build Thee More Stately Mansions

BUILD thee more stately mansions, O my soul,
  As the swift seasons roll!
  Leave thy low-vaulted past!
Let each new temple, nobler than the last,
Shut thee from heaven with a dome more vast,
  Till thou at length art free,
Leaving thine outgrown shell by life's unresting sea!
                            —*Oliver Wendell Holmes*
                            (The Chambered Nautilus)


## Build Us That Better World

THERE's but one gift that all our dead desire,
  One gift that men can give, and that's a dream,
Unless we, too, can burn with that same fire
  Of sacrifice; die to the things that seem;

Die to the little hatreds; die to greed;
  Die to the old ignoble selves we knew;
Die to the base contempts of sect and creed,
  And rise again, like these, with souls as true.

Nay (since these died before their task was finished),
  Attempt new heights, bring even their dreams to birth:-
Build us that better world, oh, not diminished
  By one true splendor that they planned on earth.

And that's not done by sword, or tongue, or pen,
There's but one way. God make us better men.

—*Anonymous*
(New Every Morning)

## The Builders

ALL are architects of Fate,
  Working in these walls of Time;
Some with massive deeds and great,
  Some with ornaments of rhyme.

Nothing useless is, or low;
  Each thing in its place is best;
And what seems but idle show
  Strengthens and supports the rest.

For the structure that we raise,
  Time is with materials filled;
Our to-days and yesterdays
  Are the blocks with which we build.

Truly shape and fashion these;
  Leave no yawning gaps between;
Think not, because no man sees,
  Such things will remain unseen.

In the elder days of art,
  Builders wrought with greatest care
Each minute and unseen part;
  For the Gods see everywhere.

Let us do our work as well,
  Both the unseen and the seen;
Make the house, where Gods may dwell
  Beautiful, entire, and clean.

Else our lives are incomplete,
  Standing in these walls of Time,
Broken stairways, where the feet
  Stumble as they seek to climb.

Build to-day, then, strong and sure,
  With a firm and ample base;
And ascending and secure
  Shall to-morrow find its place.

[ 16 ]

Thus alone can we attain
To those turrets, where the eye
Sees the world as one vast plain,
And one boundless reach of sky.
—*Henry Wadsworth Longfellow*


## Caliban in the Coal Mines

God, we don't like to complain;
We know that the mine is no lark.
But—there's the pools from the rain;
But—there's the cold and the dark.

God, You don't know what it is—
You, in Your well-lighted sky,
Watch, the meteors whizz;
Warm, with the sun always by.

God, if You had but the moon
Stuck in Your cap for a lamp,
Even You'd tire of it soon,
Down in the dark and the damp.

Nothing but blackness above—
And nothing that moves but the cars—
God, if You wish for our love,
Fling us a handful of stars!
—*Louis Untermeyer*


## Canticle of the Sun

O MOST high, almighty, good Lord God, to Thee belong praise, glory, honour, and all blessing!

Praised be my Lord God with all His creatures; and especially our brother the sun, who brings us the day, and who brings us the light; fair is he, and shining with a very great splendour: O Lord, to us he signifies Thee!

Praised be my Lord for our sister the moon, and for the stars, the which He has set clear and lovely in heaven.

Praised be my Lord for our sister the wind, and for air and cloud, calms and all weather, by the which Thou upholdest in life all creatures.

Praised be my Lord for our sister water, who is very serviceable unto us, and humble, and precious, and clean.

[ 17 ]

Praised be my Lord for our brother fire, through whom Thou givest us light in the darkness; and he is bright, and pleasant, and very mighty, and strong.

Praised be my Lord for our mother the earth, the which doth sustain us and keep us, and bringeth forth divers fruits, and flowers of many colours, and grass.

Praised by my Lord for all those who pardon one another for His love's sake, and who endure weakness and tribulation; blessed are they who peaceable shall endure, for Thou, O most Highest, shalt give them a crown!

Praised be my Lord for our sister, the death of the body, from whom no man escapeth. Woe to him who dieth in mortal sin! Blessed are they who are found walking by Thy most holy will, for the second death shall have no power to do them harm.

Praise ye, and bless ye the Lord, and give thanks unto Him, and serve Him with great humility.

—*St. Francis of Assisi; tr. by Matthew Arnold*

## Carcassonne

How old I am! I'm eighty years. I've worked both hard and long,
Yet patient as my life has been, one dearest sight I have not seen,
It almost seems a wrong. A dream I had when life was young.
Alas! our dreams, they come not true.
I thought to see fair Carcassonne,
That lovely city, Carcassonne.

One sees it dimly from the height beyond the mountain blue.
Fain would I walk five weary leagues, I do not mind the road's fatigues,
Through morn and evening's dew.
But bitter frosts would fall at night, and on the grapes that withered blight—
I could not go to Carcassonne,
I never went to Carcassonne.

They say it is as gay all times as holidays at home.
The gentles ride in gay attire, and in the sun each guilded spire
Shoots up like those at Rome.
The bishop the procession leads, the generals curb their prancing steeds.
Alas! I saw not Carcassonne.
Alas! I know not Carcassonne.

Our vicar's right. He preaches loud and bids us to beware.
He says, "Oh, guard the weakest part and most the traitor in the heart
Against ambition's snare."

[ 18 ]

Perhaps in autumn I can find two sunny days with gentle wind,
I then could go to Carcassonne,
I still could go to Carcassonne.

. . . . .

My God and Father, pardon me, if this my wish offends.
One sees some hope more high than he in age, as in his infancy
To which his heart ascends.
My wife, my son have seen Narbonne, my grandson went to Perpignan,
But I have not seen Carcassonne,
But I have not seen Carcassonne.

Thus sighed a peasant bent with age, half dreaming in his chair.
I said, "My friend, come, go with me tomorrow.
Thine eyes shall see those streets that seem so fair."
That night there came for passing soul the church bell's low and solemn
    toll.
He never saw gay Carcassonne.
Who has not known a Carcassonne?
            —*Gustave Nadau; tr. from the French by M. E. W. Sherwood*

## Carol of Beauty

PRAISE we the Lord, who made all beauty
For all our senses to enjoy;
Owe we our humble thanks and duty
That simple pleasures never cloy;
Praise we the Lord who made all beauty
For all our senses to enjoy.

Praise him who makes our life a pleasure,
Sending us things which glad our eyes;
Thank him who gives us welcome leisure,
That in our heart sweet thoughts may rise;
Praise him who makes our life a pleasure
Sending us things which glad our eyes.

Praise him who loves to see young lovers,
Fresh hearts that swell with youthful pride;
Thank him who sends the sun above us,
As bridegroom fit to meet his bride;
Praise him who loves to see young lovers,
Fresh hearts that swell with youthful pride.

Praise him who by a simple flower
Lifts up our hearts to things above;
Thank him who gives to each one power
To find a friend to know and love;

Praise him who by a simple flower
Lifts up our hearts to things above.

Praise we the Lord who made all beauty
For all our senses to enjoy;
Give we our humble thanks and duty
That simple pleasures never cloy;
Praise we the Lord who made all beauty
For all our senses to enjoy.

*—Steuart Wilson*

## Carpenter, Vagabond, Felon, Jew

· · · · ·

JESUS whose lot with us was cast,
Who saw it out from first to last:
Patient and fearless, tender, true,
Carpenter, vagabond, felon, Jew;
Who, as your hour neared, did not fail—
The world's fate trembling in the scale—
With your half-hearted band to dine,
And chat across the bread and wine;
Then went out firm to face the end,
Alone, without a single friend:
Who felt, as your last words confessed,
Wrung from a proud, unflinching breast
By hours of dull, ignoble pain,
Your whole life's fight was fought in vain:
Would I could win and keep and feel
That heart of love, that spirit of steel.

*—Anonymous*

## The Celestial Surgeon

IF I HAVE faltered more or less
In my great task of happiness;
If I have moved among my race
And shown no glorious morning face;
If beams from happy human eyes
Have moved me not; if morning skies,
Books, and my food, and summer rain
Knocked on my sullen heart in vain—
Lord, thy most pointed pleasure take
And stab my spirit broad awake;
Or, Lord, if too obdurate I,
Choose thou, before that spirit die,
A piercing pain, a killing sin,
And to my dead heart run them in!

*—Robert Louis Stevenson*

[ 20 ]

## Chant Out of Doors

GOD of grave nights,
God of brave mornings,
God of silent noon,
Hear my salutation!

For where the rapids rage white and scornful,
I have passed safely, filled with wonder;
Where the sweet pools dream under the willows,
I have been swimming, filled with life.

God of round hills,
God of green valleys,
God of clear springs,
Hear my salutation!

For where the moose feeds, I have eaten berries,
Where the moose drinks, I have drunk deep.
When the storm crashed through broken heavens—
And under clear skies—I have known joy.

God of great trees,
God of wild grasses,
God of little flowers,
Hear my salutation!

For where the deer crops and the beaver plunges,
Near the river I have pitched my tent;
Where the pines cast aromatic needles
On a still floor, I have known peace.

God of grave nights,
God of brave mornings,
God of silent noon,
Hear my salutation!

—*Marguerite Wilkinson*


## The Chapel

HERE is a quiet room!
Pause for a little space;
And in the deepening gloom
With hands before thy face,
Pray for God's grace.

Let no unholy thought
Enter thy musing mind;

Things that the world has wrought—
Unclean—untrue—unkind—
Leave them behind.

Pray for the strength of God,
Strength to obey His plan;
Rise from thy knees less clod
Than when thy prayer began,
More of a man.

—*S. Donald Cox*

## Chartless

I NEVER saw a moor,
I never saw the sea;
Yet know I how the heather looks,
And what a wave must be.

I never spoke with God,
Nor visited in heaven;
Yet certain am I of the spot
As if the chart were given.

—*Emily Dickinson*

## The Choir Invisible

O, MAY I join the choir invisible
Of those immortal dead who live again
In minds made better by their presence: live
In pulses stirred to generosity,
In deeds of daring rectitude, in scorn
For miserable aims that end with self,
In thoughts sublime that pierce the night like stars,
And with their mild persistence urge man's search
To vaster issues.

. . . . .

May I reach
That purest heaven; be to other souls
The cup of strength in some great agony,
Enkindle generous ardor, feed pure love;
Beget the smiles that have no cruelty,
Be the sweet presence of a good diffused,
And in diffusion ever more intense!
So shall I join the choir invisible
Whose music is the gladness of the world.

—*George Eliot*

[ 22 ]

## Christmas Bells

I HEARD the bells on Christmas Day
Their old familiar carols play,
   And wild and sweet
   The words repeat,
Of "Peace on earth, good will to men!"

And thought how, as the day had come,
The belfries of all Christendom
   Had rolled along
   The unbroken song,
Of "Peace on earth, good will to men!"

    . . . . .

And in despair I bowed my head;
"There is no peace on earth," I said,
   "For hate is strong
   And mocks the song
Of peace on earth, good will to men!"

Then pealed the bells more loud and deep:
"God is not dead; nor doth he sleep!
   The wrong shall fail,
   The right prevail,
With peace on earth, good-will to men!"
        —*Henry Wadsworth Longfellow*

## Christmas Carol

THE earth has grown old with its burden of care,
   But at Christmas it always is young;
The heart of the jewel burns lustrous and fair,
And its soul full of music breaks forth on the air,
   When the song of the angels is sung.

It is coming, Old Earth, it is coming tonight!
   On the snowflakes which cover thy sod.
The feet of the Christ-child fall gentle and white,
And the voice of the Christ-child tells out with delight
   That mankind are the Children of God.

On the sad and the lonely, the wretched and poor,
   That voice of the Christ-child shall fall;
And to every blind wanderer open the door
Of a hope that he dared not to dream of before,
   With a sunshine of welcome for all.

The feet of the humblest may walk in the field
　Where the feet of the Holiest trod;
This, then is the marvel to mortals revealed
When the silvery trumpets of Christmas have pealed,
　That mankind are the children of God.
—Phillips Brooks

## The Church of My Dreams

THIS is the church of my dreams:
The church of the warm heart,
Of the open mind,
Of the adventurous spirit;
The church that cares,
That heals hurt lives,
That comforts old people,
That challenges youth;
That knows no divisions of culture or class,
No frontiers, geographical or social;
The church that inquires as well as avers,
That looks forward as well as backward,
The church of the Master,
The church of the people,
High as the ideals of Jesus,
Low as the humblest human;
A working church,
A worshiping church,
A winsome church,
A church that interprets the truth in terms of truth;
That inspires courage for this life and hope for the life to come;
A church of courage,
A church of all good men,
The church of the living God.
—John Milton Moore

## City of the Light

AND the work that we have builded,
　Oft with bleeding hands and tears,
Oft in error, oft in anguish,
　Will not perish with our years:
It will live and shine transfigured
　In the final reign of Right:
It will pass into the splendors
　Of the City of the Light.
—Felix Adler
(Hail the Glorious Golden City)

[ 24 ]

## Cling to Thy Home

CLING to thy home! If there the meanest shed
Yield thee a hearth and shelter for thy head,
And some poor plot, with vegetables stored,
Be all that Heaven allots thee for thy board,
Unsavory bread, and herbs that scattered grow
Wild on the river-brink or mountain-brow;
Yet e'en this cheerless mansion shall provide
More heart's repose than all the world beside.

*—Leonidas*[1]

## Columbus

BEHIND him lay the gray Azores,
  Behind the gates of Hercules;
Before him not the ghost of shores,
  Before him only shoreless seas.
The good mate said: "Now we must pray,
  For, lo! the very stars are gone.
Brave Adm'r'l, speak; what shall I say?"
  "Why say: 'Sail on! sail on! and on!' "

"My men grow mutinous day by day;
  My men grow ghastly wan and weak."
The stout mate thought of home; a spray
  Of salt wave washed his swarthy cheek.
"What shall I say, brave Adm'r'l, say,
  If we sight naught but seas at dawn?"
"Why, you shall say, at break of day:
  'Sail on! sail on! sail on! and on!' "

They sailed and sailed as winds might blow,
  Until at last the blanched mate said:
"Why, now not even God would know
  Should I and all my men fall dead.
These very winds forget the way,
  For God from these dread seas is gone.
Now speak, brave Adm'r'l, speak and say—"
  He said: "Sail on! sail on! and on!"

They sailed. They sailed. Then spake the mate:
  "This mad sea shows his teeth to-night;
He curls his lip, he lies in wait,
  With lifted teeth as if to bite:
Brave Adm'r'l, say but one good word;
  What shall we do when hope is gone?"

[1] A Greek poet of Tarentum, c. 300 B.C.

[ 25 ]

The words leapt as a leaping sword:
"Sail on! sail on! sail on! and on!"

Then, pale and worn, he kept his deck
  And peered through darkness. Ah, that night
Of all dark nights! And then, a speck—
  A light! a light! a light! a light!
It grew, a starlight shore[1] unrolled!
  It grew to be time's burst of dawn,
He gained a world; he gave that world
  Its greatest lesson: "On! sail on!"
—Joaquin Miller

## Come, Seek a Newer World

The last lines from "Ulysses" are engraved on a cross erected when Captain Scott and a number of his party lost their lives on their return from the South Pole. The poet is saying that old age as well as youth has its adventure.

There lies the port; the vessel puffs her sail;
There gloom the dark, broad seas. My mariners,
Souls that have toil'd, and wrought, and thought with me,—
That ever with a frolic welcome took
The thunder and the sunshine, and opposed
Free hearts, free foreheads,—you and I are old;
Old age hath yet his honor and his toil:
Death closes all; but something ere the end,
Some work of noble note, may yet be done,
Not unbecoming men that strove with Gods.
The lights begin to twinkle from the rocks;
The long day wanes; the slow moon climbs; the deep
Moans round with many voices. Come, my friends,
'Tis not too late to seek a newer world.
Push off, and sitting well in order smite
The sounding furrows; for my purpose holds
To sail beyond the sunset, and the baths
Of all the western stars, until I die.
It may be that the gulfs will wash us down;
It may be we shall touch the Happy Isles,
And see the great Achilles, whom we knew.
Tho 'much is taken, much abides; and tho'
We are not now that strength which in old days
Moved earth and heaven, that which we are, we are,—
One equal temper of heroic hearts,
Made weak by time and fate, but strong in will
To strive, to seek, to find, and not to yield.
—Alfred Tennyson

[1] Two words changed.

## Cometh Earth's Latest Hour

COMETH earth's latest hour,
Evil hath mightiest power;
Nor watch we ever,
Keep we vigil!

Lo, the great Judge appears!
O'er the unfolding years,
Watching forever.

Mightest, mightiest,
He is made manifest,
Right ever crowning.

True hearts in mansion fair,
Free from all anxious care,
Ever enthroning,
Keep we vigil!

Bears he the painful goad,
Lightens the heavy load,
Heavy it must be.

Giveth the rich reward,
Meteth the penance hard,
Each given justly.
—*Anonymous, from Hora Novissima*

## The Coming of the Trees

"LET trees be made, for the Earth is bare,"
Spake the voice of the Lord in thunder.
The roots ran deep and the trees were there
And Earth was full of wonder!

For the white birch leaned, the oak held straight,
The pines marched down the mountain;
The orchards bowed with their blossomed weight
And the elms rose up like a fountain.

The palm stood proud as Aaron's rod,
The willow billowed slowly;
So came the trees at the call of God,
And all the trees are holy.
—*Arthur Guiterman*

[ 27 ]

# Content

MY CROWN is in my heart, not on my head;
Not deck'd with diamonds, and Indian stone
Nor to be seen: my crown is called Content;
A crown it is that seldom Kings enjoy.
*—William Shakespeare*
(King Henry VI)


## The Cotter's Saturday Night

THE toil-worn Cotter frae his labor goes—
This night his weekly moil is at an end,
    Collects his spades, his mattocks, and his hoes,
Hoping the morn in ease and rest to spend,
And weary, o'er the moor, his course does homeward bend.

At length his lonely cot appears in view,
    Beneath the shelter of an aged tree;
Th' expectant wee-things, toddlin, stacher through
    To meet their dad, wi'flichterin' noise and glee.
    His wee bit ingle, blinkin bonilie,
His clean hearth-stane, his thrifty wifie's smile,
    The lisping infant, prattling on his knee,
Does a'his weary kiaugh and care beguile,
And makes him quite forget his labor and his toil.

· · · · ·

The chearfu' supper done, wi' serious face,
    They, round the ingle, form a circle wide;
The sire turns o'er, wi' patriarchal grace,
    The big ha'—Bible, ance his father's pride.
    His bonnet rev'rently is laid aside,
His lyart haffets wearing thin and bare;
    Those strains that once did sweet in Zion glide,
He wales a portion with judicious care,
And 'Let us worship God!' he says, with solemn air.

· · · · ·

The priest-like father reads the sacred page,
    How Abram was the friend of God on high;
Or, Moses bade eternal warfare wage
    With Amalek's ungracious progeny;
    Or, how the royal Bard did groaning lie
Beneath the stroke of Heaven's avenging ire;
    Or Job's pathetic plaint, and wailing cry;
Or rapt Isaiah's wild seraphic fire;
Or other holy Seers that tune the sacred lyre.

[ 28 ]

Perhaps the Christian volume is the theme:
  How guiltless blood for guilty man was shed;
How he, who bore in Heaven the second name,
  Had not on earth whereon to lay his head;
  How his first followers and servants sped;
The precepts sage they wrote to many a land:
  How he, who lone in Patmos banishèd,
Saw in the sun a mighty angel stand,
And heard great Bab'lon's doom pronounc'd by Heaven's command.

Then kneeling down to Heaven's Eternal King,
  The saint, the father, and the husband prays:
Hope 'springs exulting on triumphant wing,'
  That thus they all shall meet in future days,
  There, ever bask in uncreated rays,
No more to sigh or shed the bitter tear,
  Together hymning their Creator's praise,
In such society, yet still more dear;
While circling Time moves round in an eternal sphere.

· · · · ·

From scenes like these, old Scotia's grandeur springs,
  That makes her loved at home, rever'd abroad.
                                        —*Robert Burns*


## The Courage of the Lost

THERE be who are afraid to fear,
  The myrmidons of Hope!
Their watchword cannot lend me cheer
  'Gainst that with which I cope!

There is a courage of the lost,
  Who sail uncharted seas,
Past many a firm or flying coast,
  And I must sail with these.

There is a valor of the slain,
  Who strive past mortal sight
While their spent corses strew the plain,
  And I must fight their fight.

Hast thou that courage of the lost,
  Past theirs, that reach their goal?
Whoe'er thou art, I thee accost—
  Thou Comrade of my Soul!

[ 29 ]

Thou dost not fear to fear—ah, no!
The depths wilt thou descend;
And when thy planet sinketh low
Wilt make of Night a friend!
—*Edith M. Thomas*


## A Craftsman's Creed

I HOLD with none who think not work a boon
Vouchsafed to man that he may aid his Kind
With offerings from his chisel, wheel or loom
Fashioned with loving heart and loving mind.

All of the fine traditions and the skill
Come from my elders through the long line down
Are mine to use to raise our craft's renown
And mine to teach again with reverent will.

Thus do I live to serve, though least for pay,
With fingers which are masters of the tool
And eyes which light to see the pattern's play
As it unfolds, obedient to each rule

Of our dear Art. So all my craft is praise
To God—at once part homage and part song.
My work's my prayer, I sing the whole day long
As Faith and Beauty shape the forms I raise.
—*Anonymous*


## Crossing the Bar

SUNSET and evening star,
    And one clear call for me!
And may there be no moaning of the bar,
    When I put out to sea,

But such a tide as moving seems asleep,
    Too full for sound and foam,
When that which drew from out the boundless deep
    Turns again home.

Twilight and evening bell,
    And after that the dark!
And may there be no sadness of farewell,
    When I embark;

[ 30 ]

For tho' from out our bourne of Time and Place
  The flood may bear me far,
I hope to see my Pilot face to face
  When I have crosst the bar.

—Alfred Tennyson

## Crusaders for Truth

CRUSADERS for truth!
Youth,
Untangle your banners
And set them high
Over the shoulders of
Men
Who die,
Over determined marching feet
Travelling a woodpath or
Busy street.
"Forward" the slogan
Of God, our King;
"Forward!" And youth,
You shall make it
Ring.
Crusaders for Christ,
For truth![1]

—Anonymous

(Church School Hymnal for Youth)


## Daffodils

I WANDERED lonely as a cloud
  That floats on high o'er vales and hills,
When all at once I saw a crowd,
  A host, of golden daffodils,
Beside the lake, beneath the trees,
Fluttering and dancing in the breeze.

Continuous as the stars that shine
  And twinkle on the Milky Way,
They stretched in never-ending line
  Along the margin of a bay;
Ten thousand saw I at a glance,
Tossing their heads in sprightly dance.

The waves beside them danced, but they
  Out-did the sparkling waves in glee:

[1] Slightly altered.

[ 31 ]

A poet could not but be gay
    In such a jocund company.
I gazed, and gazed, but little thought
What wealth the show to me had brought:

For oft, when on my couch I lie
    In vacant or in pensive mood,
They flash upon that inward eye
    Which is the bliss of solitude;
And then my heart with pleasure fills,
And dances with the daffodils.
                    —*William Wordsworth*


## The Dark Cat

THE dark cat, Death,
Caught me in youth and claimed me;
His sharp bright teeth bit through
Sinew and bone and maimed me—
Then let me go, to run
My staggering course, and feel
The glory of the sun
That warmed but could not heal.
—Ah, well! he had his sport, he never tamed me.

All the quicksilver, wild,
Unweighed, unstinted rapture of the child,
Filling the veins with wine,
Still, still is mine.
I loved to run, I love it yet; but now
My heart, whole and complete,
Outruns my feet
To dance where danced the shadow of the bough.
Here where the vines are laced with vivid green—
Here where are seen
The spider-webs all glittering-strung with dew,
Wheel-within-wheel of diamonds—here anew
I stand to look and feast my soul and still
I have not looked my fill.
If ever earth ran down, if any day
Was like another day,
And God forgot to make the fruit trees gay
With petalled pearl-and-rose
Spilling their windy snows—
Why then, who knows?
I might forget to feel my spirit whole,
Who have immortal April in my soul.

O Death, your mouse
Is given the freedom of so fair a house,
A house so high,
Pillared with pines, roofed with the changing sky!
Though through green leaves I see
The glimmer of your green eyes watching me,
And feel your following breath—
I cannot fear you, Death.

You should have closed my ears and shut my sight
Before I looked on light,
Before I had begun.
You should have taken me away too soon
To count the silvery changes of the moon,
To coin the golden sun.
Then, then you might have had a victory
That now belongs to me.
More lovely is the light
To one that knew the darkness, and that knows
The dark to which he goes—
A little dark, dissolved in clearer sight.
Too confident by half,
You'll snatch brief triumph from your last endeavor;
For when you pounce, I'll laugh
—The last laugh's mine!—and so escape forever.
—*Audrey Alexandra Brown*

## Day

Day!
Faster and more fast,
O'er night's brim, day boils at last;
Boils, pure gold . . .
But forth one wavelet, then another, curled,
'Till the whole sunrise, not to be suppressed,
Rose, reddened, and its seething breast
Flickered in bounds, grew gold, then overflowed the world.
—*Robert Browning*
(Pippa Passes)

## Dear Lord and Father of Mankind

Dear Lord and Father of mankind!
    Forgive our foolish ways!
Reclothe us in our rightful mind,
In purer lives Thy service find,
    In deeper reverence, praise.

[ 33 ]

In simple trust like theirs who heard
  Beside the Syrian sea,
The gracious calling of the Lord,
Let us, like them, without a word,
  Rise up and follow Thee.

O Sabbath rest by Galilee!
  O calm of hills above,
Where Jesus knelt to share with thee
The silence of eternity
  Interpreted by love!

With that deep hush subduing all
  Our words and works that drown
The tender whisper of Thy call,
As noiseless let Thy blessing fall
  As fell Thy manna down.

Drop Thy still dews of quietness,
  Till all our strivings cease;
Take from our souls the strain and stress,
And let our ordered lives confess
  The beauty of Thy peace.

Breathe through the heats of our desire
  Thy coolness and Thy balm;
Let sense be dumb, let flesh retire;
Speak through the earthquake, wind, and fire,
  O still, small voice of calm!
                —*John Greenleaf Whittier*
              (The Brewing of Soma)

## Death Thou Shalt Die

DEATH, be not proud, though some have called thee
Mighty and dreadful, for thou art not so:
For those whom thou think'st thou dost overthrow
Die not, poor Death; nor yet canst thou kill me.
From rest and sleep, which but thy picture be,
Much pleasure; then from thee much more must flow;
And soonest our best men with thee do go—
Rest of their bones and souls' delivery!
Thou'rt slave to fate, chance, kings, and desperate men,
And dost with poison, war, and sickness dwell;
And poppy or charms can make us sleep as well
And better than thy stroke. Why swell'st thou then?
  One better sleep past, we wake eternally,
  And Death shall be no more: Death, thou shalt die!
                    —*John Donne*

## The Deed, the Deed

LORD, not for light in darkness do we pray,
Not that the veil be lifted from our eyes,
Nor that the slow ascension of our day
    Be otherwise.

Not for a clearer vision of the things
Whereof the fashioning shall make us great,
Not for remission of the peril and stings
    Of time and fate.

Not for a fuller knowledge of the end
Whereto we travel, bruised yet unafraid,
Nor that the little healing that we lend
    Shall be repaid.

Not these, O Lord. We would not break the bars
Thy wisdom sets about us; we shall climb
Unfettered to the secrets of the stars
    In Thy good time.

. . . . .

Grant us the will to fashion as we feel,
Grant us the strength to labour as we know,
Grant us the purpose, ribbed and edged with steel,
    To strike the blow.

Knowledge we ask not—knowledge Thou hast lent;
But Lord, the will—there lies our bitter need,
Give us to build above the deep intent
    The deed, the deed.
            —*John Drinkwater*

## The Divine Image

To MERCY, Pity, Peace, and Love
All pray in their distress;
And to these virtues of delight
Return their thankfulness.

For Mercy, Pity, Peace, and Love
Is God, our Father dear,
And Mercy, Pity, Peace, and Love
Is man, His child and care.

For Mercy has a human heart,
Pity a human face,

And Love, the human form divine,
And Peace, the human dress.

Then every man, of every clime,
That prays in his distress,
Prays to the human form divine,
Love, Mercy, Pity, Peace.

And all must love the human form,
In heathen, Turk, or Jew;
Where Mercy, Love, and Pity dwell,
There God is dwelling too.
                              —*William Blake*

## Divinity Stirs Within Us

IT MUST be so—Plato, thou reason'st well—
Else whence this pleasing hope, this fond desire,
This longing after immortality?
Or whence this secret dread, and inward horror
Of falling into nought? Why shrinks the Soul
Back on herself, and startles at destruction?
'Tis the Divinity that stirs within us;
'Tis Heav'n itself, that points out a hereafter,
And intimates eternity to man. . . .
Here will I hold. If there's a power above us,
(And that there is, all Nature cries aloud
Through all her works,) He must delight in virtue;
And that which He delights in must be happy. . . .
The Soul, secured in her existence, smiles
At the drawn dagger, and defies its point;
The stars shall fade away, the Sun himself
Grow dim with age, and Nature sink in years;
But thou shalt flourish in immortal youth,
Unhurt amidst the war of elements,
The wreck of matter and the crash of worlds.
                              —*Joseph Addison*

## Dreamers

WHERE weary folk toil, black with smoke,
And hear but whistles scream,
I went, all fresh from dawn and dew,
To carry them a dream.
I went to bitter lanes, and dark,
Who once had known the sky—
To carry them a dream—and found
They had more dreams than I.
                              —*Mary Carolyn Davies*

[ 36 ]

## Each in His Own Tongue

A FIRE-MIST and a planet,
  A crystal and a cell,
A jelly-fish and a saurian,
  And caves where the cave-men dwell;
Then a sense of law and beauty
  And a face turned from the clod,—
Some call it Evolution,
  And others call it God.

A haze on the far horizon,
  The infinite, tender sky,
The ripe, rich tint of the cornfields,
  And the wild geese sailing high;
And all over upland and lowland
  The charm of the golden-rod,—
Some of us call it Autumn,
  And others call it God.

Like tides on a crescent sea-beach,
  When the moon is new and thin,
Into our hearts high yearnings
  Come welling and surging in:
Come from the mystic ocean
  Whose rim no foot has trod,—
Some of us call it Longing,
  And others call it God.

A picket frozen on duty,
  A mother starved for her brood,
Socrates drinking the hemlock,
  And Jesus on the rood;
And millions who, humble and nameless,
  The straight, hard pathway plod,—
Some call it Consecration,
  And others call it God.
              —*William H. Carruth*


## Early Spring

ONCE more the Heavenly Power
  Makes all things new,
And domes the red-plow'd hills
  With loving blue;
The blackbirds have their wills,
  The throstles too.

· · · · ·

[ 37 ]

The woods with living airs
　　How softly fann'd,
Light airs from where the deep,
　　All down the sand,
Is breathing in his sleep,
　　Heard by the land.

O follow, leaping blood,
　　The season's lure!
O heart, look down and up,
　　Serene, secure,
Warm as the crocus cup,
　　Like snowdrops, pure!

　　　. . . . .

For now the Heavenly Power
　　Makes all things new,
And thaws the cold, and fills
　　The flower with dew;
The blackbirds have their wills,
　　The poets too.
　　　　　　　　　*—Alfred Tennyson*


## The Earth and Man

A LITTLE sun, a little rain,
　　A soft wind blowing from the west—
And woods and fields are sweet again,
　　And warmth within the mountain's breast.

So simple is the earth we tread,
　　So quick with love and life her frame,
Ten thousand years have dawned and fled,
　　And still her magic is the same.

A little love, a little trust,
　　A soft impulse, a sudden dream—
And life as dry as desert dust
　　Is fresher than a mountain stream.

So simple is the heart of man,
　　So ready for new hope and joy;
Ten thousand years since it began
　　Have left it younger than a boy.
　　　　　　　　　*—Stopford Brooke*

## Earth's Common Things

SEEK not afar for beauty. Lo! it glows
  In dew-wet grasses all about thy feet;
  In birds, in sunshine, childish faces sweet,
In stars and mountain summits topped with snow.

Go not abroad for happiness. For see,
  It is a flower that blooms at thy door.
  Bring love and justice home, and then no more
Thou'lt wonder in what dwelling joy may be.

Dream not of noble service elsewhere wrought;
  The simple duty that awaits thy hand
  Is God's voice uttering a divine command,
Life's common deeds build all that saints have thought.

In wonder-workings, or some bush aflame,
  Men look for God and fancy him concealed;
  But in earth's common things he stands revealed
While grass and flowers and stars spell out his name.
          —*Minot J. Savage*

## Earth's Crammed with Heaven

EARTH'S crammed with heaven,
And every common bush afire with God;
But only he who sees, takes off his shoes,
The rest sit round it and pluck blackberries.
          —*Elizabeth Barrett Browning*

## An Easter Canticle

IN EVERY trembling bud and bloom
  That cleaves the earth, a flowery sword,
I see Thee come from out the tomb,
  Thou risen Lord.

In every April wind that sings
  Down lanes that make the heart rejoice;
Yea, in the word the wood thrush brings
  I hear Thy voice.

Lo! every tulip is a cup
  To hold Thy morning's brimming wine;
Drink, O my soul, the wonder up—
  Is it not Thine?

[ 39 ]

The great Lord God, invisible,
  Hath roused to rapture the green grass;
Through sunlit mead and dew-drenched dell
  I see Him pass.

His old immortal glory wakes
  The rushing streams and emerald hills;
His ancient trumpet softly shakes
  The daffodils.

Thou art not dead! Thou art the whole
  Of Life that quickens in the sod;
Green April is Thy very soul,
  Thou great Lord God!
        —*Charles Hanson Towne*

## Easter Carol

CHEER up, friends and neighbors,
  Now it's Easter tide;
Stop from endless labors
  Worries put aside:
Men should rise from sadness,
Evil, folly, strife,
When God's mighty gladness
  Brings the earth to life.

Out from snowdrifts chilly,
  Roused from drowsy hours,
Bluebell wakes, and lily;
  God calls up the flowers!
Into life he raises
  All the sleeping buds;
Meadows weave his praises,
  And the spangled woods.

All his truth and beauty,
  All his righteousness,
Are our joy and duty,
  Bearing his impress:
Look! the earth waits breathless
  After Winter's strife:
Easter shows man deathless,
  Spring leads death to life.

Ours the more and less is;
  But, changeless all the days,
God revives and blesses,
  Like the sunlight rays.

"All mankind is risen,"
  The Easter bells do ring,
While from out their prison
  Creep the flowers of Spring!
  —*Anonymous; tr. by Percy Dearmer*


## An Elegy

THE curfew tolls the knell of parting day,
  The lowing herd winds slowly o'er the lea,
The ploughman homeward plods his weary way,
  And leaves the world to darkness and to me.

Now fades the glimmering landscape on the sight,
  And all the air a solemn stillness holds,
Save where the beetle wheels his droning flight,
  And drowsy tinklings lull the distant folds;

Save that from yonder ivy-mantled tower,
  The moping owl does to the moon complain
Of such as, wandering near her secret bower,
  Molest her ancient solitary reign.

. . . . .

For them no more the blazing hearth shall burn,
  Or busy housewife ply her evening care;
No children run to lisp their sire's return,
  Or climb his knees the envied kiss to share.

Oft did the harvest to their sickle yield,
  Their furrow oft the stubborn glebe has broke;
How jocund did they drive their team afield!
  How bowed the woods beneath their sturdy stroke!

Let not ambition mock their useful toil,
  Their homely joys, and destiny obscure;
Nor grandeur hear with a disdainful smile,
  The short and simple annals of the poor.

The boast of heraldry, the pomp of power,
  And all that beauty, all that wealth e'er gave,
Await alike th' inevitable hour.
  The paths of glory lead but to the grave.

. . . . .

Full many a gem of purest ray serene
  The dark unfathomed caves of ocean bear:
Full many a flower is born to blush unseen,
And waste its sweetness on the desert air.

[ 41 ]

Some village Hampden, that, with dauntless breast
　　The little tyrant of his fields withstood;
Some mute inglorious Milton here may rest,
　　Some Cromwell guiltless of his country's blood.

. . . . .

Far from the madding crowd's ignoble strife,
　　Their sober wishes never learn'd to stray;
Along the cool sequestered vale of life
　　They kept the noiseless tenor of their way.
　　　　　　　　　　　　　　　　—*Thomas Gray*

## Enchanted Fire

I NEVER knew the earth had so much gold—
　　The fields run over with it, and this hill
Hoary and old,
　　Is young with buoyant blooms that flame and thrill.

Such golden fires, such yellow—lo, how good
　　This spendthrift world, and what a lavish God!
This fringe of wood,
　　Blazing with buttercup and goldenrod.
　　　　　　　　　　　　　　　　—*Louis Untermeyer*
　　　　　　　　　　　　　　　　(Feuerzauber)

## Endymion

A THING of beauty is a joy for ever:
Its loveliness increases; it will never
Pass into nothingness; but still will keep
A bower quiet for us, and a sleep
Full of sweet dreams, and health, and quiet breathing.
Therefore, on every morrow, are we wreathing
A flowery band to bind us to the earth,
Spite of despondence, of the inhuman dearth
Of noble natures, of the gloomy days,
Of all the unhealthy and o'er-darkened ways
Made for our searching: yes, in spite of all,
Some shape of beauty moves away the pall
From our dark spirits. Such the sun, the moon,
Trees old—and young, sprouting a shady boon
For simple sheep; and such are daffodils
With the green world they live in; the clear rills
That for themselves a cooling covert make
'Gainst the hot season; the mid forest brake,
Rich with a sprinkling of fair musk-rose blooms:
And such too is the grandeur of the dooms
We have imagined for the mighty dead;
All lovely tales that we have heard or read;

[ 42 ]

And endless fountain of immortal drink,
Pouring unto us from the heaven's brink.

Nor do we merely feel these essences
For one short hour; no, even as the trees
That whisper round a temple become soon
Dear as the temple's self, so does the moon,
The passion poesy, glories infinite,
Haunt us till they become a cheering light
Unto our souls, and bound to us so fast,
That, whether there be shine, or gloom o'ercast,
They always must be with us, or we die.

—*John Keats*

## An Epitaph

LET us not think of our departed dead
　As caught and cumbered in these graves of earth;
　But think of death as of another birth,
As a new freedom for the wings outspread,
A new adventure waiting on ahead,
　As a new joy of more ethereal mirth,
　As a new world with friends of nobler worth,
Where all may taste a more immortal bread.

So, comrades, if you pass my grave sometime,
Pause long enough to breathe this little rhyme:
　"Here now the dust of Edwin Markham lies,
But lo, he is not here: he is afar
　On life's great errands under brighter skies,
And pressing on toward some melodious star."

—*Edwin Markham*

## An Essay on Man

SEE the sole bliss Heaven could on all bestow!
Which who but feels can taste, but thinks can know:
Yet poor with fortune, and with learning blind,
The bad must miss; the good, untaught, will find;
Slave to no sect, who takes no private road,
But looks through Nature up to Nature's God;
Pursues that chain which links the immense design,
Joins heaven and earth, and mortal and divine;
Sees, that no being any bliss can know,
But touches some above, and some below;
Learns from this union of the rising whole,
The first, last purpose of the human soul;
And knows where faith, law, morals, all began,
All end, in Love of God, and Love of Man.

—*Alexander Pope*

[ 43 ]

## The Eternal Goodness

I LONG for household voices gone,
    For vanished smiles I long,
But God hath led my dear ones on,
    And He can do no wrong.

I know not what the future hath
    Of marvel or surprise,
Assured alone that life and death
    His mercy underlies.

And so beside the Silent Sea
    I wait the muffled oar;
No harm from Him can come to me
    On ocean or on shore.

I know not where His islands lift
    Their fronded palms in air;
I only know I cannot drift
    Beyond His love and care.
        —*John Greenleaf Whittier*

## Evening at Home

Now stir the fire and close the shutters fast,
Let fall the curtains, wheel the sofa round
And while the bubbles and loud hissing urn
Throw up a steaming column,
And the cup that cheers but not inebriates
Waits on each,
So let us welcome cheerful evening in.
        —*William Cowper*

## The Evening Meal

THE preparation of an evening meal
By any woman, anywhere, may be
A ceremony, beautiful to see.

Recalling clear, sweet evenings long ago
At Emmaus, or Bethany, when one
Beloved guest had come at set of sun.

And oh, that other quiet evening meal
Within an upper room—the grace he said
Above the scarlet wine, the broken bread!

[ 44 ]

An evening meal is such a gracious thing,
It matters not how plain may be the fare
So long as love and loyalty are there.

The supper hour—a magnet drawing home
The ones who have the need of food and rest!
All women know this hour of day the best.
                              —*Grace Noll Crowell*

## Ever Insurgent Let Me Be

GOD, though this life is but a wraith,
    Although we know not what we use,
Although we grope with little faith,
    Give me the heart to fight—and lose.

Ever insurgent let me be,
    Make me more daring than devout;
From sleek contentment keep me free,
    And fill me with a bouyant doubt.

Open my eyes to visions girt
    With beauty, and with wonder lit—
But let me always see the dirt,
    And all that spawn and die in it.

Open my ears to music; let
    Me thrill with Spring's first flutes and drums—
But never let me dare forget
    The bitter ballads of the slums.

From compromise and things half-done,
    Keep me, with stern and stubborn pride.
And when, at last, the fight is won,
    God, keep me still unsatisfied.
                              —*Louis Untermeyer*
                                 (Prayer)

## Evolution

OUT of the dusk a shadow,
    Then—a spark;
Out of the cloud a silence,
    Then—a lark;

Out of the heart a rapture,
    Then—a pain;
Out of the dead, cold ashes,
    Life again.
        —*John Bannister Tabb*

[ 45 ]

THE shades of night were falling fast,
As through an Alpine village passed
A youth who bore, 'mid snow and ice,
A banner with a strange device,
Excelsior!

His brow was sad; his eye beneath,
Flashed like a falchion from its sheath,
And like a silver clarion rung
The accents of that unknown tongue,
Excelsior!

In happy homes he saw the light
Of household fires gleam warm and bright;
Above, the spectral glaciers shone,
And from his lips escaped a groan,
Excelsior!

"Try not the Pass!" the old man said;
"Dark lowers the tempest overhead,
The roaring torrent is deep and wide!"
And loud that clarion voice replicd,
Excelsior!

"Oh stay," the maiden said, "and rest
Thy weary head upon this breast!"
A tear stood in his bright blue eye,
But still he answered, with a sigh,
Excelsior!

"Beware the pine-tree's withered branch!
Beware the awful avalanche!"
This was the peasant's last Good-night,
A voice replied, far up the height,
Excelsior!

At break of day, as heavenward
The pious monks of Saint Bernard
Uttered the oft-repeated prayer,
A voice cried through the startled air,
Excelsior!

A traveller, by the faithful hound,
Half buried in the snow was found,
Still grasping in his hand of ice
That banner with the strange device,
Excelsior!

There in the twilight cold and gray,
Lifeless, but beautiful, he lay,
And from the sky, serene and far,
A voice fell, like a falling star,
Excelsior!
—*Henry Wadsworth Longfellow*

## An Extra Prayer

SOMETIMES I say an extra prayer,
Besides the one for which I kneel.
I stand and look up at the stars,
And tell our Father how I feel.
I do not ask for anything;
I just feel happy through and through.
I let my heart give thanks and sing,
Till all the world seems good and true.
—*Annie Willis McCullough*

## Faith

BE LIKE the bird
That, pausing in her flight
Awhile on boughs too slight,
Feels them give way
Beneath her and yet sings,
Knowing that she hath wings.
—*Victor Hugo*

## Faith in Good

THERE is a tale of Faustus—that one day
    Lucretia the Venetian, then his love,
    Had, while he slept, the rashness to remove
His magic ring, when fair as a god he lay;

And that a sudden horrible decay
    O'erspread his face; a hundred wrinkles wove
    Their network on his cheek; while she above
His slumber crouched, and watched him shrivel away.

There is upon Life's hand a magic ring—
    The ring of Faith-in-Good, Life's gold of gold;
Remove it not, lest all Life's charm take wing;

Remove it not, lest straightway you behold
    Life's cheek fall in, and every earthly thing
Grow all at once unutterable old.
                    —*Eugene Lee-Hamilton*
                    (The Ring of Faustus)

[ 47 ]

## The Farmer

WHEN the sun rises, I go to work;
When the sun goes down, I take my rest;
I dig the well from which I drink;
I farm the soil that yields my food.
I share creation; kings do no more.[1]

—*Anonymous*
(From the Chinese)


## Farmers

I WATCH the farmers in their fields
  And marvel secretly.
They are so very calm and sure,
  They have such dignity.

They know such simple things so well,
  Although their learning's small,
They find a steady, brown content
  Where some find none at all.

And all their quarrelings with God
  Are soon made up again;
They grant forgiveness when He sends
  His silver, tardy rain.

Their pleasure is so grave and full
  When gathered crops are trim,
You know they think their work was done
  In partnership with Him.

—*William Alexander Percy*


## The First Supper

AT THE First Supper
The guests were but one;
A maiden was the hostess
The guest her son.

At the First Supper
No candles were lit;
In the darkness hay-scented
They both did sit.

[1] In China the farmer has stood next in rank to the scholar. This poem comes from about 2500 B.C.

[ 48 ]

At the First Supper
No table was spread;
In the curve of her elbow
She laid his head.

At the First Supper
They poured no wine;
On milk of the rarest
The guest did dine.

She held him very closely
Against her breast,
Her fair one, her dear one,
Her darling guest.

She held him very closely,
Guessing that this
Is the last that any mother
May know of bliss.
                    —*Jan Struther*


## *Flower Carol*

SPRING has now unwrapped the flowers
    Day is fast reviving,
Life in all her growing powers
    Towards the light is striving:
Gone the iron touch of cold,
    Winter time and frost time,
Seedlings, working through the mould,
    Now make up for lost time.

Herb and plant, that winter long
    Slumbered at their leisure,
Now, bestirring, green and strong,
    Find in growth their pleasure.
All the world with beauty fills,
    Gold the green enhancing;
Flowers make glee among the hills
    And set the meadows dancing.

Through each wonder of fair days
    God himself expresses;
Beauty follows all his ways,
    As the world he blesses:
So, as he renews the earth,
    Artist without rival,
In his grace of glad new birth
    We must seek revival.

Earth puts on her dress of glee;
　　Flowers and grasses hide her;
We go forth in charity—
　　Brothers all beside her;
For, as man this glory sees
　　In the awakening season,
Reason learns the heart's decrees,
　　And hearts are led by reason.

Praise the Maker, all ye saints;
　　He with glory girt you,
He who skies and meadows paints
　　Fashioned all your virtue;
Praise him, seers, heroes, kings,
　　Heralds of perfection;
Brothers, praise him, for he brings
　　All to resurrection!
　　　　　*—Anonymous; tr. by Percy Dearmer*

### Flower in the Crannied Wall

FLOWER in the crannied wall,
I pluck you out of the crannies,
I hold you here, root and all, in my hand
Little flower—but *if* I could understand
What you are, root and all, and all in all,
I should know what God and man is.
　　　　　*—Alfred Tennyson*

### The Friendly Beasts

JESUS our brother, strong and good,
Was humbly born in a stable rude,
And the friendly beasts around Him stood,
Jesus our brother, strong and good.

"I," said the donkey, shaggy and brown,
"I carried His mother up hill and down,
I carried her safely to Bethlehem town;
I," said the donkey shaggy and brown.

"I," said the cow all white and red,
"I gave Him my manger for His bed,
I gave Him my hay to pillow His head,
I," said the cow all white and red.

"I," said the sheep with curly horn,
"I gave Him my wool for His blanket warm,

[ 50 ]

He wore my coat on Christmas morn;
I," said the sheep with curly horn.

"I," said the dove, from the rafters high,
"Cooed Him to sleep, my mate and I;
We cooed Him to sleep, my mate and I;
I," said the dove, from the rafters high.

And every beast, by some good spell,
In the stable dark was glad to tell,
Of the gift he gave Immanuel,
The gift he gave Immanuel.

—*Anonymous*
(Twelfth Century Carol)

## Friendly Church

IF AFTER kirk you bide a wee,
There's some wad like ta speak to ye:
If after kirk you rise and flee,
We'll all seem cold and stiff to ye;
The one that's in the seat wi' ye,
Is stranger here than you, maybe.
All here hae got their fears and cares—
Add you your soul unto our prayers;
Be you our angel unawares.

—*Anonymous*

## Friendship

I HAVE a friend whose stillness rests me so,
His heart must know
How closely we together, silent, grow.

I have a friend whose brilliancy inspires
And rarely tires
When we two warm our spirits at his fires.

I have a friend whose charity delights
In others' rights,
And we two sit talking often late of nights.

I have a friend whose discipline I need,
We have agreed
That neither from this schooling shall be freed.

I have a friend whose calmness some mistake,
But we two make
Of suffering more than just its grief and ache.

[ 51 ]

I have so many friends—each one fulfills
Just what God wills,
For he through them his best in me fulfills.

And so, twice fortunate am I to find
Friends great and kind
Each one himself, yet part of God's great mind.
—*Vlyna Johnson*

## Give Me Strength

THIS is my prayer to Thee my Lord—
Strike, strike at the root of penury in my heart.
Give me the strength lightly to bear my joys and sorrows.
Give me the strength to make my love fruitful in service.
Give me the strength never to disown the poor or bend my knees before
    insolent might.
Give me the strength to raise my mind high above daily trifles.
And give me the strength to surrender my strength to Thy will with love.
—*Rabindranath Tagore*

## Give Thanks

GIVE thanks to God
   And humbly pray
To serve him well
   This new-born day.

Give thanks to God
   For friends and flowers,
For sunny days
   And cooling showers.

Give thanks to God,
   Fill well your part;
Let Love divine
   Possess your heart.

Give thanks to God,
   His bounty see;
Be still and know,
   Just grateful be.
—*Grenville Kleiser*

## God and Little Things

I COME in the little things,
Saith the Lord:
Yea! on the glancing wings
Of eager birds, the softly pattering feet

[ 52 ]

Of furred and gentle beasts, I come to meet
Your hard and wayward heart. In brown bright eyes
That peep from out the brake, I stand confest.
On every nest
Where feathery patience is content to brood
And leaves her pleasure fro the high emprise
Of motherhood—
There doth My Godhead rest.
                              —*Evelyn Underhill*


## God Give Me Joy

GOD, give me joy in the common things;
In the dawn that lures, the eve that sings.
In the new grass sparkling after rain,
In the late wind's wild and weird refrain;
In the springtime's spacious field of gold,
In the precious light by winter doled.
God give me joy in the love of friends,
In their dear home talk as summer ends;
In the songs of children, unrestrained;
In the sober wisdom age has gained.
God give me joy in the tasks that press,
In the memories that burn and bless;
In the thought that life has love to spend,
In the faith that God's at journey's end.
God, give me hope for each day that springs,
God, give me joy in the common things!
                              —*Thomas Curtis Clark*


## God Is at the Organ

GOD is at the organ;
    I can hear
A mighty music echoing,
    Far and near.

God is at the organ
    And the keys
Are storm-strewn billows,
    Moorlands, trees.

God is at the organ,
    I can hear
A mighty music, echoing
    Far and near.
                              —*Egbert Sandford*

[ 53 ]

GOD holdeth in his hand the measure of judgment;
    And all believe that he is the faithful God.

He trieth and searcheth into the most hidden secrets;
    And all believe that he knoweth the innermost thoughts.

He redeemeth from death and delivereth from the grave;
    And all believe that he is the mighty Redeemer . . .
He apportioneth life unto all his creatures;
    And all believe that he liveth and endureth.

He is good and beneficient to the wicked as well as to the good;
    And all believe that he is good unto all.

He knoweth the nature of all creatures;
    And all believe that he fashioned them all . . .

The Almighty dwelleth everywhere, even in the secret place;
    And all believe that he, alone, is One. . .
He guideth every generation with his loving kindness;
    And all believe that he keepeth mercy.

He is patient, and overlooketh the evil of the rebellious;
    And all believe that he forgiveth.

He is exalted, and he guardeth those that revere him;
    And all believe that he answereth the silent prayer.

He openeth his gate unto them that knock in repentance;
    And all believe that his hand is ever open to receive them.
He waiteth for the wicked and delighteth when they return to righteous-
    ness;
    And all believe that he is just and righteous . . .

He is perfect and dealeth truly with the pure in heart;
    And all believe that his work is perfect.

*—Yannai*
(Seventh Century Hymn)

## God Is in His Holy Temple

GOD is in his holy temple—
    The temple is the universe,
    The temple is the human heart,
    The temple is humanity.

[ 54 ]

God is in his holy temple—
    Sometimes the world seems very dark,
    Sometimes the heart of man is hard,
    Sometimes society is cruel.

God is in his holy temple—
    Truth and beauty are in God,
    Justice and mercy are in him,
    Love and friendship, these are God.

God is in his holy temple—
    The world is still aflame with God.
    May we now be aglow with love
    In all relationships of life.
                —*A. J. William Myers*

## God Keep a Clean Wind Blowing

God keep a clean wind blowing through my heart
Night and day,
Cleanse it with sunlight, let the silver rain
Wash away
Cobwebs, and the smouldering dust that years
Leave, I pray.

God keep a clean wind blowing through my heart:
Wind from far
Green pastures, and from shaded pools where still
Waters are;
Wind from spaces out beyond the first
Twilight star.

Bitterness can have no place in me,
Nor grief stay,
When the winds of God rush through and sweep
Them away.
God keep a clean wind blowing through my heart
Night and day.
                —*Grace Noll Crowell*

## God's First Temples

The groves were God's first temples. Ere man learned
To hew the shaft, and lay the architrave,
And spread the roof above them—ere he framed
The lofty vault, to gather and roll back
The sound of anthems; in the darkling wood,
Amid the cool and silence, he knelt down
And offered to the Mightiest solemn thanks

And supplication. For his simple heart
Might not resist the sacred influences,
Which, from the stilly twilight of the place,
And from the gray old trunks that high in heaven
Mingled their mossy boughs, and from the sound
Of the invisible breath that swayed at once
All their green tops, stole over him, and bowed
His spirit with the thought of boundless power
And inaccessible majesty. Ah, why
Should we, in the world's riper years, neglect
God's ancient sanctuaries, and adore
Only among the crowd, and under roofs
That our frail hands have raised? Let me, at least,
Here, in the shadow of this aged wood,
Offer one hymn—thrice happy if it find
Acceptance in his ear.

—*William Cullen Bryant*

### God's in His Heaven

THE year's at the spring—
And day's at the morn;
Morning's at seven;
The hillside's dew-pearled;
The lark's on the wing;
The snail's on the thorn;
God's in his heaven—
All's right with the world!

—*Robert Browning*

### God's Pledge to You

NOT cloudless days;
Not rose-strewn ways;
Not care-free years,
Devoid of sorrow's tears—
But—strength to bear
Your load of human care,
And grace to live aright
And keep your raiment white,
And love to see you through;
That is God's pledge to you.

—*Anonymous*

### God's World

O WORLD, I cannot hold thee close enough!
Thy winds, thy wide grey skies!
Thy mists, that roll and rise!

Thy woods, this autumn day, that ache and sag
And all but cry with colour! That gaunt crag
To crush! To lift the lean of that black bluff!
World, World, I cannot get thee close enough!

Long have I known a glory in it all,
  But never knew I this;
  Here such a passion is
As stretcheth me apart—Lord, I do fear
Thou'st made the world too beautiful this year;
My soul is all but out of me—let fall
No burning leaf; prithee, let no bird call.
                    —*Edna St. Vincent Millay*

## God the Essence of Love

GODDES love is unescapable as nature's environment, which if a man
  ignore or think to thrust it off he is the ill-natured fool that runneth
  blindly on death.

                .   .   .   .   .

God is seen as the very self-essence of love,
Creator and mover of all as active Lover, of all, self-express'd in not-self,
  without which no self were.
In thought whereof is neither beginning nor end nor space nor time; nor
  any fault nor gap therein
'twixt self and not-self, mind and body, mother and child,
'twixt lover and loved, God and man: but ONE ETERNAL.
in the love of Beauty and in the selfhood of Love.
                    —*Anonymous*

## God, Thou Art Love

IF I forget,
Yet God remembers! If these hands of mine
Cease from their clinging, yet the hands divine
Hold me so firmly that I cannot fall;
And if sometimes I am too tired to call
For him to help me, then he reads the prayer
Unspoken in my heart, and lifts my care.

I dare not fear, since certainly I know
That I am in God's keeping, shielded so
From all that else would harm, and in the hour
Of stern temptation strengthened by his power;
I tread no path in life to him unknown;
I lift no burden, bear no pain, alone;
My soul a calm, sure hiding-place has found:
The everlasting arms my life surround.

God, thou art love! I build my faith on that.
I know thee who has kept my path, and made
Light for me in the darkness, tempering sorrow
So that it reached me like a solemn joy;
It were too strange that I should doubt thy love.
—*Robert Browning*
(Paracelsus)

## Good from a Book

WE GET no good
By being ungenerous, even to a book,
And calculating profits so much help
By so much reading. It is rather when
We gloriously forget ourselves and plunge
Soul-forward, headlong into a book's profound,
Impassioned for its beauty and salt of truth,
'Tis then we get the right good from a book.
—*Elizabeth Barrett Browning*

## Good Night

SLEEP sweetly through the healing night,
O thou, whoe'er thou art,
And let no mournful yesterday
Disturb thy dreaming heart;
Nor let tomorrow mar thy rest
With fear of coming ill—
Thy maker is thy changeless Friend,
His love surrounds thee still.
Dismiss, then, every unquiet thought,
Put out each feverish light;
The stars are watching overhead,
Sleep sweetly, then—Good night!
—*Adapted by "Cheerio" from the
poem by Ellen Gates*

## The Good Shepherd with the Kid

He saves the sheep, the goats he doth not save
So rang Tertullian's sentence, on the side
Of that unpitying Phrygian sect which cried,
"Him can no fount of fresh forgiveness lave,
Who sins, once washed by the baptismal wave."
So spake the fierce Tertullian. But she sighed,
The infant Church! of love she felt the tide
Stream on her from her Lord's yet recent grave,
And then she smiled; and in the Catacombs,
With eye suffused by heart inspired true,

[ 58 ]

On those walls subterranean, where she hid
Her head 'mid ignominy, death, and tombs,
She her Good Shepherd's hasty image drew—
And on his shoulders, not a lamb, a kid.
—*Matthew Arnold*


## The Greatest Work

HE BUILT a house; time laid it in the dust;
He wrote a book, its title now forgot;
He ruled a city, but his name is not
On any table graven, or where rust
Can gather from disuse, or marble bust.
He took a child from out a wretched cot,
Who on the state dishonor might have brought,
And reared him to the Christian's hope and trust.
The boy, to manhood grown, became a light
To many souls, and preached for human need
The wondrous love of the Omnipotent.
The work was multiplied like stars at night
When darkness deepens; every noble deed
Lasts longer than a granite monument.
—*Ray M. Johnson*


## Greet the Unseen with a Cheer

AT THE midnight in the silence of the sleep-time,
    When you set your fancies free,
Will they pass to where—by death, fools think, imprisoned—
Low he lies who once so loved you, whom you loved so,
            —Pity me?

Oh to love so, be so loved, yet so mistaken!
    What had I on earth to do
With the slothful, with the mawkish, the unmanly?
Like the aimless, helpless, hopeless, did I drivel
            —Being—who?

One who never turned his back but marched breast forward,
    Never doubted clouds would break,
Never dreamed, though right were worsted, wrong would triumph,
Held we fall to rise, are baffled to fight better,
            Sleep to wake.

No, at noonday in the bustle of man's work-time
    Greet the unseen with a cheer!

[ 59 ]

Bid him forward, breast and back as either should be,
"Strive and thrive!" cry "Speed,—fight on, fare ever
        There as here!"

—*Robert Browning*
(Epilogue)

## Hallowed Ground

WHAT's hallowed ground? Has earth a clod
Its Maker meant not should be trod
By man, the image of his God,
    Erect and free,
Unscouraged by Superstition's rod
    To bow the knee?

Peace, Love! the cherubim, that join
Their spread wings o'er Devotion's shrine,
Prayers sound in vain, and temples shine,
    Where they are not—
The heart alone can make divine
    Religion's spot.

What's hallowed ground? 'Tis what gives birth
To sacred thoughts in souls of worth!—
Peace! Independence! Truth! go forth
    Earth's compass round;
And your high-priesthood shall make earth
    All hallowed ground.

—*Thomas Campbell*

## The Happiest Heart

WHO drives the horses of the sun
    Shall lord it but a day.
Better the lowly deed were done
    And kept the humble way.

The rust will find the sword of fame;
    The dust will hide the crown,
Aye, none shall nail so high his name
    Time will not tear it down.

The happiest heart that ever beat
    Was in some quiet breast
That found the common daylight sweet,
    And left to Heaven the rest.

—*John Vance Cheney*

## Happy the Man

HAPPY the man, of mortals happiest he,
Whose quiet mind from vain desires is free;
Whom neither hopes deceive, nor fears torment,
But lives at peace, within himself content;
In thought, in act, accountable to none
But to himself, and to the gods alone.

—*George Granville*


## He Dwells in All

THUS he dwells in all,
From life's minute beginnings, up at last
To man—the consummation of this scheme
Of being, the completion of this sphere
Of life—
And, man produced, all has its end thus far:
But in completed man begins anew
A tendency to God.

—*Robert Browning*


## He Had Not Where to Lay His Head

THEY borrowed a bed to lay His head
    When Christ the Lord was born;
They borrowed the ass in the mountain pass
    And he rode despite their scorn
But the Crown that He wore and the Cross that He bore
    Were His own—
The Cross was His own.


He borrowed the bread when the crowd He fed
    On the grassy mountainside;
He borrowed the dish of broken fish
    With which He satisfied;
But the Crown that He wore and the Cross that He bore
    Were His own—
The Cross was His own.


He borrowed the ship in which to sit
    To teach the multitude;
He borrowed the nest in which to rest,
    He had never a home so crude;
But the Crown that He wore and the Cross that He bore
    Were His own—
The Cross was His own.

[ 61 ]

He borrowed a room on His way to the tomb
  The Passover Lamb to eat;
They borrowed a cave for Him a grave,
  They borrowed a winding sheet;
But the Crown that He wore and the Cross that He bore
  Were His own—
The Cross was His own.[1]

—Anonymous

## He Leads Us On

HE LEADS us on,
By paths we did not know.
Upward he leads, though our steps be slow,
Though oft we faint and falter by the way,
Though storms and darkness oft obscure the day,
  Yet when the clouds are gone,
  We know he leads us on.

He leads us on
Through the unquiet years;
Past all our dreamland, hopes and doubts, and fears,
He guides our steps. Through all the tangled maze
Of sin, of sorrow, and o'er clouded days.
  We know his will is done;
  And still he leads us on.

And he, at last,
After the weary strife—
After the restless fever we call life,
After the dreariness, the aching pain—
The wayward struggles which have proved in vain,
  After all our toils are past,
  Will give us peace at last.

—Anonymous

## He Prayeth Best

HE PRAYETH best, who loveth best
All things both great and small;
For the dear God who loveth us,
He made and loveth all.
—Samuel Taylor Coleridge<br>( The Ancient Mariner )

[1] Slightly altered.

## He Saw No Sign

ONE asked a sign from God; and day by day
The sun rose in pearl; in scarlet set,
Each night the stars appeared in bright array,
Each morn the thirsting grass with dew was wet.
The corn failed not its harvest, nor the vine.
And yet he saw no sign.

—Victor Starbuck

## He Who Gives a Child a Treat

AND he who gives a child a treat
Makes joy-bells ring in Heaven's street,
And he who gives a child a home
Builds palaces in Kingdom come,
And she who gives a baby birth
Brings Savior Christ again to Earth.

—John Masefield<br>(The Everlasting Mercy)

## Heart's Desire

O, TO have a little house!
    To own the hearth and stool and all!
The heaped-up sods upon the fire,
    The pile of turf against the wall!

To have a clock with weights and chains
    And pendulum swinging up and down!
A dresser filled with shining delph,
    Speckled and white and blue and brown!

I could be busy all the day
    Clearing and sweeping hearth and floor,
And fixing on their shelf again
    My white and blue and speckled store!

I could be quiet there at night
    Beside the fire and by myself,
Sure of a bed, and loth to leave
    The ticking clock and the shining delph!

Och! but I'm weary of mist and dark,
    And roads where there's never a house or bush.
And tired I am of bog and road
    And the crying wind and the lonesome hush!

And I am praying to God on high,
    And I am praying him night and day,
For a little house—a house of my own—
    Out of the wind's and the rain's way.
                        —*Padraic Colum*

## The Heavens Are Declaring

THE heavens are declaring the Lord's endless glory,
    Through all the earth his praise is found.
The seas reecho the marvelous story,
    O man, repeat that glorious sound.

The starry host he orders and measures;
    He fills the morning's golden springs.
He wakes the sun from his night-curtained slumbers.
    O man, adore the King of Kings.

Power and splendour and wisdom and order
    In nature's mighty plan unrolled;
Through space and time to infinity's border
    What wonders vast and manifold.

The earth is his and the heavens o'er it bending.
    The Maker in his works behold.
He is and will be through ages unending
    A God of strength and love untold.
            —*An anthem arranged by Ludwig van Beethoven*

## The Hidden Years

WHAT was he doing all that time,
From twelve years old to manly prime?
Was he then idle, or the less
About his Father's business?
                    —*William Blake*
                    (The Divine Image)

## High Flight

OH! I have slipped the surly bonds of earth
    And danced the skies on laughter-silvered wings;
Sunward I've climbed, and joined the tumbling mirth
    Of sun-split clouds—and done a hundred things
You have not dreamed of—wheeled and soared and swung
    High in the sunlit silence. Hov'ring there,
I've chased the shouting wind along, and flung
    My eager craft through footless halls of air.

Up, up the long, delirious, burning blue
  I've topped the wind-swept heights with easy-grace—
Where never lark, nor even eagle flew—
And, while with silent lifting mind I've trod
  The high untrespassed sanctity of space,
Put out my hand and touched the face of God.
                              —*John Gillespie Magee, Jr.*

## The Higher Pantheism

THE sun, the moon, the stars, the seas, the hills and the plains,
Are not these, O Soul, the Vision of Him who reigns?

Is not the Vision He, tho' He be not that which He seems?
Dreams are true while they last, and do we not live in dreams?

Earth, these solid stars, this weight of body and limb,
Are they not sign and symbol of thy division from Him?

Dark is the world to thee; thyself art the reason why;
For is He not all but thou, that hast power to feel "I am I"?

Glory about thee, without thee; and thou fulfillest thy doom,
Making Him broken gleams—and a stifled splendor and gloom.

Speak to Him, thou, for He hears, and Spirit with Spirit can meet—
Closer is He than breathing, and nearer than hands and feet.

God is law, say the wise; O Saul, and let us rejoice,
For if He thunder by law the thunder is yet His voice.

Law is God, say some; no God at all, says the fool;
For all we have power to see is a straight staff bent in a pool:

And the ear of man cannot hear, and the eye of man cannot see;
But if we could see and hear, this Vision—were it not He?
                              —*Alfred Tennyson*

## His Magic

HIS magic was not far to seek—
    He was so human! Whether strong or weak,
Far from his kind he neither sank nor soared,
But sat an equal guest at every board:
No beggar ever felt him condescend,
No prince presume; for still himself he bare
At manhood's simple level, and where'er
He met a stranger, there he left a friend.
                              —*James Russell Lowell*

[ 65 ]

## The Holy Society

I DEDICATE myself to thee, O God.[1]
Would that all created things
Might understand the great life-principle
And grasp the things that come from above!

I dedicate myself to the great life-principle.
Would that all creation might immerse itself
In the depths of the scriptures and attain that wisdom
Which is vast as the sea!

I dedicate myself to the holy society
Would that all creation might in great close ranks
Stride forward toward the great assembling of all the saints!
—*Anonymous*

## Home and Love

Just Home and Love! The words are small,
Four little letters unto each;
And yet you will not find in all
    The wide and gracious range of speech
Two more so tenderly complete;
When angels talk in Heaven above
I'm sure they have no words more sweet
    Than Home and Love.

Just Home and Love! It's hard to guess
Which of the two were best to gain;
Home without Love is bitterness;
Love without Home is often pain.
No, each alone will seldom do;
Somehow they travel hand and glove:
If you win one you must have two,
    Both Home and Love.

And if you've both, well, then I'm sure
You ought to sing the whole day long;
It doesn't matter if you're poor
With these to make divine your song.
And so I praisefully repeat,
When angels talk in Heaven above,
There are no words more simply sweet
    Than Home and Love.
—*Robert W. Service*

[1] Amitabha, the great life-principle.

## Home, Sweet Home

Mid pleasures and palaces though we may roam,
Be it ever so humble, there's no place like home;
A charm from the skies seems to hallow us there,
Which, seek through the world, is ne'er met with elsewhere.

An exile from home, splendour dazzles in vain;
O, give me my lowly thatched cottage again!
The birds singing gaily, that came at my call;—
Give me them, with the peace of mind, dearer than all!

How sweet 'tis to sit 'neath a fond father's smile,
And the cares of a mother to soothe and beguile;
Let others delight 'mid new pleasures to roam,
But give me, oh, give me, the pleasures of home!

To thee I'll return, overburdened with care;
The heart's dearest solace will smile on me there;
No more from that cottage again will I roam,
Be it ever so humble, there's no place like home.

(Chorus)
Home! home! sweet, sweet home
There is no place like home.

—*John Howard Payne*

## Hope

And as, in sparkling majesty, a star
Gilds the bright summit of some gloomy cloud;
Brightening the half-veiled face of heaven afar:
So, when dark thoughts my boding spirit shroud,
Sweet Hope, celestial influence round me shed,
Waving thy silver pinions o'er my head.

—*John Keats*

## How Swift the Summer Goes

How swift the summer goes,
Forget-me-not, pink, rose.
The young grass when I started
And now the hay is carted,
And now my song is ended,
And all the summer spended;
The blackbird's second brood
Routs beech leaves in the wood;
The pink and rose have speeded,
Forget-me-not has seeded.

[ 67 ]

Only the winds that blew,
The rain that makes things new,
The earth that hides things old,
And blessings manifold.
                    —*John Masefield*
                (The Everlasting Mercy)


## Hymn of the City

Not in the solitude
Alone may man commune with Heaven, or see,
    Alone in savage wood
And sunny vale, the present Deity;
    Or only hear his voice
Where the winds whisper and the waves rejoice.

Even here do I behold
Thy steps, Almighty!—here, amidst the crowd
    Through the great city rolled,
With everlasting murmur deep and loud—
    Choking the ways that wind
'Mongst the proud piles, the work of human kind.

Thy golden sunshine comes
From the round heaven, and on their dwellings lies
    And lights their inner homes;
For them thou fill'st with air the unbounded skies,
    And givest them the stores
Of ocean, and the harvests of its shores.

Thy spirit is around,
Quickening the restless mass that sweeps along;
    And this eternal sound—
Voices and footfalls of the numberless throng—
    Like the resounding sea,
Or like the rainy tempest, speaks of thee.

And when the hour of rest
Comes, like a calm upon the mid-sea brine,
    Hushing its billowy breast—
The quiet of that moment too is thine;
    It breathes of him who keeps
The vast and helpless city while it sleeps.
                    —*William Cullen Bryant*


## Hymn to Intellectual Beauty

The day becomes more solemn and serene
    When noon is past—there is a harmony
    In autumn, and a lustre in its sky,

[ 68 ]

Which through the summer is not heard or seen,
As if it could not be, as if it had not been!
   Thus let thy power, which like the truth
   Of nature on my passive youth
Descended, to my onward life supply
   Its calm—to one who worships thee,
   And every form containing thee,
   Whom, Spirit fair, thy spells did bind
To fear himself, and love all human kind.
                    —*Percy Bysshe Shelley*


## I Have a Rendezvous with Death

I HAVE a rendezvous with Death
At some disputed barricade,
When Spring comes back with rustling shade
And apple-blossoms fill the air—
I have a rendezvous with Death
When Spring brings back blue days and fair.

It may be he shall take my hand
And lead me into his dark land,
And close my eyes and quench my breath—
It may be I shall pass him still.
I have a rendezvous with Death
On some scarred slope of battered hill,
When Spring comes round again this year
And the first meadow-flowers appear.

God knows 'twere better to be deep
Pillowed in silk and scented down,
Where Love throbs out in blissful sleep,
Pulse nigh to pulse, and breath to breath,
Where hushed awakenings are dear . . .
But I've a rendezvous with Death
At midnight in some flaming town,
When Spring trips north again this year,
And I to my pledged word am true,
I shall not fail that rendezvous.[1]
                    —*Alan Seeger*


## I Love You, Mother

"I LOVE you, mother," said little John,
Then forgetting his work his cap went on
And he was off to the garden swing
Leaving his mother the wood to bring.

[1] He was killed in Greece on St. George's Day, 1915.

"I love you, mother," said little Nell,
"I love you better than tongue can tell,"
Then she teased and pouted half the day
Till her mother rejoiced when she went to play.

"I love you, mother," said little Fan,
"To-day I'll help you all I can."
Then stepping softly she took the broom
And swept the floor and tidied the room.

"I love you, mother," again they said,
Three little children going to bed.
Now how do you think that mother guessed
Which of them really loved her best?
—*Joyce Allison*

## I Remember, I Remember

I REMEMBER, I remember—
The house where I was born,
The little window where the sun
Came peeping in at morn;
He never came a wink too soon,
Nor brought too long a day;
But now, I often wish the night
Had borne my breath away.

I remember, I remember
The roses, red and white,
The violets, and the lily-cups—
Those flowers made of light!
The lilacs where the robin built,
And where my brother set
The laburnum on his birthday,—
The tree is living yet!

I remember, I remember
Where I was used to swing,
And thought the air must rush as fresh
To swallows on the wing;
My spirit flew in feathers then
That is so heavy now,
And summer pools could hardly cool
The fever on my brow.

I remember, I remember,
The fir-trees dark and high;
I used to think their slender tops

[ 70 ]

Were close against the sky:
It was a childish ignorance,
But now 'tis little joy
To know I'm farther off from Heaven
Than when I was a boy.
                                    —*Thomas Hood*

## I Shall Not Live in Vain

IF I can stop one heart from breaking,
I shall not live in vain;
If I can ease one life the aching,
Or cool one pain,
Or help one fainting robin
Into its nest again,
I shall not live in vain.
                                    —*Emily Dickinson*

## I Will Have Faith

FAITH is not merely praying
    Upon our knees at night:
Faith is not merely straying
    Through darkness into light:
Faith is not merely waiting
    For glory that may be—
Faith is the brave endeavor,
    The splendid enterprise,
The strength to serve, whatever
    Conditions may arise.
                                    —*Anonymous*

## Ike Walton's Prayer

I CRAVE, dear Lord,
No boundless hoard
    Of gold and gear,
    Nor jewels fine
Nor lands, nor kine,
    Nor treasure-heaps of anything.
        Let but a little hut be mine
Where at the hearthstone I may hear
        The cricket sing,
        And have the shine
Of one glad woman's eyes to make,
Fur my poor sake,
    Our simple home a place divine;
Just the wee cot—the cricket's chirr—
Love, and the smiling face of her.
                                    —*James Whitcomb Riley*

[ 71 ]

## Immanence

I NEVER think of God
As a God afar
When he lifts his torch
To the first white star.
I never think of him
As a spirit aloof
When his kind rains dance
On my dark wet roof.

I never think of Jesus
As in Galilee
When I wander on the shores
Of a gold-rimmed sea.
I never think of him
On a shining throne
When I walk at high morning
In a wood, alone.

I know a path
Where the hollyhocks nod:
And when I go there
I grow friendly with God.
And when young daffodils
Dance before my eyes
I cannot think that Heaven
Is away in the skies.

I have a friend
Whose hands feel in mine
Like the very same hands
That turned water into wine.
And when, at the day's end,
I look in his face
The whole wide world
Is a God-filled place.
                    —*Wilson MacDonald*


## In Church

OFT have I seen at some cathedral door,
A laborer, pausing in the dust and heat,
Lay down his burden, and with reverent feet
Enter, and cross himself, and on the floor
Kneel to repeat his paternoster o'er;
Far off the noises of the world retreat;
The loud vociferations of the street
Become an undistinguishable roar.

So, as I enter here from day to day,
And leave my burden at this minster gate,
Kneeling in prayer, and not ashamed to pray,
The tumult of the time disconsolate
To inarticulate murmurs dies away,
While the eternal ages watch and wait.
—*Henry Wadsworth Longfellow*
(Divina Commedia)

## In Defence of Idleness

THE boy lay relaxed upon his back
Hands clasped behind his head—
Lay dreaming and star-gazing in the
Late evening, upon his back
In the sweet scented clover.

Work seemed to him flat and vulgar
And all unworthy of creative youth
And so he lay with dreaming eyes
Gazing at other worlds high lifted up
Among the twinkling stars.

He gazed dreamily as thus he lay
In scented clover upon his back
With hands loose clasped behind his head.
"There's Little Dipper; there the Goat, the
Horse, and there the Milky Way; and there the Plow."

Slowly his vision narrowed; his mind focused.
The Dipper and the Milky Way; the Goat, the Plow,
All symbols these not of day dreams
And star-gazings but of work!
Work, the basis of Worlds and Starry Kingdoms—
And of the deeds of vital youth!

And he sat erect his purpose formed!
The secret of the stars his spirit read
Day-dreaming and star-gazing
As he lay, hands clasped behind his head,
Lying relaxed upon his back
At even in sweet scented clover.
—*A. J. William Myers*

## In Flanders Fields

IN FLANDERS fields the poppies blow
Between the crosses row on row,
That mark our place; and in the sky

The larks, still bravely singing, fly
Scarce heard amid the guns below.

We are the Dead. Short days ago
We lived, felt dawn, saw sunset glow,
    Loved and were loved, and now we lie,
    In Flanders fields.

Take up our quarrel with the foe:
To you from failing hands we throw
    The torch; be yours to hold it high!
    If ye break faith with us who die
We shall not sleep, though poppies grow
    In Flanders fields.
                                    —*John M. D. McCrae*

## In Memoriam

THINE are these orbs of light and shade;
    Thou madest Life in man and brute;
    Thou madest Death; and lo, thy foot
Is on the skull which thou hast made.

Thou wilt not leave us in the dust:
    Thou madest man, he knows not why;
    He thinks he was not made to die;
And thou hast made him: thou art just.

. . . . .

Our little systems have their day;
    They have their day and cease to be;
    They are but broken lights of thee,
And thou, O Lord, art more than they.

We have but faith: we cannot know,
    For knowledge is of things we see;
    And yet we trust it comes from thee,
A beam in darkness: let it grow.

Let knowledge grow from more to more,
    But more of reverence in us dwell;
    That mind and soul, according well,
May make one music as before,

But vaster. We are fools and slight;
    We mock thee when we do not fear:
    But help thy foolish ones to bear;
Help thy vain worlds to bear thy light.

. . . . .

I held it truth, with him who sings
   To one clear harp in divers tones,
   That men may rise on stepping-stones
Of their dead selves to higher things.

. . . . .

I hold it true, whate'er befall;
   I feel it, when I sorrow most;
   'Tis better to have loved and lost
Than never to have loved at all.

. . . . .

O yet we trust that somehow good
   Will be the final goal of ill,
   To pangs of nature, sins of will,
Defects of doubt, and taints of blood;

That nothing walks with aimless feet;
   That not one life shall be destroy'd,
   Or cast as rubbish to the void
When God hath made the pile complete;

That not a worm is cloven in vain;
   That not a moth with vain desire
   Is shrivel'd in a fruitless fire,
Or but subserves another's gain.

. . . . .

Behold, we know not anything;
   I can but trust that good shall fall
   At last—far off—at last, to all,
And every winter change to spring.
                        —*Alfred Tennyson*


### In the Temple

Two went to pray? Oh, rather say
One went to brag, the other to pray;
One stands up close, and treads on high,
Where the other dares not send his eye;
One nearer to God's altar trod;
The other to the altar's God.
                        —*Richard Crashaw*


### In Time of Doubt

                              IF I stoop
Into a dark tremendous sea of cloud,
It is but for a time; I press God's lamp

[ 75 ]

Close to my breast; its splendor, soon or late,
Will pierce the gloom: I shall emerge one day.
                                —*Robert Browning*
                                        (Paracelsus)

## Indian Summer

ALONG the line of smoky hills
    The crimson forest stands,
And all the day the blue-jay calls
    Throughout the autumn lands.

Now by the brook the maple leans
    With all his glory spread,
And all the sumachs on the hills
    Have turned their green to red.

Now by great marshes wrapt in mist,
    Or past some river's mouth,
Throughout the long, still autumn day
    Wild birds are flying south.

                . . . . .

And God who paints this glorious scene
    Of meadow, wood and lee
Calls to us all in gentlest tone
    Love Beauty, Truth and Me.[1]
                        —*Wilfred Campbell*

## Ineffable

COULD we with ink the ocean fill,
Were every blade of grass a quill,
Were the world of parchment made,
And every man a scribe by trade,
    To write the love
    Of God above
Would drain that ocean dry;
    Nor would the scroll
    Contain the whole,
Though stretched from sky to sky!
        —*Nehorai Meir Ben Isaac*, 1050

## Intimations of Immortality from Recollections of Early Childhood

THERE was a time when meadow, grove, and stream,
The earth, and every common sight,
    To me did seem

[1] This stanza has been added.

Apparelled in celestial light,
The glory and the freshness of a dream.
It is not now as it hath been of yore;—
   Turn wheresoe'er I may,
    By night or day,
The things which I have seen I now can see no more.
   The Rainbow comes and goes,
   And lovely is the Rose,
   The Moon doth with delight
Look round her when the heavens are bare;
    Waters on a starry night
   Are beautiful and fair;
   The sunshine is a glorious birth;
   But yet I know, where'er I go,
That there hath past away a glory from the earth.

. . . . .

Our birth is but a sleep and a forgetting:
The Soul that rises with us, our life's Star,
   Hath had elsewhere its setting,
    And cometh from afar:
   Not in entire forgetfulness,
   And not in utter nakedness,
But trailing clouds of glory do we come
   From God who is our home:
Heaven lies about us in our infancy!
Shades of the prison-house begin to close
   Upon the growing Boy,
But he beholds the light, and whence it flows,
   He sees it in his joy;
The Youth, who daily farther from the east
   Must travel, still is Nature's Priest,
   And by the vision splendid
   Is on his way attended;
At length the Man perceives it die away,
And fade into the light of common day.
               —*William Wordsworth*

## Is It God?

Is it my God who lets children work
All day in mills and factories
And get no recompense
Except small pay in small envelopes?

Is it my God who lets children
And old and young men and women
Suffer, and see no beauty—
Only ugliness?

[ 77 ]

Is it my God who lets people live and die
Without seeing any of his Real Self;
Who disregards the saying of Jesus,
"Suffer little children to come unto me"?

Is it my God who sees the horror
Of the lives of slaves
Yet does not relieve them?
Is it your God?
Is it our God?

*—Anonymous*


## Is There for Honest Poverty

Is THERE, for honest poverty,
    That hangs his head, and a' that?
The coward-slave, we pass him by,
    We dare be poor for a' that!
        For a' that, and a' that,
            Our toils obscure, and a' that;
            The rank is but the guinea's stamp;
            The man's the gowd for a' that.

What though on hamely fare we dine,
    Wear hodden-gray, and a' that;
Gie fools their silks, and knaves their wine,
    A man's a man for a' that.
        For a' that, and a' that,
            Their tinsel show, and a' that;
            The honest man, tho' e'er sae poor,
            Is King of men for a' that.

                . . . . .

A prince can mak a belted knight,
    A marquis, duke, and a' that;
But an honest man's aboon his might,
    Guid faith, he mauna fa' that!
        For a' that, and a' that,
            Their dignities, and a' that,
            The pith o' sense, an' pride o' worth,
            Are higher rank than a' that.

Then let us pray that come it may,
    As come it will for a' that,
That sense and worth o'er a' the earth,
    May bear the gree, and a' that.
        For a' that, and a' that,
            It's coming yet, for a' that,

That a man to man, the warld o'er,
Shall brothers be for a' that.
—*Robert Burns*

## It Is a Sweet Thing, Friendship

IT IS a sweet thing, friendship, a dear balm,
A happy and auspicious bird of calm,
Which rides o'er life's ever tumultuous ocean;
A god that broods o'er chaos in commotion;
A flower which, fresh as Lapland's roses are,
Lifts its bold head into the world's pure air,
And blooms most radiantly when others die—
Health, hope, and youth, and brief prosperity;
And with the light and odour of its bloom
Shining within the dungeon and the tomb;
Whose coming is as light and music are
'Mid dissonance and gloom—a star
Which moves not 'mid the moving heavens alone—
A smile among dark frowns—a gentle tone
Among rude voices, a beloved light,
A solitude, a refuge, a delight.
—*Percy Bysshe Shelley*

## It Takes Great Strength

IT TAKES great strength to bring your life up square
With your accepted thought, and hold it there;
Resisting the inertia that drags back
From new attempts to the old habit's track.
It is so easy to drift back, to sink;
So hard to live abreast of what you think.

It takes great strength to live where you belong,
When other people think that you are wrong,
People you love, and who love you, and whose
Approval is a pleasure you would choose;
To bear this pressure and succeed at length
In living your belief—well, it takes strength,

And courage, too. But what does courage mean
Save strength to help you bear a pain foreseen?
Courage to undertake this lifelong strain
Of setting yours against your grandsire's brain:

Dangerous risk of walking lone and free
Out of the easy paths that used to be,
And the fierce pain of hurting those we love
When love meets truth, and truth must rise above!
—*Charlotte P. Stetson Gilman*

[ 79 ]

## Jack Frost

IT STARTS in the night-time, with wind, frost, and hail,
When down through a village an old man came creeping,
While all the good folk in the village were sleeping.
He took from his pocket a paint-brush, and said,
"I'm going to paint pictures—all out of my head,
And not of the world that around me I see—
I'll picture the world as I'd like it to be."

He started to paint, and he painted away
On the villagers' windows, till break of the day.
And the pictures he drew were a wonderful sight—
All sparkling and gleaming, and dainty and white.
"Ah, that's how the real world could look," he declared.
"If folk tried to make it—if only they cared!"
—*Marion St. John Webb*

## Jerusalem

BRING me my bow of burning gold!
Bring me my arrows of desire!
Bring me my spear! O clouds, unfold!
Bring me my chariot of fire!

I will not cease from mental fight,
Nor shall my sword sleep in my hand,
Till we have built Jerusalem
In England's green and pleasant land.
—*William Blake*

## Jesus' Birthday

AND did Mary bake a little cake
When Jesus' birthday came?
Did Joseph carve a wooden toy
And mark it with his name?
And did his mother make him wait
Till she could set it by his plate,
And was he happy, just the same
As you are, on your birthday?
I wish I knew! But long ago
When Jesus was a boy,
They must have had some loving ways
Of showing him their joy
When he was eight, and nine, and ten;
It wasn't very different then—
Families remembered—just the same
As yours does on your birthday!
—*Edith Kent Battle*

[ 80 ]

## The Jewish Soldier

MOTHER England, Mother England, 'mid the thousands
Far beyond the sea to-day,
Doing battle for thy honour, for thy glory,
Is there place for us, a little band of brothers?
   England, say!

Long ago and far away, O Mother England,
We were warriors brave and bold;
But a hundred nations rose in arms against us,
And the shades of exile closed o'er those heroic days of old.

Thou hast given us home and freedom, Mother England,
Thou hast let us live again,
Free and fearless, 'midst thy free and fearless children,
Sharing with them, as one people, grief and gladness,
   Joy and pain.

For the Jew has heart and hand, our Mother England,
And they both are thine to-day—
Thine for life and thine for death—yea, thine for ever!
Wilt thou take them as we give them, freely, gladly?
   England, say!

                     —*Alice Lucas*

## Joy, Shipmate, Joy!

JOY, shipmate, joy!
(Pleas'd to my soul at death I cry)
Our life is closed, our life begins,
The long, long anchorage we leave,
The ship is clear at last, she leaps!
She swiftly courses from the shore,
Joy, shipmate, joy!

                     —*Walt Whitman*

## June

AND what is so rare as a day in June?
   Then, if ever, come perfect days;
Then Heaven tries earth if it be in tune,
   And over it softly her warm ear lays;
Whether we look, or whether we listen,
We hear life murmur, or see it glisten;
Every clod feels a stir of might,
   An instinct within it that reaches and towers,
And, groping blindly above it for light,
   Climbs to a soul in grass and flowers.

Now is the high-tide of the year,
And whatever of life hath ebbed away
Comes flooding back with a ripply cheer,
Into every bare inlet and creek and bay.
—*James Russell Lowell*
(Vision of Sir Launfal)

## King Ever Glorious

KING ever glorious!
The dews of death are gathering around thee;
Upon the cross thy foes have bound thee;
Thy strength is gone.

Not in thy majesty,
Robed in heaven's supremest splendour,
But in weakness and surrender thou hangest here.
Who can be like thee?

Pilate high in Zion dwelling?
Rome with arms the world compelling? Proud though they be,
Thou art sublime, far more awful in thy weakness,
More kingly in thy meekness, thou son of God.

Glory and honour,
Let the world divide and take them,
Crown its monarchs and unmake them.
But thou wilt reign.
Here, in abasement, crownless, poor, disrobed and bleeding:
There, in glory exceeding,
Thou art King.
—*John Stainer*

## Knowledge and Wisdom

KNOWLEDGE and wisdom, far from being one,
Have oft times no connecion. Knowledge dwells
In heads replete with thoughts of other men:
Wisdom in minds attentive to their own.
Knowledge, a rude unprofitable mass,
The mere materials with which wisdom builds,
Till smoothed and squared and fitted to its place,
Does but cncumber whom it seems to enrich.
Knowledge is proud that he has learned so much;
Wisdom is humble that he knows no more.
—*William Cowper*

## The Lamb

LITTLE lamb, who made thee?
Dost thou know who made thee,
Gave thee life, and bid thee feed
By the streams and o'er the mead;
Gave thee clothing of delight,
Softest clothing, woolly, bright;
Gave thee such a tender voice,
Making all the vales rejoice?
   Little lamb, who made thee?
   Dost thou know who made thee?

Little lamb, I'll tell thee;
Little lamb, I'll tell thee:
He is callèd by thy name,
For He calls himself a lamb;
He is meek, and He is mild;
He became a little child.
I a child, and thou a lamb,
We are callèd by His name.
   Little lamb, God bless thee!
   Little lamb, God bless thee!
       —*William Blake*

## The Largest Life

THERE is a beauty at the goal of life,
   A beauty growing since the world began,
Through every age and race, through lapse and strife,
   Till the great human soul complete her span.
Beneath the waves of storm that lash and burn,
   The currents of blind passion that appal,
To listen and keep watch till we discern
   The tide of sovereign truth that guides it all;
So to address our spirits to the height,
   And so attune them to the valiant whole,
That the great light be clearer for our light,
   And the great soul the stronger for our soul:
To have done this is to have lived, though fame
Remember us with no familiar name.
       —*Archibald Lampman*

## Laus Infantium

IN PRAISE of little children I will say
God first made man, then found a better way
For woman, but his third way was the best.
Of all created things the loveliest

And most divine are children. Nothing here
Can be to us more gracious or more dear.
And though when God saw all his works were good
There was no rosy flower of babyhood,
'Twas said of children in a later day
That none could enter Heaven save such as they.

The earth, which feels the flowering of a thorn,
Was glad, O little child, when you were born;
The earth, which thrills when skylarks scale the blue,
Soared up itself to God's own Heaven in you;
And Heaven, which loves to lean down and to glass
Its beauty in each dewdrop on the grass—
Heaven laughed to find your face so pure and fair,
And left, O little child, its reflex there!
—*William Canton*

## The Leaden-Eyed

LET not young souls be smothered out before
They do quaint deeds and fully flaunt their pride.
It is the world's one crime its babes grow dull,
Its poor are ox-like, limp and leaden-eyed.

Not that they starve, but starve so dreamlessly,
Not that they sow, but that they seldom reap,
Not that they serve, but have no gods to serve,
Not that they die, but that they die like sheep.
—*Vachel Lindsay*

## L'Envoi

WHEN Earth's last picture is painted, and the tubes are twisted and dried,
When the oldest colors have faded, and the youngest critic has died,
We shall rest, and, faith, we shall need it—lie down for an aeon or two,
Till the Master of All Good Workmen shall put us to work anew.

And those that were good shall be happy: they shall sit in a golden chair;
They shall splash at a ten-league canvas with brushes of comets' hair;
They shall find real saints to draw from—Magdalene, Peter, and Paul;
They shall work for an age at a sitting, and never be tired at all!

And only the Master shall praise us, and only the Master shall blame;
And no one shall work for money, and no one shall work for fame,
But each for the joy of the working, and each, in his separate star,
Shall draw the Thing as he sees It for the God of Things as They are!
—*Rudyard Kipling*

## Let All Sing

LET all the world in every corner sing
  My God and King.

The heavens are not too high,
His praise may thither fly;
The earth is not too low,
His praises there may grow.

Let all the world in every corner sing
  My God and King.

The Church with psalms must shout,
No door can keep them out:
But, above all, the heart
Must bear the longest part.

Let all the world in every corner sing
  My God and King.
                              —*George Herbert*


## Let Me Keep the Glow of Wonder

LORD, let me keep the glow of wonder
  At the starry host's unhurrying wheel.
The drum-tapped tidings told by thunder,
  And the sea-bowl's moonlight of molten steel,

Give me, as now, to view hereafter
  A fairy's flight on the fire-fly's wing,
And to hear the lilt of elfin laughter
  In the bubbling mirth of a mountain spring.

Grant me to guard that morning splendour
  That lighted on Eden undefiled,
To walk in the garden among the tender
  Buds that dream in the heart of a child.
                              —*Anonymous*


## Let No Man Fear the Night

"PEACE I leave with you." So the lesson's read
And the Book closed. The proud recessional swells
As black-gowned figures pass the plaque that spells
A long, illustrious list of honored dead.
These were the men who bought our peace before
And paid the price in blood and sweat and tears.
These were the men who gave us careless years.

Now ends the second summer of the war.
"Not as the world gives, give I unto you."
The evening air is hushed, save for the shrill
Cicadas sounding in the grass. The light
That barred with brilliant tones the deepening blue
Fades in pale splendor on a distant hill.
But dawn will break. Let no man fear the night.
—*Gloria Lauriston*

## Let the Face of God Shine Through

THE world stands out on either side
No wider than the heart is wide;
Above the world is stretched the sky,—
No higher than the soul is high.
The heart can push the sea and land
Farther away on either hand;
The soul can split the sky in two,
And let the face of God shine through.
But East and West will pinch the heart
That can not keep them pushed apart;
And he whose soul is flat—the sky
Will cave in on him by and by.
—*Edna St. Vincent Millay*

## Letters from God

WHY should I wish to see God better than this day?
I see something of God each hour of the twenty-four, and each moment
then;
In the faces of men and women I see God, and in my own face in the glass;
I find letters from God dropped into the street,
And every one is signed by God's name.
—*Walt Whitman*

## Life

LET me but live my life from year to year,
With forward face and unreluctant soul;
Not hurrying to, nor turning from, the goal;
Not mourning for the things that disappear
In the dim past, nor holding back in fear
From what the future veils; but with a whole
And happy heart, that pays its toll
To Youth and Age, and travels on with cheer.

So let the way wind up the hill or down,
O'er rough or smooth, the journey will be joy:
Still seeking what I sought when but a boy,

[ 86 ]

New friendship, high adventure, and a crown,
My heart will keep the courage of the quest,
And hope the road's last turn will be the best.
—*Henry van Dyke*

## Life Is Ever Lord of Death

HENCEFORWARD, listen as we will,
The voices of that hearth are still;
Look where we may, the wide earth o'er
Those lighted faces smile no more.
We tread the paths their feet have worn,
We sit beneath their orchard trees,
We hear, like them, the hum of bees
And rustle of the bladed corn;
We turn the pages that they read,
Their written words we linger o'er,
But in the sun they cast no shade,
No voice is heard, no sign is made,
No step is on the conscious floor!
Yet Love will dream, and Faith will trust,
(Since He who knows our need is just)
That somehow, somewhere, meet we must.
Alas for him who never sees
The stars shine through his cypress-trees!
Who, hopeless, lays his dead away,
Nor looks to see the breaking day
Across the mournful marble play!
Who hath not learned, in hours of faith,
The truth to flesh and sense unknown,
That Life is ever Lord of Death,
And Love can never lose its own!
—*John Greenleaf Whittier*

## Life Is Too Brief

LIFE is too brief
Between the budding and the falling leaf,
Between the seedtime and the golden sheaf,
For hate and spite.
We have no time for malice and for greed;
Therefore, with love make beautiful the deed;
Fast speeds the night.

Life is too swift
Between the blossom and the white snow's drift,
Between the silence and the lark's uplift,
For bitter words.

In kindness and in gentleness our speech
Must carry messages of hope, and reach
    The sweetest chords.

                                    —*W. M. Vories*

## Life of My Life

LIFE of my life, I shall ever try to keep my body pure, knowing that thy living touch is upon all my limbs.

I shall ever try to keep all untruths out from my thoughts, knowing that thou art the truth which has kindled the light of reason in my mind.

I shall ever try to drive all evils away from my heart and keep my love in flower, knowing that thou hast thy seat in the inmost shrine of my heart.

And it shall be my endeavour to reveal thee in my actions, knowing it is thy power gives me strength to act.

                                    —*Rabindranath Tagore*

## List to the Lark

LIST to the Lark!
He soars and sings,
"Wake to your work,
The Matin rings!"
Praise God for work!
Noon-tide is near,
The board is spread;
Thanks be to Him
Who giveth bread!
Praise God for bread!
Sinks to his sleep
The pilgrim Sun,
Homeward to rest,
The day is done!
Praise God for rest!

                                    —*Anonymous*

## The Living God

THE Living God. The God that makes the world,
Makes it—is making it in all its worth;
His spirit speaking sure and slow
In the real universe we know—
God living in the earth.
I feel his breath in the blowing wind,
His pulse in the swinging sea,
And the sunlit sod is the breast of God
Whose strength we feel and see.
His tenderness in the springing grass,

His beauty in the flowers,
His living love in the sun above—
All here, and near, and ours!

Not near enough! Not near enough!
O God, come nearer still
I long for thee! Be strong for me!
Teach me to know thy will!

The Living God. The God that is the world.
The world? The world is man—the work of man.
Then—dare I follow what I see?
Then—by thy Glory—it must be
That we are in thy plan!
That strength divine in the work we do—
That love in our mother's eyes—
That wisdom clear in our thinking here—
That power to help us rise—
God in the daily work we've done—
In the daily path we've trod—
Stand still, my heart, for I am a part—
I too—of the Living God!

Ah, clear as light! As near! As bright!
O God! My God! My Own!
Command thou me! I stand for thee!
And I do not stand alone!
—*Charlotte Stetson Gilman*

## Lord God, We Lift to Thee a World Hurt Sore

LORD God, we lift to thee a world hurt sore.
    Heal it and let it be wounded no more!
Lord, when this year is done, or e'en this day,
    Many shall pray to thee who do not pray.
Let all lips comfort them, all hearts be kind,
    They who this year shall leave their joys behind.
They have thy comforting, help them to know
    That though their hopes are gone, thou dost not go.
They who shall give for thee lover and son,
    Show them thy world set free, thy battles done![1]
                                —*Anonymous*
                        (Mozarabic—before A.D. 700)

---

[1] Slightly altered.

## Love and Labor

WE DIE not at all, for our deeds remain
To crown with honor or mar with stain;
Through endless sequence of years to come
Our lives shall speak when our lips are dumb.

What though we perish, unknown to fame,
Our tomb forgotten and lost our name,
Since naught is wasted in heaven or earth,
And nothing dies to which God gives birth!

Though life be joyless and death be cold,
And pleasures pall as the world grows old,
Yet God has granted our hearts relief,
For Love and Labor can conquer grief.

Love sheds a light on the gloomy way,
And Labor hurries the weary day;
Though death be fearful and life be hard,
Yet Love and Labor shall win reward.

If Love can dry a single tear,
If life-long Labor avail to clear
A single web from before the true,
Then Love and Labor have won their due.

What though we mourn, we can comfort pain;
What if we die, so the truth be plain!
A little spark from a high desire
Shall kindle others, and grow a fire.

Labor is mortal and fades away,
But Love shall triumph in perfect day;
Labor may wither beneath the sod,
But Love lives ever, for Love is God.

*—Anonymous*


## Love Gives and Counts Not the Cost

O MOTHER, the young Prince is to pass by our door—how can I attend
to my work this morning?
Show me how to braid up my hair; tell me what garment to put on.
Why do you look at me amazed, mother?
I know well he will not glance up once at my window; I know he
will pass out of my sight in the twinkling of an eye; only the vanishing
strain of the flute will come sobbing to me from afar.
But the young Prince will pass by our door, and I will put on my
best for the moment.

O mother, the young Prince did pass by our door, and the morning sun flashed from his chariot.

I swept aside the veil from my face, I tore the ruby chain from my neck and flung it in his path.

Why do you look at me amazed, mother?

I know well he did not pick up my chain; I know it was crushed under his wheels leaving a red stain upon the dust, and no one knows what my gift was nor to whom.

But the young Prince did pass by our door, I flung the jewel from my breast before his path.

*—Rabindranath Tagore*

## Love Is of God

BELOVED, let us love: love is of God;
In God alone hath love its true abode.

Beloved, let us love: for they who love,
They only, are His sons, born from above.

Beloved, let us love: for love is rest,
And he who loveth not abides unblest.

Beloved, let us love: for love is light,
And he who loveth not dwelleth in night.

Beloved, let us love: for only thus
Shall we behold that God Who loveth us.

*—Horatius Bonar*

## Love Me for Love's Sake Only

IF THOU must love me, let it be for naught
Except for love's sake only. Do not say,
"I love her for her smile—her look—her way
Of speaking gently,—for a trick of thought
That falls in well with mine, and certes brought
A sense of pleasant ease on such a day,"—
For these things in themselves, Beloved, may
Be changed, or change for thee,—and love, so wrought
May be unwrought so.

*—Elizabeth Barrett Browning*
(Sonnets from the Portuguese, Section VII)

## Love Thou Art Mine

LOVE that I know, love I am wise in, love,
My strength, my pride, my grace, my skill untaught,
My faith here upon earth, my hope above,
My contemplation and perpetual thought:
The pleasure of my fancy, my heart's fire,

My joy, my peace, my praise, my happy theme,
The aim of all my doing, my desire
Of being, my life by day, by night my dream:

Love, my sweet melancholy, my distress,
My pain, my doubt, my trouble, my despair,
My only folly and unhappiness,
And in my careless moments still my care:
   O love, sweet love, earthly love, love divine,
Say'st thou to-day, O love, that thou are mine?
                              —Robert Bridges

## Magna Est Veritas

HERE, in this little Bay,
Full of tumultuous life and great repose,
Where, twice a day,
The purposeless, glad ocean comes and goes,
Under high cliffs, and far from the huge town,
I sit me down.
For want of me the world's course will not fail:
When all its work is done, the lie shall rot;
The truth is great, and shall prevail,
When none cares whether it prevail or not.
                              —Coventry Patmore

## Making Life Worth While

EVERY soul that touches yours—
Be it the slightest contact—
Gets therefrom some good;
Some little grace; one kindly thought;
One aspiration yet unfelt;
One bit of courage
For the darkening sky;
One gleam of faith
To brave the thickening ills of life;
One glimpse of brighter skies
Beyond the gathering mists—
To make this life worth while
And heaven a surer heritage.
                              —George Eliot

## Man and Woman

[LET] man be more of woman, she of man;
He gain in sweetness and in moral height,
Nor lose the wrestling thews that throw the world;
She mental breadth, nor fail in childward care,

Nor lose the childlike in the larger mind;
Till at the last she set herself to man,
Like perfect music into noble words;
And so these twain, upon the skirts of Time,
Sit side by side, full-summ'd in all their powers,
Dispensing harvest, sowing the To-be,
Self-reverent each and reverencing each.
Distinct in individualties,
But like each other, ev'n as those who love.
Then comes the statelier Eden back to men;
Then reigns the world's great bridals, chaste and calm;
Then springs the crowning race of human kind.
May these things be!

—*Alfred Tennyson*
(The Princess)

## Man His Own Star, or the Honest Man's Fortune

MAN is his own star; and the soul that can
Render an honest and a perfect man
Commands all light, all influence, all fate;
Nothing to him falls early, or too late.
Our acts our angels are, or good or ill,
Our fatal shadows that walk by us still.

—*John Fletcher*

## Man Shares God's Eternity

GOD created man for incorruption,
And made him an image of his own eternity.

For the souls of the righteous are in the hand of God,
And no torment shall touch them.
In the eyes of the foolish they seem to have died,
And their departure is accounted to be their hurt,
And their journeying away from us to be their ruin.
But they are in peace;
For, even if in the sight of men they be punished
Their hope is full of immortality.
Having borne a little chastening, they shall receive great good;
Because God made trial of them and found them worthy of himself,
As gold in the furnace he proved them.
They that trust in him shall understand truth,
And the faithful shall abide with him in love.

—*Wisdom of Solomon*
(From Chapters 2 and 3)

[ 93 ]

## The Man with the Hoe

IS THIS the Thing the Lord God made and gave
To have dominion over sea and land;
To trace the stars and search the heavens for power;
To feel the passion of Eternity?
Is this the dream He dreamed who shaped the suns
And marked their ways upon the ancient deep?
Down all the caverns of Hell to their last gulf
There is no shape more terrible than this—
More tongued with censure of the world's blind greed—
More filled with signs and portents for the soul—
More packed with danger to the universe.

. . . . .

O masters, lords and rulers in all lands,
Is this the handiwork you give to God,
This monstrous thing distorted and soul-quenched?
How will you ever straighten up this shape;
Touch it again with immortality;
Give back the upward looking and the light;
Rebuild in it the music and the dream;
Make right the immemorial infamies,
Perfidious wrongs, immedicable woes?

O masters, lords and rulers in all lands,
How will the future reckon with this man?
How answer his brute question in that hour
When whirlwinds of rebellion shake all shores?
How will it be with kingdoms and with kings—
With those who shaped him to the thing he is—
When this dumb Terror shall rise to judge the world,
After the silence of the centuries?[1]

—*Edwin Markham*

## Maple Sap

BEFORE a tulip lifts
    Its cup or lace
Or cherry petal sifts
    New turf to grace,
The maple makes it clear
That spring is here.

Before a robin sings
    Or phoebe calls,
Before a brown bee wings

[1] Written after seeing Millet's world-famous painting of a brutalized toiler.

[ 94 ]

Through honeyed halls,
The maple gives the sign
In proffered wine.

Before the pulsing heart
    Has aught to say,
The maple currents start
    Their eager way,
First couriers to bring
The news of spring.
                —*Lalia Mitchell Thornton*


## Mary of Nazareth

I WONDER
If Mary
Was a capable person,
Who might have written
Books—
She must have been
If the Magnificat
Came from her heart—
Or painted pictures;
Or if, perhaps,
Lofty music
Lived in her heart,
All unexpressed,
Save for the lullabies
She sang
To her wee son.

I wonder
If the village gossips
Wagged their heads,
Saying "It's a shame
The way she teaches Jesus
Idleness—
Leaving the spinning
To take him to the woods
To watch the birds build nests
And find the places
Where the little foxes
Have their holes."

I wonder
If one said,
"She even takes
The common lilies

[ 95 ]

Of the field
And tells him
That the ancient court
Of Solomon himself
Could not compare
With the pure loveliness—
An ordinary lily
Think of that!"

I wonder
If the friends
Berated her and said
They thought it was a shame—
With all her gifts—
That all she seemed to have
To give the world
Was her supreme devotion
To her son.
—*Vera Campbell Darr*

## May Spiritual Knowledge Shine

LET us all protect one the other.
Let us all enjoy together.
Let us act valiantly together.
May spiritual knowledge ever shine before us.
Let us never hate one another.
And let Peace and Peace and Peace reign everywhere.
—*The Vedas*

## Mixed

WITHIN my earthly temple there's a crowd;
There's one of us that's humble, one that's proud,
There's one that's broken-hearted for his sins,
There's one that unrepentant sits and grins;
There's one that loves his neighbor as himself,
And one that cares for naught but fame and pelf.
From much corroding care I should be free
If I could once determine which is me.
—*Edward Sanford Martin*

## Morality

WE CANNOT kindle when we will
    The fire which in the heart resides;
The spirit bloweth and is still;
    In mystery our soul abides.
But tasks in hours of insight willed
Can be through hours of gloom fulfill'd.

[ 96 ]

With aching hands and bleeding feet
  We dig and heap, lay stone on stone;
We bear the burden and the heat
  Of the long day, and wish 'twere done.
Not till the hours of light return,
All we have built do we discern.
                    —*Matthew Arnold*

## Morning

MORNING gleamed like pebbles flung
In a rapturous mountain brook;
Morning glistened, morning hung
Swinging banners, singing, "Look!
Morning is a brimming cup.
Drink it up, and up, and up!"
                    —*Rosalie Dunlap Boyle*

## Most Wonderfully Kind

SOULS of men! Why will ye scatter
Like a crowd of frightened sheep?
Foolish hearts, why will ye wander,
From a love so true and deep? . . .

It is God: his love looks mighty,
But is mightier than it seems.
'Tis our Father, and his fondness
Goes far out beyond our dreams.
There's a wideness in God's mercy
Like the wideness of the sea;
There's a kindness in his justice,
Which is more than liberty.

For the love of God is broader
Than the measure of man's mind,
And the heart of the Eternal
Is most wonderfully kind.
But we make our love too narrow
By false limits of our own,
And we magnify his strictness
With a zeal he will not own . . .

If our love were but more simple,
We should take him at his word,
And our lives would be all sunshine
In the sweetness of our Lord.
                    —*Frederick W. Faber*

[ 97 ]

## Mother

SHE never touched with skillful brush the canvas
   And left a picture that the world might praise,
Or with inspired fingers on the key board,
   Sent down an echo through the length of days;
But once with eyes tear-stained, yet looking upward,
   With smiling lips she passed beneath the rod,
Descending almost to the vail of shadows
   To bring a little new-born soul from God.

She never sang a song of joy or sadness,
   In clear, sweet tones to make us smile or weep;
Her voice, too weak to win the world's approval,
   Was only good to hush a babe to sleep.
She never penned a book whose glowing pages,
   Might lift us up, and help us in the fight,
But day by day she sought with loving patience,
   To guide two little stumbling feet aright.

And yet, mayhap, when at the gate of heaven
   She paused, God looked at her, and smiled.
With hand outstretched, his kind voice spoke a welcome
   To her, the Mother of a little child.
                    —*Mable Stevens Freer*

## The Mother

THE bravest battle that ever was fought—
Shall I tell you where and when?
In the maps of this world you will find it not—
'Twas fought by the mothers of men.
Nay, not with cannon or battle-shot,
With the sword or the mightier pen,
Nay, not with words of eloquent thought
From the lips of eloquent men,
But deep in a faithful woman's heart,
A woman that would not yield,
But bravely, nobly, bore her part,
Lo! this was the battle-field.
No rattling shot, no bivouac song,
No banners to gleam and wave,
But oh! The battle that lasted long,
From babyhood down to the grave!
For bravely there, as the silent stars,
She fights in her walled-up town,
Fights on and on in those awful wars,
Then silent, unsung, goes down.
O ye, with cannon and battle-shot,

With soldiers to shout and praise,
I tell you the noblest battles fought
Are fought in those silent ways.
O spotless woman in a world of shame,
With splendid yet silent scorn,
Go back to God as white as you came,
The kingliest warrior born!

—*Joaquin Miller*

## Music a Mystic Link

How many of us ever stop to think
Of music as a wondrous magic link
With God; taking sometimes the place of prayer,
When words have failed us 'neath the weight of care?
Music that knows no country, race or creed,
But gives to each according to his need.

—*Anonymous*

## The Music-Makers

WE ARE the music-makers,
  And we are the dreamers of dreams,
Wandering by lone sea-breakers,
  And sitting by desolate streams;
World-losers and world-forsakers,
  On whom the pale moon gleams;
Yet we are the movers and shakers
  Of the world forever, it seems.

With wonderful deathless ditties
  We build up the world's great cities,
And out of a fabulous story
  We fashion an empire's glory:
One man with a dream, at pleasure,
  Shall go forth and conquer a crown;
And three with a new song's measure
  Can trample an empire down.

We, in the ages lying
  In the buried past of the earth,
Built Nineveh with our sighing
  And Babel itself with our mirth:
And o'erthrew them with prophesying
  To the old of the new world's worth;
For each age is a dream that is dying,
  Or one that is coming to birth.

—*Arthur O'Shaughnessy*

[ 99 ]

## My Charge

THIS is the charge I keep as mine,
The goal of every hope and plan—
To cancel the dividing line
Between me and my fellow man.

The atom shock, the radared moon,
Annihilated time and space—
What were the profit or the boon
If hate be in my brother's face?

More deadly than the blackest art,
More horror-fraught than shell or bomb,
Hate dims the mind, corrodes the heart
And strikes the voice of conscience dumb.

I dare not pass the lowliest waif
With scorn or condescending pride,
For never can my path be safe
Until his want is satisfied.

My *brothers* are they across the track,
In hall of state or jungle den—
Yellow or white or brown or black—
All are my kin for all are men.

And if but one shall lack of bread
Or bleed for justice still in vain,
The guilt is heavy on my head,
And of that blood I wear the stain.

And so for me all fear shall end
Save this—that I may fail to see
My neighbor as a needed friend,
Or sense my neighbor's need of me.

Though parliaments may rise and fall,
I hold to this eternal good,
This deathless truth—that men are all
One earth-encircling brotherhood.
                    —*Leslie Pinckney Hill*

## My Garden

A GARDEN is a lovesome thing, God wot!
　　Rose plot,
　　Fringed pool,
Fern'd grot—
　　The veriest school
　　Of peace; and yet the fool
Contends that God is not—
Not God! in gardens! when eve is cool?
　　Nay, but I have a sign;
　　'Tis very sure God walks in mine.
　　　　　　　　—*Thomas Edward Brown*


## My Hereafter

Do NOT come when I am dead
To sit beside a low green mound,
Or bring the first gay daffodils
Because I love them so,
For I shall not be there.
You cannot find me there.

I will look up at you from the eyes
Of little children;
I will bend to meet you in the swaying boughs
Of bud-thrilled trees,
And caress you with the passionate sweep
Of storm-filled winds;
I will give you strength in your upward tread
Of everlasting hills;
I will cool your tired body in the flow
Of the limpid river;
I will warm your work-glorified hands through the glow
Of the winter fire;
I will soothe you into forgetfulness to the drop, drop
Of the rain on the roof;
I will speak to you out of the rhymes
Of the masters;
I will dance with you in the lilt
Of the violin,
And make your heart leap with the bursting cadence
Of the organ;
I will flood your soul with the flaming radiance
Of the sunrise,
And bring you peace in the tender rose and gold
Of the after-sunset.

[ 101 ]

All these have made me happy:
They are a part of me;
I shall become a part of them.

—Juanita de Long

## My House of Life

GIVE me wide walls to build my house of life.
The North shall be of Love, against the winds of fate;
The South of Tolerance, that I may outreach hate;
The East of Faith, that rises clear and new each day;
The West of Hope, that even dies a glorious way.
The threshold neath my feet shall be Humility;
The roof—the very sky itself—infinity.
Give me wide walls to build my house of Life!

—Anonymous

## Nature

As A FOND mother, when the day is o'er,
  Leads by the hand her little child to bed,
  Half willing, half reluctant to be led,
  And leave his broken playthings on the floor,
Still gazing at them through the open door,
  Nor wholly reassured and comforted
  By promises of others in their stead,
  Which, though more splendid, may not please him more;
So Nature deals with us, and takes away
  Our playthings one by one, and by the hand
  Leads us to rest so gently, that we go
Scarce knowing if we wish to go or stay,
  Being too full of sleep to understand
  How far the unknown transcends the what we know.

—Henry Wadsworth Longfellow

## Near God's Heart

THE kiss of the sun for pardon,
  The song of the birds for mirth,—
One is nearer God's heart in a garden
  Than anywhere else on earth.

—Dorothy Frances Gurney

## The Needy

I HAVE more food than I can eat—
They faint with hunger in the street.

I have more clothes than I can wear—
Their heads, and hands, and feet are bare.

[ 102 ]

My walls are thick, and warm, and dry—
Their walls are rain, and wind, and sky.

My heart knows love of noble souls—
Their hearts are hungry, thirsty bowls.

These things let me remember when
Cries of the needy rise again.
—*Alice Ferrin Hensey*

## New Temples

I THINK God loves new temples built to him
And watches as each stone is laid on stone,
And smiles to see them laid so straight and true,
Lifting the strong wide walls to heaven's blue.
And when the carpenters have done with them,
And each new church stands finished and alone,
When dusk sifts violet shadows through the glass
Of painted windows, I think that God must pass
Between the new dim aisles, and stopping where
The last light falls across his shining hair,
He kneels and holds his first communion there.
—*Lexie Dean Robertson*

## The Night Has a Thousand Eyes

THE night has a thousand eyes,
   And the day but one;
Yet the light of the bright world dies
   With the dying sun.

The mind has a thousand eyes,
   And the heart but one;
Yet the light of a whole life dies
   When love is done.
—*Francis William Bourdillon*

## No Faith!

"I HAVE no faith in men," you say:
No faith in men, my eye!
I saw you board a plane with ten
And ride across the sky.
"I have no faith in God," you wail:
No faith in God indeed!
Why did you dig into the sod
And scatter flower seed?
—*Anonymous*

[ 103 ]

## No Pilots We

WOULD I were one of those who preach no Cause—
Nor guide mankind with meddling fingertips;
But let each star that moves without a pause
Shine as it list—as potent when it dips
Beyond their ken in visual eclipse
As when it blazes in a darkling sky,
Regnant and beautiful, while with mute lips
Men bow the head in worship, or in shy
And inexpressive words admit that God is nigh.

We are no pilots: let us trust our bark,
Miraculous, alert, not made with hands,
That feels a magic impulse through the dark,
And leaps upon the course it understands
From shores unknown to unimagined strands;
Resists the helm we give it, but divines—
Being itself divine—divine commands;
And answers to no compass save the signs
Encircling deepest heaven where the Zodiac shines.
—*John Jay Chapman*

## No Word of Fear

DEATH stands above me, whispering low
I know not what into my ear;
Of his strange language all I know
Is, there is not a word of fear.
—*Walter Savage Landor*

## The Noble Nature

IT IS not growing like a tree
In bulk, doth make man better be;
Or standing long an oak, three hundred year,
To fall a log at last, dry, bald, and sear:
A lily of a day
Is fairer far in May,
Although it fall and die that night,
It was the plant and flower of Light.
In small proportions we just beauties see,
And in short measures life may perfect be.
—*Ben Jonson*

## Nothing Is Enough

NOTHING is enough!
No, though our all be spent—
Heart's extremest love,

[ 104 ]

Spirit's whole intent,
All that nerve can feel,
All that brain invent—
Still beyond appeal
Will Divine Desire
Yet more excellent
Precious cost require
Of this mortal stuff—
Never be content
Till ourselves be fire,
Nothing is enough.
—*Laurence Binyon*

## Nothing Is Here for Tears

NOTHING is here for tears, nothing to wail
Or knock the breast; no weakness, no contempt,
Dispraise or blame; nothing but well and fair,
And what may quiet us in a death so noble.
—*John Milton*

## Now Is the Time

Now is the time; ah, friend, no longer wait
To scatter loving smiles and words of cheer
To those around whose lives are now so dear.
They may not meet you in the coming year.
Now is the time.

Ah, friends! dear friends—if any such there be—
Keep not your loving thoughts away from me
Till I am gone.
I want them now to help me on the way,
As lonely watchers want the light of day
Ere it is morn.
—*D. F. Hodges*

## O Church of God, Divided

O CHURCH OF GOD, divided
And rent by endless strife!
Thy warring sects obscuring
The way, the truth, the life;
A stricken world, despairing,
Is calling unto thee;
O Church of Christ's evangel,
What shall thine answer be?

The subtle powers of darkness,
Like foemen in the night,
Advance upon the strongholds
Of justice, truth, and right;
The mighty sway of evil
Prevails in every land;
O Church of God's anointing,
Arise, and take thy stand!

Disperse thy warring factions,
And bid their conflict cease;
Lift high the fallen standard
Of Christ, the Prince of Peace;
One Lord, one faith, one spirit,
One God of all proclaim;
Go forth, O Church, united,
To conquer in His name!
                    —*Marion Franklin Ham*

## O Lovely Lily

O LOVELY lily clean,
O lily springing green,
O lily bursting white,
Dear lily of delight,
Spring in my heart agen
That I may flower to men.
                    —*John Masefield*
            (The Everlasting Mercy)

## O Thou Who Spreadest the Heaven Like a Tent

O THOU who spreadest the heaven like a tent,
He who depends on thee, ne'er is forspent,
Still for his might on thee he ever counteth,
On wings of eagles he, unwearied, mounteth.
Have ye not heard, have ye not known
The everlasting God
Creator is of heaven and earth,
And he alone is Lord.

So shall the glory of God be revealed,
All flesh shall see it and all shall be healed;
In word and deed declare him and adore him.
God's will is done, and all is plain before him.
Have ye not heard, have ye not known

[ 106 ]

The everlasting God
Creator is of heaven and earth,
And he alone is Lord.

—*Isaiah 40* (*Dutch Version*)


## The Oath of the Order of the Table Round

[King Arthur is telling how his power and influence have grown. He
says he drew the Knights together.]

IN THAT fair Order of my Table Round,
A glorious company, the flower of men,
To serve as model for the mighty world,
And be the fair beginning of a time.
I made them lay their hands in mine and swear
To reverence the King, as if he were
Their conscience, and their conscience as their King . . .
To ride abroad redressing human wrongs,
To speak no slander, no, nor listen to it,
To honour his own word as if his God's,
To lead sweet lives in purest chastity,
To love one maiden only, cleave to her,
And worship her by years of noble deeds,
Until they won her; for indeed I knew
Of no more subtle master under heaven
Than is the maiden passion for a maid,
Not only to keep down the base in man,
But teach high thought, and amiable words
And courtliness, and the desire of fame,
And love of truth, and all that makes a man.

—*Alfred Tennyson*


## Ode to the Northeast Wind

WELCOME, wild North-easter!
Shame it is to see
Odes to every zephyr;
Ne'er a verse to thee.
Tired we are of summer,
Tired of gaudy glare,
Showers soft and steaming,
Hot and breathless air.
Come; and strong within us
Stir the Vikings' blood;
Bracing brain and sinew;
Blow, thou wind of God!

—*Charles Kingsley*

## Of One Flesh

THE One bethought Him to make man
Of many colored dust,
And mixed the holy spirit in
In portions right and just;
Each had a part of mind and heart
From one Himself in trust;

Thus came the brown and yellow men
And black and white and red,
So different in their outer look,
Alike in heart and head—
The self-same dust before their birth,
The self-same dust when dead.

—*Pai Ta-Shun, Chinese*

## Oh, the Earth and the Air!

OH, THE earth and the air!
Honeysuckle and rose:
Fir trees tapering high
Into the deep repose
Of the fleckless sky:
Hills that climb and are strong,
Basking contented plain:
Sunlight poured out along
The sea of the grass like rain:
Spice-burdened winds that rise,
Whisper, wander and hush;
And the caroling harmonies
Of robin and quail and thrush.
O God! Thy world is fair!

And this but the place of his feet!
I had cried, "Let me see, let me hear,
Show me the ways of thy hands,"
For it all was a riddle drear
And I fainted to understand.
Canopy close curtained round,
Part not nor lift from the ground;
Move not your finger tips,
Firs, from the heaven's lips.
When this is the place of his feet
How should I bear to raise
My blasted vision to meet
The inconceivable blaze
Of his majesty complete!

—*James T. McKay*

[ 108 ]

## Old Age

IT IS too late! Ah, nothing is too late
Till the tired heart shall cease to palpitate.
Cato learned Greek at eighty; Sophocles
Wrote his grand Oedipus, and Simonides
Bore off the prize of verse from his compeers,
When each had numbered more than fourscore years;
And Theophrastus, at fourscore and ten,
Had but begun his Characters of Men.
Chaucer, at Woodstock with the nightingales,
At sixty wrote the Canterbury Tales;
Goethe, at Weimar, toiling to the last,
Completed Faust when eighty years were past.
These are indeed exceptions; but they show
How far the gulf-stream of our youth may flow
Into the arctic regions of our lives,
Where little else than life itself survives. . . .
What then? Shall we sit idly down and say
The night hath come; it is no longer day?
The night hath not yet come; we are not quite
Cut off from labour by the failing light;
Something remains for us to do or dare;
Even the oldest tree some fruit may bear. . . .
For age is opportunity no less
Than youth itself, though in another dress,
And as the evening twilight fades away
The sky is filled with stars, invisible by day.

—*Henry Wadsworth Longfellow*
(Morituri Salutamus)

## The Old Order Changeth

THE old order changeth, yielding place to new,
And God fulfils himself in many ways,
Lest one good custom should corrupt the world.
Comfort thyself: what comfort is in me?
I have lived my life, and that which I have done
May He within himself make pure! but thou,
If thou shouldst never see my face again,
Pray for my soul. More things are wrought by prayer
Than this world dreams of. Wherefore, let thy voice
Rise like a fountain for me night and day.
For what are men better than sheep or goats
That nourish a blind life within the brain,
If, knowing God, they lift not hands of prayer

Both for themselves and those who call them friend?
For so the whole round earth is every way
Bound by gold chains about the feet of God.
—*Alfred Tennyson*


## On Growing Old

BE WITH me, Beauty, for the fire is dying;
My dog and I are old, too old for roving.
Man, whose young passion sets the spindrift flying,
Is soon too lame to march, too cold for loving.
I take the book and gather to the fire,
Turning old yellow leaves; minute by minute
The clock ticks to my heart. A withered wire,
Moves a thin ghost of music in the spinet.
I cannot sail your seas, I cannot wander
Your cornland, nor your hill-land, nor your valleys
Ever again, nor share the battle yonder
Where the young knight the broken squadron rallies.
Only stay quiet while my mind remembers
The beauty of fire from the beauty of embers.

Beauty, have pity! for the strong have power,
The rich their wealth, the beautiful their grace,
Summer of man its sunlight and its flower,
Spring-time of man, all April in a face.
Only, as in the jostling in the Strand,
Where the mob thrusts or loiters or is loud,
The beggar with the saucer in his hand
Asks only a penny from the passing crowd,
So, from this glittering world with all its fashion,
Its fire, and play of men, its stirs, its march,
Let me have wisdom, Beauty, wisdom and passion,
Bread to the soul, rain where the summers parch.
Give me but these, and, though the darkness close,
Even the night will blossom as the rose.
—*John Masefield*


## The Open Door

YOU, my son,
Have shown me God.
Your kiss upon my cheek
Has made me feel the gentle touch
Of Him who leads us on.
The memory of your smile, when young,
Reveals His face
As mellowing years come on apace.

And when you went before,
You left the gates of heaven ajar
That I might glimpse,
Approaching from afar,
The glories of His grace.
Hold, son, my hand,
Guide me along the path,
That, coming,
I may stumble not,
Nor roam,
Nor fail to show the way
Which leads us home.

—*Grace Coolidge*

## Our Resolve

WE[1] WILL follow the upward road today
We will keep our face to the light,
We will think high thoughts as we go our way,
We will do what we know is right.
We will look for the flowers by the side of the road,
We will laugh and love and be strong,
We will try to lighten another's load
This day as we fare along.

—*Mary S. Edgar*

## Out of the Vast

THERE's a part of the sun in the apple,
    There's a part of the moon in a rose;
There's a part of the flaming Pleiades
    In every leaf that grows.

Out of the vast comes nearness;
    For the God whose love we sing
Lends a little of His heaven
    To every living thing.

—*Augustus Wright Bamberger*

## Over the Hills of Home

LADDIE, little laddie, come with me over the hills,
Where blossom the white May lilies and the dogwood and daffodils;
For the spirit of spring is calling to our spirits that love to roam
Over the hills of home, laddie, over the hills of home.

[1] Changed to the plural.

[ 111 ]

Brother, soldier brother, the spring has come back again,
But her voice from the windy hilltops is calling your name in vain,
For never shall we together 'mid the birds and the blossoms roam
Over the hills of home, brother, over the hills of home.

*—Lilian Leveridge*

## Overtones

I HEARD a bird at break of day
　　Sing from the autumn trees
A song so mystical and calm
　　So full of certainties,
No man, I think, could listen long
　　Except upon his knees.
Yet this was but a simple bird,
　　Alone, among the trees.

*—William Alexander Percy*

## Parents' and Teachers' Prayer

UP TO me sweet childhood looketh,
Heart and mind and soul awake;
Teach me of thy ways, O Father,
For sweet childhood's sake.

In their young hearts, soft and tender,
Guide my hand good seed to sow,
That its blossoming may praise thee,
Wheresoever they may go.

Father, order all my footsteps;
So direct my daily way,
That in following me, the children
May not, stumbling, go astray.

*—Anonymous*

## The Parliament of Man, the Federation of the World

FOR I dipt into the future, far as human eye could see,
Saw the Vision of the world, and all the wonder that would be;

Saw the heavens fill with commerce, argosies of magic sails,
Pilots of the purple twilight, dropping down with costly bales;

Heard the heavens fill with shouting, and there rain'd a ghastly dew
From the nations' airy navies grappling in the central blue;

Far along the world-wide whisper of the south-wind rushing warm,
With the standards of the peoples plunging thro' the thunder-storm;

Till the war-drum throbb'd no longer, and the battle-flags were furl'd
In the Parliament of man, the Federation of the world.

There the common sense of most shall hold a fretful realm in awe,
And the kindly earth shall slumber, lapt in universal law.

.    .    .    .    .

Yet I doubt not thro' the ages one increasing purpose runs,
And the thoughts of men are widen'd with the process of the suns.
—*Alfred Tennyson*
(Locksley Hall)

## Perfect Thy Kingdom

ETERNAL Father, who didst all create,
In whom we live, and to whose bosom move,
To all men Thy name known, which is Love,
Till its loud praises sound at heaven's high gate.
Perfect Thy kingdom in our passing state,
That here on earth Thou may'st as well approve
Our service, as Thou ownest theirs above,
Whose joy we echo and in pain await.

Grant body and soul each day their daily bread:
And should in spite of grace fresh woe begin,
Even as our anger soon is past and dead
Be Thy remembrance mortal of our sin:
By Thee in paths of peace Thy sheep be led,
And in the vale of terror comforted.
—*Robert Bridges*

## The Petrified Fern

IN A valley centuries ago
Grew a little fern leaf green and slender
Veining delicate and fibres tender
Waving when the wind crept down so low
Rushes tall and moss grew round it
Playful sunbeams darted in and found it
Drops of dew stole in by night and crowned it
But no foot of man e'er trod that way
Earth was young and keeping holiday.

Monster fishes swam the silent main
Stately forests waved their giant branches
Mountains hurled their snowy avalanches
Mammoth creatures stalked across the plain
Nature revelled in grand mysteries

[ 113 ]

But the little fern was not of these
Did not number with the hills and trees
Only grew and waved its sweet wild way
None ever came to note it day by day.

Earth one time put on a frolic mood
Heaved the rocks and changed the mighty motion
Of the deep strong currents of the ocean
Moved the plain and shook the mighty wood
Crushed the little fern in soft moist clay
Covered it, and hid it safe away. . . .
Oh the long long centuries since that day
Oh the agony! Oh life's bitter cost
Since that useless little fern was lost!

Useless? Lost? There came a thoughful man
Searching Nature's secrets far and deep.
From a fissure in a rocky steep
He withdrew o'er which there ran
Fairy pencilings a quaint design
Veinings leafage fibres clear and fine
And the fern's life lay in every line.
So, I think God hides some souls away
Sweetly to surprise us the last day.

—*Mary L. B. Branch*

## *The Pilgrim Way*

BUT once I pass this way,
And then—no more.
But once—and then, the Silent Door
Swings on its hinges—
Opens . . . Closes—
And no more
I pass this way.
So while I may,
With all my might,
I will assay
Sweet comfort and delight,
To all I meet upon the Pilgrim Way.
For no man travels twice
The Great Highway
That climbs through Darkness up to Light—
Through Night
To Day.

—*John Oxenham*

## Please God We Are Growing

THO' growing with scarce a showing,
Yet, please God, we are growing.

The twig teacheth,
The moth preacheth,
The plant vaunteth,
The bird chanteth,
God's mercy overflowing,
Merciful past man's knowing.
Please God to keep us growing. . . .
—*Christina Rossetti*

## A Poem for a New House

THIS house is built of mortar and of wood,
Of waiting long, and of our heart's desire;
Now it is finished, let us lay the hearth,
And light a fire.
(Lord, may it keep us warm when days are cold,
Though we be young, or old.)

The close-laid shingles gleam with golden light,
They are so strong, so fragrant, and so new;
The waters of the years will try them, yet
No rain drip through.
(Lord, may this shelter be a sure retreat
Through rain and snow and heat.)

The windows of our house let in the sun,
And the clean air when days are long and bright:
Wide windows through which heaven's breath may come,
And heaven's light.
(Lord, may this be a safe, sweet place to rest,
Then come, Lord, be our guest.)
—*Grace Noll Crowell*

## Poem for Sleep

TURN thou the key upon our thoughts, dear Lord,
   And let us rest;
Give us our portion of forgetfulness,
   Silent and deep.

Keep back the phantoms and the visions sad,
   The shades of grey
Like fancies that so haunt the little hours
   Before the day.

[ 115 ]

Lay Thou Thy quiet hand upon our eyes
    To close their sight;
Shut out the shining of the moon and stars
    And candle light.

Quiet the time-worn questions that are all
    Unanswered yet;
Take from the spent and troubled souls of us
    Their vain regret.

And lead us far into the silent land
    That we may go
Like children out across the field of dreams,
    Where poppies blow.

So all the saints and all the sinners too
    Wilt Thou not keep,
Since not alone unto Thy well-beloved
    Thou givest Sleep.
                              —*Virna Sheard*

## The Power of Prayer

LORD, what a change within us one short hour
Spent in Thy presence will prevail to make!
What heavy burdens from our bosoms take,
What parched grounds refresh as with a shower!
We kneel, and all around us seems to lower;
We rise, and all, the distant and the near,
Stands forth in sunny outline brave and clear;
We kneel, how weak! we rise how full of power!
Why, therefore, should we do ourselves this wrong,
Or others,—that we are not always strong,
That we are ever overborne with care,
That we should ever weak or heartless be,
Anxious or troubled, when with us is prayer,
And joy and strength and courage are with Thee!
                              —*Richard C. Trench*

## Praise Be to God

PRAISE be to God! There comes
Out of the night the day,
Out of the gloom of wintertime
Spring with its flowers gay.

Praise be to God! There comes
Out of the chrysalis dry
Yellow or blue or snowy-winged
Gay little butterfly.

[ 116 ]

Praise be to God! There comes
Out of the buried grain
Wonderful life, a hundredfold
Harvest of joy again.

Praise to our Father God.
Giver of life to all—
Wonderful life that cannot die.
Given to great and small.
—*Alice N. Pullen*

## Praise God

HARK to the sound of chiming bells
List to the song their music tells;
Praise ye, Praise God.

Praise him for life with each new day;
Praise him for joy in work and play;
Praise God for life.

Praise him for friends who help us know
Wonders of God the world may show;
Praise God for friends.
—*Jeanette Perkins Brown*

## A Prayer

O GOD, Almighty Creator,
The limitless distances of the universe tell of thy might,
The stars in their courses show forth thy power,
The worlds of the atoms suggest thy mystery.
We ascribe to thee majesty, dominion and power.

O Lord of Life, Sustainer,
The grass and flowers and trees reflect thy beauty,
The birds and beasts make joyful sounds to thy praise,
The microscope reveals new wonders of thy world.
We give thee heartfelt gratitude and praise.

O God, Father, Redeemer,
The undaunted courage of men, women, and children speaks of thee,
The faith and loyalty of friends reveal thee,
The love which sanctifies and glorifies is like thyself.
We bless and magnify thy holy name.

O God, Teacher, Leader,
For every lovely thing mankind has attempted or done,
For every beautiful hope or dream sought or attained,

For power to imagine and will to cooperate in building the Kingdom of
    Love we glorify thee,
O Lord, our strength and our Redeemer.

—A. J. *William Myers*

## A Prayer Found in Chester Cathedral

GIVE me a good digestion, Lord,
And also something to digest;
Give me a healthy body, Lord,
With sense to keep it at its best.
Give me a healthy mind, Good Lord,
To keep the good and pure in sight,
Which, seeing sin, is not appalled
But finds a way to set it right.
Give me a mind that is not bored,
That does not whimper, whine or sigh;
Don't let me worry over much
About the fussy thing called "I."
Give me a sense of humor, Lord,
Give me the grace to see a joke,
To get some pleasure out of life,
And pass it on to other folk.

—*Anonymous*

## Prayer of a New House

MAY I be full of graciousness and light, O Master Builder
A haven of refuge from the turmoil of day;
May I know all of beauty and delight,
Sweet with the sound of laughter and of joy.
May the quiet comfort of my days
The sting of sorrow blunt, and pain be calm;
May the patter of little feet within me,
And the voice of love make sweet my days;
May the whisper of scandal and of gossip
Find no lodging place within my walls.
May none in anger or in sorrow leave,
But, entering in, be glad of joyous hospitality.
May I, indeed, be like unto thy mansions—
O Master Builder, make of me a home.

—*Anonymous*

## The Present Crisis

ONCE to every man and nation comes the moment to decide;
In the strife of Truth with Falsehood, for the good or evil side;
Some great cause, God's new Messiah, offering each the bloom or blight,

Parts the goats upon the left hand, and the sheep upon the right,
And the choice goes by forever 'twixt that darkness and that light.

. . . . .

Careless seems the great Avenger; history's pages but record
One death-grapple in the darkness 'twixt old systems and the Word;
Truth forever on the scaffold, Wrong forever on the throne,—
Yet that scaffold sways the future, and, behind the dim unknown,
Standeth God within the shadow, keeping watch above his own.

. . . . .

Then to side with Truth is noble when we share her wretched crust,
Ere her cause bring fame and profit, and 'tis prosperous to be just;
Then it is the brave man chooses, while the coward stands aside,
Doubting in his abject spirit, till his Lord is crucified,
And the multitude make virtue of the faith they had denied.

Count me o'er earth's chosen heroes,—they were souls that stood alone,
While the men they agonized for hurled the contumelious stone,
Stood serene, and down the future saw the golden beam incline
To the side of perfect justice, mastered by their faith divine,
By one man's plain truth to manhood and to God's supreme design.

New occasions teach new duties; Time makes ancient good uncouth;
They must upward still, and onward, who would keep abreast of Truth;
Lo, before us gleam her camp-fires! we ourselves must Pilgrims be,
Launch our Mayflower, and steer boldly through the desperate winter sea,
Nor attempt the Future's portal with the Past's blood-rusted key.
                                        —*James Russell Lowell*

## Procrastination

SHUN delays, they breed remorse;
Take thy time while time is lent thee,
Creeping snails have weakest force,
Fly their faults lest thou repent thee;
Good is best when soonest wrought,
Ling'ring labors come to naught;
Hoist up sail while gale doth last,
Tide and wind stay no man's pleasure;
Seek not time, when time is past,
Sober speed is wisdom's leisure;
After-wits are dearly bought,
Let thy fore-wit guide thy thought.
                          —*Robert Southwell*

## The Prodigal

WHY feedest thou on husks so coarse and rude?
I could not be content with angel's food.

[ 119 ]

How camest thou companion to the swine?
I lothed the courts of heaven, the choir divine.

What sordid rags float round thee on the breeze?
I laid immortal robes aside for these.

An exile through the world, who bade thee roam?
None, but I wearied of a happy home.
—*Anonymous*

## Prospice

FEAR death?—to feel the fog in my throat,
The mist in my face,
When the snows begin, and the blasts denote
I am nearing the place,
The power of the night, the press of the storm,
The post of the foe;
Where he stands, the Arch Fear in a visible form,
Yet the strong man must go:
For the journey is done and the summit attained,
And the barriers fall,
Though a battle's to fight ere the guerdon be gained,
The reward of it all.
I was ever a fighter, so—one fight more,
The best and the last!
I would hate that death bandaged my eyes, and forebore,
And bade me creep past.
No! let me taste the whole of it, fare like my peers
The heroes of old,
Bear the brunt, in a minute pay glad life's arrears
Of pain, darkness, and cold.
For sudden the worst turns the best to the brave,
The black minute's at end,
And the elements' rage, the fiend-voices that rave,
Shall dwindle, shall blend,
Shall change, shall become first a peace out of pain,
Then a light, then thy breast,
O thou soul of my soul! I shall clasp thee again,
And with God be the rest!
—*Robert Browning*

## The Quality of Mercy

THE quality of mercy is not strain'd,
It droppeth as the gentle rain from heaven
Upon the place beneath. It is twice bless'd:
It blesseth him that gives and him that takes.
'Tis mightiest in the mightiest: it becomes

[ 120 ]

The thronéd monarch better than his crown:
His sceptre shows the force of temporal power,
The attribute of awe and majesty,
Wherein doth sit the dread and fear of kings;
But mercy is above this sceptred sway,
It is enthronéd in the hearts of kings,
It is an attribute to God himself;
And earthly power doth then show likest God's,
When mercy seasons justice.

—*William Shakespeare*
(Merchant of Venice)

## Rabbi Ben Ezra

GROW old along with me!
The best is yet to be,
The last of life, for which the first was made:
Our times are in his hand
Who saith, "A whole I planned,
Youth shows but half; trust God: see all, nor be afraid!"

. . . . .

Then, welcome each rebuff
That turns earth's smoothness rough,
Each sting that bids nor sit nor stand but go!
Be our joys three-parts pain!
Strive, and hold cheap the strain;
Learn, nor account the pang; dare, never grudge the throe!

. . . . .

Let us not always say,
"Spite of this flesh to-day
I strove, made head, gained ground upon the whole!"
As the bird wings and sings,
Let us cry "All good things
Are ours, nor soul helps flesh more, now, than flesh helps soul!"

Therefore I summon age
To grant youth's heritage,
Life's struggle having so far reached its term:
Thence shall I pass, approved
A man, for aye removed
From the developed brute; a God though in the germ.

. . . . .

But I need, now as then,
Thee, God, who mouldest men; . . .
So, take and use thy work,
Amend what flaws may lurk,

What strain o' the stuff, what warpings past the aim!
My times be in thy hand!
Perfect the cup as planned!
Let age approve of youth, and death complete the same!
—*Robert Browning*

## Red Geraniums

LIFE did not bring me silken gowns,
    Nor jewels for my hair,
Nor sight of gabled, foreign towns
    In distant countries fair;
But I can glimpse beyond my pane, a green and friendly hill,
And red geraniums aflame upon my window sill.

The brambled cares of every day,
    The tiny, humdrum things,
May bind my feet when they would stray,
    But still my heart has wings
While red geraniums are bloomed against my window glass,
And low above my green-sweet hill the gypsy wind-clouds pass.

And if my dreamings ne'er come true,
    The brightest and the best,
But leave me lone my journey through,
    I'll set my heart at rest
And thank Thee, God, for home-sweet things, a green and friendly hill,
And red geraniums aflame upon my window sill.
—*Martha Haskell Clark*

## Reflection

EACH day I rediscover this—
    What beauty means to me;
The world's so full of loveliness,
    Sometimes we fail to see,
Old-fashioned houses, airy rooms,
    Fresh mounds of new-mown hay—
Large orchards rich and bowed with fruit,
    And kittens' gentle play;
Bright silver touched by candle light,
    The merry drops of rain,
The dainty bloom of lavender,
    A country village lane;
Moon-flooded gardens, silent hills,
    A pine tree, straight and tall,
Gay wood-land carpets, soft, green moss,
    Huge bonfires in the fall,
And scarlet maples' swirling leaves;

[ 122 ]

The endless turquoise sky,
The golden mist of after-glow,
    The small birds flying high:
Deep ermine snow and frosty stars,
    The sleigh bells shining bright,
A chair beside a cheery fire
    Secure against the night!
                    —*Margaret B. Lyman*


## Render Thanks to God

THE sumac has flamed in the uplands,
The gorse flecks the meadows with gold,
The asters their violet fringes
No more by the roadsides unfold;
The rich, crimson stores of the orchards,
The grainfield's ripe, plentiful hoard;
All these have been gathered and garnered,
Come, render your thanks to the Lord.
                    —*Anonymous*


## Requiem

UNDER the wide and starry sky,
    Dig the grave and let me lie.
Glad did I live and gladly die,
    And I laid me down with a will.

This be the verse you grave for me:
    Here he lies where he longed to be;
Home is the sailor, home from sea,
    And the hunter home from the hill.
                    —*Robert Louis Stevenson*


## Requirement

WE LIVE by Faith; but Faith is not the slave
Of text and legend. Reason's voice and God's,
Nature's and Duty's, never are at odds.
What asks our Father of His children, save
Justice and mercy and humility,
A reasonable service of good deeds,
Pure living, tenderness to human needs,
Reverence and trust, and prayer for light to see
The Master's footprints in our daily ways?
No knotted scourge nor sacrificial knife,
But the calm beauty of an ordered life

[ 123 ]

Whose very breathing is unworded praise!—
A life that stands as all true lives have stood,
Firm-rooted in the faith that God is Good.
—*John Greenleaf Whittier*

## Resignation

THERE is no flock, however watched and tended,
  But one dead lamb is there!
There is no fireside, howsoe'r defended,
  But has one vacant chair!

. . . . .

She is not dead—the child of our affection—
  But gone unto that school
Where she no longer needs our poor protection,
  And Christ himself doth rule.

. . . . .

And though at times impetuous with emotion
  And anguish long suppressed,
The swelling heart heaves moaning like the ocean,
  That cannot be at rest,

We will be patient, and assuage the feeling
  We may not wholly stay;
By silence sanctifying, not concealing,
  The grief that must have way.
—*Henry Wadsworth Longfellow*

## Resurrection

YE WHO fear death,
  Behold the buds bursting;
    Ye who fear death,
      Hark, how the robins sing;
Ye who fear death,
  Go, hear the crocus crying,
    Eternal Spring!

Ye who fear death,
  See how the trees are greening,
    Risen to life before the April sun;
Ye who fear death,
  Give way to joy and gladness,
    New Life's begun!

So it has been
Since days first had beginning,

[ 124 ]

Glad prophecies of Resurrection Morn;
  Weep not before a closed tomb
  In Joseph's garden,
  Life is reborn!
          —*Ralph Spaulding Cushman*

## *Revelation*

I MADE a pilgrimage to find the God!
I listened for his voice at holy tombs,
Searched for the print of his immortal feet
In dust of broken altars; yet turned back
With empty heart. But on the homeward road,
A great light came upon me, and I heard
The God's voice singing in a nesting lark;
Felt his sweet wonder in a swaying rose;
Received his blessing from a wayside well;
Looked on his beauty in a lover's face;
Saw his bright hand signal from the sun.
          —*Edwin Markham*

## *Ring Out the Old, Ring in the New*

RING out, wild bells, to the wild sky,
  The flying cloud, the frosty light:
  The year is dying in the night;
Ring out, wild bells, and let him die.

Ring out the old, ring in the new,
  Ring happy bells, across the snow:
  The year is going, let him go;
Ring out the false, ring in the true.

Ring out the grief that saps the mind,
  For those that here we see no more;
  Ring out the feud of rich and poor,
Ring in redress to all mankind.

Ring out a slowly dying cause,
  And ancient forms of party strife;
  Ring in the nobler modes of life,
With sweeter manners, purer laws.

Ring out the want, the care, the sin,
  The faithless coldness of the times;
  Ring out, ring out my mournful rhymes,
But ring the fuller minstrel in.

[ 125 ]

Ring out false pride in place and blood,
The civic slander and the spite;
Ring in the love of truth and right,
Ring in the common love of good.

Ring out old shapes of foul disease;
Ring out the narrowing lust of gold;
Ring out the thousand wars of old,
Ring in the thousand years of peace.

Ring in the valiant man and free,
The larger heart, the kindlier hand;
Ring out the darkness of the land,
Ring in the Christ that is to be.
—*Alfred Tennyson*

## Rules of Life

SLIGHT those who say, amidst their sickly healths,
"Thou liv'st by rule." What doth not so but man?
Houses are built by rule, and Common-Wealths.
Entice the trusty sunne, if that you can,
From his ecliptick line; becken the skie!
Who lives by rule, then, keeps good companie.

Who keeps no guard upon himself is slack,
And rots to nothing at the next great thaw.
Man is a shop of rules, a well-truss'd pack,
Whose every parcell under-writes a law.
Loose not thyself, nor give thy humours way;
God gave them to thee under lock and key.
—*George Herbert*

## The Rune of Hospitality

I SAW a stranger yestreen;
I put food in the eating place,
Drink in the drinking place,
Music in the listening place,
And, in the sacred name of the Father,
He blessed myself and my house,
My cattle and my dear ones.
And the lark sang in her song,
Often, often, often,
Goes the Christ in the stranger's guise;
Often, often, often,
Goes the Christ in the stranger's guise.
—*Anonymous; recovered by Kenneth MacLeod*
(Old Gaelic Rune)

## The Salutation of Dawn

LISTEN to the Exhortation of the Dawn!
Look to this Day!
For it is Life, the very Life of Life.
In its brief course lie all the
Verities and Realities of your Existence;
    The Bliss of Growth,
    The Glory of Action,
    The Splendor of Beauty;
For Yesterday is but a Dream,
And Tomorrow is only a Vision;
But Today well-lived makes
Every yesterday a Dream of Happiness,
And every tomorrow a Vision of Hope.
Look well therefore to this Day!
Such is the Salutation of the Dawn.

                              —*Anonymous*
                        (From the Sanskrit)


## Santa Filomena

WHENE'ER a noble deed is wrought,
Whene'er is spoken a noble thought,
    Our hearts, in glad surprise,
    To higher levels rise.

The tidal waves of deeper souls
Into our inmost being rolls,
    And lifts us unawares
    Out of all meaner cares.

Honour to those whose words or deeds
Thus help us in our daily needs,
    And by their overflow
    Raise us from what is low!

Thus thought I, as by night I read
Of the great army of the dead,
    The trenches cold and damp,
    The starved and frozen camp,—

The wounded from the battle-plain,
In dreary hospitals of pain,
    The cheerless corridors,
    The cold and stony floors.

Lo! in that house of misery
A lady with a lamp I see

Pass through the glimmering gloom,
And flit from room to room.

And slow, as in a dream of bliss,
The speechless sufferer turns to kiss
    Her shadow, as it falls
    Upon the darkening walls.

As if a door in heaven should be
Opened, and then closed suddenly,
    The vision came and went,
    The light shone and was spent.

On England's annals, through the long
Hereafter of her speech and song,
    That light its ray shall cast
    From portals of the past.

A Lady with a lamp shall stand
In the great history of the land,
    A noble type of good,
    Heroic womanhood.

Nor even shall be wanting here
The palm, the lily, and the spear,
    The symbols that of yore
    Saint Filomena bore.
                —*Henry Wadsworth Longfellow*
                    (Florence Nightingale)


## Say Not the Struggle Naught Availeth

SAY not the struggle naught availeth,
    The labor and the wounds are vain,
The enemy faints not, nor faileth,
    And as things have been they remain.

If hopes were dupes, fears may be liars;
    It may be, in yon smoke conceal'd,
Your comrades chase e'en now the fliers,
    And, but for you, possess the field.

For while the tired waves, vainly breaking,
    Seem here no painful inch to gain,
Far back, through creeks and inlets making,
    Comes silent, flooding in, the main.

[ 128 ]

And not by eastern windows only,
      When daylight comes, comes in the light;
   In front, the sun climbs slow, how slowly!
   But westward, look, the land is bright!
                      —*Arthur Hugh Clough*


## The Sea Is Mighty

THE sea is mighty, but a mightier sways
His restless billows. Thou, whose hands have scooped
His boundless gulfs and built his shore, thy breath,
That moved in the beginning o'er his face,
Moves o'er it evermore. The obedient waves
To its strong motion roll, and rise and fall.
      . . . Thou dost look
On thy creation and pronounce it good.
Its valleys, glorious in their summer green
Praise thee in silent beauty, and its woods,
Swept by the murmuring winds of ocean, join
The murmuring shores in a perpetual hymn.
                      —*William Cullen Bryant*


## See Thyself

   IN THEE
   In me
   In all men
   There dwelleth the One God

   In all
   He suffers
   And he suffers
   For all;

   In all everywhere,
   See thyself.
   Abandon this thy ignorant conceit,
   Which holds that thou art separate from
         other men.
         —*Anonymous; tr. by Mohandas Gandhi*
            (From an ancient Sanskrit poem)


## Seeds

WHAT shall we be like when
We cast this earthly body and attain
To immortality?
What shall we be like then?

[ 129 ]

Ah, who shall say
What vast expansions shall be ours that day?
What transformations of this house of clay
To fit the heavenly mansions and the light of day?
Ah, who shall say?

But this we know . . .
We drop a seed into the ground,
A tiny, shapeless thing, shrivelled and dry,
And, in the fullness of its time, is seen
A form of peerless beauty, robed and crowned
Beyond the pride of any earthly queen,
Instinct with loveliness, and sweet and rare
The perfect emblem of its Maker's care.

This from a shrivelled seed? . . .
Then may man hope indeed!

For man is but the seed of what he shall be,
When, in the fullness of his perfecting,
He drops the husk and cleaves the upward way,
Through earth's retardings and the clinging clay
Into the sunshine of God's perfect day.
No fetters then! No bonds of time or space!
But powers as ample as the boundless grace
That suffered man, and death, and yet, in tenderness,
Set wide the door and passed himself before . . .
As he had promised . . . to prepare a place.

Yea, we may hope!
For we are seeds,
Dropped into earth for heavenly blossoming.
Perchance, when comes the time of harvesting,
His loving care
May find some use for even a humble tare.

We know not what we shall be . . . only this . . .
That we shall be like him . . . as he is.
                                        —John Oxenham


## Seize This Minute

Lose this day loitering, 'twill be the same old story,
Tomorrow, and the next, move dilatory.
Each indecision brings its own delays,
And days are lost, lamenting o'er lost days.
Are you in earnest? Seize this very minute!
What you can do, or dream you can, begin it.

Boldness has genius, power and magic in it.
Only engage, and then the mind grows heated.
Begin, and then the work will be completed.

—Johann W. von Goethe

## Send Me

W<small>HAT</small> was his name? I do not know his name.
I only know he heard God's voice and came,
  Brought all he had across the sea
  To live and work for God and me;
    Felled the ungracious oak;
    Dragged from the soil
    With horrid toil
  The thrice-gnarled roots and stubborn rock; . . .

      . . . . .

And I?
Is there some desert or some pathless sea
Where Thou, good God of angels, wilt send me?
  Some oak for me to rend, some sod,
    Some rock for me to break;
    Some handful of His corn to take
      And scatter far afield,
      Till it, in turn, shall yield
        Its hundredfold
        Of grains of gold
  To feed the waiting children of my God?
Show me the desert, Father, or the sea.
Is it Thine enterprise? Great God, send me.
And though this body lies where ocean rolls,
Count me among all Faithful Souls.

—Edward Everett Hale

## Shall I Take Away Pain?

T<small>HE</small> cry of men's anguish went up unto God:
"Lord, take away pain—
The shadow that darkens the world thou hast made,
The close-coiling chain
That strangles the heart: the burden that weighs
On the wings that would soar—
Lord, take away pain from the world Thou hast made,
  That it love Thee the more!"

Then answered the Lord to the cry of the world:
"Shall I take away pain,
And with it the power of the soul to endure,
Made strong by the strain?

[ 131 ]

Shall I take away pity that knits heart to heart,
And sacrifice high?
Will ye lose all your heroes that lift from the fire
White brows to the sky?
Shall I take away love, that redeems with a price
And smiles at its loss?
Can ye spare from your lives, that would climb unto mine,
The Christ on his cross?"

*—Anonymous*

## The Shepherd's Song in the Valley of Humiliation

He that is down needs fear no fall,
    He that is low, no pride;
He that is humble ever shall
    Have God to be his guide.

I am content with what I have,
    Little be it or much;
And, Lord, contentment still I crave,
    Because Thou savest such.

Fullness to such a burden is
    That go on pilgrimage;
Here little, and hereafter bliss,
    Is best from age to age.

*—John Bunyan*

## Snowdrops

There they stand—
A tiny band—
Mid slush and mud and sodden leaves.
Their snowy heads so humbly bent,
They do not seem to know
They're sent as promise,
To a world which grieves.
All summer's glory cannot bring
The thrill . . .
Of these small reaching fingers of the spring.

*—Mary Murdock*

## The Snowflake Fairies

Snowflakes, falling, falling,
    Can you hear the fairies calling?
The fairies in the woods, among the trees?

They watch you dropping, dropping.
And call you, without stopping,
   To ask, "Have you a message for us, please?"

Snowflakes, twirling, twirling,
You are fairy postcards, whirling
   From the fairies in the clouds to those below.
You float, each light and airy,
Down to a waiting fairy,
   Who grasps and reads her postcard made of snow.
                     —*Marion St. John Webb*

## So Long as There Are Homes

So LONG as there are homes to which men turn
At close of day;
So long as there are homes where children are,
Where women stay—
If love and loyalty and faith be found
Across those sills—
A stricken nation can recover from
Its gravest ills.

So long as there are homes where fires burn
And there is bread;
So long as there are homes where lamps are lit
And prayers are said;
Although people falter through the dark—
And nations grope—
With God himself back of these little homes—
We have sure hope.
                     —*Grace Noll Crowell*

## The Soldier

IF I should die, think only this of me:
   That there's some corner of a foreign field
That is for ever England. There shall be
   In that rich earth a richer dust concealed;
A dust whom England bore, shaped, made aware,
   Gave, once, her flowers to love, her ways to roam,
A body of England's breathing English air,
   Washed by the rivers, blest by suns of home.

And think, this heart, all evil shed away,
   A pulse in the eternal mind, no less
      Gives somewhere back the thoughts by England given;

Her sights and sounds; dreams happy as her day;
And laughter, learnt of friends; and gentleness,
In hearts at peace, under an English heaven.
—*Rupert Brooke*

## *Something There Is That Doesn't Love a Wall*

THERE where it is we do not need the wall:
He is all pine and I am apple orchard.
My apple trees will never get across
And eat the cones under his pines, I tell him.
He only says, "Good fences make good neighbors."
Spring is the mischief in me, and I wonder
If I could put a notion in his head:
"Why do they make good neighbors? Isn't it
Where there are cows? But here there are no cows.
Before I built a wall I'd ask to know
What I was walling in or walling out,
And to whom I was like to give offence.
Something there is that doesn't love a wall,
That wants it down."
—*Robert Frost*

## *Song of the New Year*

ONE song for thee, New Year,
One universal prayer;
Teach us—all other teachings far above—
To hide dark hate beneath the wings of love;
To slay all hatred, strife,
And live the larger life!
To bind the wounds that bleed;
To lift the fallen, lead the blind
As only love can lead—
To live for all mankind!
—*James Whitcomb Riley*

## *The Soul That Loves God Finds Him Everywhere*

O THOU by long experience tried,
Near whom no grief can long abide;
My Love! how full of sweet content
I pass my years of banishment!

All scenes alike engaging prove,
To souls impressed with sacred love;
Wher'er they dwell, they dwell in Thee;
In heaven, in earth, or on the sea.

[ 134 ]

To me remains nor place nor time;
My country is in ev'ry clime;
I can be calm and free from care
On any shore since God is there.
—*William Cowper*

## The Stirrup-Cup

DEATH, thou'rt a cordial old and rare:
   Look how compounded, with what care!
Time got his wrinkles reaping thee
   Sweet herbs from all antiquity.

David to thy distillage went,
   Keats, and Gotama excellent,
Omar Khayyam, and Chaucer bright,
   And Shakspere for a king-delight.

Then, Time, let not a drop be spilt:
   Hand me the cup whene'er thou wilt;
'Tis thy rich stirrup-cup to me;
   I'll drink it down right smilingly.
—*Sidney Lanier*

## Stradivarius

         BUT God be praised
Antonio Stradivari has an eye
That winces at false work and loves the true,
With hand and arm that play upon the tool
As willingly as any singing bird
Sets him to sing his morning roundelay,
Because he likes to sing and likes the song . . .

         When any master holds
'Twixt chin and hand a violin of mine,
He will be glad that Stradivari lived,
Made violins, and made them of the best.
The masters only know whose work is good:
They will choose mine, and while God gives them skill
I give them instruments to play upon,
God choosing me to help him . . .

         My work is mine,
And, heresy or not, if my hand slacked
I should rob God—since he is fullest good—
Leaving a blank instead of violins.
I say, not God Himself can make man's best
Without best men to help Him . . .

'Tis God gives skill,
But not without men's hands: He could not make
Antonio Stradivari's violins
Without Antonio.

*—George Eliot*

## Strains of Joy

LET all the strains of joy mingle in my last song—
The joy that makes the earth flow over in the riotous excess of the grass,
The joy that sets the twin brothers, life and death, dancing over the wide
 world,
The joy that sweeps in with the tempest, shaking and waking all life with
 laughter,
The joy that sets still with its tears on the open red lotus of pain,
And the joy that throws everything it has upon the dust, and knows not
 a word.

*—Rabindranath Tagore*

## Strength in Wisdom

WHAT is strength without a double share
Of wisdom? vast, unwieldly, burdensome,
Proudly secure, yet liable to fall
By weakest subtleties, not made to rule,
But to subserve where wisdom bears command!

*—John Milton*
(Sampson Agonestes)

## Summer Joy

THE summer days are come again,
 With sun and clouds between,
And, fed alike by sun and rain,
 The trees grow broad and green:
Spreads broad and green the leafy tent,
 Upon whose grassy floor
Our feet, too long in cities pent,
 Their freedom find once more.

The summer days are come again;
 Once more the glad earth yields
Her golden wealth of rip'ning grain;
 And breath of clover fields,
And deep'ning shade of summer woods,
 And glow of summer air,
And winging thoughts, and happy moods
 Of love and joy and prayer.

[ 136 ]

The summer days are come again;
　　The birds are on the wing;
God's praises, in their loving strain,
　　Unconsciously they sing:
We know who giveth all the good
　　That doth our cup o'erbrim,
For summer joy in field and wood
　　We lift our song to him.
　　　　　　　　　*—Samuel Longfellow*


## Sweet Church Fellowship

O SWEETER than the marriage-feast,
'Tis sweeter far to me,
To walk together to the kirk
With a goodly company!—

To walk together to the kirk,
And all together pray,
While each to his great Father bends,
Old men, and babes, and loving friends,
And youths and maidens gay!
　　　　　　*—Samuel Taylor Coleridge*
　　　(The Rime of the Ancient Mariner)


## Taps

FADING light
Dims the sight
And a star
Gems the sky
Gleaming　bright
From afar;
Drawing nigh
Falls　the　night.

Day is done,
Gone the sun
From the hills,
From the lake,
From the sky;
All is well,
Safely rest,
God is nigh.
　　　　*—Anonymous*

[ 137 ]

## Teach Me, Father, How to Go

TEACH me, Father, how to go
Softly as the grasses grow;
Hush my soul to meet the shock
Of the wild world as a rock;
But my spirit, propt with power,
Make as simple as a flower.
Let the dry heart fill its cup,
Like a poppy looking up;
Let life lightly wear her crown,
Like a poppy looking down,
When its heart is filled with dew,
And its life begins anew.

Teach me, Father, how to be
Kind and patient as a tree.
Joyfully the crickets croon
Under shady oak at noon;
Beetle, on his mission bent,
Tarries in that cooling tent.
Let me, also, cheer a spot,
Hidden field or garden grot—
Place where passing souls can rest
On the way and be their best.
                    —*Edwin Markham*


## The Teacher

LORD, who am I to teach the way
To little children day by day,
So prone myself to go astray?

I teach them KNOWLEDGE, but I know
How faint they flicker and how low
The candles of my knowledge glow.

I teach them POWER to will and do,
But only now to learn anew
My own great weakness through and through.

I teach them LOVE for all mankind
And all God's creatures, but I find
My love comes lagging far behind.

Lord, if their guide I still must be,
Oh, let the little children see
The teacher leaning hard on Thee.
                    —*Leslie Pinckney Hill*

## Tears

AH, TEARS! Unbidden tears!
Familiar friends since childhood's lonely years,
Long separated we,
Why dost thou come again to dwell with me?
At midnight, dawn, midday,
Ye come; nor wait thy coming nor delay;
Nay, fearless with what scorn,
Ye picture China by my brothers torn.
Thy scorn I must accept,
But I'm no coward; pray heed ere more ye've wept;
I love Japan so fair,
And China too; this war I cannot bear.

"Is there no other way?"
Thus do I search my spirit all the day
Nor ever reach a goal;
I live, but only as a phantom soul,
Like Christ who bore our sins upon the cross,
I, too, must bear my country's sins and dross;
Land of my love! Thy sins are grievous to be borne,
My head hangs low upon my form forlorn.
Ah, tears! Unbidden tears!
Alas! Has come another day
When I must dwell with thee.

*—Toyohiko Kagawa*


## Tell God's Love in Action

LISTEN, all ye young people,[1] and go
Out into the sorrow-filled world,
Preach that all can now attain salvation,
Relief, and strength on the way.
The fire of mercy
Lights all hearts.
The law of salvation they must hear,
Then the closed doors are opened.
Glorious is the law from first to last,
Glorious in the middle parts!
Glorious is the wording—and sure.
Bringing salvation and happiness.
Therefore, ye young people; tell in action and words
How immeasurably great is the love of God.

*—Anonymous*

[1] The original means religious students in training—'pi-ch'iu'.

## Thanatopsis

So LIVE that when thy summons comes to join
The innumerable caravan, which moves
To that mysterious realm, where each shall take
His chamber in the silent halls of death,
Thou go not, like the quarry-slave at night,
Scourged to his dungeon, but, sustained and soothed
By an unfaltering trust, approach thy grave
Like one who wraps the drapery of his couch
About him, and lies down to pleasant dreams.
—*William Cullen Bryant*

## Thank God for Everything

O GOD, we thank thee for everything.
For the sea and its waves, blue, green, and gray and always wonderful;
For the beach and the breakers and the spray and the white foam on the
rocks;
For the blue arch of heaven; for the clouds in the sky, white and gray
and purple;
For the green of the grass; for the forests in their spring beauty; for the
wheat and corn and rye and barley.
We thank thee for all thou hast made and that thou hast called it good;
For all the glory and beauty and wonder of the world.
We thank thee that thou hast placed us in the world to subdue all things
to thy glory
And to use all things for the good of thy children.
Amen.
—*Edward Everett Hale*

## Thanks to God for a Little House

LORD, thou hast given me a cell
  Wherein to dwell;
A little house whose humble roof
  Is weather-proof;
Under the spars of which I lie
  Both soft and dry;
Where thou my chamber for to ward
  Hast set a guard
Of harmless thoughts, to watch and keep
  Me, while I sleep.
—*Robert Herrick*

## That I May See God

As A FLOWER that suddenly bursts into bloom,
So is my eye opened,
That I may see God
And understand his perfect law.

[ 140 ]

Again in a moment,
See how my soul is filled
With perfect wisdom and an earnest desire
To have a part in the great work of salvation
For the redemption of the whole creation.

—*Anonymous; tr. by Karl Ludvig Reichelt*
(From the Chinese)

## There Always Will Be Gardens

THERE always will be gardens
Where such as you and I
May keep alive our faith in him
Whose love can never die.
Men hate and fear each other,
And wars and griefs abound;
But peace abides with beauty here
Within our garden ground.

There always will be gardens
For he who planted flowers
In Eden long and long ago,
Still takes a hand in ours.
And still he walks at eventide
In gardens cool and sweet.
The raptured roses touch his robe,
The violets kiss his feet.

There always will be gardens
Where men his steps may trace,
And find, though they perceive him not,
The comfort of his grace.
For loveliness shall bud and bloom
To all eternity.
The Lord of gardens keeps the seed
Alive for you and me.

—*Lilian Leveridge*

## There Is No Death

THERE is no death! The stars go down
  To rise upon some other shore,
And bright in heaven's jeweled crown
  They shine for evermore.

There is no death! The dust we tread
  Shall change beneath the summer showers
To golden grain, or mellow fruit,
  Or rainbow-tinted flowers.

. . . . .

[ 141 ]

And ever near us, though unseen,
　The dear immortal spirits tread;
For all the boundless universe
　Is life—there are no dead.
                    —*John L. McCreery*

## There Is No Death—There's Immortality

THERE is a plan far greater than the plan you know;
There is a landscape broader than the one you see.
There is a haven where storm-tossed souls may go—
You call it death—we, immortality.

You call it death—the seeming endless sleep;
We call it birth—the soul at last set free.
'Tis hampered not by time or space—you weep.
Why weep at death? 'Tis immortality.

Farewell, dear voyageur—'twill not be long.
Your work is done—now may peace rest with thee.
Your kindly thoughts and deeds—they will live on.
This is not death—'tis immortality.

Farewell, dear voyageur—the river winds and turns;
The cadence of your song wafts near to me,
And now you know the thing that all men learn:
There is no death—there's immortality.
                    —*Anonymous*

## There's Immeasurably More

WE CAN only see a little of the ocean,
　Just a few miles distant from the rocky shore;
But out there—far beyond our eye's horizon,
　There's more, immeasurably more.

We can only see a little of God's loving—
　A few rich treasures from his mighty store;
But out there—far beyond our eyes' horizon,
　There's more—immeasurably more.
                    —*Anonymous*

## These Are Treasure

WHAT is more worth than rubies? Is it wisdom?
What is wisdom? To know the springs of joy.
And what are they? They are the things we live by.
And what are they? They are four for the body:
Air, light, food, and water;

[ 142 ]

And four for the soul:
Work and play, love and worship.
These are treasure:
All else is trash and treason to the City of Mansoul.

—*Monica Saleeby*

## They Also Serve Who Only Stand and Wait

WHEN I consider how my light is spent,
E're half my days, in this dark world and wide,
And that one Talent[1] which is death to hide,
Lodg'd with me useless, through my Soul more bent
To serve therewith my Maker, and present
My true account, lest he returning chide,
Doth God exact day-labour, light deny'd,

I fondly ask; but patience, to prevent
That murmur, soon replies, God doth not need
Either man's work or his own gifts, who best
Bear his mild yoke, they serve him best, his State
Is Kingly. Thousands at his bidding speed,
And post o'er Land and Ocean without rest:
They also serve who only stand and wait.

—*John Milton*

## Things I Prize

THESE are the things I prize
And hold of dearest worth:
Light of the sapphire skies,
Peace of the silent hills,
Shelter of forests, comfort of the grass,
Music of birds, murmur of little rills,
Shadows of cloud that swiftly pass,
And, after showers
The smell of flowers
And of the good brown earth—
And, best of all, along the way,
friendship and mirth.

—*Anonymous*

## Things That Cannot Be Bought

I BOUGHT a gay-roofed little house upon a sunny hill,
Where heaven is very close to earth and all the world is still.
It took my savings, every cent, although the cost was small,
But, oh, the lovely things I bought, and paid for not at all!
The sleepy valleys that below in tawny sunshine lie,
The oaks that sprawl across their slopes and climb to meet the sky,

[1] An allusion to the parable in Matthew 25.

[ 143 ]

Stray winds that sing of other things than those our eyes may see,
Blue wisps of mist, and raveled clouds that, fleeing, beckon me.
White suns of mad, glad April, October's wine to quaff,
On crystal winter mornings my hearth fire's crackling laugh,
The silent stars that march at night so close above my head,
The sound of raindrops on the roof when I am snug in bed.
For joist and beam and shingles gay I spent my savings small,
But on the lovely things God gave He put no price at all!

—*Rose Darrough*
(Only Heaven Is Given Away)

## This Is the Day of Light

THIS is the day of light:
Let there be light today;
O Dayspring, rise upon our night,
And chase its gloom away.
This is the day of rest:
Our failing strength renew;
On weary brain and troubled breast
Shed thou thy freshing dew.
This is the day of peace:
Thy peace our spirits fill;
Bid thou the blasts of discord cease,
The waves of strife be still.
This is the first of days:
Send forth thy quickening breath,
And wake dead souls to love and praise,
O Vanquisher of death!

—*Arranged as an anthem by William Berwald*

## Thou

O LORD
Where shall I find thee
And where shall I not find thee!
If all is well, I owe it to thee,
And when ill arises, it too is from thee.
To the east, thou
To the west, thou
To the north, thou
To the south, thou
Upward, thou
Downward, thou
Thou, thou, thou, thou,
Thou, thou, thou, thou,
Everywhere thou.

—*Isaac Levi ben Meir; tr. by Rabbi Louis Finkelstein*
(Russian, Nineteenth Century)

[ 144 ]

## Thou Perfect Master

THOU perfect master,
Who shinest upon all things and all men,
As gleaming moonlight plays upon a thousand waters at the same time!
Thy great compassion does not pass by a single creature;
Steadily and quietly sails the great ship of compassion across the sea of
  sorrow.
Thou art the great physician for a sick and impure world,
In pity giving the invitation to the "Paradise of the West."

*—Anonymous*
(From the Chinese)


## Thou Who Sendest Sun and Rain

THOU who sendest sun and rain,
Thou who sendest bliss and pain,
Good with bounteous hand bestowing,
Evil for our will allowing
Though thy hand we cannot see,
All is just that comes from thee.

In the peace of hearts at rest
Is the child at mother's breast;
In the lives that now surround us,
In the deaths that sorely wound us,
Though we may not understand,
Father, we behold thy hand.

Hear the happy hymn we raise,
Take the love which is thy praise,
Give content in each condition,
Blend our hearts in sweet submission,
All the faithful children prove
Worthy of the Father's love.

*—An anthem arranged by George Chadwick*


## Thoughts Too Deep for Tears

I LOVE the Brooks which down their channels fret,
Even more than when I tripped lightly as they;
The innocent brightness of a new-born Day
  Is lovely yet;
The Clouds that gather round the setting sun
Do take a sober colouring from an eye
That hath kept watch o'er man's mortality;
Another race hath been, and other palms are won.

[ 145 ]

Thanks to the human heart by which we live,
Thanks to its tenderness, its joys, and fears,
To me the meanest flower that blows can give
Thoughts that do often lie too deep for tears.
—*William Wordsworth*
(Ode on Intimations of Immortality)

## Threshing Time

WHERE the tilled earth, with all its fields set free,
    Naked and yellow from the harvest lies,
By many a loft and busy granary,
    The hum and tumult of the threshers rise;
There the tanned farmers labour without slack,
    Till twilight deepens round the spouting mill,
    Feeding the loosened sheaves, or with fierce will,
Pitching waist-deep upon the dusty stack.
—*Archibald Lampman*

## A Tide in the Affairs of Men

THERE is a tide in the affairs of men
Which, taken at the flood, leads on to fortune;
Omitted, all the voyage of their life
Is bound in shallows and in miseries:
On such a full sea are we now afloat,
And we must take the current when it serves,
Or lose our ventures.
—*William Shakespeare*
(Julius Caesar)

## To a Bereaved Mother

OH, SAY not that your little son is dead;
The word too harsh and much too hopeless seems.
Believe, instead,
That he has left his little trundle bed
To climb the hills
Of morning, and to share the joy that fills
    God's pleasant land of dreams.

Nay, say not that your little son is dead.
It is not right, because it is not true.
Believe, instead,
He has but gone the way that you must tread,
And, smiling, waits
In loving ambush by those pearly gates,
    To laugh and leap at you.

[ 146 ]

No knight that does you service can be dead,
Nor idle is this young knight gone before.
Believe, instead,
Upon an envoy's mission he hath sped
That doth import
Your greatest good; for he at heaven's court
  Is your ambassador.

—T. A. Daly


## To a Waterfowl

WHITHER, midst falling dew,
While glow the heavens with the last steps of day,
Far, through their rosy depths, dost thou pursue
    Thy solitary way?

Vainly the fowler's eye
Might mark thy distant flight to do thee wrong,
As, darkly painted on the crimson sky,
    Thy figure floats along.

Seek'st thou the plashy brink
Of weedy lake, or marge of river wide,
Or where the rocking billows rise and sink
    On the chafed ocean-side?

There is a Power whose care
Teaches thy way along that pathless coast—
The desert and illimitable air—
    Lone wandering, but not lost.

.   .   .   .   .

And soon that toil shall end;
Soon shalt thou find a summer home, and rest,
And scream among thy fellows; reeds shall bend
    Soon, o'er thy sheltered nest.

Thou'rt gone, the abyss of heaven
Hath swallowed up thy form; yet, on my heart
Deeply hath sunk the lesson thou hast given,
    And shall not soon depart.

He who, from zone to zone,
Guides through the boundless sky thy certain flight,
In the long way that I must tread alone,
    Will lead my steps aright.

*William Cullen Bryant*

## To Be a Girl

To BE a girl, and see
Beauty in flower, bird and tree;
To follow truth and right, and know
The emptiness of outward show.

To be a girl, and thrill
When climbing windblown up the hill;
To think the Father's love and care
Are round about, and everywhere.

To be a girl, and aim
Above the mark of self and fame;
To pass through, strong, and pure, and good,
The gate which leads to womanhood.

To be a girl, and heed
The call to meet the world's great need
Put Beauty, Truth and Goodness first,
Bring in the Kingdom of our God.

—*Anonymous*
(Adapted from a Camp Fire poem)


## To-Day

WITH every rising of the sun
Think of your life as just begun.

The Past has cancelled and buried deep
All yesterdays. There let them sleep.

Concern yourself with but To-day.
Grasp it, and teach it to obey

Your will and plan. Since time began
To-day has been the friend of man.

You and To-day! A soul sublime
And the great heritage of time.

With God Himself to bind the twain,
Go forth, brave heart! Attain! Attain!
—*Ella Wheeler Wilcox*

[ 148 ]

## To God, the Architect

Who thou art I know not,
  But this much I know:
Thou hast set the Pleiades
  In a silver row;

Thou hast sent the trackless winds
  Loose upon their way;
Thou hast reared a colored wall
  'Twixt the night and day;

Thou hast made the flowers to blow
  And the stars to shine;
Hid rare gems of richest ore
  In the tunneled mine;

But chief of all Thy wondrous works,
  Supreme of all Thy plan,
Thou hast put an upward reach
  In the heart of man.

*—Harry Kemp*


## To the Fringed Gentian

Thou blossom bright with autumn dew,
And colored with the heaven's own blue,
That openest when the quiet light
Succeeds the keen and frosty night.

Thou comest not when violets lean
O'er wandering brooks and springs unseen,
Or columbines, in purple dressed,
Nod o'er the ground-bird's hidden nest.

Thou waitest late and com'st alone,
When woods are bare and birds are flown,
And frosts and shortening days portend
The aged year is near his end.

Then doth thy sweet and quiet eye
Look through its fringes to the sky,
Blue—blue—as if that sky let fall
A flower from its cerulean wall.

I would that thus, when I shall see
The hour of death draw near to me,
Hope, blossoming within my heart,
May look to heaven as I depart.

*William Cullen Bryant*

[ 149 ]

## The Tomb of the Unknown Soldier

TRUE symbol of equality in worth
Of valour crowned in arms by patriot death
That knows no rank of place or breed or birth,
But levels all in dust of common fate,
And equal dignity in burial state
Of sculptured tomb and amaranthine wreath—
Hold thou in sacred trust the unknown name
Of him who sleeps in reverent silence here,
As lesson to mankind's vain pride of fame
And pomp of earthly power. Do not fear
That he will be forgot: in Heaven's scroll
Is writ the name of every valiant soul.
God hath his name, to fellowmen unknown,
Guard thou thy secret; He will find his own.

—*Thomas White*

## The Troubadours of God

WHO are these
That run along the highways of the world,
And seek its meanest suburbs with their feet?

They are the troubadours of God,
Blowing an airy melody along earth's aisles
As solid as the masonry of dreams;

They are the wise eccentrics
Who reason with divine hilarity;

They are the canny merchants
Who buy the hearts of nations for their Prince;

They are the vivid tailors
Who push the threads of ages through their hands,
Who take no blood to spill it but their own;

They are the blessed coolies
Who lift the loads of folly on their backs
And dump them into truth's dissolving streams.

They are the blithe outrunners
Who trek the world's long reaches for old trails
Whereon to lay the pavement of new years.

They are the grave cross-carriers
Who bear stern wooden gibbets on their backs,
And nail their loves and treasures to the beams.

[ 150 ]

They are our princely brothers,
Born of the womb which bore us,
Who speak for Christ amid the courts of life.
—*Anonymous*


## Trumpet Song of King Arthur's Knights

AND Arthur's knighthood sang before the King:

"Blow trumpet, for the world is white with May;
Blow trumpet, the long night hath roll'd away!
Blow thro' the living world—'Let the King reign!'

"Shall Rome or Heathen rule in Arthur's realm?
Flash brand and lance, fall battleaxe upon helm,
Fall battleaxe, and flash brand! Let the King reign!

"Strike for the King and live! his knights have heard
That God hath told the King a secret word.
Fall battleaxe, and flash brand! Let the King reign!

"Blow trumpet! he will lift us from the dust.
Blow trumpet! live the strength and die the lust!
Clang battleaxe, and clash brand! Let the King reign!

"Strike for the King and die! and if thou diest,
The King is king, and ever wills the highest.
Clang battleaxe, and clash brand! Let the King reign!

"Blow, for our Sun is mighty in his May!
Blow, for our Sun is mightier day by day!
Clang battleaxe, and clash brand! Let the King reign!

"The King will follow Christ, and we the King,
In whom high God hath breathed a secret thing.
Fall battleaxe, and clash brand! Let the King reign!"
—*Alfred Tennyson*


## Two Gods

### I

A BOY was born 'mid little things,
Between a little world and sky—
And dreamed not of the cosmic rings
Round which the circling planets fly.

[ 151 ]

He lived in little works and thoughts,
　　Where little ventures grow and plod,
And paced and ploughed his little plots,
　　And prayed unto his little God.

But as the mighty system grew,
　　His faith grew faint with many scars;
The Cosmos widened in his view—
　　But God was lost among His stars.

## II

Another boy in lowly days,
　　As he, to little things was born,
But gathered lore in woodland ways,
　　And from the glory of the morn.

As wider skies broke on his view,
　　God greatened in his growing mind;
Each year he dreamed his God anew,
　　And left his older God behind.

He saw the boundless scheme dilate,
　　In star and blossom, sky and clod;
And as the universe grew great,
　　He dreamed for it a greater God.
　　　　　　　　　*—Sam Walter Foss*

## Two Temples

A BUILDER builded a temple,
　　He wrought it with grace and skill;
Pillars and groins and arches,
　　All fashioned to work his will.
Men said, as they saw its beauty,
　　"It shall never know decay;
Great is thy skill, O Builder!
　　Thy fame shall endure for aye."

A Teacher builded a temple
　　With loving and infinite care,
Planning each arch with patience,
　　Laying each stone with prayer.
None praised her unceasing efforts,
　　None knew of her wondrous plan,
For the temple the Teacher builded
　　Was unseen by the eyes of man.

[ 152 ]

Gone is the Builder's temple,
  Crumbled into the dust;
Low lies each stately pillar,
  Food for consuming rust.
But the temple the Teacher builded
  Will last while the ages roll,
For that beautiful unseen temple
  Was a child's immortal soul.
                    —*Hattie Vose Hall*

## Unbelief

THERE is no unbelief;
Whoever plants a seed beneath the sod
And waits to see it push away the clod—
  He trusts in God.

Whoever says when clouds are in the sky,
"Be patient, heart; light breaketh by and by,"
  Trusts the Most High.

Whoever sees 'neath Winter's field of snow
The silent harvest of the future grow,
  God's power must know.

Whoever lies down on his couch to sleep,
Content to lock each sense in slumber deep,
  Knows God will keep.

Whoever says, "Tomorrow," "The unknown,"
"The future," trusts that Power alone
  He dares disown.

The heart that looks on when the eyelids close,
And dares to live when life has only woes—
  God's comfort knows.

There is no unbelief;
For thus by day and night, unconsciously
The heart lives by that faith the lips deny.
  God knoweth why!
                    —*Lizzie York Case*

## Valiant's Song

WHO would true valour see,
  Let him come hither;
One here will constant be,
  Come wind, come weather,

[ 153 ]

There's no discouragement
Shall make him once relent
His first avow'd intent
    To be a Pilgrim.

Whoso beset him round
    With dismal stories,
Do but themselves confound,—
    His strength the more is.
No lion can him fright,
He'll with a giant fight,
But he will have a right
    To be a Pilgrim.

Hobgoblin nor foul fiend
    Can daunt his spirit;
He knows he at the end
    Shall life inherit.
Then fancies fly away;
He'll fear not what men say;
He'll labour night and day
    To be a Pilgrim.
                —*John Bunyan*
              (Pilgrim's Progress)


## Vestigia

I TOOK a day to search for God,
And found him not. But as I trod
    By rocky ledge, through woods untamed,
    Just where one scarlet lily flamed,
I saw His footprint in the sod.

Then suddenly, all unaware,
Far off in the deep shadows, where
    A solitary hermit thrush
    Sang through the holy twilight hush—
I heard His voice upon the air.

And even as I marveled how
God gives us Heaven here and now,
    In a stir of wind that hardly shook
    The poplar leaves beside the brook—
His hand was light upon my brow.

At last with evening as I turned
Homeward, and thought what I had learned
                [ 154 ]

And all that there was still to probe—
I caught the glory of His robe
Where the last fires of sunset burned.

Back to the world with quickening start
I looked and longed for any part
In making saving Beauty be. . . .
And from the kindling ecstasy
I knew God dwelt within my heart.

—*Bliss Carman*

## Vitae Lampadu

THERE's a breathless hush in the close to-night—
Ten to make and the match to win—
A bumping pitch and a blinding light,
An hour to play and the last man in.
And it's not for the sake of a ribboned coat,
Or the selfish hope of a season's fame,
But his captain's hand on his shoulder smote
"Play up! play up! and play the game!"

The sand of the desert is sodden red—
Red with the wreck of a square that broke;
The gatling's jammed and the colonel dead,
And the regiment blind with dust and smoke:
The river of death has brimmed his banks,
And England's far, and honour a name,
But the voice of a schoolboy rallies the ranks,
"Play up! play up! and play the game!"

This is the word that year by year,
While in her place the school is set,
Every one of her sons must hear,
And none that hears it dare forget.
This they all with a joyful mind
Bear through life like a torch in flame,
And falling, fling to the host behind—
"Play up! play up! and play the game!"

—*Henry Newbolt*

## The Voice of Our Town

OUR Town is full of aliens, Moroccans and Australians,
Brazilians and Sicilians and the swarthy Hindustans,
Inhabited by Phoenicians, Peruvians, Vesuvians,
Our Town is full of Russians—
Full of Prussians—

[ 155 ]

Full of Swedes,
Bavarians, Hungarians
And all the old-world creeds;
The populace of every place from Johannesburg to Rome—
Our Town is full of everything but folk to whom it's home.
Our Town has its Bulgarians, its Polish and Ontarians,
Parisians and Silesians and the folk of sunny Spain.
Our Town has its Rumanians as well as Lithuanians,
Our people come from China, Carolina, Greece, and Maine,
Our Town is full of Spartans,
Full of Tartans,
Full of Greeks,
Croatians
And Dalmatians. . . .
How many a nation speaks!

—Margaret T. Applegarth

## The Voice unto Pharaoh or Any Tyrant

PHARAOH, Pharaoh, let my people go!

My fettered children toil with aching limbs
  And wearied fingers, brain and spirit bound.
Their puny forms are bent; the shadow dims
  Their straining eyes; their ears are choked with sound
And thick with reek is every breath they draw.
  I gave them light to see and song to hear;
I gave them Truth for guide and Love for law;
  And thou hast given darkness, blight and fear.

  Pharaoh, Pharaoh, let my people go!

In chains, unseen but strong, my children slave,
  Too dull for hopes or dreams, too dumb for prayers;
Thou, thou hast robbed them of the youth I gave,
  The world I made, the joy that should be theirs;
These lives are coined to swell thy glittering store;
  Then darest thou plead, "Nay, Lord,
    I did not know!"—
Still heaping up their burdens more and more?
The sand is running. Let my people go.

Pharaoh, Pharaoh, let my people go!

Thy heart is hard. Be warned: The Plagues shall come.
  This wrong thou dost shall breed yet fouler wrong.
Those lips shall speak in flame that now are dumb;
  Those feeble hands, through wrath and hatred strong,

Shall rend where they have wrought. Yea, once again
Disease, Rebellion, Crime shall overthrow
The selfishness that bred them. Sons of men,
For dread of vengeance, let my people go!
—*Arthur Guiterman*


## Waking Prayer

I THANK Thee, dear God,
For this new day,
Another chance
To do Thy way.

I pray Thee, dear God,
So to teach me
That, childlike, I
May humble be.

When it is night
May I then say—
I know I walked
With God today.
—*Grenville Kleiser*


## Walk with God

So I GO ON, not knowing,
I would not, if I might—
I would rather walk in the dark with God
Than go alone in the light;
I would rather walk with Him by faith
Than walk alone by sight.
—*Mary Gardner Brainard*


## The Wanderer of Liverpool

HERSELF is not there, being Beauty Eternal, alive,
She wanders the waters of thought, past disasters, past hates,
Past the world's disapproval, across the black seas of despair,
And on, beyond anquish to havens of peace whence she brings
Hope, Mercy and Courage, all gentle and beautiful things.
She shines on the waters, in summer's mid-daylight she shines
For the hand-shielded brow of her gazer is crowned with a star
And gently and surely she sweeps through the waters of thought
Up, over the curve of the planet, uplifting a song:—

"Adventure on, companions, the attempt
At high adventure brings reward undreamt.

The raging sea is grim with reefs unconn'd:
There is a way, a haven is beyond.

Way for yourself, a harbourage for you,
Where every quarry spirit can pursue
Is, in the glory of the dream come true."

So, singing, she wanders the waters with white wing on wing
Star-lighted, star-guided, the sea-gleaming beautiful thing.
—*John Masefield*

## The Way of God

MY HEART seeks after thee, O God
As famished deer the water brooks
For in thee is refreshment, and healing, and life.

Come unto me all weary ones
And peace and rest ye both shall find
For the way of life is friendship with God.

Our unjust deeds to fellow men
Bring woe and pain to human hearts
For if we love not man neither do we love God.

But kindness, helpfulness, and love
Bring health, and joy, and peace, and power
And thus is built God's Kingdom in the earth.
—*A. J. William Myers*

## We Are Such Stuff as Dreams Are Made On
(The Tempest)

THE cloud-capp'd towers, the gorgeous palaces,
The solemn temples, the great globe itself,
Yea, all which it inherit, shall dissolve;
And, like this insubstantial pageant faded,
Leave not a rack behind. We are such stuff
As dreams are made on, and our little life
Is rounded with a sleep.
—*William Shakespeare*

## The Weaver

MY LIFE is but a weaving
Between my Lord and me,
I cannot choose the colors
He worketh steadily.
Oft times he weaveth sorrow,

And I, in foolish pride,
Forget he sees the upper
And I, the under side.

Not till the loom is silent,
    And the shuttles cease to fly,
Shall God enroll the canvas
    And explain the reason why
The dark threads are as needful
    In the Weaver's skillful hand,
As the threads of gold and silver
    In the pattern he has planned.
                —*John Bannister Tabb*


## The Weavers

YES, I am a weaver, and each day
The threads of life I spin.
And be the colors what they may,
I still must weave them in.
With morning light there comes the thought
As I my task begin,
My Lord to me new threads has brought,
And bids me weave them in.

Sometimes he gives me threads of gold
To brighten up the day
Then sombre tints so bleak and cold
That change the gold to grey.
And so my shuttle swiftly flies
With threads both gold and grey
And on I toil till daylight dies
And fades in night away.

Oh when my day of toil is o'er
And I have ceased to spin
He'll open wide my Father's door
And bid me rest within.
When safe at home in heavenly light
How clearly I shall see
That every thread—the dark, the light,
Each one had need to be.
                —*Anonymous*


## What Do You Here?

IN A great quarry, once I chanced upon,
Three workmen chiselling each a slab of stone.

Monotonous task, confining, dusty, slow!
And while I gazed something I longed to know:
"What do you here?" I asked one quietly,
"I shape these blocks," he answered literally.

His neighbor stared as my request was made,
"Why, thus I earn my living; 'tis my trade."

"What do you, friend?" though easily I guessed,
He was an artist, artisans the rest.

One deep stroke more. He paused, then raised his head,
"I build cathedrals, sir," he proudly said.
—*Frances Grosby Hamlet*


## What Is Death?

WHAT is death? A little broadening of a ripple
Upon the Eternal shore.
A little loosening of the bands that cripple—
This and nothing more.
What's death? A parting of the cloud above us
Which hides the sun,
A golden vision of the souls that love us
And labor done.
What's death? The opening of a perfect flower;
No watcher sees
The silent spirit, who at twilight hour
The bondman frees.
What's death? God's mercy strange
Uncomprehended;
The undiscovered goal;
The land of promise when the toil
Is ended—
The day-dawn of the soul.
—*Anonymous*


## What Is the Coming Year?

It is a door,
By which we reach new fields
Of service for our God and fellow man;
A door by which we can explore
Wide spheres of usefulness our world to bless
And reap the sheaves God's Word of witness yields.
—*Anonymous*

## Where Did You Come from, Baby Dear?

Where did you come from, baby dear?
Out of the everywhere into here.

Where did you get those eyes so blue?
Out of the sky as I came through.

What makes the light in them sparkle and spin?
Some of the starry spikes left in.

Where did you get that little tear?
I found it waiting when I got here.

What makes your forehead so smooth and high?
A soft hand stroked it as I went by.

What makes your cheek like a warm, white rose?
I saw something better than anyone knows.

Whence that three-cornered smile of bliss?
Three angels gave me at once a kiss.

Where did you get this pearly ear?
God spoke and it came out to hear.

Where did you get those arms and hands?
Love made itself into bonds and bands.

Feet, whence did you come, you darling things?
From the same box as the cherub's wings.

How did they all come to be you?
God thought about me, and so I grew.

How did you come to us, you dear?
God thought about you, and so I am here.
—George MacDonald

## Where God Is

God dwells among the lowiest of men.
He sits on the dust heap among the prison convicts.
With the juvenile delinquents he stands at the door begging bread.
He throngs with the beggars at the place of alms.
He is among the sick. He stands in line with the unemployed in front of
the free employment bureaus.
Therefore, let him who would meet God visit the prison cell before going
to the temple.
Before he goes to church let him visit the hospital.
Before he reads his Bible let him help the beggar standing at his door.
—Toyohito Kagawa

## Wherever Through the Ages

WHEREVER through the ages rise
The altars of self-sacrifice,
Where love its arms hath opened wide,
Or man for man has calmly died,

I see the same white wings outspread
That hovered o'er the Master's head;
And the great marvel of his death
To the one order witnesseth.

Up from undated time they come,
The martyr-souls of heathendom,
And to his cross and passion bring
Their fellowship of suffering;

Each in his measure but a part
Of the unmeasured Over-Heart—
Guide, Comforter, and inward Word,
The eternal Spirit of the Lord!
                    —*John Greenleaf Whittier*
                    (The Brewing of Soma)


## Whist a Wee

"WHIST A WEE!"
Little brown Dee
Peers from her shelter
Of bush and tree.
Her time she is biding
To leap from her hiding.
And she says unto me:
"Don't look this way, big man, or they'll see
You are looking at me:
Please, please look out at the sea:
Whist a wee!"

And I walked up the sands,
And three little rebels took hold of my hands;
And they said: "Do you know
Where a little brown maid,
In a little brown plaid,
Did go?"
And I lied and said: "No."
And they scampered away
Like young squirrels at play;
And looked all over and under the rocks
For a glimpse of brown frocks.

[ 162 ]

And I heard a quick cry
From the shade of the tree
Saying to me—
Yes, saying to me:
"You're a dear, you're a dear."
And I said, "Whist a wee;
The rebels are all returning for thee."
And she hugged to the tree.

. . . . .

"Whist a wee," just three little words:
But I heard them to-day in the song of the birds.
And the waters all sang as I walked by the sea:
"Whist a wee, whist a wee."
And I looked behind bush and I looked behind tree;
And the birds still were there and the busy song bee.
But little brown Dee,
With her solemn "Whist a wee,"
Spake not unto me.

And over the hills I went,
And a gentle mound
I found;
Lying like some fairy's lost pillow upon the ground.
And I knelt on my knee
And wrote on the sand,
With a sorrowing hand:
"Little brown Dee
Sleeps here by the sea:
All ye who pass,
Whist a wee!"

—*Wilson MacDonald*

## The White Road

WHEN all our earth is winter on a morn,
And the unbroken road lies trackless white
Between the dark-hued spruces decked with snow,
Step forth. What thrill of life in the keen air!
What vibrant light! What lift of the high heart!
What ecstasies the fragrant boughs bring home
Of early carols and of glad surprise,—
Sense of God's truce, the whiteness of his dream!
This is the mystic preparation spread
To meet the miracle of incarnate love,
It's Lord's nativity in the world of men,
That Christ may walk the common road anew,
In each one's guise with his ineffable smile
Speeding his peace o'er a rejoicing world.

—*Bliss Carman*

## Who Are Life's Victors?

SPEAK, History! Who are Life's victors? Unroll thy long annals, and say,
Are they those whom the world called the victors—who won the success
 of a day?
The martyrs, or Nero? The Spartans who fell at Thermopylae's tryst,
Or the Persians and Xerxes? His judges or Socrates? Pilate or Christ?

—*William Wetmore Story*

## Who Would Excel in Strength

WHO would in strength excel
Must first his passions quell,
His lusts control:
Were India's mighty realm,
His hand upon the helm,
Her wealth to roll
Before his conquering feet
And Thule's island greet
Him Lord. The Goal
Could not be reached or seen,
Until, with conquest keen,
He won his soul.

—*Boethius*
(Consolations of Philosophy)

## Wings for Easter

THE radiant symbol of Easter is wings,
Not life of the flower come up from the soil
But life of the spirit that soars as it sings;
That lifts us above the stark dullness of toil
And sets our hearts dreaming of heavenly things.

Strange glories too bright for our dim human eyes.
There's something within us forever must call
For life everlasting, for strength to arise
Above what is mortal, or petty and small,
And reach for the wideness and light of the skies.

—*Frances McKinnon Morton*

## The Winds of Fate

ONE ship drives east and another drives west,
With the selfsame winds that blow.
'Tis the set of the sails
And not the gales
Which tell us the way to go.

Like the winds of the sea are the ways of fate,
  As we voyage along through life:
    'Tis the set of the soul
    That decides its goal,
  And not the calm or the strife.
                    —*Ella Wheeler Wilcox*


## World-Brotherhood

My COUNTRY is the world;
My flag with truth impearled,
Fills all the skies;
All the round earth I claim;
Peoples of every name;
And all inspiring fame
My heart would prize.

Mine are all lands and seas,
All flowers, shrubs and trees,
All life's design.
My heart within me thrills,
For all uplifted hills,
And for all streams and rills;
The world is mine.

And all men are my kin,
Since every man has been;
Blood of my blood.
I glory in the grace
And strength of every race,
And joy in every trace
Of brotherhood.

The days of pack and clan
Shall yield to love of man,
When war-flags are furled;
We shall be done with hate,
And strife of state with state,
And man with man create
A brave new world.
                    —*Anonymous*


## The World One Neighborhood

WE THANK thee, Lord, for eyes to see
  The beauty of the earth;
For ears to hear warm words of love,
  Or happy sounds of mirth;

[ 165 ]

For minds that find new thoughts to think,
    New wonders to explore;
For health and freedom to enjoy
    The good thou hast in store.

May we remember that to some
    The eye and ear and mind
Bring sights and sounds of ugliness,
    And only sadness find;
May we remember that to them
    The world has seemed unfair;
That we must strive to bring to them
    The beauty all may share!

Oh may our eyes be open, Lord,
    To see our neighbors' need,
And may our ears be kept alert
    Their cries for help to heed;
Keen be our minds to plan the best
    For one another's good,
That all the world shall be at last
    One friendly neighborhood.
        —*Jeanette Perkins Brown*

## Years of the Modern

YEARS of the modern! years of the unperform'd!
Your horizon rises—I see it parting away for more august dramas;
I see not America only, . . . but other nations preparing;
I see tremendous entrances and exits, new combinations, the solidarity
    of races. . . .

I see men marching and countermarching by swift millions;
I see the frontiers and boundaries of the old aristocracies broken;
I see the landmarks . . . removed
I see this day the People beginning their landmarks,      (all others give
    way)
Never such sharp questions ask'd as this day,
Never was average man, his soul, more energetic, more like a God,
Lo! how he urges and urges, leaving the masses no rest! . . .

No one knows what will happen next, such portents fill the days and
    nights;
Years prophetical! the space ahead as I walk, as I vainly try to pierce it,
    is full of phantoms,
Unborn deeds, things soon to be, project their shapes around me,
This incredible rush and heat, this strange ecstatic fever of dreams, O
    years!
Your dreams, O years, how they penetrate through me! (I know not
    whether I sleep or wake)

The unperform'd America and Europe grow dim, retiring in shadow
   behind me,
The unperform'd, more gigantic than ever, advance, advance upon me.
                                                —*Walt Whitman*

## The Yigdal[1]

PRAISE to the living God!
   All praiséd be his name,
Who was, and is, and is to be,
   For aye the same!
The one Eternal God,
   Ere aught that now appears;
The first, the last; beyond all thought
   His timeless years!
                                                —*Anonymous*

## Youth, Fill Up the Gaps!

SEE! in the rocks of the world
Marches the host of mankind,
A feeble, wavering line.
Years they have been in the wild!
Sore thirst plagues them, the rocks
Rising all round overawe;
Factions divide them, their host
Threatens to break, to dissolve.

Then, in such hour of need,
Ye like angels appear,
Radiant with ardour divine.
Ye alight in our van! At your voice
Panic, despair, flee away.
Ye move through the ranks, recall
The stragglers, refresh the outworn,
Praise, re-inspire the brave.

Order, courage, return;
Eyes rekindling, and prayers,
Follow your steps as ye go.
Ye fill up the gaps in the files,
Strengthen the wavering line,
Stablish, continue our march,
On to the bound of the waste,
On to the City of God.
                                                —*Matthew Arnold*

[1] The Yigdal, the great credal statement of the Jewish Articles of Faith formu-
lated about A.D. 1400, was put into verse by Rev. Newton Mann and revised by
Rev. William C. Gannett. It is sometimes made to begin, wrongly, "The God of
Abraham praise." It is found in the *Jewish Union Prayer Book*.

[ 167 ]

## Youth, or the Cynic

THE cat stretched himself
He gaped, opening his mouth big and wide,
Then suddenly he sprang;
He chased his own tail in giddy whirl.
Meanwhile the mouse ate the cheese.
And this is Youth—
And life!

*—A. J. William Myers*

## Youth's Prayer

OLD Man Great Chief,
Spirit of the mountain,
Hear a young brave's prayer.
Hear a prayer for kindness,
Hear a prayer for cleanness,
Keeper of the strong rain
Drumming on the mountain.
Lord of the small rain
That restores in newness;
Keeper of the clean rain,
Hear a prayer for wholeness.

Oh Man Great Chief,
Spirit of the mountain,
Keeper of the deer's way
Reared among the eagles,
Make my feet run faster,
Keep my feet from slowness.
Keeper of the ways of men,
Hear a prayer for fleetness.
Keeper of the hearts of men,
Hear a prayer for straightness.

Old Man Great Chief,
Hear a prayer for courage.
Lord of the thin peaks,
Reared among the thunders!
Keeper of the headlands,
Holding up the harvest,
Keeper of the paths of men,
Give me plenty courage.
Keeper of the hearts of men,
Hear a prayer for staunchness!

*—Anonymous*
(From the Navajo)

[ 168 ]

# BOOK II

# THE PSALMS
# FOR CHRISTIAN WORSHIP

•

## INTRODUCTION

THE PSALMS have had a long history. They have been used in worship for centuries. But each age has selected those parts that were suitable for its own purpose and adapted them to its needs.

It is necessary to make such selection today if the Psalms are to be saved for worship. In their present form it often happens that sections of deep religious value are lost because they are mixed in with elements that by their expression or content are unacceptable to religious people today. Sentiments such as those expressed in "Happy shall he be, that taketh and dasheth thy little ones against the stones" (137:9), and the imprecatory and narrowly nationalistic Psalms, are impossible for Christian worship. As a matter of fact, devout people have used few of the Psalms for either private or public worship.

The Psalms went through a long evolution before assuming their present form. The main lines of this development have been established and published in many books which should be read by anyone interested in the subject. Prof. Julius A. Bewer, in *The Literature of the Old Testament*, Chapter XX, deals with the Psalms. He says in part:

"The collections that we now have in our Psalter date from the period of the second temple." [Not earlier than 521 B.C.]

"It has always been fascinating to connect the various psalms with the circumstances in history out of which they appear to come. . . . But these guesses[1] are without value, there is not one of them that can be accepted as correct."[2]

He continues, "When after the rebuilding of the temple . . . a collection of hymns, old and new, was made, and it was called 'the Psalms of David.' It was only the first of a number. We can still point out the various collections which are now parts of our Psalter:

1. The first David Psalter in Ps. 2-41.
2. The second David Psalter in Ps. 51-72.
3. The Korah Psalter in Ps. 42-49.
4. The Asaph Psalter in Ps. 50, 73-83.
5. An appendix to the Korah Psalter in Ps. 84-89.

[1] On 14 psalms, 3, 7, 18, 30, 34, 51, 52, 54, 56, 57, 59, 60, 63, 142.
[2] Bewer, op. cit., rev. ed., pp. 341, 342.

6. The Hallelujah Psalter in Ps. 105-107, 111-118, 146-150.
7. The Pilgrim Psalter in Ps. 120-134.
8. Another David Psalter in Ps. 138-145.
9. The hymns in Ps. 93, 95-100 appear to have formed a special collection also.

"In the final edition of the Psalter these collections were put together and the whole was divided into five books, each closing with a special doxology. (I. Ps. 1-41. II. Ps. 42-72. III. Ps. 73-89. IV. Ps. 90-106. V. Ps. 107-150). Psalm 150 serves as a doxology for the whole Psalter. This division coincides with the earlier collections in Books I-III, but it is artificial in the last two books. It appears to have been made in imitation of the Pentateuch in order that the five Books of the Law might find their response in the five Books of Praises. Psalm 1 was prefixed to the whole Psalter to emphasize its legal character, and Psalm 2 to emphasize its Messianic character."[3]

He adds in a footnote: "The total number of psalms (150) is also gotten artificially. Originally some psalms, now counted as two, were one, e.g., Ps. 9 and 10 . . . In other psalms two or more originally unrelated poems are combined, e.g., in Ps. 19, 24, 27, 144 . . .

"The Greek version counts Ps. 9 and 10 as one, also Ps. 114 and 115, but it divides Ps. 116 and 147 each into two psalms."[4]

Isaac Watts is one of the greatest figures in Christian hymnody. A number of his hymns are included in every good modern hymn book. His famous *Hymns and Spiritual Songs* is a landmark in church worship. In the preface to this work, dated "March 3rd, 1719-20" he says:

"To see the dull indifference, the negligent and thoughtless air, that sits upon the faces of a whole assembly while the Psalm is on their lips, might tempt even a charitable observer to suspect the fervency of inward religion; and it is much to be feared that the minds of most of the worshippers are absent or unconcerned. Perhaps the modes of preaching in the best churches still want some degrees of reformation; nor are the methods of prayer so perfect as to stand in need of no correction or improvement; but of all our religious solemnities Psalmody is the most unhappily managed; that very action, which should elevate us to the most delightful and divine sensations doth not only flat our devotion, but too often awakens our regret, and touches all the springs of uneasiness within us."

He then makes this penetrating observation, which is as true today as it was over two centuries ago, and every church ought to take cognizance of it. He writes:

"I have long been convinced that one great occasion of this evil arises from the matter and words to which we confine all our songs. Some of them are almost opposite to the spirit of the gospel; many of them foreign to the state of the New Testament, and widely different from the present circumstances of Christians."

The case is clear in regard to the Psalms at least, as every thoughtful

[3] *Ibid.*, pp. 343-4.
[4] *Ibid.*, p. 344.

person has experienced for himself. The most elevated thoughts and aspirations may be followed in the next verse by something which clashes with every Christian ideal. Watts puts the case most convincingly:

"While we are kindling into divine love by the meditations of the loving kindness of God and the multitude of his tender mercies within a few verses some dreadful curse against men is proposed to our lips; that God would add iniquity unto their iniquity, nor let them come into his righteousness but blot them out of the book of the living. Psalm 69:26-28 which is so contrary to the new commandment of loving our enemies; and even under the Old Testament is best accounted for by referring it to the spirit of prophetic vengeance. Some sentences of the Psalmist that are expressive of the temper of our own hearts, and the circumstances of our lives, may compose our spirits to seriousness, and allure us to a sweet retirement within ourselves; but we meet with a following line, which so peculiarly belongs to one action or hour of the life of David or Asaph, that breaks off our song in the midst; and our consciences are affrighted lest we should speak a falsehood unto God; thus the powers of our souls are shocked on a sudden, and our spirits ruffled, before we have time to reflect, that this may be sung only as a history of ancient saints; and, perhaps, in some instances, that salvo is hardly sufficient neither; besides it almost always spoils the devotion, by breaking the uniform thread of it; for while our lips and our hearts run on sweetly together, applying the words to our own case, there is something of divine light in it; but at once we are forced to turn off the application abruptly, and our lips speak nothing but the heart of David. Thus our own hearts are, as it were, forbid the pursuit of the song, and then the harmony and the worship grow dull of necessity.

"Many ministers, and many private Christians have long groaned under this inconvenience, and have wished rather than attempted a reformation.

"Far be it from my thoughts," he continues, "to lay aside the Book of Psalms in public worship; few can pretend so great a value for them as myself; it is the most artful, most devotional, and divine collection of poesy; and nothing can be supposed more proper to raise a pious soul to heaven than some parts of that book; never was a piece of experimental divinity so nobly written, and so fully reverenced and admired; but it must be acknowledged still, that there are a thousand lines in it which were not made for a church in our days to assume as its own; there are also many deficiences of light and glory, which our Lord Jesus and his apostles have supplied in the writings of the New Testament."

This section entitled "The Psalms for Christian Worship" preserves all in the psalms that is in keeping with Christian teaching, and provides a body of worship material that is rich in historical significance and in spiritual inspiration.

The Authorized Version is followed, except where otherwise stated, but sometimes modified in the light of other translations, especially Moffatt's.

## 1. *The Moral Life*

BLESSED is the man that walketh not in the counsel of the ungodly, nor standeth in the way of sinners, nor sitteth in the seat of the scornful. But his delight is in the law of the Lord; and in his law doth he meditate day and night. And he shall be like a tree planted by the rivers of water, that bringeth forth his fruit in his season; his leaf also shall not wither; and whatsoever he doeth shall prosper.

The ungodly are not so: but are like the chaff which the wind driveth away. Therefore the ungodly shall not stand in the judgment, nor sinners in the congregation of the righteous. For the Lord knoweth the way of the righteous: but the way of the ungoldly shall perish.  —*1:1-6*

## 2. *A Morning Prayer*

I CRY unto the Lord with my voice, and he hears me out of his holy hill. I laid me down and slept; and this morning I awaked; for the Lord sustained me.  —*3:4-5*

## 3. *Little Less than Divine*

O LORD our Lord, how excellent is thy name in all the earth! who hast set thy glory above the heavens. Let me sing of this, thy heavenly strength like tiny children lisping out thy praise.

When I consider thy heavens, the work of thy fingers, the moon and the stars, which thou hast ordained; what is man, that thou art mindful of him? and the son of man, that thou visitest him? For thou has made him little less than divine, and hast crowned him with glory and honor. Thou madest him to have dominion over the works of thy hands; thou hast put all things under his feet: all sheep and oxen, yea, and the beasts of the field; the fowl of the air, and the fish of the sea, and whatsoever passeth through the paths of the seas.

O Lord our Lord, how excellent is thy name in all the earth!
—*8:1-2, 3-9*

## 4. *With My Whole Heart*

I WILL praise thee, O Lord, with my whole heart; I will show forth all thy marvelous works. I will be glad and rejoice in thee: I will sing praise to thy name, O thou most High.  —*9:1-12*

## 5. *The Fool*

THE fool has said in his heart, There is no God.  —*14:1; 53:1*

## 6. *Who Shall Abide?*

LORD, who shall abide in thy tabernacle? who shall dwell in thy holy hill?

He that walketh uprightly, and worketh righteousness, and speaketh the truth in his heart. He that backbiteth not with his tongue, nor doeth evil to his neighbor, nor taketh up a reproach against his neighbor. In whose eyes a vile person is despised; but he honoreth them that reverence the Lord. He that sweareth to his own hurt, and changeth not; he who will take no interest on a loan; he who will not be bribed against the innocent; he that doeth these things shall never be moved.        —15

## 7.   What I Get from Life

PRESERVE me, O God: for in thee do I put my trust. O my soul, thou hast said unto the Lord, Thou art my lord: my welfare rests on thee alone. Thou art what I get from life, O Lord, thou thyself art my share. Fair prospects have fallen to me; yea, I have a goodly heritage.

I have set the Lord always before me; because he is at my right hand, I shall not be moved. Therefore my heart is glad, and my soul rejoiceth: my body rests secure. For thou wilt never let me sink to death, nor leave thy loyal one to the grave; thou wilt show me the path of life; in thy presence is fullness of joy; at thy right hand there are pleasures forever.
                                                                    —16:1, 5-6, 8-11

## 8.   The Lord Is My Rock

I WILL love thee, O Lord, my strength. The Lord is my rock, and my fortress, and my deliverer; my God, my strength, in whom I will trust; my buckler, my saving strength, and my high tower.

The sorrows of death compassed me, and the floods of destruction made me afraid. Deadly nets entangled me, and fatal snares surprised me.

In my distress I called upon the Lord, and cried unto my God: he heard my voice out of his temple, and my cry came before him, even into his ears.

He brought me forth also into a large place; he delivered me, because he delighted in me. For all his judgments were before me, and I did not put away his statutes from me. I was also upright before him, and I kept myself from mine iniquity.

With the merciful thou wilt show thyself merciful; with an upright man thou wilt show thyself upright; with the pure thou wilt show thyself pure; and with the froward thou wilt show thy self froward. For thou wilt save the afflicted people; but wilt bring down high looks.

For thou wilt light my candle: the Lord my God will enlighten my darkness. For by thee I have run through a troop; and by my God have I leaped over a wall.

As for God, his way is perfect: the word of the Lord is tried: he is a buckler to all those that trust in him. For who is God save the Lord? or who is a rock save our God? It is God that girdeth me with strength, and maketh my way perfect. Thou hast also given me the shield of salvation; and thy right hand hath holden me up, and thy gentleness hath made me

[ 173 ]

great. Thou hast enlarged my steps under me, that my steps did not slip. Therefore will I give thanks unto thee, O Lord.

—18:1-2, 4, 6, 19-21, 25-32, 35-36, 50

## 9. *The Heavens Declare the Glory of God*

THE heavens declare the glory of God; and the firmament showeth his handiwork.

Day after day takes up the tale, night after night makes him known. Their speech has never a word, not a sound for the ear, yet their message spreads the wide world over, their meaning carries to earth's end. There hath he set a tabernacle for the sun, which is as a bridegroom coming out of his chamber, and rejoiceth as a strong man to run a race. He sets out from one end of heaven, and round he passes to the other, and there is nothing hid from the heat thereof.

The law of the Lord is perfect, reviving life: the testimony of the Lord is sure, making wise the open-minded. The statutes of the Lord are right, rejoicing the heart: the commandment of the Lord is pure, a light to the mind. The Lord's faith is clean enduring for ever: the judgments of the Lord are true and righteous altogether.

More to be desired are they than gold, yea, than much fine gold: sweeter also than honey and the honeycomb. Moreover by them is thy servant warned: and in keeping them there is great reward.

Who can understand his errors? cleanse thou me from secret faults. Keep back thy servant also from wilful sins, from giving way to them: then shall I be upright, and I shall be innocent from many a transgression.

Let the words of my mouth, and the meditation of my heart, be acceptable in thy sight, O Lord, my strength, and my redeemer. —19

## 10. *The Lord Is My Shepherd*

THE Lord is my shepherd; I shall not want. He maketh me to lie down in green pastures: he leadeth me beside the still waters. He restoreth my soul: he leadeth me in the paths of righteousness for his name's sake.

Yea, though I walk through the valley of the shadow of death, I will fear no evil: for thou art with me; thy rod and thy staff they comfort me.

Thou preparest a table before me in the presence of mine enemies: thou annointest my head with oil; my cup runneth over.

Surely goodness and mercy shall follow me all the days of my life: and I will dwell in the house of the Lord for ever. —23

## 11. *The King of Glory*

THE earth is the Lord's, and the fullness thereof; the world, and they that dwell therein. For he hath founded it upon the seas, and established it upon the floods.

Who shall ascend into the hill of the Lord? or who shall stand in his holy place?

[ 174 ]

He that hath clean hands, and a pure heart; who hath not lifted up his soul unto vanity, nor sworn deceitfully. He shall receive the blessing from the Lord, and righteousness from the God of his salvation. Such are they that seek him, who seek the presence of the God of Jacob.

Lift up your heads, O ye gates; and be ye lifted up, ye everlasting doors; and the King of glory shall come in.

Who is this King of glory? The Lord strong and mighty, the Lord mighty in battle.

Lift up your heads, O ye gates; even lift them up, ye everlasting doors; and the King of glory shall come in.

Who is this King of glory? The Lord of hosts, he is the King of glory.
—24

## 12. *Show Me Thy Ways*

Unto thee, O Lord, do I lift up my soul. O my God, I trust in thee.

Show me thy ways, O Lord; teach me thy paths. Lead me in thy truth, and teach me: for thou art God my help; on thee do I wait all the day.

Remember, O Lord, thy tender mercies and thy loving-kindnesses; for they have been ever of old. Remember not the faults of my youth, nor my transgressions: according to thy mercy remember thou me for thy goodness' sake, O Lord.

Good and upright is the Lord: therefore will he teach any who go astray, guiding humble souls aright: and the meek will he teach his way.

The secret of the Lord is with them that revere him. Mine eyes are ever toward the Lord; for he shall help me out of perplexities. Turn thee unto me, and have mercy upon me; for I am desolate and afflicted. Relieve the anguish of my heart: O bring thou me out of my distresses. Look upon mine affliction and my pain; and forgive all my sins.

May my devotion and my loyalty preserve me; for I am waiting for thyself, O Lord.                   —25:1-2, 4-9, 14, 15-18, 21

## 13. *Test Me and Prove Me*

Judge me, O Lord; for I have walked in mine integrity: I have trusted also in the Lord; therefore I shall not slide.

Test me, O Lord, and prove me; try my mind and my heart. For thy loving-kindness is before mine eyes: and I have walked in thy truth.

I love to sing my thanks aloud, and tell of all thy wondrous works. Lord, I have loved the habitation of thy house, and the place where thine honor dwelleth.                   —26:1-2, 3, 7-8

## 14. *The Lord Is My Light*

The Lord is my light and my salvation; whom shall I fear? the Lord is the strength of my life; of whom shall I be afraid?

One thing have I desired of the Lord, that will I seek after; that I may dwell in the house of the Lord all the days of my life, to behold the

[ 175 ]

beauty of the Lord, and to inquire in his temple. For in the time of trouble he shall hide me in his pavilion: in the secret of his tabernacle shall he hide me; he shall set me up upon a rock. Therefore will I offer in his tabernacle sacrifices of joy; I will sing, yea, I will sing praises unto the Lord.

Hear, O Lord, when I cry with my voice: have mercy also upon me, and answer me. My heart cries, Thy face, Lord, do I seek.

Even when my father and my mother forsake me, the Lord will take me up.

Teach me thy way, O Lord, and lead me in a plain path.

I do believe I shall yet see the goodness of the Lord in the land of the living.

Wait on the Lord: be of good courage, and he shall strengthen thine heart: wait, I say, on the Lord.                —27:1, 4-5, 6-8, 10-11, 13-14


## 15.  *Worship the Lord in the Beauty of Holiness*

GIVE unto the Lord, O ye mighty, give unto the Lord glory and strength. Give unto the Lord the glory due unto his name; worship the Lord in the beauty of holiness.

The voice of the Lord is upon the waters: the God of glory thundereth: the Lord is upon many waters.

The voice of the Lord is powerful; the voice of the Lord is full of majesty.

The voice of the Lord breaketh the cedars; yea, the Lord breaketh the cedars of Lebanon, till Lebanon leaps like a calf and Sirion like an antelope.

The voice of the Lord splits the rocks, splits them with flashes of fire.

The voice of the Lord whirls the sand, the Lord whirls the desert of Kadesh.

The voice of the Lord twists the trees, and strips the forests: while in his temple all are chanting, "Glory!"

The Lord sitteth upon the flood; yea, the Lord sitteth King for ever. The Lord will give strength unto his people; the Lord will bless his people with peace.                —29


## 16.  *Joy Cometh in the Morning*

I WILL extol thee, O Lord; for thou hast lifted me up. O Lord my God, I cried unto thee, and thou hast healed me. O lord, thou hast brought up my soul from the grave: thou hast kept me alive, that I should not go down to the world below.

Sing unto the Lord, O ye saints of his, and give thanks at the remembrance of his holiness. For his anger only lasts a moment; his favor lasts a lifetime. Weeping may endure for a night, but joy cometh in the morning.

Hear, O Lord, and have mercy upon me: Lord, be thou my helper. Thou hast turned for me my mourning into dancing: thou hast put off my sackcloth, and girded me with gladness that my soul might sing praise to thee without ceasing.

O Lord my God, I will give thanks unto thee forever.

*—30:1, 2-5, 10-12*

## 17. *Thou Art My God*

I PUT my life into thy hands,[1] and O God, O thou faithful God, thou savest me.

On thee, O Lord, I rely: I say, Thou art my God. My times are in thy hand.

O love the Lord, all ye his saints. Be of good courage, and he shall strengthen your heart, all ye that hope in the Lord.     *—31:5, 14, 23, 24*

## 18. *Glad in the Lord*

BLESSED is he whose transgression is forgiven, whose sin is pardoned. Blessed is the man unto whom the Lord imputeth not iniquity, and in whose spirit there is no guile.

I acknowledged my sin unto thee, and mine iniquity have I not hid. I said, I will confess my transgressions unto the Lord; and thou forgavest the iniquity of my sin.

So let each loyal heart pray to thee in trouble: surely in the floods of great waters they shall not come nigh unto him.

Be ye not as the colt, or as the mule, which do not understand the bridle, unbroken creatures that must be held in with a halter, or they will not come near thee.

Be glad in the Lord, and rejoice, ye righteous: and shout for joy, all ye that are upright in heart.     *—32:1-2, 5-6, 9, 11*

## 19. *A New Song*

REJOICE in the Lord, O ye righteous: for praise is comely for the upright. Praise the Lord with harp: sing unto him with the psaltery and an instrument of ten strings. Sing unto him a new song; play skilfully with a loud noise. For the word of the Lord is right; and all his works are done in truth. He loveth righteousness and judgment: the earth is full of the goodness of the Lord.

By the word of the Lord were the heavens made; and all the host of them by the breath of his mouth. He gathereth the waters of the sea together as a heap: he layeth up the depth in storehouses. Let all the earth fear the Lord: let all the inhabitants of the world stand in awe of him. For he spake, and it was done; he commanded, and it stood fast.

The purpose of the Lord standeth forever, the thoughts of his heart to all generations.

Blessed is the nation whose God is the Lord; and the people whom he hath chosen for his own.

[1] A.V. Into thine hand I commit my spirit.

No king is saved by the multitude of his armies: a mighty man is not delivered by much strength. A horse is a vain thing for safety: neither shall he deliver any by his great strength.

Our soul waiteth for the Lord: he is our help and our shield. For our heart shall rejoice in him, because we have trusted in his holy name. Let thy mercy, O Lord, be upon us, according as we hope in thee.

—*33:1-9, 11-12, 16-17, 20-22*

## 20.  *O Magnify the Lord*

I WILL bless the Lord at all times: his praise shall continually be in my mouth. My soul shall make her boast in the Lord: the humble shall hear thereof, and be glad. O magnify the Lord with me, and let us exalt his name together.

I sought the Lord, and he heard me, and delivered me from all my fears. They looked unto him, and were bright with joy: and their faces were not ashamed. This poor man cried, and the Lord heard him, and saved him out of all his troubles. The angel of the Lord encampeth round about them that fear him, and delivereth them.

O taste and see that the Lord is good: blessed is the man that trusteth in him. O revere the Lord, ye his saints: for there is no want to them that revere him. The young lions do lack, and suffer hunger: but they that seek the Lord shall not want any good thing.

Come ye children, hearken unto me: I will teach you true religion. What man is he that desireth life, and loveth many days, that he may see good? Keep thy tongue from evil, and thy lips from speaking guile. Depart from evil and do good; seek peace and pursue it.

The Lord is nigh unto them that are of a broken heart; and saveth such as be of a contrite spirit. The Lord redeemeth the soul of his servants: and none of them that trust in him shall be desolate.

—*34:1-14, 18, 22*

## 21.  *Fret Not Thyself*

FRET not thyself because of evildoers, neither be thou envious against the workers of iniquity.

Trust in the Lord, and do good; be loyal to him within his land. Delight thyself also in the Lord; and he shall give thee the desires of thine heart.

Rest in the Lord, and wait patiently for him: fret not thyself because of him who prospereth in his way, because of the man who bringeth wicked devices to pass. Cease from anger, and forsake wrath: fret not thyself in any wise to do evil.

The meek shall inherit the earth; and shall delight themselves in the abundance of peace.

A little that a good man hath is better than the great riches of the wicked.

When one's life pleases God he gives him a sure footing; he may fall, but he never falls down, for the Lord holds him by the hand. I have seen the wicked in great power, and spreading himself like a green bay tree. Yet he passed away, and, lo, he was not: yea, I sought him, but he could not be found.

Mark the perfect man, and behold the unright: for the end of that man is peace. —37:1, 3-4, 7-8, 11, 16, 23-24, 35-37

## 22. *Forsake Me Not*

I AM ON the verge of a collapse; my plight is always present to my mind. Forsake me not, O Lord: O my God, be not far from me. Make haste to help me, to rescue me, O Lord. —38:17, 21-22

## 23. *My Hope Is in Thee*

I SAID, I will take heed to my ways, that I sin not with my tongue: I will keep my mouth with a bridle.

Lord, make me to know mine end, the number of my days, how long I have to live! Behold, thou hast made my days as a hand-breadth; and mine age is as nothing before thee, no better than an empty breath. Man's busy life indeed is but a phantom, making an empty ado, amassing wealth and knowing not who is to have his hoard.

What then can I expect? My hope is in thee. —39:1, 4-7

## 24. *On a Rock*

I WAITED patiently for the Lord, and he turned and heard my cry. He brought me up also out of a horrible pit, out of the miry clay, and set my feet upon a rock, and established my goings. And he put a new song in my mouth, even praise unto our God.

—40:1-3

## 25. *My Prayer*

MY PRAYER is, O Lord, be merciful unto me: heal me; for I have sinned against thee.

Blessed be the Lord God of Israel from everlasting, and to everlasting. Amen, and Amen.

—41:4, 13

## 26. *Athirst for God*

As THE hart panteth after the water brooks, so panteth my soul after thee, O God. My soul thirsteth for God, for the living God: when shall I come and appear before God? My tears have been my meat day and night, while they continually say unto me, Where is thy God?

Why art thou cast down, O my soul? and why art thou disquieted in me?

Wait, wait for God; I shall again be praising him, my saving help, my God.

O send out thy light and thy truth: let them lead me; let them bring me unto thy holy hill, to where thou dwellest! Let me come to the altar of God, unto God my exceeding joy, singing thy praise on the harp, O God my God.

Why art thou cast down, O my soul? and why art thou disquieted within me? Wait, wait for God; I shall again be praising him, my saving help, my God. —42:1-3, 5, 7; 43:3-5

## 27. *The Palace of the King*

O DAUGHTER take good heed,
　Incline, and give good ear;
Thou must forget thy kindred all,
　And father's house most dear.
Thy beauty to the King,
　Shall then delightful be:
And do thou humbly worship him,
　Because thy Lord is he.

(Chorus)
With gladness and with joy,
　Thou all of them shalt bring,
And they together enter shall
　The palace of the King,
The palace of the King, the palace of the King;
　And they together enter shall,
　The palace of the King.

The daughter then of Tyre
　There with a gift shall be,
And all the wealthy of the land
　Shall make their suit to thee.
The daughter of the King
　All glorious is within;
And with embroideries of gold
　Her garments wrought have been.

She cometh to the King
　In robes with needle wrought;
The virgins that do follow her
　Shall unto thee be brought.
With gladness and with joy,
　Thou all of them shalt bring,
And they together enter shall
　The palace of the King.

[ 180 ]

And in thy father's stead,
Thy children thou shalt take,
And in all places of the earth
Them noble princes make.
I will show forth thy name
To generations all:
The people therefore evermore
To thee give praises shall.[1]                    —45:10-16


## 28.  God Our Refuge and Strength

GOD is our refuge and strength, a very present help in trouble; therefore will we not fear though the earth be removed, and though the mountains sink deep in the sea. Let the waters roar and foam, let the mountains shake under the storm: the Lord of hosts is with us; the God of Jacob is our refuge.

There is a river the streams whereof make glad the city of God, the holy place of the tabernacles of the most High. God is in the midst of her; she shall not be moved: God shall help her and that right early. Though nations rage and kingdoms be shaken; though his thunders melt the earth, the Lord of hosts is with us; the God of Jacob is our refuge.

Come, behold the works of the Lord, the desolation he hath wrought on earth; he maketh wars to cease to the ends of the earth; he breaketh the bow and snappeth the spear in sunder; he burneth the chariot in the fire. Be still, he cries, and know that I am God, high over the nations, high over the world. The Lord of hosts is with us; the God of Jacob is our refuge.                    —46


## 29.  Sing Praises

SING praises to God, sing praises: sing praises to our King, sing praises. For God is the King of all the earth: sing ye praises with understanding. God reigneth over the nations: God sitteth on the throne of his holiness.
                    —47:6-8


## 30.  Like Beasts That Perish

WHY should I be afraid when times are bad and all around I see those who rely on their riches and boast themselves in their abounding wealth? Why, none can buy himself off; not one can purchase for a price from God a life that shall never end.

What? Never die? But die they must—the clever have to die, the stupid and the senseless perish, leaving their money to others.

[1] Psalm 45 is a love song ascribed to the King and Queen—or to the bridegroom and bride—the King and Queen of Love for the moment. But this hymn, "The Palace of the King," also known as "The King's Daughters Hymn," a paraphrase of Psalm 45:10-16, is ascribed to God. It is found in Gospel Hymns No. 6, Copp, Clark Co., Ltd., for William Briggs, Toronto, 1891.

[ 181 ]

Be not thou afraid when one is made rich, when the glory of his house is increased; for, when he dieth he can take nothing with him: his glory shall not descend after him. In life he flatters himself on his fortune, praising himself for his prosperity; but down he goes to where his fathers dwell, who see no light to all eternity.

Man that is in honor, and understandeth not, is like the beasts that perish. —*49:5-7, 10, 16-20*

## 31.  *I Am God*

THE mighty God, even the Lord, speaks and calls the earth from the rising of the sun unto the going down thereof.

Hear, O my people and I will speak; O Israel, and I will testify against thee: I am God, even thy God. I do not reprove thee for lack of sacrifices or burnt offerings; daily your offerings are put before me. I need no bullock out of thy house, no goats out of thy folds: for every beast of the forest is mine, and the cattle upon a thousand hills. I know all the fowls of the mountains: and the wild beasts of the fields are mine. If I were hungry, I would not tell thee: for the world is mine, and the fullness thereof. Will I eat the flesh of bulls or drink the blood of goats? Offer unto God thanksgiving; and pay thy vows unto the most High: and call upon me in the day of trouble: I will deliver thee and thou shalt glorify me. —*50:1, 7-15*

## 32.  *Create in Me a Clean Heart*

HAVE mercy upon me, O God, according to thy loving-kindness: according unto the multitude of thy tender mercies blot out my transgressions. Wash me thoroughly from mine iniquity, and cleanse me from my sin. For I acknowledge my transgressions: and my sin is ever before me. Against thee, thee only, have I sinned, and done this evil in thy sight: that thou mightest be justified when thou speakest, and be clear when thou judgest.

It is inward truth that thou desirest, grant me then wisdom in my secret heart.

Purge me with hissop, and I shall be clean: wash me, and I shall be whiter than snow. Make me to hear joy and gladness; that the life thou hast broken may rejoice.

Create in me a clean heart, O God; and renew a right spirit within me.

Gladden me with thy saving aid again, and give me a willing spirit as my strength, that I may teach transgressors thy ways; and sinners may turn back to thee.

O Lord, open thou my lips; and my mouth shall show forth thy praise. For thou desirest not sacrifice; else would I give it: thou delightest not in burnt offerings. The sacrifices of God are a broken spirit: a broken and a contrite heart, O God, thou wilt not despise.

—*51:1-4, 7-8, 10, 12-13, 15-17*

## 33. *Trust*

CAST thy burden upon the Lord, and he shall sustain thee. —55:22

## 34. *The Sunshine of Life*

WHAT time I am afraid, I will trust in thee. In God I trust; I will not fear what man will do unto me. For thou hast saved my life from death, my feet from falling, that I may walk ever mindful of God in the sunshine of life. —56:3, 4, 13

## 35. *Awake the Dawn!*

UP, O God, high over heaven! Up with thy glory over all the earth! My heart is ready, ready, O God, for song and melody.
Awake my soul! Awake my lute and lyre! Let me awake the dawn!
I will praise thee, O Lord, among the people; I will sing unto thee among the nations. For thy love is high over heaven, and thy truth soars to the skies.
Up, O God, high over heaven! Up with thy glory over all the earth!
—57:5, 7-11 (Moffatt)

## 36. *He Is My Rock*

MY SOUL, wait thou only upon God; for my expectation is from him. He only is my rock and my salvation; he is my defense; I shall not be moved. In God is my salvation and my glory: the rock of my strength, and my refuge, is in God. Trust in him at all times; ye people, pour out your heart before him: God is a refuge for us. —62:5-8

## 37. *Thy Love Is More Than Life*

O GOD, thou art my God; early will I seek thee: my soul thirsteth for thee, my flesh longeth for thee like a dry and thirsty land, where no water is. As I have seen thee in the sanctuary, with visions of thy power and majesty, so will I bless thee while I live: I will lift up my hands in thy name.
Because thy loving-kindness is better than life, my lips shall praise thee. My soul shall be satisfied as with marrow and fatness; and my mouth shall praise thee with joyful lips.
When I remember thee upon my bed, and meditate on thee by night, my soul clings close to thee: thy right hand upholdeth me. Because thou hast been my help, therefore in the shadow of thy wings will I rejoice.
—63:1, 2, 4, 3, 5, 6, 8, 7

## 38. *The Valleys Shout for Joy*

PRAISE waiteth for thee, O God, in Zion: and unto thee shall the vow be performed. O thou that hearest prayer, all man shall come to thee.

[ 183 ]

Thou art good to the earth, giving water, enriching her greatly with rain from brimming streams divine; thou providest the grain when thou hast so prepared for it, watering the ridges abundantly, soaking the furrows: making it soft with showers, and blessing all her growth.

Thou crownest the year with thy goodness; and thy paths drop fatness. The very pastures overflow, and the little hills rejoice on every side. The meadows are clothed with flocks; the valleys also are covered over with grain; they shout for joy, they also sing.                —65:1-2, 9-13

### 39.  Make His Praise Glorious

MAKE a joyful noise unto God, all ye lands: sing forth the honor of his name: make his praise glorious. All the earth shall worship thee, and shall sing unto thee; they shall sing to thy name.

O bless our God, ye people, and make the voice of his praise to be heard: who keeps us safe in life and suffereth not our feet to be moved. For thou, O God, hast proved us: thou hast tried us, as silver is tried. Come, all ye worshippers of God, hear what he did for me: no sooner had I called to him than I was praising him for answering me.

Blessed be God, which hath not turned away my prayer, nor his mercy from me.                —66:1-2, 4, 8-10, 16-17, 20

### 40.  Let All the People Praise Thee

GOD be merciful unto us, and bless us; and cause his face to shine upon us; that thy way may be known upon earth, thy saving health among all nations.

Let the people praise thee, O God; let all the people praise thee. O let the nations be glad and sing for joy: for thou rulest the people righteously, and guidest the nations upon earth.

Let the people praise thee, O God; let all the people praise thee. The earth has yielded her harvest by the blessing of God, our God. God shall bless us; and all the ends of the earth shall revere him.                —67

### 41.  Dominion from Sea to Sea

GIVE the king thy judgments, O God, and thy righteousness unto the king's son. He shall rule thy people with righteousness, and assure justice to the poor.

May justice bring the people peace, from the very hills and mountains! He shall judge the poor of the people, he shall save the children of the needy, and shall break in pieces the oppressor.

Long may he live, as long as the sun and moon endure, throughout all generations. May his rule be like rain upon the mown grass: as showers that water the earth. In his days shall justice flourish; and abundance of peace so long as the moon endureth.

He shall have dominion also from sea to sea, and from the river unto the ends of the earth.

All kings shall fall down before him: all nations shall serve him. For he saves the needy when he crieth; the poor also, and him that hath no helper. He shall spare the poor and needy, and shall save the souls of the needy. He rescues them from oppression and violence: and precious are their lives in his sight.

May the land be rich in waving grain, right up to the top of the hills. May the people flourish like trees in Lebanon, may citizens flourish like grass of the earth!

His name shall endure forever: his name shall continue as long as the sun: and men shall be blessed in him: all nations shall call him blessed.

Blessed be the Lord God, the God of Israel, who only doeth wondrous things. And blessed be his glorious name forever: and let the whole earth be filled with his glory. Amen, and Amen.    —72:1-8, 11-14, 16-19

## 42.  When My Heart Was Sour

TRULY God is good to Israel, even to such as are of a clean heart. But as for me, my feet were almost gone; my steps had well nigh slipped. For I was envious at the foolish, when I saw the prosperity of the wicked.

When I thought to know this it was too painful for me; until I went into the sanctuary of God; then understood I their end.

Thus my heart was sour, when I felt sore, I was a dull, stupid creature no better than a brute before thee. Whom have I in heaven but thee? and there is none upon the earth that I desire besides thee. Body and soul may fail: but God is the strength of my heart, and my portion for ever.

Those that leave thee are lost. But to be near God is my bliss. I put my trust in the Lord.         —73:1-3, 16-17, 21, 22, 25, 26, 27, 28

## 43.  The Day Is Thine

THE day is thine, the night also is thine: thou hast prepared starlight and sun; thou hast arranged the earth in due order: thou hast made summer and winter.                              —74:16-17

## 44.  'Tis God Who Rules

WE OFFER thanks to thee, O God,
    we offer thanks to thee,
telling of all thy wondrous deeds.
God says, "Through all the long delay
I am still ruling in my justice;
when men in any panic melt away,
I still uphold the order of the world.
I tell the boastful, 'Do not boast.'
I tell the impious, 'Never flaunt your power.'"
No, never flaunt your power thus proudly,
    defy not God thus loudly;

[ 185 ]

rely not upon east or west,
    on the south desert or the northern hills—
'tis God who rules o'er men,
    this one he lowers, this one he lifts.
But I will rejoice for ever,
    I will sing praise to Jacob's God,
for lopping the power of evil men,
    and rallying the power of the upright.

                 —75:1-7, 9-10 (Moffatt)

## 45. *The Sparrow Hath Found a House*

How amiable are thy tabernacles, O Lord of hosts! My soul longeth, yea, even fainteth for the courts of the Lord: my heart and my flesh cry out for the living God.

Yea, the sparrow hath found a house, and the swallow a nest for herself, where she may lay her young, even thine altars, O Lord of hosts, my King, and my God.

Blessed are they that dwell in thy house, praising thee all day long. For a day in thy courts is better than a thousand. I had rather be a doorkeeper in the house of my God, than to dwell in the tents of wickedness. For the Lord God is a sun and shield: the Lord will give grace and glory: no good thing will he withhold from them that walk uprightly.

O Lord of hosts, blessed is the man that trusteth in thee.

                 —84:1-4, 10-12

## 46. *Teach Me Thy Way*

Bow down thine ear, O Lord, hear me: for I am poor and needy. Preserve my soul; for I am true to thee: O thou my God save thy servant that trusteth in thee. Be merciful unto me, O Lord: for I cry unto thee daily. Rejoice the soul of thy servant: for unto thee, O Lord, do I lift up my soul. For thou, Lord, art good, and ready to forgive; and plenteous in mercy unto all them that call upon thee.

Give ear, O Lord, unto my prayer; and attend to the voice of my supplications. In the day of my trouble I will call upon thee: for thou wilt answer me. Among the gods there is none like unto thee, O Lord; neither are there any works like unto thy works. All nations whom thou hast made shall come and worship before thee, O Lord; and shall glorify thy name. For thou art great, and doest wondrous things: thou art God alone.

Teach me thy way, O Lord: how to walk in thy truth; unite my heart to reverence thy name. With all my heart I thank thee, O my God, and I will glorify thy name forever. For great is thy love toward me: and thou hast delivered me from the very depths of death.

But thou, O Lord, art a God full of compassion, and gracious, long-suffering, and plenteous in mercy and truth.    —86:1-13, 15

## 47. Thy Love Endures

I WILL sing of the love of the Lord for ever: making known thy faithfulness to all generations; for thy love thou has promised to endure for ever: thy faithfulness shalt thou establish in the very heavens. For who in the heaven can be compared unto the Lord? who among the sons of the mighty can be likened with the Lord?

Thou rulest the raging of the sea: when the waves thereof arise, thou stillest them. The heavens are thine, the earth also is thine: as for the world and the fulness thereof, thou hast founded them.

Thy throne rests upon equity and justice, love and truth are thine attendants. Blessed is the people that know thy festal songs: they walk, O Lord, in the sunshine of thy favor. For the Lord is our defense; and the Holy One of Israel is our King.

Remember, Lord, what life is—how frail and futile thou hast made all men. Who can live on and die not, who can escape the grave?

Blessed be the Lord for ever and ever. Even so, even so!

—89:1-2, 6, 9, 11, 14-15, 18, 47-48, 52

## 48. The Lord Our Dwelling Place

LORD, thou has been our dwelling place in all generations. Before the mountains were brought forth, or ever thou hadst formed the earth and the world, even from everlasting to everlasting, thou art God.

Thou turnest man to destruction summoning them back to the dust. For a thousand years in thy sight are but as yesterday when it is past, and as a watch in the night.

Year after year thou sowest men like grass that grows anew. In the morning it flourisheth, and groweth up; in the evening it is cut down, and withereth.

The days of our years are threescore years and ten; and if by reason of strength they be fourscore years, yet is their strength labor and sorrow; for it is soon cut off, and we fly away.

So teach us to number our days, that we may apply our hearts unto wisdom.

Let thy love dawn on us undimmed, that we may rejoice and be glad all our days. Let thy servants see thee at thy saving work, and let their children see thy glorious power. And let the beauty of the Lord our God be upon us: and the work of our hands establish thou it.

—90:1-6, 10, 12, 14, 16, 17

## 49. The Secret Place of the Most High

HE THAT dwelleth in the secret place of the most High shall abide under the shadow of the Almighty. I will say of the Lord, He is my refuge and my fortress; my God; in him will I trust. Surely he shall deliver thee from the snare of the fowler, and from the noisome pestilence. He shall cover thee with his feathers, and under his wings shalt thou trust: his truth shall be thy shield and buckler.

Thou shalt not be afraid for the terror by night; nor for the arrow that flieth by day: nor for the pestilence that walketh in darkness; nor for the destruction that wasteth at noonday. A thousand shall fall at thy side and ten thousand at thy right hand; but it shall not come nigh thee. Only with thine eyes shalt thou behold and see the reward of the wicked. Because thou hast made the Lord, which is my refuge, even the most High, thy habitation, there shall no evil befall, thee, neither shall any plague come nigh thy dwelling.

For he shall give his angels charge over thee, to keep thee in all thy ways. They shall bear thee up in their hands, lest thou dash thy foot against a stone. Thou shalt tread upon the lion and adder; the young lion and the dragon shalt thou trample under feet.

Because he hath set his love upon me, therefore will I deliver him: I will set him on high, because he hath known my name. He shall call upon me, and I will answer him: I will be with him in trouble: I will deliver him, and honor him. With long life will I satisfy him, and show him my saving care.                                                                    —91

## 50.  *I Sing for Joy*

It is a good thing to give thanks unto the Lord, and to sing praises unto thy name, O most High: to show forth thy loving kindness in the morning, and thy faithfulness every night, upon an instrument of ten strings, and upon the psaltery; upon the harp with a solemn sound. For thou, Lord, hast made me glad through thy work: I sing for joy at all that thou hast done.

Those that be planted in the house of the Lord shall flourish in the courts of our God. They shall still bring forth fruit in old age, still fresh and green, showing that the Lord is upright; he is my strength, there is no unrighteousness in him.                                               —92:1-4, 13-15

## 51.  *The Lord Reigneth*

The Lord reigneth, he is clothed with majesty; the Lord is clothed with strength, wherewith he hath girded himself: the world also is established, that it cannot be moved. Thy throne is established of old: thou art from everlasting.

The floods may storm, O Lord, the floods may storm aloud, the floods may storm and thunder; but high above the ocean breakers, the Lord stands supreme. Thy testimonies are ever sure: holiness becometh thine house, O Lord, for ever.                                                           —93:1-5

## 52.  *The Lord My Help*

He that made the ear, does he not hear? he that formed the eye, does he not see? he that traineth the nations, can he not correct them?

[ 188 ]

has he no knowledge, he who teaches man? Knowledge! The Lord knoweth that the thoughts of man are but an empty breath.

Blessed is the man whom thou chastenest, O Lord, and teachest him out of thy law. For the Lord will not cast off his people, neither will he forsake his own. No, goodness shall have justice done to it, the future is with men of upright mind.

Unless the Lord had been my help, my soul had almost dwelt in silence. When I think my foot is slipping thy goodness, Lord, holds me up; when doubts crowd into my mind, thy comforts cheer me.

Can evil rulers have thee for an ally, who work us injury by law, who attack honest men, and doom the innocent to death? No, my God is my protection, my God is my strength and safety.

*—94:9-12, 14-15, 17-19, 20-22*

## 53.  *O Come Let Us Worship*

O COME, let us sing unto the Lord: let us make a joyful noise to the rock of our salvation. Let us come before his presence with thanksgiving, and make a joyful noise unto him with psalms.

For the Lord is a great God, and a great King above all gods. In his hands are the deep places of the earth: the strength of the hills is his also. The sea is his, and he made it: and his hands formed the dry land.

O come, let us worship and bow down: let us kneel before the Lord our maker. For he is our God; and we are the people of his pasture, and the sheep of his hand. *—95:1-7*

## 54.  *The Beauty of Holiness*

PRAISE the Lord, O ye kindreds of the people, praise the Lord for his glory and strength. Praise the Lord for the glory due unto his name. O worship the Lord in the beauty of holiness. *—96:7, 8, 9*

## 55.  *Light Dawns*

THE Lord reigneth; let the earth rejoice; let the multitude of isles be glad thereof. Clouds and darkness are round about him; his throne rests on equity and justice. His lightnings illumine the world: the earth sees and trembles. The hills melt like wax at the presence of the Lord, at the presence of the Lord of the whole earth. The heavens declare his righteousness, and all the people see his glory.

Light dawns for the righteous, and gladness for the upright in heart. Rejoice in the Lord, ye righteous; and give thanks at the remembrance of his holiness. *—97:1-2, 4-6, 11-12*

## 56.  *Sing a New Song*

O SING unto the Lord a new song; for he hath done marvelous things: his right hand, and his holy army hath gotten him the victory.

Make a joyful noise unto the Lord, all the earth: make a loud noise, and rejoice, and sing praise. Sing unto the Lord with the harp; with the harp, and the voice of a psalm. With trumpets and sound of cornet make a joyful noise before the Lord, the King.

Let the sea roar, and the fulness thereof; the world, and they that dwell therein. Let the rivers clap their hands: let the hills be joyful together before the Lord; for he cometh to rule the earth: with right-eousness shall he rule the world, and the people with equity. —*98:1, 4-9*

## 57. *The Lord Is Good*

MAKE a joyful noise unto the Lord, all ye lands. Serve the Lord with gladness: come before his presence with singing. Know ye that the Lord he is God: it is he that hath made us, and not we ourselves; we are his people, and the sheep of his pasture. Enter into his gates with thanksgiving, and into his courts with praise: be thankful unto him, and bless his name. For the Lord is good; his mercy is everlasting; and his truth endureth to all generations. —*100*

## 58. *Bless the Lord*

BLESS the Lord, O my soul: and all that is within me, bless his holy name. Bless the Lord, O my soul, and forget not all his benefits: who forgiveth all thine iniquities; who healeth all thy diseases; who redeemeth thy life from destruction; who crowneth thee with loving-kindness and tender mercies; who satisfieth thy mouth with good things; so that thy youth is renewed like the eagle's.

The Lord vindicates the cause of any who are wronged. He made known his ways unto Moses, his acts unto the children of Israel.

The Lord is merciful and gracious, slow to anger, and plenteous in mercy. He hath not dealt with us after our sins; nor rewarded us according to our iniquities. For as the heaven is high above the earth, so great is his mercy toward them that fear him. As far as the east is from the west, so far hath he removed our transgressions from us.

Like as a father pitieth his children, so the Lord pitieth them that fear him. For he knoweth our frame; he remembereth that we are dust.

As for man, his days are as grass: as a flower of the field, so he flourisheth. For the wind passeth over it, and it is gone; and the place thereof shall know it no more. But the mercy of the Lord is from everlasting to everlasting upon them that fear him, and his righteousness unto children's children; to such as keep his covenant, and to those that remember his commandments to do them.

Bless the Lord, ye his angels, that excel in strength, that do his commandments, hearkening unto the voice of his word. Bless ye the Lord, all ye his hosts, ye ministers of his that do his pleasure. Bless the Lord, all his works in all the places of his dominion: bless the Lord, O my soul. —*103:1-8, 10-18, 20-22*

[ 190 ]

## 59.  *He Sendeth Streams into the Valleys*

BLESS the Lord, O my soul.

O Lord, my God, thou art very great; thou art clothed with honor and majesty: who coverest thyself in a robe of light: who stretchest out the heavens like a tent: who buildest thy chambers on the waters above: who maketh the clouds his chariot: who ridest upon the wings of the wind: who maketh winds thy messengers, fire and flame thy servants.

He sendeth the streams into the valleys, which flow between the hills. They give drink to every beast of the field: the wild asses quench their thirst. There the wild birds settle, singing among the branches. He watereth the hills from his chambers and rains abundantly upon the land, causing the grass to grow for the cattle, and herb for the service of man: that he may bring forth food out of the earth; and wine that maketh glad the heart of man, and oil to make his face to shine, and bread which strengtheneth man's heart. The great trees drink their fill; the cedars of Lebanon, which the Lord hath planted; where the birds make their nests: the stork with her home in the cypress. The high hills shelter the wild goats; and the conies hide in the rocks.

He marks the seasons by the moon, he tells the sun when it must set. Thou makest darkness, and it is night: when all the beasts of the forest creep forth. The lions roar for their prey, and claim their food from God. When the sun rises then they slink away, and lay them down in their dens. Man goeth forth unto his work and labors till the evening.

O Lord, how manifold are thy works! in wisdom hast thou made them all: the earth is full of thy riches. So is the great and wide sea, with its countless swarms, with creatures small and great. There go the ships: there is leviathan at his play. These wait all upon thee; that thou mayest give them their meat in due season. What thou givest, that they gather, feasting from thine open hand. Thou hidest thy face, they are troubled: when thou takest away their breath, they die. Yet a breath from thee brings them into being, renewing the face of the earth.

May the glory of the Lord endure for ever: may the Lord rejoice in his own works. He looketh on the earth, and it trembleth: he toucheth the hills, and they smoke.

I will sing unto the Lord as long as I live: I will sing praise to my God while I have my being. May these my thoughts please him: I find my joy in the Lord.

Bless the Lord, O my soul. Praise ye the Lord.     —104:1-4, 10-34, 35

## 60.  *Seek Ye the Lord*

O GIVE thanks unto the Lord; call upon his name: make known his deeds among the people. Sing unto him, sing psalms unto him: talk ye of all his wondrous works. Glory ye in his holy name: let the heart of them rejoice that seek the Lord. Seek the Lord, and his strength: seek his face evermore. Remember his marvellous works that he hath done; his wonders, and the judgments of his mouth.

He is the Lord our God, supreme over all nations.     —105:1-5, 7

[ 191 ]

## 61. Hold to What Is Right

PRAISE ye the Lord.

Happy are they who hold to what is right, who do their duty at all times.

Blessed be the Lord God of Israel from everlasting to everlasting: and let all the people say, Amen. Praise ye the Lord. *—106:1, 3, 48*

## 62. His Mercy Endureth for Ever

O GIVE thanks unto the Lord, for he is good: for his mercy endureth for ever. Let the redeemed of the Lord say so, whom he hath redeemed from the hand of the enemy; and gathered them out of the lands, from the east, and from the west, from the north, and from the south. They wandered in the wilderness in a solitary way; they found no city to dwell in. Hungry and thirsty, their soul fainted in them. Then they cried unto the Lord in their trouble to save them from their evil plight, and he led them forth by the right way, that they might go to a city of habitation.

Oh that men would praise the Lord for his goodness, and for his wonderful works to the children of men! For he satisfieth the longing soul, and filleth the hungry soul with goodness. Such as sit in darkness and in the shadow of death, being bound in affliction and iron; because they rebelled against the words of God, and scorned the counsel of the most High. Hard labor crushed their spirit; they fell down, and there was none to help. Then they cried unto the Lord in their trouble, and he saved them out of their distresses. He brought them out of their distresses. He brought them out of darkness and the shadow of death, and brake their chains in sunder.

Oh that men would praise the Lord for his goodness, and for his wonderful works to the children of men! For he breaks the gates of brass, and cuts the bars of iron in sunder. Some, weakened by their sinful ways, were sick and suffering by evildoing; they had a loathing for all food, and they were on the verge of death. Then they cry unto the Lord in their trouble to save them out of their distresses. He sent his word, and healed them, and delivered them from their destructions.

Oh that men would praise the Lord for his goodness and for his wonderful works to the children of men! And let them offer sacrifices of thankgiving, and declare his works with rejoicing.

Some crossed the sea in ships, trading in great waters; these saw the works of the Lord, and his wonders in the deep. For he commandeth, and raiseth the stormy wind, which lifteth up the waves thereof. They mount up to the heaven, they go down again to the depths: their courage melting, they reeled and staggered, like a drunken man, and were at their wits' end. Then they cried to the Lord in their trouble, to save them out of their distresses. He made the wind to calm, so that the waves thereof were still. Then were they glad because of the calm; so he brought them to their desired haven.

Oh that men would praise the Lord for his goodness, and for his wonderful works to the children of men! Let them exalt him also in the congregation of the people, and praise him in the assembly of the elders. He turneth rivers into a desert and the watersprings into dry ground; a fruitful land into barrenness, for the wickedness of them that dwell therein. He turneth a desert into pools of water, and dry ground into watersprings. And there he maketh the hungry dwell, to build a city to settle in; and to sow the fields, and plant vineyards, gathering in the harvest. He blesseth them also, so that they are multiplied greatly; and suffereth not their cattle to decrease.

He lifteth poor men from their woes, and maketh their household like a fruitful flock. Good men rejoice to see this, and wrong-doers are silenced. Whoso is wise and will observe these things, even they shall understand the loving-kindness of the Lord.        *—107:1-38, 41-43*

## 63.  *The Beginning of Wisdom*

REVERENCE for the Lord is the beginning of wisdom: it is sound sense for everyone. His praise endures for ever.        *—111:10*

## 64.  *Where Is That God of Theirs?*

NOT unto us, O Lord, not unto us, but unto thy name give glory, for thy mercy, and for thy truth's sake. Wherefore should the heathen say, Where is now their God? But our God is in the heavens: he hath done whatsoever he hath pleased.

Their idols are silver and gold, the work of men's hands. They have mouths, but they speak not: eyes have they, but they see not: they have ears, but they hear not: noses have they, but they smell not: they have hands, but they handle not: feet have they, but they walk not: neither speak they through their throat. They that make them are like unto them; so is every one that trusteth in them.

O Israel, trust thou in the Lord: he is their help and their shield. O house of Aaron, trust in the Lord: he is their help and their shield. The Lord hath been mindful of us: he will bless us.

We will bless the Lord from this time forth and for evermore. Praise ye the Lord.        *—115:1-12, 18*

## 65.  *I Love the Lord*

I LOVE the Lord, because he hath heard my voice and my supplications. Because he hath inclined his ear unto me, therefore will I call unto him as long as I live.

The sorrows of death compassed me, I was in desperate straits. I found trouble and sorrow. Then called I upon the name of the Lord; O Lord, I beseech thee, deliver my soul. Gracious is the Lord, and righteous; yea, our God is merciful. The Lord preserveth the simple: I was brought low, and he helped me.

Return unto thy rest, O my soul; for the Lord hath dealt bountifully with thee. For thou hast saved my life from death, mine eyes from tears, and my feet from falling. I will walk before the Lord in the land of the living. I believed, therefore have I spoken: I was greatly afflicted: I said in my haste, All men are liars. What shall I render unto the Lord for all his benefits toward me? I will take the cup of salvation, and call upon the name of the Lord. I will pay my vows unto the Lord now in the presence of all his people.

Precious in the sight of the Lord is the death of his saints.

O Lord, truly I am thy servant; I am thy servant and the son of thine handmaid: thou hast loosed my bonds.

I will offer to thee the sacrifice of thanksgiving, and will call upon the name of the Lord. I will pay my vows unto the Lord now in the presence of all his people, in the courts of the Lord's house, in the midst of thee, O Jerusalem.

Praise ye the Lord.                                                —116

## 66.   O Give Thanks

O GIVE thanks unto the Lord; for he is good: because his mercy endureth for ever. Let Israel say, that his mercy endureth for ever. Let the house of Aaron now say, that his mercy endureth for ever. Let them now that worship the Lord say, that his mercy endureth for ever.

I called upon the Lord in distress: the Lord answered me, and set me free. The Lord is on my side; I will not fear: what can man do unto me? It is better to trust in the Lord than to put confidence in man. It is better to trust in the Lord than to put confidence in princes.

The voice of rejoicing and triumph is in the tents of the righteous: the right hand of the Lord doeth valiantly. The right hand of the Lord is exalted: the right hand of the Lord doeth valiantly. I shall not die, but live, and declare the works of the Lord. The Lord hath chastened me sore: but he hath not given me over unto death.

Open me the gates of righteousness: I will go into them, and I will praise the Lord: this gate of the Lord, into which the just alone can enter. I will praise thee: for thou hast heard me, and hast delivered me.

The stone which the builders refused is become the head stone of the corner. This is the Lord's doing; it is marvelous in our eyes.

This is the day which the Lord hath made; we will rejoice and be glad in it.

Thou art my God, and I will praise thee: thou art my God, I will exalt thee. O give thanks unto the Lord; for he is good: for his mercy endureth for ever.                        —118:1-6, 8-9, 15-24, 28-29

## 67.   A Lamp for My Feet

BLESSED are the undefiled in the way, who walk in the law of the Lord. Blessed are they that keep his testimonies, and that seek him with the whole heart, who do no wrong: they walk in his ways.

Thou hast commanded us to keep thy precepts diligently. O that my

[ 194 ]

ways were directed to keep thy statutes! No shame befalls me when I heed thy commands.

As I learn the justice of thy rulings, I thank thee with unfeigned heart. I will obey thee: never do thou forsake me.

How can a young man keep life clean? By keeping thy word. With my whole heart have I sought thee: O let me not wander from thy commandments. Thy word have I hid in mine heart, that I might not sin against thee. Blessed art thou, O Lord: teach me thy will. With my lips have I declared all the judgments of thy mouth. I find more joy in the way of thy testimonies than in all riches. I meditate in thy precepts, and have respect unto thy ways. I delight in thy will: I never forget thy word.

It is good for me that I have been in trouble—to learn thy will. Thy law means more to me than thousands of gold and silver.

Though shrivelled like a wineskin in the smoke, I never forget thine orders. Never shall I forget thy laws, for they put new life into me.

Thy law is a lamp for my feet, and a light on my path. The interpretation of thy words enlightens and instructs the openminded.

*—119:1-16, 71-72, 83, 93, 105, 130*

## 68.  *Unto the Hills*

I will lift up mine eyes unto the hills, ah, where is help to come from? My help cometh from the Lord, which made heaven and earth.

He will not suffer thy foot to be moved: he that keepeth thee will not slumber. Behold, he that keepeth Israel shall neither slumber nor sleep.

The Lord is thy keeper: the Lord is thy shade upon thy right hand. The sun shall not smite thee by day, nor the moon by night.

The Lord shall preserve thee from all evil: he shall preserve thy soul. The Lord shall preserve thy going out and thy coming in from this time forth, and even for evermore.  *—121*

## 69.  *The House of the Lord*

I am glad whenever they say to me, Let us go into the house of the Lord, glad when our feet stand at last inside Jerusalem. Jerusalem is now rebuilt, a city solid and unbroken, whither the tribes go up, the tribes of the Lord, to give thanks unto the name of the Lord.

Pray for the peace of Jerusalem: they shall prosper that love thee. Peace be within thy walls, and prosperity within thy palaces.

For my brethren and companions' sakes, I will now say, Peace be within thee. Because of the house of the Lord our God I will seek thy good.  *—122:1-4, 6-9*

## 70.  *Mount Zion*

They that trust in the Lord shall be as mount Zion, which cannot be removed, but abideth for ever. As the mountains are round about Jerusalem, so the Lord is round about his people now and evermore.

*—125:1-2*

## 71. *The Exiles' Song*

WHEN the Lord brought back the exiles to Zion, we were like them that dream. Then was our mouth filled with laughter, and our tongue with singing: the very heathen said, The Lord hath done great things for them.

The Lord hath done great things for us; whereof we are glad.

O Lord, bring back now the rest of our exiles, to fill us up, like streams in the dry south.

They that are sowing in tears shall reap in joy. Sadly they bear seed to the field, gladly they bear home the sheaves.                    —*126*

## 72. *A Pilgrim Song*

EXCEPT the Lord build the house, they labor in vain that build it: except the Lord keep the city, the watchman waketh but in vain.

—*127:1*

## 73. *Wait for the Lord*

OUT of the depths have I cried unto thee, O Lord. Lord, hear my voice: let thine ears be attentive to the voice of my supplications. If thou, Lord, shouldest mark iniquities, O Lord, who shall stand? But there is forgiveness with thee, that thou mayest be worshipped.

I wait for the Lord, my soul doth wait, and in his promise do I hope. My soul waiteth for the Lord more eagerly than watchmen for the dawn.

Let Israel hope in the Lord: for with the Lord there is love, there is wealth of saving power.                    —*130:1-7*

## 74. *Praise the Lord*

PRAISE ye the Lord. Praise ye the name of the Lord; praise him, O ye servants of the Lord. Ye that stand in the house of the Lord, in the courts of the house of our God, praise the Lord; for the Lord is good: sing praises unto his name; for he is gracious.                    —*135:1-3*

## 75. *His Kindness Never Fails*

O GIVE thanks unto the Lord; for he is good: his kindness never fails.

O give thanks unto the God of gods: his kindness never fails.

O give thanks to the Lord of Lords: his kindness never fails.

To him who alone does wonders: his kindness never fails.

To him whose wisdom made the heavens: his kindness never fails.

To him that stretched out the earth above the waters: his kindness never fails.

To him that made great lights: his kindness never fails.

The sun to rule by day: his kindness never fails.

[ 196 ]

The moon and stars to rule by night: his kindness never fails.
Who furnishes us all with food: his kindness never fails.
O give thanks unto the God of heaven: his kindness never fails.

*—136:1-9, 25-26*

## 76.  *The Captives' Song*

BY THE rivers of Babylon, there we sat and wept, at the thought of
Zion. There on the willows we hung up our harps when our captors asked
for a song, and those who had harried us bade us to be merry. "Sing us
a song of Zion," they said. But how can we sing the Lord's songs here,
in a foreign land! Jerusalem, if ever I forget thee, withered be this my
hand! May my tongue cleave to my mouth if I do not remember thee;
if I prefer not Jerusalem above my chief joy!          *—137:1-6*

## 77.  *Lead Me in the Way Everlasting*

O LORD, thou hast searched me, and known me. Thou knowest my
downsitting and mine uprising; thou understandest my thoughts from
afar. Thou compassest my path and my lying down, and my life to thee
lies open. Ere even a word comes to my tongue, O Lord, thou knowest
it altogether. Thou art on everyside, behind me and before, laying thy
hand on me. Such knowledge is too wonderful for me; it is far, far
beyond me.

Where could I go from thy spirit, where could I flee from thy presence? If I climb to heaven, thou art there: if I crouch in the lower world,
thou art there. If I take the wings of the morning, and dwell in the utter-
most parts of the sea; even there thy hand would fall on me, and thy
right hand would reach me. If I say, Surely the darkness will screen me,
the night will hide me in its curtains; yet the darkness hideth not from
thee; the night is clear as daylight.

I praise thee for the awful wonder of my birth; thy work is wonderful.
Thou knowest all about my soul; my body was no mystery to thee.

What mysteries I find in thee, O God! How vast the number of thy
purposes! If I should count them, they are more in number than the
sand: I awake from my reverie, and I am still lost in thee.

Search me, O God, and know my heart: try me, and know my thoughts:
and see if there be any wicked way in me, and lead me in the way
everlasting.          *—139:1-15, 17-18, 23-24*

## 78.  *Happy That People Whose God Is the Lord*

LORD, what is man, that thou takest knowledge of him! or the son of
man, that thou makest account of him! Man is like a passing breath, his
days are as a flitting shadow.

I will sing a new song unto thee, O God: and on an instrument of ten
strings will I sing praises unto thee.

May our sons be straight and strong like saplings, our daughters like cornices carved in a palace!

May our barns be bursting with all sorts of produce, may our sheep in the fields multiply in myriads!

May our rulers be strong, may nothing go wrong—no raids or retreats, no panic in our streets! Happy is that people, that is in such a case: happy that people, whose God is the Lord!

—*144:3-4, 9, 12-15* (Moffatt)

## 79.  *Gracious and Full of Compassion*

I WILL extol thee, my God, O King; and I will bless thy name for ever and ever. Every day will I bless thee; and I will praise thy name for ever and ever.

Great is the Lord, and greatly to be praised; and his greatness is unsearchable. One generation shall praise thy works to another, and shall declare thy mighty acts.

I will speak of the glorious honor of thy majesty, and of thy wondrous works. And men shall speak of the might of thy terrible act; and declare thy greatness.

The Lord is gracious, and full of compassion; slow to anger and of great mercy. The Lord is good to all: and his tender mercies are over all his works.

All thy works shall praise thee, O Lord; and thy saints shall bless thee. They shall speak of the glory of thy kingdom, and talk of thy power: to make known to the sons of men thy mighty acts, and the glorious majesty of thy kingdom. Thy kingdom is an everlasting kingdom, and thy dominion endureth throughout all generations.

The Lord upholdeth all that fall, and raiseth up all those that be bowed down.

The eyes of all wait upon thee; and thou givest them their meat in due season. Thou openest thine hand, and satisfiest the desire of every living thing.

The Lord is faithful in all his ways, and loving in all he does. The Lord is near all who call on him, to all who call on him in truth. He satisfies his worshippers: he also hears their cry, and helps them.

My mouth shall speak the praise of the Lord: and let all flesh bless his holy name for ever and ever.                    —*145:1-19, 21*

## 80.  *The Lord Is King*

PRAISE ye the Lord. Praise the Lord, O my soul. While I live will I praise the Lord: I will sing praises unto my God while I have any being.

Put not your trust in great men—mere mortals who can give no help. When their breath goes they return to dust, on that very day their projects perish.

Happy is he that hath the God of Jacob for his help, whose hope is in the Lord his God: which made heaven, and earth, the sea, and all that therein is. He remains ever true: he rights those who are wronged, he feeds those who are hungry. The Lord sets the captives free.

The Lord giveth the blind their sight: the Lord raiseth them that are bowed down: the Lord loveth the righteous.

The Lord preserves poor foreigners: he relieves the widow and the orphan: but the way of the wicked he turneth upside down.

The Lord shall reign for ever, even thy God, O Zion, unto all generations. Praise ye the Lord. —146

## 81. *He Healeth the Broken in Heart*

PRAISE ye the Lord, for he is good: make melody to our God for he is gracious. He healeth the broken in heart, and bindeth up their wounds. He fixes the number of the stars and gives a name to each. Great is our Lord, and of great power: his understanding is infinite.

Sing to the Lord with thanksgiving; sing praise on the harp to our God: who covereth the heaven with clouds, who prepareth rain for the earth till grass grows on the very hills, and fodder for the beasts that serve mankind; who gives wild animals their food, that cry for it at eventide.

He cares not for the strength of the warhorse: he delights not in man's armour. The Lord delights in those who revere him, who trust in his goodness.

Praise the Lord, O Jerusalem; praise thy God, O Zion: for he hath fortified your gates and blessed your citizens within. He has made peace in thy borders, and filleth thee with the finest of the wheat.

He sendeth forth his commendment upon earth: his word runneth very swiftly. He giveth snow like wool: he scattereth the hoar frost like ashes. He casteth down hailstones like morsels: the waters freeze; he sendeth out his order and they melt; he causeth his wind to blow, and the waters flow.

Praise ye the Lord. —147:1, 3-5, 7-18, 20b

## 82. *Praise Him*

PRAISE the Lord.
Praise the Lord from the heavens,
Praise him in the heights,
Praise him, all his angels
Praise him, all his hosts,
Praise him, sun and moon,
Praise him, all stars of light,
Praise him, heaven of heavens, ye waters that be above the heavens!

Let them praise the name of the Lord: for he commanded and they were created; he established them for ever and ever; he set them boundaries that they should not pass.

Praise the Lord from the earth, ye depths of ocean and ye water-spouts; lightning and hail and snow and ice; storms carrying out his will; moun-

[ 199 ]

tains and all hills; fruit trees and all cedars; wild beasts and all cattle;
creeping things and flying fowl; kings of the earth and all the peoples;
princes and all authorities; both young men and maidens, old people
and children; let them praise the name of the Lord, for his name only
is excellent; his glory is above earth and heaven.
Praise ye the Lord. —148:1-13, 14

## 83.  *Hallelujah*

PRAISE ye the Lord.
Sing unto the Lord a new song, and his praise where his followers
gather. Let Israel rejoice in their Maker; let the children of Zion be
joyful in their King. Let them dance in praise of him, and make melody
to him with drum and harp; for the Lord delights in his people.
Praise ye the Lord. —149:1-4, 9

## 84.  *Praise Ye the Lord*

Praise ye the lord.
Praise God in his sanctuary,
Praise him in the firmament of his power,
Praise him for his mighty acts,
Praise him for his excellent greatness;
Praise him with a bugle blast,
Praise him with the lute and lyre,
Praise him with the drum and dance,
Praise him with stringed instruments and organs,
Praise him with resounding cymbals,
Praise him with the clash of cymbals.
Let everything that breathes praise the Lord!
Praise ye the Lord. —150

# BOOK III

# PROSE

•

## INTRODUCTION

It is more difficult to find brief quotations in prose than in poetry. It was thought wise to gather the quotations from as wide a variety of sources as possible. Some are from ancient times, some from medieval, and some are contemporary. The subjects are likewise varied. The variety in time, place, national and religious background, and subject, itself suggests that people of all times and all lands are loved of God and respond to him, and that all worthy human interests are of God and may justly give their mead of praise and devotion to our Christian worship.

## As I Grow Old

I used to wonder a little at the serene faith of the old . . . I wonder no more. I can see that the day is far spent, and I begin to feel that serenity of faith which had excited my wonder. I feel, more and more, like one going home. Going home is a good part of the occupation of every living thing. Home is the pole-star of this planet. It is a universal, ever present, force.
*—Irving Bacheller*

## Bad Temper

The first thing that hinders the prayer of a good person from obtaining its effects is bad temper[1] and a violent storm in the spirit of him who prays. For bad temper sets the house on fire. It is an eternal enemy to discourse, and sober counsels, and fair conversation; it is fever in the heart, and a fire in the face, and a sword in the hand, and a fury all over; and therefore can never suffer a person to be in a disposition to pray. For prayer is an action, and a state of intercourse and desire, exactly contrary to this character of bad temper.

Prayer is the peace of our spirit, the stillness of our thoughts, the evenness of recollection, the seat of meditation, the rest of our cares, and the calm of our tempest; prayer is the issue of a quiet mind, of untroubled thoughts. It is the daughter of charity, and the sister of meekness; and he that prays to God with an angry, that is, with a troubled and decomposed spirit, is like him that retires into a battle to meditate!

[1] The original is translated "anger," but "bad temper" seems nearer the meaning.

Bad temper is a perfect alienation of the mind from prayer, and therefore is contrary to that attention which presents our prayers in a right line to God.                                                   —*Jeremy Taylor*

## Be Not Afraid

HEAR ye, Israel; hear what the Lord speaked: Oh, hadst thou heeded my commandments! Who hath believed our report; to whom is the arm of the Lord revealed? Thus saith the Lord, the Redeemer of Israel, and his holy one, to him oppressed by tyrants: I am he that comforteth; be not afraid, for I am thy God, I will strengthen thee . . . Who art thou, that thou art afraid of a man that shall die; and forgettest the Lord, thy Maker, who hath stretched forth the heavens, and laid the earth's foundations? Be not afraid, for I, thy God, will strengthen thee.
                                        —*Felix Mendelssohn-Bartholdy*
                                                             (Elijah)

## Be Patient with Yourself

BE PATIENT with every one, but above all with yourself. I mean, do not be disturbed because of your imperfections, and always rise up bravely from a fall. I am glad that you daily make a new beginning; there is no better means of progress in the spiritual life than to be continually beginning afresh, and never to think that we have done enough.
                                                —*St. Francis of Sales*

## Be Ye All of One Mind

BE YE all of one mind, having compassion one of another, love as brethren, be pitiful, be courteous: not rendering evil for evil, or railing for railing: but contrariwise blessing; knowing that ye are thereunto called, that ye should inherit a blessing. For he that will love life, and see good days, let him refrain his tongue from evil, and his lips that they may speak no guile; let him eschew evil, and do good; let him seek peace, and ensue it. . . . And who is he that will harm you, if ye be followers of that which is good? But and if ye suffer for righteousness' sake, happy are ye: and be not afraid of their terror, neither be troubled; but sanctify the Lord God in your hearts: and be ready always to give an answer to everyman that asketh you a reason of the hope that is in you. . . .                                    —*I Peter 3:8-11, 13-15*

## The Beauty of Snow

IN THE range of inorganic nature, I doubt if any object can be found more perfectly beautiful than a fresh, deep snowdrift, seen under warm light. Its curves are of inconceivable perfection and changefulness, its surface and transparency alike exquisite, its light and shade of inexhaustible variety and inimitable finish, the shadows sharp, pale and of heavenly color, the reflected lights intense and multitudinous, and mingled with the sweet occurrences of transmitted light.　　　　　　—*John Ruskin*

## *Because He Will Not Return*

You are sitting in the room he left. The open cupboard shows all his workaday and best clothes hanging cleaned and pressed against his return. . . . And now the paper in your hand says he will not return.

If I might do so I would sit in that clean, still, empty room with you. But after that I wish we might leave the empty room and go out where the children play and the birds sing and flowers grow in the sunshine, where they are all alive with the first taste of life.

The paper says that he is dead, but that is not true. The truth is that he will not return. He went adventuring out ahead of us, following the call to give his life—no, not his real life but that part of it which he shared with us here. That part of life he gave wholly and freely, not careless of us but because he was so mindful of us all. So he no longer needs the body we knew. It is folded away in Mother Earth or in the clean salt sea.

His first taste of life, his apprentice work, is over. We had not thought of him as following us in our long monotone of work and care, his vigor like ours slowing down at last to the anxious step of advancing age. We had no adventure, only a steady plodding through many years. But for him a trumpet sounded! We had thought the days of chivalry gone forever, and yet in an hour our plain man went away like a knight to rescue the innocent and the distressed. He has done his devoir and now the trumpets are sounding for him on the other side. He is now wonderfully, tremendously alive.

We taught him the faith of the Everlasting Arms and the Everlasting Life. In that faith he went out, not speaking of it so openly as we do but holding to it and proving it like a man. Now it is our turn to believe that faith as never before and to practise it. He is alive in the paradise of God. What that means passes all imagining, but surely it means that his love for us is illuminated by a great light.

Do you think that, delighted and full of wonder as he is, he would want us to sit and mourn with folded hands in his old empty room? To grieve and harden and grow bitter? To turn the room where once he was so gay into a museum and a morgue? No! He wants us to lift up our hearts and catch a glimpse of the vision so clear around him.

Wouldn't he say?—"If you could know what I do now, you would have no grief. You would put on festive clothes and sing to God in church and out. I've been promoted. I am busy in a great service. The old frustrations are all gone. We do great things here. Let someone into my old room. Give my things to someone who needs them. And when you get going in your new happiness, go to other houses where men like me will not return and get the truth across to the people there.

[ 203 ]

Where we are, we can see better how God is working his purpose out. It costs a great price and we have paid a little of it, and you are paying some of it, but it is all marvelously worth while." —*Gilbert P. Symons*

## Blessing in External Work

LET everyone lovingly cast all his thoughts and cares, and his sins too, as it were, on the will of God. Moreover, if a man, while busy in this lofty inward work, were called by some duty in the Providence of God to cease therefrom, and cook a broth for some sick person, or any other such service, he should do so willingly and with great joy. If I had to forsake such work, and go out to preach or aught else, I should go cheerfully, believing not only that God would be with me, but that he would vouchsafe me it may be even greater grace and blessing in that external work undertaken out of true love in the service of my neighbor, than I should perhaps receive in my season of loftiest contemplation.

—*John Tauler*

## Blessing of Work

THANK God every morning, when you get up, that you have something to do that day which must be done, whether you like it or not. Being forced to work and forced to do your best, will breed in you temperance, and self-control, diligence and strength of will, cheerfulness and content and a hundred virtues which the idle man will never know.

—*Charles Kingsley*

## The Boy with the Lunch

"MOTHER!" cried David, bursting into the house, "Jesus, the teacher, is to be at the lakeside today and the whole village is going there. May we go too?"

"You know, David, I long to see and hear him almost more than anything else in the world, but your grandmother is ill and I cannot go."

"That's always the way! We never can do anything like other people!" and the little lad turned his back, bitter with disappointment.

"But if Mr. Peter is going," continued his mother, "and will take you along, you could go with him."

"Oh, may I? Thanks mother!" and away he flew. He came back breathless. "Mr. Peter says he'll be glad to have me come with them, and they're leaving at once!" He started for the door.

"But, David," said the mother, "you will be away all day and will need something to eat. Come, it will not take a minute to get it ready."

She went to the crock where she kept the delicious barley buns or rolls and picked out five that were brown and crisp, the kind he liked best, and from another crock she took several little pickled fish, very tasty for a cold meal, and packed them in his shepherd's pouch.

[ 204 ]

"Mother, that's a big lunch. I'll never need all that," said David.

"Perhaps not," agreed the mother, "but there may be some there who forgot to bring anything and you can share with them."

The boy threw his arms impulsively around his mother's neck as he kissed her good-bye and said, "You always think of everything a fellow needs!"

It was a long, tiresome, lonely day for the mother. It was not till late evening that she saw them coming back along the path that wound through the fields.

David came in sunburnt and very weary, and as he ate the lovely hot dinner she had ready for him he told her snatches of the day's events.

"When we got there there was quite a crowd around Jesus, but you know how boys are. I wiggled in until I was close to the men who are with him. He talked so simply that I could understand all he said and he told some of the most wonderful stories. One was about a lamb that got lost and another about a hen and her little chickens that I'll tell you sometime.

"I began to get hungry and I heard one of the men say to him, 'Master, you are talking too long. Everybody is starving. Stop and let them go away and get something to eat.'

"And Jesus said, 'Can we not give them something to eat?' The men laughed and replied, 'It would take over a hundred dollars to serve light refreshments, and where would we ever get that much money?'

"Then I remembered what you said. I pulled the sleeve of one of the men, Andrew, I think, and said, 'You may have my lunch to share with others,' and the man laughed and said, 'This kid is willing to give his lunch!'

"But Jesus took it as if it had been the gift of a king. He held it up before the people and said, 'A lad here offers to share his lunch with others. Perhaps we could all do that and there would be plenty for all.'

"Then, I do not know how it happened, but everybody was sitting down in little groups and sharing with each other and passing things around and talking and laughing just as we do on a picnic, and everyone seemed happy. That's the way, the teacher said, to make a happy world."

By this time the little boy was curled up on his sleeping rug. As his mother tucked him in, he murmured, "He was so kind and had such lovely eyes—he reminded me of you, Mother."

And the last words she heard as he fell asleep were, "I want to be like him."

—A. J. William Myers

## Bread

Two men I honor, and no third. First, the toil-worn craftsman that with earth-made implement laboriously conquers the earth and makes her man's. . . . Hardly-entreated brother! For us was the back so bent, for us were thy straight limbs and fingers so deformed; thou wert our conscript, on whom the lot fell, and fighting our battles wert so marred. . . . Yet toil on, toil on: thou art in thy duty, be out of it who may; thou toilest for the altogether indispensable, for daily bread.

A second man I honor, and still more highly: Him who is seen toiling for the spiritually indispensable; not daily bread, but the bread of Life. . . . Highest of all, when his outward and his inward endeavor are one: when we can name him Artist; not earthly Craftsman only, but inspired Thinker, who with heaven-made Implement conquers Heaven for us! . . .

Unspeakably touching is it, however, when I find both dignities united; and he that must toil outwardly for the lowest of man's wants is also toiling inwardly for the highest. Sublimer in this world know I nothing than a Peasant Saint, could such now anywhere be met with. Such a one will take thee back to Nazareth itself; thou wilt see the splendor of Heaven spring forth from the humblest depths of Earth, like a light shining in great darkness. *—Thomas Carlyle*

*(Sartor Resartus)*

## The Burma Road

WITHIN our recent memory this swift order for a highway has been carried out for all the world to watch—for the Burma Road is a spiritual symbol of all the pluck and grit and ingenuity which a people can muster: made by part of a nation to save all of a nation.

For when China's port cities were cut off by Japan as a source of supplies, this "back way in" from Burma became an immediate necessity; and the 700 miles from Lashio in Burma to Kun Ming in China saw a drama of tremendous significance. For this had been the olden route for caravans which Marco Polo traveled in the thirteenth century— full of curves where the mules of many decades had ambled on their ancient silk route: quite unfit for modern trucks, of course. So the new road was begun in the late autumn of 1937, by village clansmen most of whom had never seen a wheeled vehicle in all their lives. Moreover, they had no modern tools, but hammered the rocks with crude implements, not understanding at all why speed was urgent—so remote were they from war and news. . . .

In the end nearly a million men and women helped to build it, and within a year it was ready for use: although each worker needed to be a Hercules, so demanding was the labor and so great the risks. For rugged mountains towered ten thousand feet above, giant gorges fell a thousand feet below, and out of the face of such rocks the road had to be chipped away, inch by inch, by hand. No dynamite. No machinery. No cranes. Just the patient constant bending and lifting of human backs and human arms—landslides endangering them, washouts and malaria and mosquitoes molesting them. If it has been done once for an earthly kingdom, is there not hope of conscripting the rest of us for work upon the King's highway?

Through desert ways, dark fen and deep morass,
Through jungles, sluggish seas, and mountain pass,

Build ye the road, and falter not, nor stay,
Prepare across the earth the King's highway.

—*H. D. Friberg*
(West China and the Burma Road)

## Captain Scott

CAPTAIN Robert Falcon Scott of the Royal Navy was chosen leader of the South Pole expedition in 1910. The utmost care was taken to insure success and to provide against every emergency. Four men and the commander made the last dash from the "farthest south" depot, travelling as light as possible, depending on the supplies in each succeeding depot.

With nine days' provision they set out and reached the pole on January 17. The long-sought goal was achieved! But to their great disappointment they found that Amundsen had been there first. They found his Norwegian flag. This disappointment must have sapped their vitality and greatly depressed them. They built a cairn and put up the Union Jack.

Early next morning they started back on their fatal journey. There was a strong head wind, it was bitterly cold, and they had before them "800 miles of solid dragging."

One misfortune after another dogged them. Evans fell sick. If they had left him the others could have got through. They would not. Then Oates sickened and begged them to go on without him. They laughed at the suggestion. One night in the fearful blizzard he crawled out and could not be found. He gave his life for his friends.

The continuous blizzards and intense cold—40 below zero—were most unusual at that time of year. Besides, the stored gasoline had wasted in the continued intense cold so there was not enough for heat and fuel!

The courage of the five men, their consideration for each other, their thought for their loved ones make a glorious page of history. On such expeditions the party carries poison; but these men, though they knew the end to be inevitable, decided not to use it.

Scott's journal is an amazing document written under such conditions. There is no repining, no fault-finding, only thoughtfulness for others, courage and faith. His letters to his mother and to his wife and their little boy reveal something of what a beautiful home life and faith in God mean in facing reality.

### I. Scott's Last Camp

[When the relief expedition discovered their tent, this is what they found:]

Bowers and Wilson were sleeping in their bags. Scott had thrown back the flaps of his bag at the head. His left hand was stretched over

Wilson, his lifelong friend. Beneath the head of his bag, between the bag and the floor cloth, was the green wallet in which he carried his diary. The brown books of diary were inside, and on the floor cloth were some letters.

Everything was tidy. The tent had been pitched as well as ever, taut and shipshape. There was no snow inside the inner lining. There were some loose pannikins from the cooker, and a few more letters and records—personal and scientific. Near Scott was a lamp formed from a tin and some lamp wick off a finnesco. It had been used to burn the little methylated spirit which remained. I think that Scott had used it to help him to write up to the end. I feel sure that he had died last—and once I had thought he would not go so far as some of the others. We never realized how strong that man was, mentally and physically, until now. . . .

Nothing that they had accomplished was wasted; all their records were faithfully preserved; even the geological specimens, two stone weight of them, more than the ordinary man cares to carry, had been dragged all along their weary marches from the Beardmore Glacier. Then, at the end, the team as a team, rejecting the alternative death by opium, for which they were provided, quietly lay down to take what came. But the leader's work was not done while life remained in him. On him rested the whole responsibility, and he felt that his power to affect events would not be ended by death. He counted with certainty that search would find them; the written word therefore remained; and there were duties to be done with the last flicker of his strength, while the cold gnawed at his fingers.

[Suffering extremely and dying, his thoughts were only of the great purpose of the expedition, and the sufferings of others. All his writing is full of tenderness and strength. These are excerpts from his diary:]

For four days we have been unable to leave the tent—the gale howling about us. We are weak, writing is difficult, but for my own sake I do not regret this journey, which has shown that Englishmen can endure hardships, help one another, and meet death with as great a fortitude as ever in the past. We took risks, we knew we took them; things have come out against us, and therefore we have no cause for complaint, but bow to the will of Providence, determined still to do our best to the last. But if we have been willing to give our lives to this enterprise, which is for the honour of our country, I appeal to our countrymen to see that those who depend on us are properly cared for.

Had we lived, I should have had a tale to tell of the hardihood, endurance and courage of my companions which would have stirred the heart of every Englishman. These rough notes and our dead bodies must tell the tale, but surely, surely, a great rich country like ours will see that those who are dependent on us are properly provided for.

R. Scott

[Britain did provide for them.]

## II. Scott's Last Letters to His Wife

[Scott knew the end was near; so he wrote:]

To My Widow,
We are in a very tight corner and have doubts of pulling through. In our short lunch hours I take advantage of a very small measure of warmth to write letters preparatory to a possible end. The first is naturally to you on whom my thoughts mostly dwell, waking or sleeping.

If anything happens to me I should like you to know how much you have meant to me, what pleasant recollections are with me as I depart.

I should like you to take what comfort you can from these facts also. I shall not have suffered any pain, but leave the world fresh from harness and full of good health and vigour. This is decided already. When provisions come to an end we simply stop unless we are within easy distance of another depot. Therefore you must not imagine a great tragedy . . .

We have a chance to get through, but the cold weather doesn't let up at all. We are 20 miles from a depot but we have very little food and fuel.

I want you to take the whole thing very sensibly, as I am sure you will. The boy will be your comfort. I had looked forward to helping you to bring him up, but it is a satisfaction to know that he will be safe with you . . .

I must write a little letter for the boy if time can be found, to be read when he grows up. The inherited vice from my side of the family is indolence—above all he must guard, and you must guard him, against that. I had to force myself into being strenuous, as you know—had always an inclination to be idle. . . .

You know I cherish no sentimental rubbish about re-marriage. When the right man comes to help you in life, you ought to be your happy self again—I wasn't a very good husband, but I hope I shall be a good memory. Certainly the end is nothing for you to be ashamed of, and I like to think that the boy will have a good start in his parentage, of which he may be proud.

It isn't easy to write because of the cold—40 below zero and nothing but the shelter of our tents. You must know that quite the worst aspect of this situation is the thought that I shall not see you again. The inevitable must be faced; you urged me to be leader of this party, and I know you felt it would be dangerous. I have taken my place throughout, haven't I?

God bless you. I shall try and write more later—I go on across the back pages.

Since writing the above, we got within 11 miles of our depot with one hot meal and two days' cold food. We should have got through but have been held for four days by a frightful storm. I think the last chance has gone. We have decided not to kill ourselves but to fight to the last for that depot, but in fighting there is a painless end, so don't worry, I have written letters on odd pages of this book. Will you manage to get them sent? You see, I am anxious for you and the boy's future. Make

[ 209 ]

the boy interested in natural history if you can. It is better than games. They encourage it at some schools. I know you will keep him in the open air. Try and make him believe in a God, it is comforting. . . . .

There is a piece of the Union Jack I put up at the South Pole in my private kit-bag, together with Amundsen's black flag and other trifles. Send a small piece of the Union Jack to the King, a small piece to Queen Alexandra, and keep the rest—a poor trophy for you. What lots and lots I could tell you of this journey. How much better has it been than lounging in too great comfort at home. What tales you would have for the boy, but oh what a price to pay.

[The letter ends with messages to his mother and friends. The terrible storm continued for eleven days.]

On the 20th. they had fuel to make two cups of tea apiece and bare food for two days. Yet Scott was able to write on the 29th., and apparently all were then still alive. The last words in his diary are:

Every day we have been ready to start for our depot 11 *miles* away, but outside the door of the tent it remains a scene of whirling drift. I do not think we can hope for any better things now. We shall stick it out to the end, but we are getting weaker, of course, and the end cannot be far.

It seems a pity, but I do not think I can write more.

R. Scott

[Last entry:]

For God's sake look after our people.

### III. Captain Scott's Letter to his Mother

My Own Darling Mother,

The Great God has called me, and I feel that the news of it will add a fearful blow to the heavy ones that have fallen on you in life. But take comfort that I die at peace with the world, and I myself not afraid —not perhaps believing in all that you hold to so splendidly, but still believing that there is a God—a merciful God. I wish I could remember that I had been a better son to you, but I think you will know that you were always very much in my heart and that I strove to put you into more comfortable circumstances.

I join dear old Arch, both of us having given the life you gave us to our country. The country owes you the debt—Willy will look after you, but you will have the small sum of money I was able to save, and Willy will buy an annuity.

[It had been agreed between him and his wife that his whole personal fortune, the small savings of ten years, should go to his mother, if she outlived him.]

I hope so that you remain in your. . . .

[So the letter ends; and then there is this final farewell:]

My Dear, Dear Mother,
I wish you could have been spared this blow and indeed it has been most supremely unfortunate, for the risks I have taken never seemed excessive.
For myself I am not unhappy, but for Kathleen, you, and the rest of the family my heart is very sore.
Still, I hope for all that I leave a memory to be proud of—we have done a very big journey and failed only by a very narrow margin.
God bless you, dear—I die feeling that your material comfort will be looked after to the end. I wish I had been a greater comfort to you.

Your loving son

Con.

—*Gwynn Stephen*
(Captain Scott)

## Christ and History's Voices

GREECE said, "Be moderate—know thyself."
Rome said, "Be strong—order thyself."
Confucianism says, "Be superior—correct thyself."
Shintoism says, "Be loyal—suppress thyself."
Buddhism says, "Be disillusioned—annihilate thyself."
Hinduism says, "Be separated—merge thyself."
Mohammedanism says, "Be submissive—assert thyself."
Judaism says, "Be holy—conform thyself."
Materialism says, "Be industrious—enjoy thyself."
Dilettantism says, "Be broad—cultivate thyself."
Christianity says, "Be Christlike—give thyself."

—*E. Stanley Jones*
(The Christ of the Indian Road)

## Christ of the Andes

THE Christ of the Andes stands on the border between Argentina and Chile. It was made from cannon abandoned by the Spaniards and bears this inscription: "Sooner shall these mountains crumble into dust than the people of Argentina and Chile break the peace to which they have pledged themselves at the feet of Christ, the Redeemer" . . .

—*J. Warshaw*
(The New Latin America)

## Christian Nurture

CHILD life in the Bible is always represented as a constant growth [Joseph, Samuel, David, John the Baptist, Jesus, Timothy].

[ 211 ]

The child is to grow up a Christian, and never know himself as being otherwise [is the aim of the Christian home and church].

For be it never forgotten, that in the divine plan, the culture of child-piety stands first in importance in furnishing the materials out of which the Church, God's spiritual temple, is to be built up in the world.

We ask then of every parent: Let family religion be a domestic minia-ture of heaven, not a dull formality. Let him be there, as the gardener among his opening flowers, expecting their fragrance and beauty, not that they will all be thistles—expecting it, because God hath promised, and the dews of his grace are perpetually felt.

No mock piety, no sanctimony of phrase, or longitude of face on Sundays will suffice. You must live in the light of God and hold such a spirit in exercise as you wish to see translated into your children.

Religion never thoroughly penetrates life, till it becomes domestic. Like that patriotic fire, which makes a nation invincible, it never burns with inextinguishable devotion, till it burns at the hearth.

Growth, not conquest, is the true means of extending the Kingdom.

According to the opinion of Christ himself, the church is as a grain of mustard seed, and its future spread is to be as the growth of a tree. It is a creature whose vitality is spiritual life, and it can have its increase only by the same law which pertains in all organic living bodies, *i.e.*, by development from within, not by external accretion.

The very nature of childhood teaches us that there is a place for children in the church; the very nature of the church proves that there ought to be a place for children within it.          —*Horace Bushnell*


## A Christmas Carol

[Scrooge's nephew is speaking to him:]

I have always thought of Christmas time, when it has come around . . . as a good time; the only time I know of, in the long calendar of the year, when men and women seem by one consent to open their shut-up hearts freely, and to think of people below them as if they really were fellow-passengers to the grave, and not another race of creatures bound on other journeys. And therefore . . . though it has never put a scrap of gold or silver in my pocket, I believe that it *has* done me good, and *will* do me good; and I say, God bless it!

[Marley's ghost visits Scrooge and exclaims, wringing its hands:]

Business! . . . Mankind was my business. The common welfare was my business; charity, mercy, forbearance and benevolence, were all my business. The dealings of my trade were but a drop of water in the comprehensive ocean of my business!

[Tiny Tim is a little boy cripple who thinks of others:]

Tiny Tim said that he hoped people would see him in the church on Christmas Day because he was a cripple, because they then would be thankful they were not cripples.

[And it was Tiny Tim who spoke the great universal Christmas prayer:]

God bless us every one! said Tiny Tim.      —*Charles Dickens*
(A Christmas Carol)

## Christmas Memories

AND numerous indeed are the hearts to which Christmas brings a brief season of happiness and enjoyment. How many families whose members have been dispersed and scattered far and wide in the restless struggles of life are then reunited, and meet once again in that happy state of companionship and mutual good-will which is a source of such pure and unalloyed delight; and one so incompatible with the cares and sorrows of the world that the religious belief of the most civilized nations and the rude traditions of the roughest savages alike number it among the first joys of a future condition of existence provided for the blessed and happy! How many old recollections, and how many dormant sympathies, does Christmas awaken!

We write these words now, many miles distant from the spot at which we met on that day a merry and joyous circle. Many of the hearts that throbbed so gaily then have ceased to beat; many of the looks that shone so brightly then have ceased to glow; the hands that we grasped have grown cold; the eyes we sought have hid their lustre in the grave; and yet the old house, the room, the merry voices and smiling faces, the jest, the laugh, the most minute and trivial circumstances connected with those happy meetings, crowd upon our mind at each recurrence of the season, as if the last assemblage had been but yesterday! Happy, happy Christmas, that can win us back to the delusions of our childish days; that can recall to the old man the pleasures of his youth; that can transport the sailor and the traveller, thousands of miles away, back to his own fireside and his quiet home!      —*Charles Dickens*
(Pickwick Papers)

## Clarions of God

HIGH hearts are never long without hearing some new call, some distant clarion of God, even in their dreams; and soon they are observed to break up the camp of ease, and start on some fresh march of faithful service. . . . (These are they) who do the good only to see the better, and see the better only to achieve it; . . . whose worship is action, and whose action is ceaseless aspiration.      —*James Martineau*
(Hours of Thought)

[ 213 ]

## A Confession of Faith

WE BELIEVE that God hath made man in his own image and that all men are therefore brothers.

Spirit, that is what God is, and they that worship him must worship him in spirit and in truth.

We believe that God is love and that every one that loveth is born of God and knoweth him.

We believe that God is light and that if we walk in the light, as he is in the light, we have fellowship one with another.

We believe that we are children of God and that he is our Father.

We believe that Jesus embodies most fully in his life and teaching the purpose of God for mankind and so has shown us the way of life.

We believe that if we walk with God and in fellowship with others we can make this world the family of God.

We believe the world passeth away, and the lust thereof, but that he that doeth the will of God abideth forever.

We believe that Jesus summed up the Christian creed in the two commandments: Thou shalt love the Lord with all thy heart, strength, soul and mind; and thy neighbor as thyself; and that assent to these is sufficient for full membership in the Church. —*Anonymous*

## The Cosmic Order

THIS sovereignty of God we sometimes speak of as the cosmic order. It is the realm of the fixed and unalterable, within which all our life moves, which sets limits to all our freedom. It is the moral order which underlies all human life, as well as the order of nature which rules the process of the suns. It is not, however, something abstract or impersonal. It is the direct expression of the mind and will of God and of his sustaining power. Apart from this there could be no science, no purposive and effective action; indeed, no reason in man or freedom for man or any life at all. This sovereign rule of God is then not so much a barrier to human action as a necessary condition, through its all-including order, of any free and effective life.

But it is more than this: it is the power and purpose of God active in the restraint of evil and in the support of good. It holds before men the unchangeable values which give meaning to life, at once rewarding our loyalty and judging our disobedience. It is as surely a part of God's creative-redemptive process as is his reconciling love. In its light alone can history find meaning. It sets its sure limits to the power of evil and works against this. —*Harris Franklin Rall*
(According to Paul)

## The Cross as Symbol

THESE, then, are some of the meanings of the cross to all who use it as a symbol:

[ 214 ]

1. The unfailing, unchanging, undying love of God. That love is with us in disappointment, defeat, and death, as well as in prosperity, joy, and abundant life.

2. The ability of man, in his dependence on and co-operation with God, to face life and death without faltering and without bitterness or despair. The spirit of man may be triumphant *in love.*

3. The awful result of actions, deliberate or otherwise, growing out of prejudice and hate, that are not in keeping with God's purpose of good and of respect for persons.

Those who use this symbol, the cross, thereby declare that it is their deliberate purpose to live the adventurous life in mutuality with their fellows and with God.

Some people speak and sing about taking up the cross as if it meant little more than pinning a decoration on one's coat. To take up the cross means to live the adventurous life day by day. It means practicing faith in God and in his unchanging love and purpose for good; a deep and abiding faith in the intrinsic worth of every person, and in his ability to live and endure for God; and the determination to venture to live in this faith, to follow the way of love and of service at all costs, even to risking life itself in the defence of one's fellow men. —A. J. *William Myers*
(Religion for Today)

## The Daily Grind

WE MUST be continually sacrificing our own wills, as opportunity serves, to the will of others; bearing, without notice, sights and sounds that annoy us; setting about this or that task when we had far rather be doing something very different; persevering in it, often, when we are thoroughly tired of it; keeping company for duty's sake, when it would be a great joy to us to be by ourselves; besides all the trifling untoward accidents of life; bodily pain and weakness long continued, and perplexing us often when it does not amount to illness; losing what we value, missing what we desire; disappointment in other persons, wilfulness, unkindness, ingratitude, folly, in cases where we least expect it.
—*John Keble*

## The Death of Socrates

[SOCRATES was condemned to death by drinking the hemlock, a deadly poison. His friends, broken in grief, were with him. The following excerpts give parts of one of the most beautiful and moving stories ever written:]

[Crito, one of the friends, had asked Socrates, How shall we bury you?]

Just as you please, he said, if only you can catch me, and I do not escape from you. And at the same time smiling gently, and looking

[ 215 ]

around on us, he said; I cannot persuade Crito, my friends, that I am that Socrates who is now conversing with you, and who methodizes each part of the discourses; but he thinks that I am he whom he will shortly behold dead, and asks how he should bury me. But that which I some time since argued at length, that when I have drunk the poison I shall no longer remain with you, but shall depart to some happy state of the blessed, this I seem to have urged to him in vain, though I meant at the same time to console both you and myself. . . . But do you be sureties that, when I die, I shall depart . . . and when he sees my body either burnt or buried, may not be afflicted for me, as if I suffered some dreadful thing, nor say at my interment that Socrates is laid out, or is carried out, or is buried. . . . You must have a good courage then, and say that you bury my body, and bury it in such a manner as is pleasing to you, and as you think is most agreeable to our laws.

When he had bathed . . . he sat down, and did not speak much afterwards; then the officer of the Eleven came in, and standing near him, said, "Socrates, I shall not have to find that fault with you that I do with others, that they are angry with me, and curse me, when, by order of the archons, I bid them drink the poison. But you, on all other occasions during the time you have been here, I have found to be the most noble, meek, and excellent man of all that ever came into this place; and, therefore, I am now well convinced that you will not be angry with me, for you know who are to blame, but with them. Now, then, for you know what I came to announce to you, farewell, and endeavour to bear what is inevitable as easily as possible." And at the same time, bursting into tears, he turned away and withdrew.

And Socrates, looking after him, said, And thou, too, farewell, we will do as you direct. At the same time, turning to us, he said, How courteous the man is; during the whole time I have been here he has visited me, and conversed with me sometimes, and proved the worthiest of men; and now how generously he weeps for me. But come, Crito, let us obey him, and let some one bring the poison, if it is ready pounded, but if not, let the man pound it.

Then Crito said, But I think, Socrates, that the sun is still on the mountains, and has not yet set. Besides, I know that others have drunk the poison very late, after it had been announced to them, and have supped and drunk freely, and some even have enjoyed the objects of their love. Do not hasten then, for there is yet time.

Upon this Socrates replied, These men whom you mention, Crito, do these things with good reason, for they think they shall gain by so doing, and I too with good reason shall not do so; for I think I shall gain nothing by drinking a little later, except to become ridiculous to myself, in being so fond of life, and sparing of it when none any longer remains. Go then, he said, obey, and do not resist.

Crito having heard this, nodded to the boy that stood near. And the boy having gone out, and staid for some time, came, bringing with him the man that was to administer the poison, who brought it ready pounded in a cup. And Socrates, on seeing the man, said, Well, my good friend, as you are skilled in these matters, what must I do?

Nothing else, he replied, than when you have drunk it walk about, until there is a heaviness in your legs, then lie down; thus it will do its purpose. And at the same time he held out the cup to Socrates. And he received it very cheerfully, Echecrates, neither trembling, nor changing at all in colour or countenance . . . [and] drank it off readily and calmly. Thus far, most of us were with difficulty able to restrain ourselves from weeping, but when we saw him drinking, and having finished the draught, we could do so no longer; but in spite of myself the tears came in full torrent, so that, covering my face, I wept for myself, for I did not weep for him, but for my own fortune, in being deprived of such a friend. . . . But he said, What are you doing, my admirable friends? I indeed, for this reason chiefly, sent away the women, that they might not commit any folly of this kind. For I have heard that it is right to die with good omens. Be quiet, therefore, and bear up.

When we heard this we were ashamed, and restrained our tears. But he, having walked about, when he said that his legs were growing heavy, laid down on his back; for the man so directed him. And at the same time he who gave him the poison, taking hold of him, after a short interval examined his feet and legs; and then having pressed his foot hard, he asked if he felt it; he said that he did not. And after this he pressed his thighs; and thus going higher, he showed us that he was growing cold and stiff. Then Socrates touched himself, and said, that when the poison reached his heart he should then depart. But now the parts around the lower belly were almost cold; when uncovering himself, for he had been covered over, he said, and they were his last words, Crito, we owe a cock to Aesculapius; pay it, therefore, and do not neglect it.

It shall be done, said Crito, but consider whether you have anything else to say.

To this question he gave no reply; but shortly after he gave a convulsive movement, and the man covered him, and his eyes were fixed; and Crito, perceiving it, closed his mouth and eyes.

This, Echecrates, was the end of our friend, a man, as we may say, the best of all of his time that we have known, and moreover, the most wise and just. —*Plato*
(Phaedo)

## Deathless Love

IN THE volcanic ashes of Pompeii, in one of the excavations, a little invalid child was found with his mother's arm around him. The mother, plainly enough from her ring of a noble family, had had plenty of chance to escape and save herself, as everybody else did in that section, but she had gone back to rescue this helpless deformed boy. And through all these years this mother's arm has lain there underneath this little child she died to save—a mute and tender token of deathless love. So in greater fashion, for which no human illustration is adequate, through all the confusions of the world, the din and noise of our busy and material lives, the darkness and mystery of time and space, the everlasting arms of the love of God are underneath us. He is with us in our agonies and our struggles, in our follies and frustrations, striving to finish his creation and to bring to fulfilment the expectation of the sons of God.

—*Rufus M. Jones*

## Do Thy Work

HE HAS especial tenderness of love towards thee for that thou art in the dark and hast no light, and his heart is glad when thou dost arise and say, "I will go to my Father." For he sees thee through all the gloom through which thou canst not see him. Say to him, "My God, I am very dull and low and hard; but thou art wise and high and tender, and thou art my God. I am thy child. Forsake me not." Then fold the arms of thy faith, and wait in quietness until light goes up in the darkness. Fold the arms of thy Faith, I say, but not of thy Action: bethink thee of something that thou oughtest to do, and go and do it, if it be but the sweeping of a room, or the preparing of a meal, or a visit to a friend; heed not thy feelings: do thy work.
—*George Macdonald*

## Endure Suffering

ST. FRANCIS being once sorely afflicted with his eyes, Cardinal Ugolino, protector of the Order, for the great love he bore him, wrote to him that he should come to him at Rieti, where were the best doctors for the eyes. . . .

(The only treatment these "best doctors for the eyes" knew, was searing with a white-hot iron.

In his prayer Francis thought God said to him, "Be of good cheer, Francis"; so, bidding farewell, he went on to Rieti.)

But when he was counselled by the physicians, and earnestly besought by the brethren, to suffer cautery for his relief, the man of God humbly yielded, because he saw that this would be at once both salutary and grievous. The surgeon, therefore, being sent for, came and placed his iron in the fire to heat it. But the servant of Christ, comforting his body, which was shuddering with dread, began to speak to the fire as a friend, saying, "O Brother Fire, before all other things the most High hath created thee of exceeding comliness, powerful, beauteous, and useful; be thou to me, in this my hour, merciful, be courteous. I beseech the Great Lord who hath created thee, that he may temper for me thy heat, that I may be able patiently to endure thy burning me." And when he had finished his prayer over the iron, glistening white with heat, he made the sign of the cross, and then remained stedfastly unflinching. The hissing iron was plunged into the tender flesh, and from the ear to the eyebrow the cautery was drawn. When he was asked concerning the pain of the fire, the holy man made answer: "Praise," said he to the brethren, "praise ye the most High; for I truly tell you I neither felt the fire's

[ 218 ]

heat, nor pain of body." And turning to the physician "If it be not well burnt," said he, "thrust in again." And the physician, beholding in the weakness of the flesh such wondrous strength of spirit, marvelled and extolled the miracle of God, and said, "I tell you, brethren, I have seen a strange thing to-day." For since to so great a purity had he come, that flesh with spirit, and spirit with God, agreed in wondrous harmony, it was by God's ordering, that the creature, obeying its Creator, was in a wondrous manner subject to his will and command.

—*Margaret Oliphant*
(Francis of Assisi)

## Endure Trouble

So LONG as we live in this world we cannot be without trouble and trial. . . .

Yet, notwithstanding, temptations turn greatly unto our profit, even though they be great and hard to bear; for through them we are humbled, purified, instructed. All Saints have passed through much tribulation and temptation, and have profited thereby. And they who endured not temptation became reprobate and fell away. There is no position so sacred, no place so secret, that it is without temptations and adversities. . . .

The beginning of all temptations to evil is instability of temper and want of trust in God.           —*Thomas à Kempis*
(Imitation of Christ)

## The Eternal God of Love

OUT in front of us is the drama of men and of nations, seething, struggling, laboring, dying. Upon this tragic drama in these days our eyes are all set in anxious watchfulness and in prayer. But within the silences of the souls of men an eternal drama is ever being enacted, in these days as well as in others. And on the outcome of this inner drama rests, ultimately, the outer pageant of history. It is the drama of the Hound of Heaven baying relentlessly upon the track of man. It is the drama of the lost sheep wandering in the wilderness, restless and lonely, feebly searching, while over the hills comes the wiser Shepherd. For his is a shepherd's heart, and he is restless until he holds his sheep in his arms. It is the drama of the Eternal Father drawing the prodigal home to himself, where there is bread enough and to spare. . . . And always its chief actor is— the Eternal God of Love.                    —*Thomas R. Kelly*

## Faith Is Better Than Doubt and Love Is Better Than Hate

(LAURIER, after forty years of public life, was speaking to "you who stand today on the threshold of life.")

Let me tell you that for the solution of these problems you have a safe guide, an unfailing light, if you remember that faith is better than doubt and love is better than hate.

Banish doubt and hate from your life. Let your souls be ever open to the promptings of faith and the gentle influence of brotherly love. Be adamant against the haughty, be gentle and kind to the weak. Let your aim and purpose, in good report or ill, in victory or defeat, be so to live, so to strive, so to serve as to do your part to raise ever higher the standard of life and of living. —*Oscar Douglas Skelton*
(Life and Letters of Sir Wilfred Laurier)

## A Faithful Friend

SWEET words multiply friends . . . A faithful friend is a strong defence. He that hath found such an one hath found a treasure. There is nothing that can be taken in exchange for a faithful friend, and his excellency is beyond price. He is the medicine of life, and they that fear the Lord shall find him.

Love thy friend, and keep faith with him. But, if thou reveal his secrets, follow no more after him. For thou wilt not catch him again; he is gone and hath escaped as a gazelle out of a snare. A wound may be bound up, and after reviling there may be a reconcilement; but he that revealeth secrets hath lost hope.

He that feareth the Lord, directeth his friendship aright.
—*Ecclesiasticus 6:5, 14-16; 27:17, 20-21; 6:17*

A friend loveth at all times, and in adversity is reborn a brother.
—*Proverbs 17:17*

## Footpath to Peace

AND he shall judge among many people, and rebuke strong nations afar off; and they shall beat their swords into plowshares, and their spears into pruninghooks: nation shall not lift up a sword against nation, neither shall they learn war any more.

But they shall sit every man under his vine and under his fig tree; and none shall make them afraid: for the mouth of the Lord of hosts hath spoken it. —*Micah 4:3-4*

## Freedom

IF A nation values anything more than freedom, it will lose its freedom; and the irony of it is that if it is comfort or money that it values more, it will lose that too. And when a nation has to fight for its freedom, it can only hope to win if it possesses certain qualities: honesty, courage, loyalty, vision and self-sacrifice. If it does not possess them, it has only itself to blame if it loses its freedom.[1] —*W. Somerset Maugham*
(Strictly Personal)

[1] This passage follows a description of the collapse of France in 1941.

[ 220 ]

## Giovanni's Letter

I SALUTE you.
I am your friend, and my love for you goes deep. There is nothing I can give you which you have not; but there is much, very much, that while I cannot give it, you can take. No heaven can come to us unless our hearts find rest in it today. Take heaven! No peace lies in the future which is not hidden in this present little instant. Take peace! The gloom of the world is but a shadow. Behind it yet within our reach is Joy. Take Joy. There is radiance and glory in the darkness could we but see; and to see, we have only to look. I beseech you to look. Life is so generous a giver, but we, judging the gifts by their covering, cast them away as ugly or heavy or hard. Remove the covering and you will find beneath it a living splendor, woven of Love, by Wisdom, with Power. Welcome it, grasp it, and you touch the angel's hand that brings it to you. Everything we call a trial, a sorrow, or a duty, believe me, that angel's hand is there; the Gift is there, and the wonder of an overshadowing Presence. Our joys, too; be not content with them as joys. They, too, conceal diviner Gifts. Life is so full of Meaning and Purpose, so full of Beauty, beneath its covering, that you will find earth but cloaks your Heaven. Courage then, to claim it; that is all! But together, wending through unknown country, Home.

And so at this time I greet you, not quite as the World sends greetings, but with profound esteem, and with the Prayer that for you, now and forever, the day breaks, and the shadows flee away.

—*Fra Angelico*

## God Known Through Nature

SURELY vain are all men by nature, who are ignorant of God, and could not out of the good things that are seen know him that is: neither by considering the works did they acknowledge the workmaster; but deemed either fire, or wind, or the swift air, or the circle of the stars, or the violent water, or the lights of heaven, to be the gods which govern the world. . . . Let them know how much better the Lord of them is: for the first author of beauty hath created them. . . . For by the greatness and beauty of the creatures proportionably the maker of them is seen . . .

He who is ignorant of God his heart is ashes, his hope is more vile than earth, and his life of less value than clay: Forasmuch as he knew not his Maker, and him that inspired into him an active soul, and breathed in a living spirit.

—*The Wisdom of Solmon, 13:1-3, 5; 15:10-11*

## God's Emerging Plan

THE study of the characteristics of man fits in with the observed facts about the universe. There is clearly revealed a cosmic drift or, rather, an

[ 221 ]

emerging plan and purpose, from the inorganic on up to self-conscious man. In man, a new element arises. The cosmic process is as inevitable as ever, but now man perceives in himself this same urge toward self-judgment in seeking ends and a gradual clarification of these ends in terms of human personality, both for himself and his fellows. Since God is not an autocratic absentee, imposing his will upon men, religion and morality are not imposed from "above" but are both as inherent as life. These facts are discovered by observation as truly as any in any laboratory test tube. They are as mighty in freeing the mind from the sense of artificially imposed religion and morals as in science they free the mind of superstition with regard to disease or other natural events. Kinship with God, the sense of the sacredness of persons, the freedom to say "Yes" or "No" even to God, and the longing for a more perfect society— these are the basis of democracy.      —A. J. William Myers

(Religion for Today)

## God the Father

INCLUDING both the Old Testament and the books of the Apocrypha we find 2,685 references to God, of which only twelve in the Old Testament use the word Father in any sense, and six more in the Apocrypha. Of these twelve Old Testament passages, six refer plainly to God as Father of the Hebrew people. One refers to him as Father of the Messiah, and one as Father of the king's son; one as step-father of the fatherless, and the other three use the word only as a simile, not a statement. Of the Apocryphal passages, two refer to God as Father of the tribes or nation, one as Father of the Messiah, and the remaining three as Father of the writer of the book in a personal sense.

Not a single one of these passages uses the term Father in the deeply intimate sense of Jesus' experience; yet the word does occur, in these exceedingly few and scattered verses in Jesus' Bible.

—George Walter Fiske

## Golden Sayings of Confucius

THE principles of the Higher Education are to unfold the great virtue, to be on familiar terms with the people, and to rest in the highest good.

Happiness is Heaven-sent.

You may deceive man; you cannot deceive Heaven.

Man proposes but God disposes.[1]

To do evil is to transgress the laws of Heaven.

It is not hard to talk about good works, but to do them.

When a word has left the mouth, a four-horse team cannot overtake it.

Better be hungry and have a pure mind, than be filled and have an evil mind.

You are solicitous for food and clothing; seek not only material wealth,

[1] A famous remark of K'ung Ming.

[ 222 ]

but also (real) happiness; you desire fame and gain; better seek these in yourself than from others.

To relieve men's calamities is ten times better than to worship Buddha.

He who associates with the virtuous becomes good; he who associates with the wicked becomes evil.

Take care of your mind; thus can you help your country.

He who has true learning never boasts.

Sincerity and patience—these are the things that matter most.

The happiest people in the world are those who do many good deeds.

When you have food to eat, remember the misery of those who are starving.

[This old saying is good:] "He who is content, does not bind himself with possessions; he who understands freedom is not afraid of being poor; he who cultivates virtue is not ashamed of not having office."

The learner must first understand love, for love is a feeling of kinship with (all) creation. Justice, propriety, knowledge and sincerity are all manifestations of love.

All within the four seas are brothers. (An oftheard quotation from the Chinese classics.)

What you would not wish done to yourself never do to others.

In the State of Sung there was a man who was very impatient for the little plants he had set out, to grow faster. So he pulled on each one to make it a little bigger, then hurried home and told his family: "I am tired out to-day: for I have been helping my little plants to grow." His son ran out to see them and found each one withered to the roots!

## The Great Way

WHEN the Great Way is followed, all under Heaven will work for the common good. They will choose the virtuous and the able (for rulers). They will advocate sincerity, and cultivate peace. Men will not limit their friendship to their relatives nor their love to their own sons. The aged will have provision made for them: the able in body will serve: youth will have respect for its elders. There will be sympathy for the widows and the orphans, and care for the afflicted. The women will be properly provided for. The accumulation of earthly goods will be discountenanced; hoarding for one's self will be done away. Idleness on the part of those who can work will be frowned upon. No one will be for himself. Thus self-aggrandizement will no longer be known, and robbery and thieving will cease. When this time comes the front door may be left open. Then will be the true Brotherhood of Mankind. —*Li Ki*[1]

## Greater Love (and Heroism) Has No One Than This . . .

I HEARD that among certain groups of Englishmen walking from Burma to India[2] there has silently developed a solemn compact. Who-

[1] Li Ki was a Chinese philosopher before Confucius.
[2] During the heroic withdrawal before the Japanese.

[ 223 ]

ever should find himself too ill or too lame to go further is to drop back little by little and permit his fellows to pass beyond him, perhaps forever, without notification or the indulgence of a farewell. He is to do this in such a way that his companions will not detect his absence until it is too late to turn back. Thus they insure beforehand that the safety of the larger group shall not be imperiled by the loyalties of the members for one another. Whoever arranges that the group shall not be endangered for the sake of one, runs the risk that he may be that one.

—*Paul Geren*
(Burma Diary)

## Harmony, Self-Discipline, Peace

THE men of old, when they wished their virtues to shine throughout the land, first had to govern their states well. To govern their states well, they first had to establish harmony in their families. To establish harmony in their families, they first had to discipline themselves. To discipline themselves, they first had to set their minds in order. To set their minds in order, they first had to make their purpose sincere. To make their purpose sincere, they first had to extend their knowledge to the utmost. Such knowledge is acquired through a careful investigation of things. For with things investigated knowledge becomes complete. With knowledge complete the purpose becomes sincere. With the purpose sincere the mind is set in order. With the mind set in order there is real self-discipline. With real self-discipline the family achieves harmony. With harmony in the family the state becomes well governed. With the state well governed there is peace throughout the land.     —*Confucius*

## Having Eyes We See Not

IT IS more difficult to teach ignorance to think than to teach an intelligent blind man to see the grandeur of Niagara. I have walked with people whose eyes are full of light, but who see nothing in wood, sea, or sky, nothing in the city streets, nothing in books. What a witless masquerade is this seeing! It were better far to sail for ever in the night of blindness, with sense and feeling and mind, than to be thus content with the mere act of seeing. They have the sunset, the morning skies, the purple of distant hills, yet their souls voyage through this enchanted world with a barren stare.     —*Helen Keller*
(The World I Live In)

## He Doeth Much Who Loveth Much

FOR no worldly good whatsoever, and for the love of no man must anything be done which is evil, but for the help of the suffering a good work must sometimes be postponed, or be changed for a better; for herein a good work is not destroyed, but improved. Without love no work profiteth, but whatsoever is done in love, howsoever small and of no reputation it be, bringeth forth good fruit; for God verily considereth what a man is able to do, more than the greatness of what he doth.

He doth much who loveth much. He doth much who doth well. He doth well who ministereth to the public good rather than to his own. Oftentimes that seemeth to be love which is rather carnality, because it springeth from natural inclination, self-will, hope of repayment, desire of gain.

He who hath true and perfect love, in no wise seeketh his own good, but desireth that God alone be altogether glorified. He envieth none, because he longeth for no selfish joy; nor doth he desire to rejoice in himself, but longeth to be blessed in God as the highest good. He ascribeth good to none save to God only, the Fountain whence all good proceedeth, and the End, the Peace, the Joy of all Saints. Oh, he that hath a spark of true love, hath verily learned that all worldly things are full of vanity.[1]

—*Thomas à Kempis*
(Imitation of Christ)

## Heaven or Hell

A MODERN morality play gives an amusing caricature of the future life. The following is much abbreviated.

There are two characters, a modern man who has just been killed in an automobile accident and an experienced inhabitant or official of the other world. The deceased, gradually coming to himself and wondering where he is, calls out in the misty twilight that surrounds him:

"Is anybody there?"

The mist clears away, revealing a shining Presence. The Presence asks: "Can I do anything for you, Sir?"

The deceased wants to know what's to be had here.

"Anything you like," is the reply. "Anticipating your desires, I have already taken thirty years from your age."

"Perpetual youth, eh?" exclaims the newcomer. "It looks as if I had come to the good place, after all. But what about the golden crown?"

"You can have one if you like," comes the answer, and presto! a starry golden crown encircles the stranger's brow . . .

"And now, what else have you got here?" "Anything you like," replies the Angel. "I can have everything I desire? Absolutely everything?" asks the soul excitedly.

"Subject only to certain restrictions imposed by the nature of the place," is the reply. "There is neither pain, nor suffering, nor struggle here. Anything else that you desire I will procure for you."

There follows a succession of requests and realizations: The best of things to eat and drink; luxurious living quarters; "period" furniture and decorations; masterpieces of painting and statuary; the society of beauteous women. But each of these exalted experiences proves to be insufficient and finally cloying, and the experimenter demands a change. "This everlasting perfection and satisfaction of desires without effort

[1] The word "charity" has been changed to "love."

[ 225 ]

palls on me," he says. "The sights are too uniformly beautiful, the ladies too uniformly clever, charming and obliging . . . I know what I want! I want some work." But he discovers that, since work is something one cannot have merely by wanting it, that is out of the question.

Then his mind clears. "Hold on!" he exclaims, "I've got it! I want some pain; that's it."

"I'm sorry, Sir," comes the polite answer, "but no one is allowed to have any pain in this place. You'll get used to the restriction after you've been here a few thousand years."

"But," ejaculates the neophyte, "I can't stand this everlasting bliss! I'd rather be in hell."

The Presence, stepping back and looking at him in astonishment, asks, "And wherever do you think you are, Sir?"　　　*—John L. Balderston*
(A Morality Play for the Leisured Class)

## His Name Alone Is Excellent

HE SENDETH the springs into the valleys, which run among the hills. He watereth the hills from his chambers, the earth is satisfied with the fruit of thy works. Thus it shall be in the midst of the land among the people, there shall be as the shaking of an olive tree, and as the gleaming grapes when the vintage is done. For as the earth bringeth forth her bud, and as the garden causeth the things that are sown in it to spring forth; so the Lord God will cause righteousness and praise to spring forth before all the nations. Praise the Lord from the earth, ye dragons, and all deeps: fire, and hail, snow, and vapour; stormy wind, fulfilling his word: mountains and all hills; fruitful trees and all cedars: let them praise the name of the Lord: for his name alone is excellent; his glory is above the earth and heaven.[1]

*—From Psalm 104:10, 13; Isaiah 17:13; 61:1; and Psalm 148:7-9 and 13*

## The House of Beauty and Light

SURELY we would not weep if some beloved friend had the good fortune to move from a humble and uncomfortable house to a mansion into which the sunlight had streamed, and whose grounds are a never-ending maze of beauty and wonder and delight. We would say that that was a fortunate friend, and a bit wistfully we would look forward to the time when we, too, might leave the burden of our daily tasks and join him in his house of beauty and light.　　　*—Helen Keller*
(The World I Live In)

## How Excellent Is Thy Loving Kindness

How excellent is thy loving kindness, O God. Thou visiteth the earth and maketh it soft with showers. Thou crownest the year with thy good-

[1] An anthem, arranged by Herbert Wareing.

[ 226 ]

ness and thy paths drop fatness. They drop upon the pastures of the wilderness and the little hills are girded with joy. The valleys also are covered over with corn, they shout for joy and sing. God hath given me of the dew of heaven and the fatness of the earth and plenty of corn and wine. The hills were girded with joy, the valleys are covered over with corn. They shout for joy and sing.[1]

—*Psalm 36:7; Genesis 27:28; Psalm 65:9-13*

## How Scrooge Spent Christmas

"It's Christmas Day!" said Scrooge to himself. "I haven't missed it. The Spirits have done it all in one night. Hallo, my fine fellow!"

"Hallo!" returned the boy.

"Do you know the poulterer's, in the next street but one, at the corner?" Scrooge inquired.

"I should hope I did," replied the lad.

"An intelligent boy!" said Scrooge. "A remarkable boy! Do you know whether they've sold the prize turkey that was hanging up there?"

"It's hanging there now," replied the boy.

"Is it?" said Scrooge. "Go and buy it."

"Walk-ER!" exclaimed the boy.

"No, no," said Scrooge, "I am in earnest. Go and buy it, and tell 'em to bring it here, that I may give them the directions where to take it. Come back with the man, and I'll give you a shilling."

The boy was off like a shot.

"I'll send it to Bob Cratchit's," whispered Scrooge, rubbing his hands, and splitting with a laugh. "He shan't know who sends it. It's twice the size of Tiny Tim."

The hand in which he wrote the address was not a steady one; but write it he did, somehow (and went downstairs to open the street door, ready for the coming of the poulterer's man).

The chuckle with which he paid for the turkey, and the chuckle with which he recompensed the boy, were only to be exceeded by the chuckle with which he sat down breathless in his chair again, and chuckled till he cried.

He dressed himself "all in his best," and got out into the streets. The people were by this time pouring forth, as he had seen them with the Ghost of Christmas Present. . . .

He went to church, and walked about the streets and watched the people hurrying to and fro, and patted the children on the head, and looked down into the kitchens of houses, and up to the windows; and found everything could yield him pleasure. In the afternoon, he turned his steps toward his nephew's house.

He passed the door a dozen times, before he had the courage to go up and knock. But he made a dash, and did it.

"Is your master at home, my dear?" said Scrooge to the girl. Nice girl! Very.

[1] Arranged for an anthem by Frederick Cowen.

"Yes, sir."

"Where is he?" said Scrooge.

"He's in the dining-room, sir, along with mistress. I'll show you upstairs, if you please."

"Thank'ee. He knows me," said Scrooge, with his hand already on the dining-room lock. "I'll go in here, my dear."

He turned it gently, and sidled his face in, round the door. They were looking at the table (which was spread out in great array); for these young housekeepers are always nervous on such points, and like to see that everything is right.

"Fred!" said Scrooge.

"Why, bless my soul!" cried Fred, "who's that?"

"It's I. Your Uncle Scrooge. I have come to dinner. Will you let me in, Fred?"

Let him in! It is a mercy he didn't shake his arm off. He was at home in five minutes. Nothing could be heartier.

But he was early at the office next morning. Oh, he was early there. If he could only be there first, and catch Bob Cratchit coming late! That was the thing he had set his heart upon.

And he did it; yes, he did! The clock struck nine. No Bob. A quarter past. No Bob. He was full eighteen minutes and a half behind his time. Scrooge sat with his door wide open, that he might see him come into the bank.

His hat was off, before he opened the door, his comforter, too. He was on his stool in a jiffy; driving away with his pen, as if he were trying to overtake nine o'clock.

"Hallo!" growled Scrooge, in his accustomed voice as near as he could feign it. "What do you mean by coming here at this time of day?"

"I am very sorry, sir," said Bob. "I am behind my time."

"You are!" repeated Scrooge. "Yes. I think you are. Step this way, sir, if you please."

"It's only once a year, sir," pleaded Bob, appearing from the tank. "It shall not be repeated. I was making rather merry yesterday, sir."

"A Merry Christmas, Bob!" said Scrooge, with an earnestness that could not be mistaken, as he clapped him on the back. "A Merrier Christmas, Bob, my good fellow, than I have given you for many a year! I'll raise your salary, and endeavor to assist your struggling family, and we will discuss your affairs this very afternoon. Make up the fires, and buy another coal scuttle before you dot another 'i,' Bob Cratchit!"

Scrooge was better than his word. He did it all, and infinitely more, and to Tiny Tim, who did not die, he was a second father. . . . And it was always said of him, that he knew how to keep Christmas well, if any man alive possessed the knowledge. May that be truly said of us, and all of us! And so, as Tiny Tim observed, God Bless Us, Every One!

—*Charles Dickens*
(A Christmas Carol)[1]

[1] The condensed version of the last stave.

[ 228 ]

## How to Treat People

[THE disciples of Confucius were talking:]

Tsze-lu said: "When people treat me well, I treat them well; when people treat me badly, I also treat them badly."

Tsze-kung said: "When people treat me well, I also treat them well; when they treat me badly, I treat them justly, but with indifference."

Yen Hui said: "When people treat me well, I also treat them well; when people treat me badly, I still treat them well."

Since the three disciples each held a different view, they asked the master about it.

The master said: "The words of Tsze-lu are those of a barbarian; the words of Tsze-kung are those of a friend; the words of Yen Hui are those of a member of the family."

—*Confucius*

## Hunger for Truth

THE desire and love of knowledge we believe has been implanted in us undoubtedly by God, and just as the eye naturally seeks light and vision, and just as our body desires meat and drink, so our mind exhibits its own natural desire of knowing the truth of God and understanding the causes of things; but we have received this desire from God not in order that it should never by any possibility be fulfilled, for it would seem that the love of truth has been implanted in our mind to no purpose by our Creator if the desire is never to find fulfilment.

—*Origen*
(De Principiis)

## In the Haven of Her Arms

THE wind fretted the black sea until it broke all roundabout; and the punt healed to the gusts and endlessly flung her bows up to the big waves; and the spray swept over us like driving rain, and was bitter cold; and the mist fell swift and thick upon the coast beyond. Jacky, forward with the jib-sheet in his capable little fist and the bail bucket handy, scowled darkly at the gale, being alert as a cat, the while; and the skipper, his mild smile unchanged by all the tumult, kept a hand on the main-sheet and tiller, and a keen, quiet eye on the canvas and on the vanishing rocks whither we were bound. And forth and back she went, back and forth, again and again, without end—beating up to the harbour.

"Dear man!" said Skipper Tommy, with a glance at the vague black outline of the Watchman, "but 'tis a fine harbour!"

" 'Tis that," sighed Jacky, wistfully, as a screaming little gust heeled the punt over; "an'—an'—I wisht we was there!"

Skipper Tommy laughed at his son.

"I does!" Jacky declared.

"I—I—I'm not so sure," I stammered, taking a tighter grip on the gunwhale, "but I wisht we was—there—too."

"You'll be wishin' that often," said Skipper Tommy, pointedly, "if you live to be so old as me."

We wished it often, indeed, that day—while the wind blustered yet more wildly out of the north and the waves tumbled aboard our staggering little craft and the night came apace over the sea—and we have wished it often since that old time, have Jacky and I, God knows! I had the curious sensation of fear, I fancy—though I am loath to call it that—for the first time in my life; and I was very much relieved when, at dusk, we rounded the looming Watchman, ran through the white waters and thunderous confusion of the Gate, with the breakers leaping high on either hand, sharply turned Frothy Point and came at last into the ripples of Trader's Cove. Glad I was, you may be sure, to find my mother waiting on my father's wharf, and to be taken by the hand, and to be led up the path to the house, where there was spread a grand supper of fish and bread, which my sister had long kept waiting; and, after all, to be rocked in the broad window, safe in the haven of my mother's arms, while the last of the sullen light of day fled into the wilderness and all the world turned black. . . .

The feeling of harbour—of escape and of shelter and of brooding peace—was strong upon me while we sat rocking in the failing light. I have never since made harbour—never since come of a sudden from the toil and frothy rage of the sea by night or day, but my heart has felt again the peace of that quiet hour—never once but blessed memory has given me once again the vision of myself, as a little child, lying on my mother's dear breast, gathered close in her arms, while she rocked and softly sang. . . . I protest that I love my land, and have from that hour, barren as it is and as bitter the sea that breaks upon it; for I then learned —and still know—that it is as though the dear God himself made harbours with wise, kind hands for such as have business in the wild waters of that coast. . . .

And I fell asleep in my mother's arms, and by and by my big father came in and laughed tenderly to find me lying there; and then, as I have been told, laughing softly still they carried me up and flung me on my bed, flushed . . . and limp with sound slumber, where I lay like a small sack of flour, while together they pulled off my shoes and stockings and jacket and trousers and little shirt, and bundled me into my night-dress, and rolled me under the blanket, and tucked me in, and kissed me good-night.

When my mother's lips touched my cheek I awoke. "Is it you, mama?" I asked.

"Ay," said she; " 'tis your mother, lad."

Her hand went swiftly to my brow, and smoothed back the tousled, wet hair.

"Is you kissed me yet?"

"Oh, ay!" said she.

"Kiss me again, please, mum," said I, "for I wants—t' make sure—you done it."

She kissed me again, very tenderly; and I sighed and fell asleep, content.                              —*Norman Duncan*
(Dr. Luke of the Labrador)

## Intellectual Death

It is perfectly possible for you and me to purchase intellectual peace at the price of intellectual death. The world is not without refuges of this description; nor is it wanting in persons who seek their shelter, and try to persuade others to do the same. The unstable and the weak have yielded and will yield to this persuasion, and they to whom repose is sweeter than the truth. But I would exhort you to refuse the offered shelter, and to scorn the base repose—to accept, if the choice be forced upon you, commotion before stagnation, the breezy leap of the torrent before the foeted stillness of the swamp.            —*John Tyndall*
(The Belfast Address)

## Interdependence and Charity

But at least I have learned this lesson of our interdependence. The lesson that all mankind now must learn. The twin lessons of interdependence and charity. No one of us can move any more, can sigh or sneeze, cough or whisper—without disturbing the rest of us. . . .

Unless we have fellowship together we have nothing. It seems to me that until we learn this fellowship—the fellowship, generous and understanding—of all living men on this earth, made so essential now by our close quarters, the impossibility of our escape from one another, there will be no peace.

I must not judge my neighbors, and the children must be trained . . . to grow straight into light and loveliness, and I must not lose myself in selfish attempts to save my own soul—and for why? Because we are all brothers together under God and are all of us, one with another, our brother's keeper.

[Then he adds the final word from *The Dream of John Ball*:]

Forsooth, brothers, fellowship is heaven, and lack of fellowship is hell; fellowship is life, and lack of fellowship is death; and the deeds that ye do upon the earth, it is for fellowship's sake that ye do them, and the life that is in it, that shall live on forever and ever, and each one of you part of it, while many a man's life upon the earth from the earth shall wane. Therefore, I bid you not dwell in hell but in heaven, or while ye must, upon earth, which is a part of heaven, and forsooth no foul part.
—*Hugh Walpole*
(The Blind Man's House)

[ 231 ]

## An International Creed

WE BELIEVE in (our country) everlasting
And in her sons conceived of the Spirit and not of the flesh alone,
Who suffered for the Rights of Man, were crucified and buried,
Descended into Hell, but will rise again and push aside their tombstone.
They will ascend into the Heaven of freedom,
Be honored in their country everlasting
As they pardon the living and honor the dead.
We believe in Supreme Righteousness
In justice universal,
In the Communion of Nations,
In mutual forgiveness of sins,
In the life more abundant of the Soul,
And in Peace eternal.—Amen.

—*Anonymous*
(Polish)

## Joan of Arc

[JOAN of Arc wants to go at once to complete the freeing of France of enemy strongholds. But as always she is hampered by the jealousy of military officers and by the archbishop. Again, as so often in the past, she feels she is alone but for God.]

### I. Alone with God

JOAN: There is no help, no counsel, in any of you. Yes: I am alone on earth: I have always been alone. My father told my brothers to drown me if I would not stay to mind his sheep while France was bleeding to death: France might perish if only our lambs were safe. I thought France would have friends at the court of the King of France; and I find only wolves fighting for pieces of her torn body. I thought God would have friends everywhere, because he is the friend of everyone; and in my innocence I believed that you who now cast me out would be like strong towers to keep harm from me. But I am wiser now; and nobody is any the worse for being wiser. Do not think you can frighten me by telling me that I am alone. France is alone; and God is alone; and what is my loneliness before the loneliness of my country and my God? I see now that the loneliness of God is his strength: what would he be if he listened to your jealous little counsels? Well, my loneliness shall be my strength too: it is better to be alone with God: his friendship will not fail me, nor his counsel, nor his love. In his strength I will dare, and dare, and dare, until I die.

### II. Martyrdom of Joan of Arc

[At the trial Joan was promised her life if she would recant. After weary weeks of prison and persecution that would have broken the courage and strength of a giant and without an advocate or friend by her side, and persuaded by treacherous priests posing as her friends, she at last consented and signed the prepared document. But she was horrified to find it was a trap, that she was not to be set free but to be sentenced by the holy fathers to imprisonment for life! The following depicts the scene in the court room]

JOAN (*rising in consternation and terrible anger*): Perpetual imprisonment! Am I not then to be set free? . . . Give me that writing. (*She rushes to the table; snatches up the paper; and tears it into fragments.*) Light your fire: do you think I dread it as much as the life of a rat in a hole? My voices were right. . . . Yes: they told me you were fools, . . . and that I was not to listen to your fine words nor trust to your charity. You promised me my life; but you lied. . . . You think that life is nothing but not being stone dead. It is not the bread and water I fear: I can live on bread: when have I asked for more? It is no hardship to drink water if the water be clean. Bread has no sorrow for me, and water no affliction. But to shut me from the light of the sky and the sight of the fields and flowers; to chain my feet so that I can never again ride with the soldiers nor climb the hills; to make me breathe foul damp darkness, and keep from me everything that brings me back to the love of God: . . . all this is worse than the furnace in the Bible that was heated seven times. I could do without my war-horse; I could drag about in a skirt; I could let the banners and the trumpets and the knights and soldiers pass me and leave me behind as they leave the other women, if only I could still hear the wind in the trees, the larks in the sunshine, the young lambs crying through the healthy frost, and the blessed church bells that send my angel voices floating to me on the wind. But without these blessed things I cannot live; and by your wanting to take them away from me, or from any human creature, I know that your counsel is from the devil and that mine is of God. . . . His ways are not your ways. He wills that I go through the fire to his bosom; for I am his child, and you are not fit that I should live among you. That is my last word to you. . . .

[Proceeding within the law, the Church court had her burnt at the stake. Even a cross was denied her. She has since been created a saint! An English soldier broke a stick, tied it in the form of a cross, and put it in her hand. Then a monk tells what happened]

LADVENU: I took the cross from the church for her that she might see it to the last: she had only two sticks that she had put into her bosom. When the fire crept around us, and she saw that if I held the cross before her I should be burnt myself, she warned me to get down and save myself. My Lord: a girl who could think of another's danger in such a moment was not inspired by the devil. When I had to snatch the cross from her sight, she looked up to heaven. And I do not believe that the

[ 233 ]

heavens were empty. I firmly believe that God[1] appeared to her then in his tenderest glory. She called to him and died. This is not the end of her but the beginning.                                   —*George Bernard Shaw*
(St. Joan)

## John Hus

ON JUNE 10 (1415)—two days after the second hearing—Hus wrote the letter which of all his letters has obtained, and rightly obtained, the greatest fame. It is addressed "To the whole Bohemian Nation." Hus writes (in part): Master John Hus, in good hope a servant of God, hopes that the Lord God will grant to all true Bohemians who love and will love the Lord God, to live and die in his grace, and to reside forever in celestial joy. Amen.

Faithful in God, men and women, rich and poor! I beg and entreat you to love the Lord God, praise his word, gladly hear it and live according to it. Cling, I beg you, to the divine truth, which I have preached to you according to God's law. . . . I beg the nobles to treat the poor people kindly and rule them justly. I beg the burghers to conduct their business honestly. I beg the artisans to perform their duties conscientiously and joyfully. I beg the servants to serve their masters and mistresses faithfully. I beg the teachers to live honestly, to instruct their pupils carefully, to love God above all; for the sake of his glory and the good of the community, not from avarice and worldly ambition should they teach. I beg the students and other scholars to obey and follow their masters in everything that is good, and to study for the . . . praise of God, for their own salvation, and that of others. . . .

I write this letter to you in prison and in fetters, expecting to-morrow the sentence of death, full of hope in God, resolved not to recede from the divine truth, nor to recant the errors which false witnesses have invented and attributed to me.[2]                        —*Franz Heinrich Luetzow*
(The Life and Times of Master John Hus)

## The Journey's End

[IN THE last chapter of *Beside the Bonnie Briar Bush*, Ian Maclaren gives a wonderful picture of Dr. John MacLure, a family physician of the old type. He was not married and had no family connections; but all the people on the Scottish hills are his people and their children are his children. He has given his life for them. He took what they gave him in fees, and he kept no books. Utterly worn out, he is now on his last journey. He knows the end is near and that none can help him. His bosom friend, Drumsheugh, sits beside him. The doctor tells him how to dispose of his few things and that he is not to send any bills to anyone. He wants his faithful mare, old Jess, taken care of. He says:]

[1] One word changed.
[2] Soon after this letter was written Hus was burned at the stake for his faith.

[ 234 ]

"But a' wuldna like tae sell Jess, for she's been a faithfu' servant, an' a friend tae. There's a note or twa in that drawer a' savit, and if ye kent ony a man that wud gie her a bit o' grass and a sta' in his stable till she followed her maister—"

"Confoond ye, Weelum," broke out Drumsheugh, "it's doonricht cruel o' ye to speak like this tae me. Whar wud Jess gang but tae Drumsheugh? Shei'll hae her run o' heck an' manger sae lang as she lives; the Glen wudna like tae see anither man on Jess, and nae man 'ill ever touch the auld mare."

"Dinna mind me, Paitrick, for a' expeckit this; but ye ken we're no verra gleg wi' oor tongues in Drumtochty, an' dinna tell a' that's in oor hearts."

[And now, having thought of everybody else and having secured comfort for old Jess, he thinks of himself. He asks Drumsheugh to read from his mither's Bible but to come close, for he cannot hear so well now. He asks his friend to pray. Drumsheugh wants to get the minister but he says there is not time. Besides, he wants him to pray.

So Drumsheugh knelt and prayed with many pauses.]

"Almichty God—dinna be hard on Weelum MacLure, for he's no been hard wi' onybody in Drumtochty. . . . Be kind tae him as he's been tae us a' for forty years. . . . Forgive him for what he's dune wrang, an' dinna cuist it up tae him. . . . Mind the fouk he's helpit—the weemen and bairnies—and gie him a welcome hame, for he's sair needin't after a' his wark—Amen."

"Thank ye, Paitrick, and gude nicht tae ye. Ma ain true freend, gie's yir hand, for a'll maybe no ken ye again.

"Noo a'll say ma mither's prayer and hae a sleep, but ye'ill no leave me till a' is ower."

Then he repeated his childhood prayer as he had done every night. In his delirium he was fighting storms and drifts with old Jess until he thought he had come to the journey's end.

"Yon's the licht in the kitchen window; nae wonder ye're nickering;—it's been a stiff journey; a'm tired, lass . . . a'm tired tae deith," and the voice died into silence.

Drumsheugh held his friend's hand, which now and again tightened in his, and as he watched, a change came over the face on the pillow beside him. The lines of weariness disappeared, as if God's hand had passed over it; and peace began to gather round the closed eyes.

The doctor is back in his childhood. He is tired, but as soon as he memorizes the psalm his mother will come and give him his good night kiss and tuck him in.

" 'The Lord's my Shepherd, I'll not want,' "

he repeated, till he came to the last verse, and then he hesitated . . .

Drumsheugh, in an agony, whispered into his ear, " 'My dwelling-place,' Weelum."

"That's it, that's it a' noo; wha said it?

'And in God's house for evermore
My dwelling-place shall be.'

"A'm ready noo, an' a'll get ma kiss when mither comes; a' wish she wud come, for a'm tired and wantin' tae sleep.

"Yon's her step—an' she's carryin' a licht in her hand; 'see it through the door.

"Mither! a' ken ye wudna forget yir laddie, for ye promised tae come, an' a've feenished ma psalm.

'And in God's house for evermore
My dwelling-place shall be.'

"Gie me the kiss, mither, for a've been waitin' for ye, an' a'll sune be asleep."

The gray morning light fell on Drumsheugh, still holding his friend's cold hand, and staring at a hearth where the fire had died down into white ashes; but the peace on the doctor's face was of one who rested from his labors. —*Ian MacLaren*
(Beside the Bonnie Briar Bush)


## The Joyful Passing of the Righteous

Now the day drew on that Christiana must be gone. So the road was full of people to see her take her journey. But behold all the banks beyond the river were full of horses and chariots, which were come down from above to accompany her to the city gate. So she came forth and entered the river, with a beckon of farewell to those that followed her to the river-side. The last word she was heard to say here was, I come, Lord, to be with thee, and bless thee. . . . So she went and called, and entered in at the gate with all . . . ceremonies of joy. . . .

After this Mr. Ready-to-halt called for his fellow-pilgrims, and told them, saying, I am sent for, and God shall surely visit you also. . . . When he came at the brink of the river, he said, Now I shall have no more need of these crutches, since yonder are chariots and horses for me to ride on. The last words he was heard to say were, Welcome life! So he went his way. . . .

When days had many of them passed away, Mr. Despondency was sent for. . . . Now Mr. Despondency's daughter, whose name was Much-afraid, said . . . that she would go with her father. Then Mr. Despondency said to his friends, Myself and my daughter, you know what we have been, and how troublesomely we have behaved ourselves in every company. My will and my daughter's is, that our desponds, and slavish fears, be by no man ever received, from the day of our departure, for ever. . . . For, to be plain with you, they are ghosts, the which we entertained when we first began to be pilgrims, and could never shake them off after; and they will walk about and seek entertainment of the pilgrims; but for our sakes shut ye the doors upon them.

When the time was come for them to depart, they went to the brink of the river. The last words of Mr. Despondency were, Farewell night; welcome day! . . .

After this it was noised abroad that Mr. Valiant-for-truth was taken with a summons. . . . Then said he, I am going to my fathers, and though with great difficulty I am got hither, yet now I do not repent me of all the trouble I have been at to arrive where I am. My sword I give to him that shall succeed me in my pilgrimage, and my courage and skill to him that can get it. My marks and scars I carry with me, to be a witness for me that I have fought his battles who now will be my rewarder. When the day that he must go hence was come, many accompanied him to the river-side, into which as he went he said, "Death, where is thy sting?" And as he went down deeper, he said, "Grave, where is thy victory?" So he passed over, and all the trumpets sounded for him on the other side. . . .

Then came forth a summons for Mr. Stand-fast. . . . Now there was a great calm at that time in the river; wherefore Mr. Stand-fast, when he was about half-way in, he stood a while, and talked to his companions that had waited upon him thither. And he said:

This river has been a terror to many; yea, the thoughts of it also have often frightened me. But now methinks I stand easy. . . . The thoughts of what I am going to, and of the conduct that awaits for me on the other side, doth lie as a glowing coal at my heart.

I see myself now at the end of my journey, my toilsome days are ended. . . . I have formerly lived by hearsay, and faith, but now I go where I shall live by sight and shall be with him in whose company I delight myself. . . .

Now, while he was thus in discourse, his countenance changed . . . and after he had said, Take me, for I come unto thee, he ceased to be seen of them.

But glorious it was, to see how the open region was filled with horses and chariots, with trumpeters and pipers, with singers and players on stringed instruments, to welcome the pilgrims as they went up, and followed one another in at the beautiful gate of the city.

—*John Bunyan*
(Pilgrim's Progress)

## Keep Thyself in Peace

FIRST keep thyself in peace, and then shalt thou be able to be a peacemaker towards others. A peaceable man doth more good than a well-learned. A passionate man turneth even good into evil; a peaceable man converteth all things into good. He who dwelleth in peace is suspicious of none, but he who is discontented and restless is tossed with many suspisions, and is neither quiet himself nor suffereth others to be quiet. He often saith what he ought not to say, and omitteth what it were more expedient for him to do. . . . Thou knowest well how to excuse and to colour thine own deeds, but thou wilt not accept the excuses of others. It would be more just to accuse thyself and excuse thy brother. If thou wilt that others bear with thee, bear thou with others. Behold how far thou art as yet from the true charity and humility which knows not how to be angry or indignant against any save self alone.

—*Thomas à Kempis*
(Imitation of Christ)

## Lincoln and the Church

I DOUBT the possibility of, or propriety of, settling the religion of Jesus Christ in . . . creeds and dogmas. It was a spirit in the life that he laid stress on and taught, if I read aright. . . .

I cannot without mental reservations assent to long and complicated creeds and catechisms. If the church would ask simply for assent to the Savior's statement of the substance of the law: "Thou shalt love the Lord thy God with all thy heart and with all thy soul, and with all thy mind, and thy neighbor as thyself"—that church would I gladly unite with. —*Abraham Lincoln*

## A Little Girl Who Was Sick

RUTH was sick. Her father and mother had done all they could to relieve her suffering. Now they looked worried and sad and said to each other, "Ruth is not going to get better!" and they could not keep back the tears.

Sometimes Ruth wished that her friend Jesus might come, for she loved him dearly. Then one day glad cries of children were heard as they rushed up the street. Jesus had come to the village! They crowded around him. He called them all by name—Mary, John, Jonathan, Naomi, David. He asked them about all they had been doing and told them about some of the places he had visited and the things he had seen. Then, looking around, he asked, "Where's Ruth?" "She's very sick," they answered, "She'll not get better!" "She's dying!" said a little one proudly, not knowing what it meant. "I must go and see her," said Jesus. Quickly he selected a few beautiful and fragrant flowers and hastened away.

When he got to the house it was full of people and almost unbearably hot. Some were weeping and wailing and making a great noise, for that was what the people believed would drive away evil spirits when a loved one was very sick. They thought that Ruth could not get better; that she was dying. The child was hot, flushed and fevered, and seemed so weak and ill. Jesus said sternly, "You must all go out and away to your homes. She must have perfect quiet. I will stay with her. Send everyone away!" and all the people scattered. Jesus sat down beside the little girl and put his cool hand on her fevered brow. She loved the flowers, too, and he told her about his travels. Then he gave her a few grapes, ripe and luscious. Soothed and interested, she said, "Tell me a story, please." "Which one would you like to hear?" "Tell me about the little lamb that was lost." And he told her the wonderful story of the good shepherd and the sheep that was lost.

[ 238 ]

When he had finished he said, "Let me see if we cannot make you feel better." With tender care he settled her more comfortably on her little bed. Then taking cold water, he bathed her face and her hands and her little hot feet. She gave a contented sigh as she held his hand in her own.

"Now," he said, "you must sleep. If you sleep you shall do well. You will grow strong, and, perhaps, you may wake up hungry! I have this new story for you:

"The mother hen and her baby chickens had been up and busy since break of day. The chicks had run and scratched and frolicked since early morning. She knew they were tired and that they must have good rest and sleep if they were to wake up refreshed and hungry and grow big. So she found a nice place, settled herself down, and called them to bed.

"But they did not want to go. One was chasing a big, fat fly and was sure he would catch it in a minute. Another was scratching in nice soft earth. The mother hen called again in her soft, comforting voice, coaxing and clucking, 'Come to bed under my wings.' One very tired baby staggered in and snuggled under her feathers with a contented 'cheep, cheep!' and was asleep before he could tuck his head under his wing. Then others came running, and soon all were warm and cosy in their feather bed. All the time she crooned to them her lullaby 'Currroh, currroh!' At first six or seven answered with shrill 'cheep, cheep!' She crooned again, and only two or three very sleepy babies answered. The rest were all quiet. Her own eyes closed, for she was very tired. She roused herself again and 'currrch, currroh!' Only one little chick was awake. He whispered 'cheep, c-hee-p,' and was sound asleep before he had finished, for they all felt so safe and happy under the mother's wings, surrounded by the friendly dark and in the loving Father's care."

When Jesus had finished the story little Ruth was sound asleep. After a while Jesus slipped away. He charged the parents to keep everything perfectly quiet all night, and to let no one disturb or waken her.

In the early morning Jesus was back. It was much later when Ruth woke up. She was so much better after the refreshing sleep. She looked up lovingly and shyly into Jesus' face and said, "I was like the little baby chicks. I fell asleep too and woke up a little bit—hungry!" What a delight it was to hear her say that and to see her enjoy a taste of food. Day by day she grew stronger and was soon able to play again. Is it any wonder that the children and their parents loved their friend Jesus?

—*A. J. William Myers*

## The Living Church

You must understand that this is no dead pile of stones and unmeaning timber. *It is a living thing.* . . .

When you enter it, you hear a sound—a sound as of some mighty poem chanted. Listen long enough and you will learn that it is made up of the beating of human hearts, of the nameless music of men's souls—that is, if you have ears. If you have eyes, you will presently see the church itself—a looming mystery of many shapes and shadows, leaping sheer from floor to dome. The work of no ordinary builder . . .

The pillars of it go up like the trunks of brawny heroes; the sweet human flesh of men and women is moulded about its bulwarks, strong, impregnable; the faces of little children laugh out from every corner-stone; the terrible spans and arches of it are the joined hands of comrades; and up in the heights and spaces there are inscribed the number-less musings of all the dreamers of the world. It is yet building—building and built upon. Sometimes the work goes forward in deep darkness: sometimes in blinding light: now beneath the burden of unutterable anguish: now to the tune of a great laughter and heroic shoutings like the cry of thunder. . . . Sometimes, in the silence of the night-time, one may hear the tiny hammerings of the comrades at work up in the dome—the comrades that have climbed ahead.

—*Charles Rann Kennedy*
(The Servant in the House)

## The Living God

THE living God: that is the message of Christianity; that is the hope of the world. "My Father is working even up to now," said Jesus. He that has eyes to see and ears to hear can see and hear God's message in the experiences of his daily life. Mankind everywhere has always been witness to his presence. That has been sufficient at every age for all who responded to his love. But the character of God is expressed incomparably more perfectly in Jesus than in anyone else. That revelation is so convincing that people with spiritual insight have testified that Jesus is like God. The essential qualities of God's love, of his character, are seen in Jesus. How much the eternal God is beyond anything that could ever have been compassed in a human frame in power and wisdom and purpose the mind cannot conceive. It is enough to know, with an assurance nothing can shake, that his purpose for good is steadfast and that his love never fails.

Jesus did not close revelation . . . but what he did and thought and experienced is the key to God and also, one may add, to man. Jesus opened and is opening men's eyes. At present they dimly see men as trees walking. The confidence that clearer vision will come if he is true to the highest, gives man courage and strength in a world of frustration and confusion. Jesus interpreted and revealed God "so that God may be everything to everyone," thereby strengthening faith, so that man may go on to the realization of untold good if he will but be true to the vision, and incarnate his knowledge of God and of the good life in the practical affairs of the everyday world.　　　—*A. J. William Myers*
(Religion for Today)

## Love Is Stronger Than Death

(THE hunter was returning with his dog from hunting. Suddenly the dog saw a young sparrow that had fallen from its nest and was flapping helplessly on the ground.)

My dog was slowly approaching it, when, suddenly darting down from a tree close by, an old dark-throated sparrow fell like a stone right before his nose, and all ruffled up, terrified, with disparing and pitiful cheeps, it flung itself twice towards the open jaws of shining teeth.

It sprang to save; it cast itself before its nestling, but all its tiny body was shaking with terror; its note was harsh and strange. Swooning with fear, it offered itself up!

What a huge monster must the dog have seemed to it! And yet it could not stay on its high branch out of danger. A force stronger than its will flung it down.

My Tresor stood still, drew back. Clearly he too recognized this force. I hastened to call off the disconcerted dog, and went away, full of reverence.

Love, I thought, is stronger than death or the fear of death. Only by it, by love, life holds together and advances.

—*Ivan Sergiewich Turgenev*
(Dream Tales and Prose Poems, translated by Constance Garnett)


## Love Never Fails

[LITTLE Emily had disappeared. It was surmised she had run off with Steerforth. She was cast off by every one except her old uncle, Mr. Peggotty. "My dooty here, sir, . . . is done. . . . I'm going to seek her. That's my dooty evermore."

His old housekeeper, Mrs. Gummidge, was to remain and keep the house just as it was when Emily left it, while he went everywhere in search of her. This was his explanation:]

"My wishes is, sir, as it shall look, day and night, winter and summer, as it has always looked, since she fust know'd it. If ever she should come a wandering back, I wouldn't have the old place seem to cast her off, you understand, but seem to tempt her to draw nigher to 't, and to peep in, maybe, like a ghost, out of the wind and rain, through the old winder, at the old seat by the fire. Then, maybe, Mas'r Davy, seein' none but Missis Gummidge there, she might take heart to creep in, trembling; and might come to be laid down in her old bed, and rest her weary head where it was once so gay. . . ."

"Every night," said Mr. Peggotty, "as reg'lar as the night comes, the candle must be stood in its old pane of glass, that if ever she should see it, it may seem to say, 'Come back, my child, come back!'"

[And that is like the love of God.]
—*Charles Dickens*
(David Copperfield)

## The Love of What Is Good

KUNG-SUN CHOW asked, "Is Yo-ching a man of vigor?" and was answered, "No."

"Is he wise in council?"

"No."

"Is he possessed of much information?"

"No."

"What then made you so glad that you could not sleep?"

"He is a man who loves what is good."

"Is the love of what is good sufficient?"

"The love of what is good is more than a sufficient qualification for the government of the empire. . . . If a minister love what is good, all within the four seas will count a thousand li but a small distance, and will come to lay their good thoughts before him."  —*Mencius*

## Love Together

OUR whole duty is contained in these words, "Love together." Therefore St. Paul saith, "He that loveth another, fulfilleth the whole law"; so it appeared that all things are contained in this word Love. This love is a precious thing: Jesus saith, "By this shall all men know that ye are my disciples, if ye shall love one another."

So that he maketh love his cognizance, his badge, his livery. Like as every lord most commonly giveth a certain livery to his servants, whereby they may be known that they pertain unto him; and so we say, "Yonder is this lord's servants, because they wear his livery": so God which is the Lord above all lords, would have his servants to be known by their liveries and badge, which badge is love alone. Whosoever now is endued with love and charity, is God's servant . . . for love is the token whereby you know such a servant; . . . so that love may be called the very livery of Christ.  —*Hugh Latimer*

## Man: Son of God

WHEN a man therefore has learned to understand the government of the universe and has realized that there is nothing so great or sovereign or all-inclusive as this frame of things wherein men and God are united, and that from it come the seeds from which are sprung not only my own father or grandfather, but all things that grow upon the earth, and rational creatures in particular—for these alone are by nature fitted to share in the society of God, being connected with him by the bond of reason—why should he not call himself a citizen of the universe and son of God? Why should he fear anything that can happen to him among men?  —*Epictetus; tr. by P. E. Matheson*

## Master

IT AWES me when I think of the great company that no one can number who have studied the character of Jesus. Let your mind roam

[ 242 ]

over the last nineteen hundred years, and think of the artists who have stood before him, seeing in him new revelations of beauty; think of the poets who have stood before him and have caught inspiration for their songs; think of the musicians who have stood before him and who have worked the impression which he made upon them into tones which lift the heart and set it dreaming; think of the philosophers who have stood before him and meditated on the great ideas which found expression on his lips; think of the unlettered men and women, the great crowd of peasants, plain working people, descendents of the shepherds, . . . who have bowed in adoration before him and found rest from their weariness and strength in their weakness. And then let your mind run out into the centuries that are coming and think of the countless generations of men and women who are still to stand before this matchless figure, drinking in inspiration with which to live their life and to do their work. If you can see in your imagination this great procession which has been and the greater procession which is yet to be, you will take your places with reverent spirit as followers of him who compels the heart to cry out, "Master!"  —*Charles Edward Jefferson*
(The Character of Jesus)

## Misunderstanding

OH, MY dear friends, you who are letting miserable misunderstandings run on from year to year, meaning to clear them up some day; you who are keeping wretched quarrels alive because you cannot quite make up your mind that now is the day to sacrifice your pride and kill them; you who are passing men sullenly upon the street, not speaking to them out of some silly spite, and yet knowing that it would fill you with shame and remorse if you heard that one of these men were dead tomorrow morning; you who are letting your neighbor starve, till you hear that he is dying of starvation; or letting your friend's heart ache for a word of appreciation or sympathy, which you mean to give him some day—if you only could know and see and feel, all of a sudden, that "the time is short," how it would break the spell! How you would go instantly and do the thing which you might never have another chance to do!
—*Phillips Brooks*

## The Most Certain Sign That We Love God

OUR Lord asks but two things of us: love for God and for our neighbour. . . .

I think the most certain sign that we keep these two commandments is that we have a genuine love for others. We cannot know whether we love God, although there may be strong reasons for thinking so, but there can be no doubt about whether we love our neighbour or no. Be sure that in proportion as you advance in fraternal charity, you are increasing in your love of God, for his majesty bears so tender an affection for us that I cannot doubt he will repay our love for others by augment-

[ 243 ]

ing, in a thousand different ways, that which we bear for him. We should watch most carefully over ourselves in this matter, for if we are perfect on this point we have done all.  —*St. Teresa*

## My Symphony

To LIVE content with small means; to seek elegance rather than luxury; and refinement rather than fashion; to be worthy, not respectable; and wealthy, not rich; to study hard, think quietly, talk gently, act frankly; to listen to stars and birds, to babes and sages, with open heart; to bear all cheerfully, do all bravely; await occasion, hurry never; in a word, to let the spiritual, unbidden and unconscious, grow up through the common—this is to be my symphony.  —*William Henry Channing*

## The New World

AND many nations shall come, and say, Come, and let us go up to the mountain of the Lord . . . and he will teach us of his ways, and we will walk in his paths. . . . And he shall judge among many people, and rebuke strong nations afar off; and they shall beat their swords into plowshares, and their spears into pruninghooks: nation shall not lift up a sword against nation, neither shall they learn war any more.

But they shall sit every man under his vine and under his fig tree; and none shall make them afraid: for the mouth of the Lord of hosts hath spoken it.  —*Micah 4:2-4*

## A New World Is Being Born

WHAT, it may be asked, are my own views and desires in respect of these things? They are capable of very simple statement. I want change. I want a social order that is truly moral where the great masses of toiling humanity can be liberated to creative activity. I want this change to come, if possible, peacefully and with a minimum of social upheaval and dislocation. The way of violence inevitably creates fresh injustices and deepens the wells of bitterness.

I look out from my window on one of the fairest scenes in England's green and pleasant land. I see the gardens, the lawns, the flowers and behind them the Cathedral that I love; a poem in stone, fashioned by England's craftsmen throughout the ages, one of man's noblest offerings to God. Today it trembles beneath the blast of war. Below, in the exquisite undercroft chapel, little children, sheltering for safety, sing their songs, whilst above machine guns rattle and bullets descend from the blue vault of a perfect September sky.

This is the world, beauteous and hideous, that mankind has made. What divine purpose runs through it? Must man ever learn only through suffering? One thing seems sure. In this brutal and bloody travail a new world is being born. These are the pangs of birth—not death. Purged by this anguish, men may find, as find I feel convinced they will, that only through community, fellowship and love can be applied all those noble gifts that God has given for the enrichment of human life.

—*Hewlett Johnson*
(The Soviet Power)

## The Nobility of "Common" Men

[On one of its voyages the brigantine "Louise," 227 tons, John J. Bain master, sailing from Bridgewater, N.S., for the Barbados with a cargo of lumber, encountered a terrific storm. The lumber got loose and acted as battering rams. The boats were all carried away and the men huddled around the broken stump of a mast seeing the ship disintegrate under their feet. When the storm abated they found that their stove in the galley was intact. Frozen and numb, they made a fire and] kept a kettle of seawater boiling, a man standing by to lift off the cover every few minutes and hold it upside down until the steam attached thereto condensed into a drop of fresh water. In this way, out of the immensity of water around them, they secured a pitiful drinking supply—enough to allow each of the eleven men two teaspoonfuls at evening and two more in the morning.

[For six days they drifted helplessly, enduring all the torments of thirst, until they were so weak they could barely stand, and their throats swollen from thirst.

Captain Bain said afterwards] I learned also that there are some ordeals which a man can remember without brooding bitterness, without feeling that all human suffering is mere vanity, the needless and purposeless imposition of a mad world. I came out of that experience with a new respect for my fellowmen. [All of the men were quite ordinary folk.] But the way they endured that ordeal was a thing to wonder at. . . .

When huddled together men helped one another to massage the cramps out of one-another's limbs, and the annoyance and pain of being hurled into one-another's ribs by a boarding sea caused no expressions of ill-feeling. . . .

When a man was condensing tiny drops of drinking water, we felt that he did not need watching; that though every atom of his body was burning with fierce fever of thirst, that though he craved with a terrific craving to cool the fire of his tongue by licking the condensing steam, he would treasure each tiny drop—that must have looked to him vaster than a lake—for the common supply, waiting patiently for his share.

—*C. McKay*
(Windjammers and Bluenose Sailors)

## O Come Let Us Sing Unto the Lord

O come, let us sing unto the Lord; let us raise our voice in joy to the rock of our salvation.

O sing unto the Lord a new song; sing unto the Lord, all the earth.

[ 245 ]

Sing unto the Lord; bless his name; proclaim his salvation from day to day.

Honor and majesty are before him; strength and beauty are in his sanctuary.

Worship the Lord in the beauty of holiness; tremble before him, all the earth.

The Lord reigneth; the world is established that it cannot be moved.

Let the heavens be glad, and the earth rejoice; let the field exult, and all that is therein.

He will judge the world with righteousness; and the peoples in his faithfulness.

O ye that love the Lord, hate evil; he preserveth the souls of his servants.

Light is sown for the righteous, and gladness for the upright in heart.

Be glad in the Lord, ye righteous; and give thanks to his holy name.

He hath remembered his mercy and his faithfulness toward the house of Israel.

All the ends of the earth have seen the salvation of our God.

The Lord our God is holy.                    —*From Psalms 95, 96, 97, 98*

## Only with God

RELIGION is the first thing and the last thing, and until a man has found God and been found by God, he begins at no beginning, he works to no end. He may have his friendships, his partial loyalties, his scraps of honour. But all these things fall into place, and life falls into place only with God. Only with God. God who fights through man against Blind Force and Night and Non-Existence; who is the end, who is the meaning. He is the only King. . . . And before the coming of the true King, the inevitable King, the King who is present whenever just men foregather, this bloodstained rubbish of the ancient world, these puny kings and tawdry emperors, these wily politicians and artful lawyers, these men who claim and grab and trick and compel, these war makers and oppressors, will presently shrivel and pass—like paper thrust into a flame.

—*H. G. Wells*

(*Mr. Britling Sees It Through*)

## The Palace of the King

FROM a well-known fairy tale of our English childhood there comes the legend of the King who lived in a plain house, although once he had lived in a magic palace of great beauty. This, however, had been destroyed in an earthquake, and he did not want a new palace because the old one had been built from music, and that was what had made it so unbelievably beautiful. However, the people knew perfectly well that the King ought to have a palace; so one by one they invited all the musicians of the kingdom to come and play—hoping the walls might begin to rise up as before. But although each man outdid himself in brilliance and skill, nothing whatever happened!

Then a little lame boy stepped forward and suggested that maybe if they all played something together the walls would rise; but they laughed him to scorn—*what! play something for which no one could ever get sole credit? Not they!* But the little boy was wise as only a little child can be, and, with another small lad, began to blow through a home-made wooden whistle the national anthem, which was so familiar that all the people found themselves humming it softly, and suddenly the musicians seized their harps and lyres and flutes and trumpets to join in also, until such a glorious harmony was achieved that lo! the palace walls began to rise.

For that was the only way the King could ever have his palace again: each person sinking his own importance to create a larger national beauty —a house not made with hands.

That was no mere legend! For let me tell you about the actual Peace Palace at the Hague, which went up as if by magic in the year 1913, adorned by gifts from many nations—granite for the base from Norway; granite for the terraces from Denmark; granite for the balustrades of the terraces from Sweden; statuary from the United States; tapestries from France; iron entrance gates from Germany; silk hangings from Japan; bronze doors from Belgium; precious woods from South America; crystal chandeliers from Austria; pictures from Holland; jasper and gold vases from Russia; two ancient lovely vases from China; four stained-glass windows from England; and a great crucifix from Argentina, a copy of the famous one held in the arms of the statue of Christ in the Andes. Yes, with great rejoicing this palace actually went up to music from all the kingdoms of the earth. —*Margaret T. Applegarth*
(Bound in the Bundle of Life)

## Paul's Work

ASSUREDLY Paul was one of history's most interesting men: thoroughly human; vigorous; undaunted by handicaps and difficulties and opposition; wholeheartedly devoted to his master and unreservedly given to his cause; genuinely interested in people, especially in his converts; not satisfied with the initial step of conversion but seeking constantly to shepherd his inexperienced Christians until they grew in spiritual grace and in moral fidelity; deeply enriched by present spiritual fellowship with God, but always thrilled by the prospect of an ever-enlarging experience and horizon; living, speaking, and writing for the one aim of furthering the cause of his master. It was he who, more than any other leader in the Apostolic Age, realized the full meaning of the gospel of love and grace. He stated most clearly and championed most effectively the universal gospel. —*Floyd V. Filson*
(Pioneers of the Primitive Church)

[ 247 ]

## Peace at Last!

OVER a world dyed dark with suffering breathes the deep sweet sigh of Peace; and countless hearts are lifted up in praise and unutterable Thanksgiving to him who was our shield and our shelter when the earth did tremble . . . which now is still.

May the sacrifice of . . . lives spent and sorrow endured commend us to him who sustained a righteous cause that he may order the beginning, direct the progress and perfect the achievement of the work which Peace makes paramount today.[1]                                         —*Anonymous*


## The Picture of Jesus

THE picture of Jesus that emerges (from this critical study of the Gospels) can be drawn in lines and colors that fit the picture of human experience as modern people know it. It is the picture of a living man who walked this earth in joy and hope as we have done; who knew what it was to have popular approval, and who knew what it was to fail, as men count failure; who knew discouragement and pain; who found the answer to all life's hardships in unfailing love for people who hated only because they did not understand; a man who found his solution for life's bitterest problems in unshaken faith in the long purposes of God; who found his way at last through utter darkness by virtue of an inner light that guided all his way; who found the answer to deep loneliness in the sure knowledge that he was never really alone. The modern man may well remember him, because in so doing he may perchance recover a half-forgotten way of living that runs deeper than all the troubled surface of our world; an understanding of people that transcends all hatreds by the ancient power of love; a serenity of spirit that rests on certainties which time and change have left unshaken through the years. This was Jesus Christ, who has shown us how a man might live, who felt himself a child of God; and how a man might die, who knew that only through death could man enter into life.          —*David E. Adams*
(Man of God)


## Pledge of the Seven Men of Preston

[EVEN a very few people working together can do great things.]

In 1830 the British Government passed a bill giving free trade in beer to decrease the drinking of spirits. The policy was mistaken. The results were disastrous.

In the midst of this deluge of beer, two men stood talking one Thursday afternoon, late in August, 1832, in the door of a cheese-shop in Church Street, Preston. One was a Methodist clogger, John King by name. The other was the proprietor of the shop, a Baptist called Joseph

[1] Published in the *Globe and Mail*, Aug. 15, 1945, by the T. Eaton Company, Toronto, the day after Japan surrendered.

[ 248 ]

Livesey. Both were in great concern, for reports of visitation among members of the Preston Temperance Society, of which Livesey was head, and King, the "captain" of a district, showed a sorry tale of members who had fallen away through beer-drinking. Livesey's own record shall continue the story:

"One Thursday, August 23rd, 1832, John King was passing by my shop in Church Street, and I invited him in, and after discussing this question, upon which we were both agreed, I asked him if he would sign a pledge of *total* abstinence, to which he consented. I then went to the desk and wrote one out, the precise words of which I do not remember. He came to the desk, and I said: 'Thee sign it first.' He did so, and I signed after him. This first step led to the next, for in the course of a few days, notice of a special meeting was given, to be held in the Temperance Hall, the Cock-pit, the following Saturday night, September 1st, at which this subject was warmly discussed. At the close of the meeting, I remember well a group of us gathering together still further debating the matter, which ended in *seven* persons' signing a new pledge, it being opposed by others. I subjoin the pledge and the names:

'We agree to abstain from all liquors of an intoxicating quality, whether Ale, Porter, Wine, or Ardent Spirits, except as medicines.

| John Gratrix | Joseph Livesey |
| Edward Dickenson[1] | David Anderton |
| Thomas Broadbelt | John King' " |
| Thomas Smith | |

That famous pledge of the Seven Men of Preston became the spring of a moral reformation that spread through the whole of England, and its momentum is not yet exhausted. The Preston Temperance Society, indeed, became a band of apostles, proclaiming the gospel of total abstinence around Preston, through Lancashire and through Cheshire. Livesey himself travelled England. Others felt the contagion of their enthusiasm, and new movements sprang up, all of which owed something to the new movement for temperance and sobriety.

—*E. C. Urwin*
(Temperance and Self Control)

## The Principle of Loving All

Do THOSE who hate and do harm to others hold the principle of loving all, or that of distinctions between man and man? It must be replied: They make distinctions. . . . There is a principle of loving all, which is able to change that which makes distinctions. If the nations were as much for other states as for their own, which one among them would raise force to attack another? . . . So then it is the principle of universal mutual love which gives rise to all that is beneficial to the world.

—*Motse*

[1] In copying this, Mrs. Myers recognized her grandfather's name.

[ 249 ]

## Reasons for Family Worship

IT SWEETENS home life and enriches home relationships.

It helps to resolve misunderstanding and to relieve friction that may enter the home.

It tends to hold our boys and girls to the Christian ideal and to determine their lasting welfare.

It gives strength to meet bravely any disappointments and adversities as they come.

It reinforces the influence and work of the Church, the Church school, and agencies helping to establish the Kingdom of Love in the world.

It honors our Father and is a means of expressing together our gratitude and our love to our God. — *Anonymous*

## Religion and Health

IF WE may assume that the keynote of a normal Christian life is not the thought of sin, or of penitence, or of suffering, or of anxiety of any sort, but rather that of a joyous realization of the highest good, a realization begun now and growing ever toward greater fullness—if we may assume this, then it follows that the Christian mode of life tends directly toward physical health. Other things being equal, a religion that ruled by fear would have less robust votaries than one ruled by love. Faith, hope and love are all full of constructive suggestion; for the first two take the attention away from present evil to present and future good; and love—the out-going of self toward others for their own good—is the very antithesis of that brooding and self-contemplation whence grow the rankest weeds of unhealthful auto-suggestion. With persons of certain temperaments, if not of all, selfishness is distinctly unhealthful; and so it comes to pass that he who fails to use his health for the bettering of the world is in danger of losing even that which he hath.

—George A. Coe
(The Spiritual Life)

## Religion Basic

OF ALL the dispositions and habits, which lead to political prosperity, Religion and morality are indispensable supports. In vain would that man claim the tribute of Patriotism who should labor to subvert these great Pillars of human happiness, these firmest props of the duties of Men and Citizens. The mere Politician, equally with the pious man, ought to respect and to cherish them.—A volume could not trace all their connections with private and public felicity.—Let it simply be asked where is the security for property, for reputation, for life, if the sense of religious obligation *desert* the oaths, which are the instruments of investigation in Courts of Justice? And let us with caution indulge the supposition, that morality can be maintained without religion.—Whatever may be conceded to the influence of refined education on minds of peculiar structure—reason and experience both forbid us to expect, that national morality can prevail in exclusion of religious principle.

—*George Washington*
(From the Farewell Address)

## Rest and Work

MY GOD, in everything I see thy hand; in every passage thy gracious discipline.

Thou wisely governest the house thou hast built, and preventest with thy mercy all our wants.

Thou callest us up in the early morning, and givest us light by the beams of the sun;

To labour every one in their proper office, and fill the place appointed them in the world.

Thou providest a rest for our weary evening; and favorest our sleep with a shady darkness;

To refresh our bodies in the peace of night, and repair the waste of our decaying spirits.

Again thou awakest our drowsy eyes, and biddest us return to our daily task.

Thus has thy wisdom mixed our life, and beauteously interwoven it of rest and work.

Whose mutual changes sweeten each other, and each prepares us for our greatest duty,

Of finishing here the work of our salvation, to rest hereafter in thy holy peace.

—*John Austin*
(Devotions for Everyday in the Week)

## Roses in Our Hearts

"GIVE us this day our daily bread. . . ."

This is the simplicity of asking that the moon and the sun still rise. Give beauty to women, and grace to children, and songs for poets to sing. Let not the green tree wither, but send it rain. And give a little softness to the hearts of callous men. And remind us that widows live, and that there are fatherless. Teach us to guide youth wisely and give us gentleness. And when roses grow on the walls in June, put a bud in our hearts.[1]

—*Donn Byrne*

## Roses in the Heart

HE WHO would have beautiful Roses in his garden must have Roses *in his heart.* He must love them well and always. . . . He must have not only the glowing admiration, the enthusiasm, and the passion, but the tenderness, the thoughtfulness, the reverence, the watchfulness of love.

—*S. R. Hole*

[1] Adapted.

## Saint Anthony's Cobbler

WE READ a pretty story of St. Anthony, who, being in the wilderness, led there a very hard and straight life, insomuch that none at that time did the like, to whom came a voice from heaven, saying, Anthony, thou art not so perfect as is a cobbler that dwelleth at Alexandria. Anthony hearing this, rose up forthwith, and took his staff and went till he came to Alexandria, where he found the cobbler. The cobbler was astonished to see so reverend a father come to his house. Then Anthony said unto him, Come and tell me thy whole conversation, and how thou spendest thy time? Sir, said the cobbler, as for me, good works have I none, for my life is but simple and slender; I am but a poor cobbler: in the morning when I rise, I pray for the whole city wherein I dwell, specially for all such neighbours and poor friends as I have: after, I set me at my labour, where I spend the whole day in getting my living, and I keep me from all falsehood, for I hate nothing so much as I do deceitfulness: wherefore, when I make to any man a promise, I keep it and perform it truly; and thus I spend my time poorly, with my wife and children, whom I teach and instruct, as far as my wit will serve me, to love and serve God. And this is the sum of my simple life.

In this story, you see how God loveth those that follow their vocation and live uprightly, without any falsehood in their dealing. This Anthony was a great holy man, yet this cobbler was as much esteemed before God as he. —*Hugh Latimer*

## Satisfactions from Gardens

WHEN any of us may be tired, worried, or even discouraged by the troubles of the world which oppress us so threateningly in these anxious times, what can be more heartening or pleasant than to turn aside for a brief moment from the problems of the gold standard, unemployment, war debts, reparations, and all the anxieties of the post-war world, and devote our thoughts to the beauty of our gardens.

—*Vere Brabazon Ponsouby*
(Lord Bessborough)

## Saving Life

### 1. Pasteur's Discoveries

(PASTEUR, by his marvellous discoveries, saved the wine industry. He also discovered an inoculation to immunize sheep from the deadly anthrax. His enemies scoffed at his discovery; so a great public test was made on forty-eight sheep—twenty-four inoculated, twenty-four not. Then all were given anthrax germs. On the day set the crowds gathered. The inoculated sheep were all alive and well; the others all dead!

His discovery saved the sheep industry of France and of the world.

Then Pasteur turned his attention to the awful disease produced by the bite of a mad dog. He discovered a serum which worked with animals. But would it save human beings?)

From all over the world came letters, urgent telegrams, from physicians, from poor fathers and mothers who were waiting terror-smitten for their children, mangled by mad dogs, to die—frantic messages poured in on Pasteur, begging him to send them his vaccine to use on threatened humans.

Never was any microbe hunter faced with a worse riddle. "Not a single one of all my dogs has ever died from the vaccine," Pasteur pondered. "All of the bitten ones have been perfectly protected by it. . . . It must work the same on humans—it must . . . but—"

At last, mercifully, the worried Mrs. Meister from Miessengott in Alsace took the dreadful decision out of Pasteur's hands. This woman came crying into the laboratory, leading her nine-year-old boy, Joseph, gashed in fourteen places two days before by a mad dog. He was a pitifully whimpering, scared boy—hardly able to walk.

"Save my little boy, Mr. Pasteur," this woman begged him.

Pasteur told the woman to come back at five in the evening, and meanwhile he went to see the two physicians, Vulpian and Grancher—admirers who had been in his laboratory, who had seen the perfect way in which Pasteur could guard dogs from rabies after they had been terribly bitten. That evening they went with him to see the boy, and when Vulpian saw the angry festering wounds he urged Pasteur to start his inoculations: "Go ahead," said Vulpian, "if you do nothing it is almost sure that he will die."

And that night of July 6, 1885, they made the first injection of the weakened microbes of hydrophobia into a human being. Then, day after day, the boy Meister went without a hitch through his fourteen injections—which were only slight pricks of the hypodermic needle into his skin.

And the boy went home to Alsace and had never a sign of that dreadful disease.

Then all fears left Pasteur. Pasteur shouted to the world that he was prepared to guard the people of the world from hydrophobia. This one case had completely chased his fears, his doubts—those vivid but not very deep-lying doubts of the artist that was in Louis Pasteur.

The tortured bitten people of the world began to pour into the laboratory of the miracle-man of the Rue d'Ulm . . . polyglot crowds of mangled ones, babbling in a score of tongues: "Pasteur—save us!" . . .

From Smolensk in Russia came nineteen peasants, moujiks who had been set upon by a mad wolf nineteen days before, and five of them were so terribly mangled they could not walk at all. . . .

Then Paris went mad—as only Paris can—with excited concern about these bitten Russians who must surely die—it was so long since they had been attacked. . . .

Perhaps, indeed, it was too late. Pasteur could not eat nor did he sleep at all. He took a terrible risk, and morning and night, twice as quickly as he had ever made the fourteen injections—twice a day to make up for lost time—he and his men shot the vaccine into the arms of the Russians.

And at last a great shout of pride went up for this man Pasteur, went up from the Parisians, and all of France and all the world raised a paean of thanks to him—for the vaccine marvelously saved all but three of the doomed peasants. The moujiks returned to Russia and were welcomed with the kind of awe that greets the return of helpless sick ones who have been healed at some miraculous shrine. And the Tsar of All the Russias sent Pasteur the diamond cross of Ste. Anne, and a hundred thousand francs to start the building of that house of microbe hunters in the Rue Dutot in Paris—that laboratory now called the Institut Pasteur. From all over the world—it was the kind of burst of generosity that only great disasters usually call out—from every country in the earth came money, piling up into millions of francs for the building of a laboratory in which Pasteur might have everything needed to track down other deadly microbes, [and] to invent weapons against them.

## 2. What Have You Done for Humanity?

Pasteur died in 1895 in a little house near the kennels where they now kept his rabid dogs, at Villeneuve l'Etang, just outside of Paris. . . . Madame Pasteur was there and these men who had risked their lives in the carrying out of his wild forays against death [and who] would now have died to save him, if they could.

That was the perfect end of this so human . . . saver of lives.

But there is another end of his career that I like to think of more— and that was the day, in 1892, of Pasteur's seventieth birthday—when a medal was given to him at a great meeting held to honor him, at the Sorbonne in Paris. . . . There was a great buzz of young voices—all at once a hush, as Pasteur limped up the aisle, leaning on the arm of the President of the French Republic. . . .

At last the old microbe hunter gave his speech. . . . It was to the students, to the boys of the high schools he was calling:

". . . Do not let yourselves be tainted by a deprecating and barren skepticism, do not let yourselves be discouraged by the sadness of certain hours which pass over nations. Live in the serene peace of laboratories and libraries. Say to yourselves first: What have I done for my instruction? and, as you gradually advance, What have I done for my country? until the time comes when you may have the immense happiness of thinking that you have contributed in some way to the progress and good of humanity."                                            —*Paul DeKruif*
                                                                    (Microbe Hunters)

## Sayings from Thomas à Kempis

AND this should be our endeavour, even to master self, and thus daily to grow stronger than self, and go on unto perfection.

Devout conversation on spiritual things helpeth not a little to spiritual progress, most of all where those of kindred mind and spirit find their ground of fellowship in God.

Consider now the lively examples of the holy fathers. . . . They were strangers to the world, but unto God they were as kinsmen and friends. Blessed are they who long to have leisure for God, and free themselves from every hindrance of the world. Think on these things, O my soul, and shut the doors of thy carnal desires, so mayest thou hear what the Lord God will say within thee.

God who is eternal and incomprehensible, and of infinite power, doth great and inscrutable things in heaven and in earth, and his wonderful works are past finding out. If the works of God were of such sort that they might easily be comprehended by human reason, they should no longer be called wonderful or unspeakable.             —*Thomas à Kempis*
                                                                  (Imitation of Christ)

## Sensitiveness to God

IT WOULD seem as though tens of thousands today were thoroughly "pagan," in the sense that they have no conscious feeling for God and delight in nothing but creature comforts. That sort of life seems most tragic. These people are not only deaf and blind but insensate to the pulsing, living spirit of the universe. They have the house, but without the warmth and glow of the home; they have the corpse, but not life; they have the material world, but not the radiating love of a glowing, living God. The writer of Ecclesiastes expressed a universal law when he discovered that, although he had mastered all knowledge, acquired wealth, and tested the delights of fame, without God, life was all vanity.

The person who is sensitive to God understands something of the mystery and beauty of life. Day by day he communes with God, sees things from the point of view of the Eternal, and enters with insight and intelligence into his plans and purposes. It is his to know God and enjoy him, now and forever; and one who faces the problems of his own life and the burdens of the world . . . must be filled with despair unless he feels that, in working for the best, he is co-operating with the almighty power and wisdom of God. . . .

This sensitiveness to God is communion. It is prayer in reality. Words are not prayer, but prayer may be expressed—though always inadequately —in words. . . . To one who is sensitive to God, all nature, the cosmos, human history, and all human life are instinct with God.
                                                              —*A. J. William Myers*
                                                                  (Religion for Today)

## Shakespeare's Memorial

I HAVE now made a pilgrimage to Stratford-on-Avon. . . . At the age of thirty-two, he (Shakespeare) is a successful, well-to-do man. . . . At fifty-two, his health fails. He makes business-like arrangements in the event of death, and faces the darkness of the long sleep like any other good citizen. . . .

I walked through the churchyard, vocal with building rooks, and came to the noble church full of the evidences of wealth and worship and honour. I do not like to confess the breathless awe with which I drew near to the chancel and gazed on the stone that, nameless, with its rude rhyme, covers the sacred dust. I cannot say what my thoughts were, but I was lost in a formless, unuttered prayer of true abasement before the venerable relics of the highest achievements of the human spirit. There beneath my feet slept the dust of the brain that conceived *Hamlet* and *Macbeth* and the hand that traced the *Sonnets* and the eye that had plumbed the depths of life. That was a solemn moment, and I do not think I ever experienced so deep a thrill of speechless awe. I could not tear myself away; I could only wonder and desire.

I do not think I ever realized before the humanity of Shakespeare. He seemed to me before to sit remote, enshrined aloof, the man who could tell all the secrets of humanity that could be told, and whose veriest hints still seem to open doors into mysteries both high and sweet and terrible. But now I feel as if I had been near him, had been able to love what I had only admired. . . .

And I am glad that . . . Shakespeare could be silent, and buy and sell, and go in and out among his fellow townsmen, and make merry. . . .

God give me and all uneasy natures grace to know when to hold our tongues; and to take the days that remain with patience and wonder and tenderness; not making haste to depart, but yet not fearing the shadow out of which we come and into which we must go; to live wisely and bravely and sweetly, and to close our eyes in faith, with a happy sigh, like a child after a long summer day of light and delight.

—*Arthur Christopher Benson*
(The Upton Letters)


## Socrates on Immortality

[PLATO represents Socrates, immediately preceding his death, talking with his friends. They ask him about what happens after death, and he replies:]

But those who are found to have lived an eminently holy life, these are they who, being freed and set at large from these regions in the earth, as from a prison, arrive at the pure abode above and dwell on the upper parts of the earth. And among these, they who have sufficiently purified themselves by philosophy [the love of wisdom] shall live without bodies, throughout all future time, and shall arrive at habitations yet more beautiful than these, which it is neither easy to describe, nor at present is there sufficient time for the purpose.

But for the sake of these things which we have described, we should use every endeavor . . . so as to acquire virtue and wisdom in this life; for the reward is noble, and the hope great.

To affirm positively, indeed, that these things are exactly as I have described them does not become a man of sense; that however either this, or something of the kind, takes place with respect to our souls and their habitations—since our soul is certainly immortal—this appears to me most fitting to be believed, and worthy the hazard for one who trusts in its reality; for the hazard is noble, and it is right to allure ourselves with such things. —*Plato*

(Phaedo)

## Socrates' Speech at His Trial

IF YOU were to say to me, "Socrates, this time we will let you go, but on this condition, that you cease from carrying on this search of yours [for truth], and from philosophy [love of wisdom]; if you are found following these pursuits again, you shall die": I say, if you offered to let me go on these terms, I should reply, "Athenians, I hold you in the highest regard and love, but I will obey God rather than you; and as long as I have breath and strength I will not cease from philosophy, and from exhorting you, and declaring the truth to every one of you whom I meet saying, as I am wont, 'You are a citizen of Athens, a city which is very great and very famous for wisdom and power of mind. Are you not ashamed of caring so much for the making of money, and for reputation? Will you not think or care about wisdom, and truth, and the perfection of your soul?' And therefore, Athenians, either acquit me, or do not acquit me; but be sure that I shall not alter my way of life; no, not if I have to die for it many times."

[He was condemned to death.] —*Plato*

(The Trial and Death of Socrates)

## Spending Ourselves, Not Getting

FOR me, then, to have the sense of Divine Vocation means that in the daily life of each of us there should be something done, not by instinct, but more and more consciously, without thought of reward, whether it is part of our paid work or not. There should be something that is spending ourselves, not getting anything. There should be something that in marking the brotherhood and sisterhood of man, leads to the fatherhood of God. —*William H. Beveridge*

(The Pillars of Security)

## Sunday

I AM always very well pleased with a country Sunday; and think if keeping holy the [Sunday] were only a human institution, it would be the best method that could have been thought of for the polishing and civilizing of mankind. It is certain [that] . . . people would soon degenerate into a kind of savages and barbarians, were there not such frequent returns of a stated time, in which the whole village meet together with their best faces, and in their cleanliest habits, to converse with one another upon indifferent subjects, hear their duties explained to them, and join together in adoration of the Supreme Being. —*Joseph Addison*

(Sir Roger de Coverley)

[ 257 ]

## Sundays

GOD must have known that there would be need of Sundays. When life is very lovely, and one has been living with trees and stars and sky, there must be Sundays. To have made the wonder and beauty of the earth and not to set apart a holy day wherein the people whom he had created might rejoice over the work of his fingers, the moon and the stars which he had ordained, this would have meant poverty of spirit indeed.

What a heritage of Sabbath Ceremonies has been bequeathed to us— music and incense and priestly vestments and flaming altars, prayers, sacrifices and visions, and holy sacraments. I, too, would have my ceremonials of seeing God in his world, and of worshipping him.

I would not have Sunday be an ordinary day. On no day are things so much loved as on Sunday, but there is a subtle difference in motives. Sunday is my Festival of Beauty, of Loved Things, of Leisure, and of Worship. I reserve for it whatever I most enjoy—flowers, blue china at breakfast, books, important letters, special walks, colored candles at supper and waffles, pine incense and colored flames in my fire. On Sunday I would not do any work, nor say nor think nor do unworthy things. I may this day announce to the people whom I like the fact that I do like them.

I think God must take pleasure in the joyousness that awakens me on Sunday mornings. —*Abbie Graham*
(Ceremonials of Common Days)

## Sure of God's Help

A ROOT set in the finest soil, in the best climate, and blessed with all that sun and air and rain can do for it, is not in so sure a way of its growth to perfection as every man may be whose spirit aspires after all that which God is ready and infinitely desirous to give him. For the sun meets not the springing bud that stretches towards him with half the certainty with which, as God, the source of all good, communicates himself to the soul that longs to partake of him. —*William Law*

## Suspicion

A CERTAIN man lost an axe. He at once suspected that the son of his neighbor had stolen it. When he saw the boy walking by, the boy looked like a fellow who had stolen an axe; when he listened to the boy's words, they sounded like those of a boy who had stolen an axe. All his actions and manners were those of a boy who had stolen an axe. Later, when digging a ditch, he found the lost axe. The next day the man saw again his neighbor's son, but in all his manners and actions, there was nothing like a boy who had stolen an axe. The boy had not changed, but the man himself had changed! And the only reason for this change lay in his suspicion. —*Anonymous*
(From the Chinese)

[ 258 ]

## Thank You

DANTE Gabriel Rossetti once said that the most miserable moment for an atheist was when he really felt grateful for the universe, and had nobody to thank. Most of us have passed through experiences which enable us to understand what he meant; occasions when joy itself would have become sour and stagnant if it could have no satisfying outlet in gratitude. Such a moment I recall when, having with a friend walked from Kendal up to Grassmere in a day of ceaseless rain, we discovered in the morning that the clouds had been swept away as though by magic. The sun was just topping the everlasting hills, and a delicate mist lay like a benediction upon the level of the lake. Every twig and leaf and blade of grass was gemmed with sparkling water-drops. . . . If ever I felt the need for prayer it was then. To share such beauty with a friend overwhelmed me with a sense of thankfulness.

"I hate ingratitude more in a man than lying vainness, babbling drunkenness, or any taint of vice." So said great Shakespeare, denouncing elsewhere the fault as "monstrous." Yet to be thankful is not an altogether easy thing.

Rather it is an art in which we need to school ourselves. When little children ask me the right time, and scamper off without a word of thanks for my uncertain hazard, I feel a little dashed in spirit; not because I want their thanks, but because I feel there is something wanting in their training, for the lack of which they will themselves become impoverished. —*F. E. Christmas*

## There Is No Real Death

IT HAS been my lot in life to have to stand by many deathbeds, and to be called in to dying men and women almost as a routine in my profession. Yet I am increasingly convinced their spirits never die at all. I am sure that there is no real death. Death is no argument against, but rather for, life. Eternal life is the complement of all my unsatisfied ideals; and experience teaches me that the belief in it is a greater incentive to be useful and good than any other I know.

Perhaps the critic is a shallower fool than he [thinks]. . . . It may be that there is no such thing as matter. . . . The spiritual may be far more real than the material. . . .

Immortality may be the complement of mortality as water becomes steam and steam becomes power, and power becomes heat and heat becomes light. The conclusion that life beyond is the conservation of energy of life here may be as scientific as the great natural laws for material things. I see Knowledge *become Service, Service become Joy.* . . . [I have seen] hope bring back color to the face and tone to the blood. . . . I have seen *love* do physical things which mere intellectual convictions cannot. . . . I prefer to stand with Moses in his belief in the Promised Land and that we can reach it; than to believe that the Celestial City is a mirage. —*Wilfred Thomason Grenfell*

## There Is None Greater

WILL great originality be born again, or will the world content itself henceforth with following the ways opened by the bold creators of the ancient ages? We know not. But whatever may be the unexpected phenomena of the future, Jesus will not be surpassed. . . . The tale of his life will cause ceaseless tears, his sufferings will soften the best hearts; all the ages will proclaim that, among the sons of men, there is none born who is greater than Jesus.    —*Ernest Renan*
(The Life of Jesus)

## There Is Work to Do

[THIS is what the resurrection of Jesus means to the Unknown Disciple: There is work to do and I must do it. He, like the other disciples, was completely crushed by the death of Jesus. Mary's story of the resurrection seemed an idle tale and the Good News only a dream. Finally, leaving him alone, Mary said:]

"It does not matter whether you believe that I saw Jesus or dreamed. What matters is that we must spread the news of his kingdom. Cannot a dream alter the face of the world? There is a power within me that forces me to go on, that makes me want to suffer everything for everybody. What matter how it came? Shall I not yield to it? And you, too, when it comes to you?"

And she went away and left me there under the tree of God.

It was in Galilee, on the mountain where I had first heard Jesus teach, that hope came back to me. After a hard day's work I had wandered away from the village, and climbed the mountain and sat looking down on the great plain with its vineyards and olive gardens, and the thin grey smoke that rose in the air as the women made ready the evening meal. The voices of the children driving the cattle home came from the plain, and far in the distance a cow lowed to her calf and the sheep baaed to their lambs. Darkness was falling, but I could not go. The light faded and blackness covered the land. I bowed my head on my arms and sat on, too tired for sleep, too hopeless for pain, too sad for tears. The wild beasts cried aloud in the night, but I did not move. All night I sat there, and in the morning came the dawn. First there came the stillness. No bird cheeped, no wild beast cried aloud. A faint glimmer of light showed the dark masses of the forests on the hills, and the dim silver line of the sea. The golden light spread and touched the land and colour awoke again in earth and sky. The sun came up behind the mountains and the shadows lay from east to west along the plain. It was then that the vision came to me. I saw nothing. I heard nothing, but as the dawn spread slowly over the land, waking the earth to beauty, something awoke in my heart. I do not know what it was. I have no words to tell of it. The earth lay before me bathed in a light that men seldom saw, a clear radiance that transfigured each familiar place and gave the world the beauty of a dream. And yet it was still the earth. The forests and moors, the mountains and valleys, were the same, but another light lay upon them. So it was with my soul. An intense, still joy awoke in my heart, a joy in which there was no shadow of restlessness or disturbance, and the old gay sense of something added to life came back to me. It seemed as though Jesus had watched by me all night and I had not known it. The place was full of his presence. Or was it only that the earth was my healer?

The glory of the vision blinded me, and I hid my eyes. There was no death. Each night the beauty of the earth died into darkness, each dawn in wonder the light rose again on it. It was so with the spirit of man. In tribulation and in agony happiness died, but in beauty and glory joy lived again. I rolled over on my face on the course mountain grass and lay there thinking. The greatest miracle in the world had happened to me. I had seen the transfiguration in the look of life that an emotion brings. A remembrance of beauty and love and immortal passion, the romance of the earth and of life had taken hold of me. The smallest, meanest things had gained a power of signifying the greatest, noblest things. The world was full of wonders. Nothing was impossible to love.

The children had begun to drive the cattle out. Their shrill cries rose in the air before I stirred. When I sat up and looked at the earth again it was broad, garish day. The beauty of the world no longer caught my breath away. In the bustle of life my vision must fade, but I did not mind. I had seen the eternal beauty that lies hidden in the commonplace. There was a work to do, and like Peter and the disciples I must do it, no matter what the cost. So I rose to my feet to go back to my village and take up my job again. —*By an Unknown Disciple*

## Three Properties

HE SHOWED a little thing, the quantity of a hazel-nut, lying in the palm of my hand, as meseemed, and it was as round as a ball. I looked thereon with the eye of my understanding, and thought, "What may this be?" and it was answered generally thus, "It is all that is made." I marvelled how it might last; for methought it might suddenly have fallen to naught for littleness. And I was answered in my understanding, "It lasteth and ever shall: For God loveth it. And so hath all things being by the Love of God." In this little thing I saw three properties. The first is, that God made it. The second is, that God loveth it. The third is, that God keepeth it. For this is the cause which we be not all in ease of heart and soul: for we seek here rest in this thing which is so little, where no rest is in: and we know not our God that is all Mighty, all Wise and all Good, for he is very rest. —*Mother Juliana* (A.D. 1373)

(Daily Strength)

## To the Worshipper

WHOEVER you are that worships here, in whatever household of faith you were born, whatever creed you now profess, if you come to this sanctuary to seek the God in whom you may believe or to rededicate yourself to the God in whom you do believe, you are welcome.

Leave not this church without a prayer for yourself, your friends, and all who worship here; for our nation in these days of sacrificial burdens and difficult decisions; for all hapless victims of the world's catastrophe, and for the coming of God's world-wide Kingdom of justice and peace; for the fellowship of the Christian Church universal among all nations and races; and for men and women of every faith who sincerely desire one human family under the Fatherhood of one God.[1]     —*Anonymous*

## The Tomb Opens on the Dawn

I FEEL in myself the future life. . . .

You say the soul is nothing but the resultant of the bodily powers. Why, then, is my soul more luminous when my bodily powers begin to fail? Winter is on my head, but eternal spring is in my heart. I breathe at this hour the fragrance of the lilacs, the violets and the roses, as at twenty years. The nearer I approach the end the plainer I hear around me the immortal symphonies of the worlds which invite me. It is marvelous yet simple. It is a fairy tale, and it is history.

For half a century I have been writing my thoughts in prose and in verse; history, philosophy, drama, romance, tradition, satire, ode and song; I have tried them all. But I feel I have not said the thousandth part of what is in me. When I go down to the grave I can say, like many others, "I have finished my day's work." But I cannot say, "I have finished my life." My day's work will begin again the next morning. The tomb is not a blind alley; it is a thoroughfare. It closes on the twilight, it opens on the dawn.     —*Victor Hugo*

## True Ambition

To BE honest, to be kind, to earn a little, and to spend a little less, to make upon the whole, a family happier for his presence, to renounce when that shall be necessary and not to be embittered, to keep a few friends, but these without capitulation; above all, on the same condition, to keep friends with himself, here is a task for all a man has of fortitude and delicacy.     —*Robert Louis Stevenson*

## Turning Grief into Loving Service

I WAS in the depths of grief. I might almost say of despair, for the light and sunshine of my house had been extinguished. All that was left on earth of my young wife, except the memory of a sainted life and a too brief happiness, was lying still and cold in the chamber above us. Mr. Cobden called upon me as his friend, and addressed me, as you might suppose, with words of condolence. After a time he looked up and said, "There are thousands of houses in England at this moment where wives, mothers, and children are dying of hunger. Now," he said,

[1] Riverside Church Calendar, Sunday, June 9, 1946.

"when the first paroxysm of your grief is past, I would advise you to come with me, and we will never rest till the Corn Law is repealed."

I accepted his invitation. I knew that the description he had given of the homes of thousands was not an exaggerated description. I felt in my conscience that there was a work which somebody must do, and therefore I accepted his invitation, and from that time we never ceased to labor hard on behalf of the resolution which we had made.

Now, do you suppose that I wish you to imagine that he and I, when I say "we," were the only persons engaged in this great question? We were not even the first, though afterwards, perhaps, we became the foremost before the public. But there were others before us; and we were joined, not by scores, but by hundreds, and afterwards by thousands, and afterwards by countless multitudes; and afterwards famine itself, against which we had warred, joined us; and a great minister (of the Crown) was converted, and minorities became majorities, and finally the barrier was entirely thrown down. And since then though there has been suffering in many homes in England, yet no wife and no mother and no little child has been starved to death as the result of a famine made by law.

—*G. M. Trevelyan*
(Life of John Bright)

## United in Love Though Differing in Opinion

ALTHOUGH a difference in opinions or modes of worship may prevent an entire external union, need it prevent our union in affection? Though we cannot think alike, may we not love alike? May we not be of one heart, though we are not of one opinion? Without all doubt we may. Herein all the children of God may unite, notwithstanding these smaller differences. These remaining as they are, they may forward one another in love and in good works. . . . I dare not presume to impose my mode of worship on any other. . . . I ask not therefore of him with whom I would unite in love, Are you of my church? Of my congregation? Do you receive the same form of church-government? . . . Do you receive the supper of the Lord in the same posture and manner as I do? Nor, whether in the administration of baptism, you agree with me . . . in the manner of administering it, or the age of those to whom it should be administered. Nay, I ask not of you (as clear as I am in my own mind) whether you allow baptism and the Lord's Supper at all. Let all these things stand by: we will talk of them, if need be, at a more convenient season. My only question at present is, Is thine heart right as my heart is with thy heart? If it be, give me thy hand. I do not mean, Be of my opinion. You need not. I do not expect or desire it. Neither do I mean, I will be of your opinion. I cannot. . . . Keep you your opinion, I mine: and that as steadily as ever. You need not even endeavour to come over to me, or bring me over to you. I do not desire you to dispute those points, or to hear or speak one word concerning them. Let all opinions alone on one side and on the other. Only give me thine hand.

—*John Wesley*

[ 263 ]

## The Unwritten Law of the Lodge

BE HOSPITABLE.
Always give your guest the place of honor.
Never sit while your guest stands.
Go hungry rather than stint your guest.
Protect your guest as one of the family.
Never walk between persons who are conversing.
Never interrupt persons talking.
Speak softly, especially before your elders or in the presence of strangers.
Show respect to all men but grovel to none.
Thank the Great Spirit for each day and each meal. —*Anonymous*
(North American Indian)

## Wanted: Workers

THE lazy and idle seldom hear the call of God. It is often when intent on some useful work and while pursuing a helpful calling that God's voice is heard. Here are a few examples from the Bible:
Moses was busy with his flocks at Horeb.
Gideon was busy threshing wheat by the wine press.
Saul was busy searching for his father's lost beasts.
Elisha was busy plowing with twelve yoke of oxen.
David was busy caring for his father's sheep.
Nehemiah was busy bearing the king's wine-cup.
Amos was busy caring for his sheep and sycamore fruit and attending the market.
Peter and Andrew were busy casting their nets into the sea.
Lydia was busy preparing and selling her purple fabrics.
James and John were busy mending their nets.
Matthew was busy collecting customs duties.
Mary and Elizabeth were busy with their homemaking.
Jesus was busy probably in the carpenter shop and about his Father's business.[1] —*Anonymous*

## We Believe

WE BELIEVE that God is spirit and they that worship him must worship him must worship him in spirit and in truth.
We believe that God hath made of one blood all nations of men to dwell on the face of the whole earth.
We believe that God is love, and everyone that loveth is born of God and knoweth God.
We believe that Jesus is a son of God, and as many as are led by the spirit of God, they are the sons of God.
We believe that Jesus reveals the way, the truth and the life.

[1] Slightly altered.

[ 264 ]

We believe that if we walk in the light, as he is in the light, we have fellowship one with another.

We believe that our highest joy and greatest glory is to love God, to follow the Master, and to serve our fellow men. —*S. Angus*
(Essential Christianity)

## We Cannot Choose Happiness

WE CANNOT choose happiness either for ourselves or for another; we cannot tell where that will lie. We can only choose whether we shall indulge ourselves in the present moment, or whether we will renounce that for the sake of obeying the Divine voice within us—for the sake of being true to all the motives that sanctify our lives. I know this belief is hard; it has slipped away from me again and again; but I have felt that if I let it go forever, I should have no light through the darkness of this life. —*George Eliot*

## We Worship for Sheer Delight

WE WORSHIP for sheer delight. It is akin to the intense enjoyment given us by the countryside on a spring morning or the forest-clad hills gorgeous in the sunlight on an October day. We "glorify God, and . . . enjoy him." For many people formal public worship may be an acquired taste, developed by exposure to it, like the taste for good music. But whether cultivated or seemingly native-born, it affords its possessors intense delight. To stand before God, viewing his glory in the face of Jesus Christ, with our faculties raised to their height of acute perception by a company of fellow devotees, is the acme of bliss—the beatific vision. "One thing have I desired of the Lord, that will I seek after; that I may dwell in the house of the Lord all the days of my life, to behold the beauty of the Lord." Thou shalt make me "drink of the river of thy pleasures."

Such appreciation is inexpressibly satisfying. It is its own justification. When one hears the question raised, "Why go to church?" one would like to ask parallel questions: "Why enjoy music? Why read poetry? Why find happiness in being with one's dearest?" We worship for the sheer pleasure of it, or we do not really worship. A service is rightly termed "a celebration." It is a sobering experience for sinful creatures to face their holy God. "How dreadful is this place!" We are humbled before him. But God is also fascinating . . . He is our "exceeding joy." In genuine worship men feel that "it is good for us to be here." They no more think of reasons why it is good than they do when they are rapt by an exquisite melody. Worship, like all other appreciation of the lovely, finds that "beauty is its own excuse for being." To "enjoy" God is man's "chief end."

Appreciation craves expression and grows by it. A clasp of the hand both shows and intensifies friendship. At a public meeting applause utters and multiplies enthusiasm. Muted appreciation runs the risk of

[ 265 ]

being stifled. A family celebrates birthdays, wedding anniversaries, and other festivals at the prompting of affection, and the celebrations strengthen family feeling . . . Did we not worship, and worship reasonably often, we should lose our sense of relationship with the blessed and blessing One. "To have a God," wrote Martin Luther, "is to worship him". . .

The primary element in Christian worship is this adoring recognition of the most dear Father, the august Lord of all worlds. Every service should begin by setting men before him. A sentence of Scripture, a prayer, a hymn which confronts us with God in his majesty, his righteousness, his compassion, and evokes reverence, pentience, gratitude, devotion—this is a fitting start for an appreciation of God in a glad solemnity. Worshipers must become engrossed in him. Victor Hugo says of his Bishop Bienvenu: "He did not study God: he was dazzled by him." The more completely we are taken out of ourselves and become oblivious of our problems, our feelings, our desires, the better. At the outset of worship it is inappropriate to dwell on our needs or on our obligations, much less on our awareness or forgetfulness of the divine presence. God, as he has revealed himself, should grasp and absorb attention.

—*Henry Sloane Coffin*

## What Happens after Death? (Socrates)

[After being condemned to death Socrates consoles his friends:]

IF WE reflect we shall see that we may well hope that death is a good. For the state of death is one of two things: either the dead man ceases to be, and loses all sensation; or, according to the common belief, it is a change and a migration of the soul into another place. And if death is the absence of all sensation, and like the sleep of one whose slumbers are unbroken by any dreams, it will be a wonderful gain. If that is the nature of death, I for one count it a gain. For then it appears that eternity is nothing more than a single night.

But if death is a journey to another place, and the common belief be true, that there are all who have died, what good could be greater than this, my judges? What would you not give to converse with Orpheus and Hesiod and Homer? I am willing to die many times, if this be true.

And you, too, judges, must face death with a good courage, and believe this as a truth, that no evil can happen to a good man, either in life or after death.                                                                —*Plato*

(The Trial and Death of Socrates)

## What Is Dying?

I AM standing upon the seashore. A ship at my side spreads her white sails to the morning breeze and starts for the blue ocean. She is an object of beauty and strength and I stand and watch her until at length she hangs like a speck of white cloud just where the sea and sky come down to mingle with each other. Then someone at my side says: "There! She's gone."

Gone where? Gone from my sight—that is all. She is just as large in mast and hull and spar as she was when she left my side, and just as able to bear her load of living freight to the place of destination. Her diminished size is in me, not in her; and just at the moment when someone at my side says, "There! She's gone," there are other eyes watching her coming, and other voices ready to take up the glad shout, "There she comes!"

And that is dying. —*Anonymous*

## Where Love Is There God Is

IN A certain town in Russia there lived a cobbler, Martin Avdéitch by name. He had a tiny room in a basement the one window of which looked out onto the street. Here he slept, cooked, had his meals and worked. He had plenty to do, for he worked well, used good material, did not charge too much, and could be relied on. If he could do a job by the day required he undertook it; if not, he told the truth and gave no false promises.

After his long day's work he always read the Bible and this night the story was about Simon in Luke's Gospel. "He must have been like me, that Pharisee," thought Martin. "He, too, thought only of himself—how to get a cup of tea, how to keep warm and comfortable." Then Martin laid his head on both his arms and fell asleep.

"Martin!" he suddenly heard, as if someone had breathed the word above his ear. "Look for me tomorrow, for I shall come." He did not know whether he had heard these words in a dream or awake. He put out the lamp and lay down to sleep.

Next morning he rose, as usual, before daylight, and after saying his prayers, he lit the fire and prepared his cabbage soup and buckwheat porridge. Then he lit the samovár, put on his apron, and sat down by the window to his work and thought over the strange message of the night before. He wondered if he would recognize God if he came. So he sat at his work and kept his eye on the passers-by on the street.

Presently an old soldier, Stepánitch, began to clear away the snow from the sidewalk. He was old and broken down, and had evidently not enough strength to shovel the heavy snow. Martin tapped on the window and beckoned to him to come in, and went himself to open the door.

"Come in," he said, "and warm yourself a bit. I'm sure you must be cold." He came in, but as he did so, he tottered and nearly fell. "Come, friend, sit down and have some tea," said Martin. As the old soldier drank his tea Martin told him his strange dream. Stepánitch finished his tumbler and laid it on its side; but Martin stood it up again and refilled it for him. As Stepánitch left he said, "You have given me food and comfort both for soul and body. God bless you, Martin."

Martin stitched away, thinking about the heavenly Father and his doings. A woman passed by the window. She was a stranger, poorly dressed and with a baby in her arms. She stopped by the wall with her back to the wind trying to wrap her baby up though she had hardly anything to wrap it in. Martin heard the baby crying and the woman trying to soothe it but unable to do so. Martin went to the door and called to her, "Come inside. You can wrap him up better in a warm place." As they went down the steps, Martin said, "There, sit down near the stove. Warm yourself and feed the baby."

He brought out a basin and some bread. Then he opened the oven door and poured some cabbage soup into the basin. "Sit down and eat, my dear," said he, "and I'll mind the baby. Why, bless me, I've had children of my own; I know how to manage them."

When the woman had finished Martin brought an old cloak and said, "Though it's a worn-out old thing, it will do to wrap the baby up in. The woman looked at the cloak, then at the old man, and taking it, burst into tears and said, "The Lord bless you, friend. Surely God must have sent me to your window, else the child would have frozen." Martin smiled and said, "It is quite true; it was he made me do it," and he told the woman his dream. Then he pressed sixpence into her hand, saying, "Take this and get your shawl out of pawn."

It was now evening and Martin saw an apple-woman stop just in front of his window. On her back she had a sack full of chips. She put it down, and placing her basket on a post, began to shake down the chips in the sack. While she was doing this a boy in a tattered cap ran up and snatched an apple, but she caught him. The boy screamed and the woman scolded. Martin ran out and caught the boy and said, "Let him go, Granny. Forgive him. He won't do it again. I will pay you for the apple." The woman let him go, and the boy wished to run away, but Martin stopped him.

"Ask the Granny's forgiveness!" said he, "and don't do it another time. I saw you take the apple." The boy began to cry, and asked her pardon. She smiled and said, "Oh, all right," but she added, "He should be whipped." "Oh Granny, Granny," said Martin, "That's our way—but it's not God's way. If he should be whipped for stealing an apple, what should be done to us for our sins?" "That's true enough," said she.

As the old woman was about to hoist the sack on her back, the lad sprang forward to her, saying, "Let me carry it for you, Granny. I'm going your way." The old woman nodded her head, and put the sack on the boy's back, and they went down the street together. Martin smiled as he watched them talking together like old friends.

When they were out of sight he went back to the house and worked till late. Then he took the Gospels from the shelf. As he opened it he thought he heard the words, "Martin, didn't you know me?" He mused over the day and saw again the old soldier, the woman and baby, the apple-woman and the boy, and his soul grew glad. He put on his spectacles and began reading just where it had opened; and at the top of the page he read:

"I was an hungered, and ye gave me meat: I was thirsty, and ye gave me drink: I was a stranger, and ye took me in."

And at the bottom of the page he read: "Inasmuch as ye did it unto one of these my brethren, even these least, ye did it unto me."

And Martin understood that his dream had come true; and that the heavenly Father had really come to him that day, and that he had welcomed him.[1]

—*Leo Tolstoy*
(Twenty-Three Tales)

## Why Were the Saints, Saints?

WHY were the saints, saints?

Because they were cheerful when it was difficult to be cheerful, patient when it was difficult to be patient; and because they pushed on when they wanted to stand still; and kept silent when they wanted to talk, and were agreeable when they wanted to be disagreeable. That was all.

It was quite simple and always will be. —*Anonymous*

## Women and Christianity

I WILL say again that when Jesus was come, women rejoiced in him before either man or angel. I read not that ever any man did give unto Christ so much as one groat; but the women followed him, and ministered to him of their substance. It was a woman that washed his feet with tears, and a woman that anointed his body to the burial. They were women that wept when he was going to the cross, and women that followed him from the cross, and that sat by his sepulchre when he was buried. They were women that were first with him at his resurrection-morn, and women that brought tidings first to his disciples that he was risen from the dead. Women, therefore, are highly favored, and show by these things that they are sharers . . . in the grace of life.

—*John Bunyan*
(Pilgrim's Progress)

## The Wonderful Power of Love

LOVE is a great thing, a good above all others, which alone maketh every burden light, and equaliseth every inequality. For it beareth the burden and maketh it no burden, it maketh every bitter thing to be sweet and of good taste. . . .

Nothing is sweeter than love, nothing stronger, nothing loftier, nothing broader, nothing pleasanter, nothing fuller nor better in heaven nor in earth, for love was born of God and cannot rest save in God above all created things. . . .

Love oftentimes knoweth no measure, but breaketh out above all measure; love feeleth no burden, reckoneth not labours, striveth after more than it is able to do, pleadeth not impossibility, because it judgeth all things which are lawful for it to be possible. It is strong therefore for all things, and it fulfilleth many things, and is successful where he who loveth not faileth and lieth down.

[1] This story as it appears here has been abbreviated and condensed by the editor.

[ 269 ]

Love is watchful, and whilst sleeping still keepeth watch; though fatigued it is not weary, though pressed it is not forced, though alarmed it is not terrified. . . .

Let me love thee more than myself, not loving myself except for thy sake, and all men in thee. —*Thomas à Kempis*
(Imitation of Christ)

## Workmen, Craftsmen, Teachers: Inspired and Called of God

THEN said Moses to the Israelites, "God has specially chosen Bezalêl the son of Uri, the grandson of Hur, who belongs to the clan of Judah, inspiring him with skill and knowledge and competence in every craft, to devise artistic works in gold, silver, and bronze, in cutting jewels to be set, and in wood-carving, that he may work at any skilled craft. He has also given him and Oholiab the son of Ahisamak, belonging to the clan of Dan, ability to teach others, endowing them with skill in every skilful craft, in engraving, in decorating, in handling violet, purple, and scarlet yarn, in working with fine linen, in weaving, and in all sorts of trades and arts. Bezalêl and Oholiab are to do the work, along with any skilful craftsman who is inspired by God with skill and knowledge for carrying out all the work upon the sanctuary, as God has given orders."

Moses then called Bezalêl and Oholiab and all the skilful craftsmen whom God had endowed with skill, men who had felt moved to undertake the work.[1] —*Exodus 35:30-36:2* (Moffatt)

## The World Is Good

FOR my part, I find the world is good. It is a most reliable paymaster, whichever way you make your investment, and I am glad to be in it. Everything seems to have a purpose, and from that fact I deduce a purposer. The world seems reasonable, and therefore likely to end reasonably. The evolution of love, the development of intellect, the unceasing metabolism of the body, considered with the principle of the conservation of energy, always seemed to me to argue against the annihiliation of personality . . . Some men hate the whole universe, because they realize how brief the tenure of things they love in life is. But I am no pessimist. Knowing that I only stay for a time alongside of what I call my property, I am still delighted with all I get, enjoying immensely the use of it while I have it, and believing, as Christ teaches, that so-called death cannot rob me of spiritual friendships and assets. If I count what I can contribute to life, and not what I can get out of it, that of itself makes it worth while. The gauge is not what we have, but what we do with what we have.

I am sure that I am not my body and I am sure that I am not my house. But for all that, I know that I am I, and that I shall always continue to be so is sufficiently probable to satisfy me.
—*Wilfred Thomason Grenfell*
(The Adventure of Life)

[1] Slightly altered.

## The World Says, but Jesus Says

### The World Says:

HAPPY are the proud and the rich.
Happy are they who are free from sorrow.
Happy are the self-assertive and ambitious.
Happy are [those who have] no Puritan conscience.
Happy are the "hard-boiled" realists.
Happy are the voluptuaries of pleasure.
Happy are the heroes of war and the field of honor.
Happy are the prudent who avoid persecution.
Happy are they who escape slander, insults, and ridicule.

### But Jesus Says:

Happy are the humble, the poor in spirit.
Happy are the mourners, the penitent.
Happy are the unassuming, the self-controlled.
Happy are they who long earnestly for goodness.
Happy are the kind and merciful.
Happy are the pure-minded.
Happy are the peacemakers.
Happy are the martyrs to a great cause.
Happy are you who bear insults and slanders because you are Christians.
—*George Walter Fiske*
(A Study of Jesus' Own Religion)

## Youth

YOUTH is not a time of life; it is a state of mind. It is not a matter of red cheeks and supple knees; it is a temper of will, a quality of the imagination, a vigor of the emotions; it is a freshness of the deep springs of life.

Youth means a predominance of courage over timidity, of the spirit of adventure over the love of ease. This sometimes exists in a person of fifty more than in one of twenty.

Nobody grows old by merely living a number of years; people grow old by deserting their ideals. Years may wrinkle the skin but to give up enthusiasm wrinkles the soul. Worry, doubt, distrust, fear and despair—these are the long, long years that bow the head and turn the growing spirit back to dust.

We are as young as our faith, as old as our doubt; as young as our confidence, as old as our fear; as young as our hopes, as old as our despair.

As long as the central place of your heart receives messages of beauty, hope, cheer, courage, grandeur, and power from the earth, from men, and from the Infinite, so long are we young.

When the heart is covered with the snows of pessimism and the ice of cynicism, then are we grown old indeed.                    —*Anonymous*

# BOOK IV

# PRAYERS

•

## INTRODUCTION

It is a central teaching of the Christian religion that God, the Father, loves everyone with a depth and intensity that even the imagination of man cannot fully fathom, and that he is ever seeking to inspire, guide, and teach all mankind. Therefore it does not seem to be in keeping with Christian faith to beg, beseech and urge God to remember the needy, to visit the sick, to redeem the erring, to feed the hungry and to comfort the dying. The problem is never with God; it is always with us. His love and inspiration and guidance are for all who respond to his love. He first and always loves us.

A large number of the quoted prayers in the following pages have therefore been slightly altered so that it will not appear that one is seeking to persuade an unwilling God, but that he is affirming faith in God's eternal love.

Most of the individual prayers that could be adapted to group worship have been changed to the plural, and some, by the change of a word or reference have been brought into harmony with the Christian teaching about God. But whenever prayers have been altered the phrasing and the main purpose of the prayer have been maintained.

## Abide in God

O thou from whom to be turned away is to fall; to whom to be turned is to rise, and in whom to abide is to stand fast forever; thou wilt give us in all our duties thy help; in all our perplexities thy guidance; in all our dangers thy protection; and in all our sorrows thy peace. Amen.

—*John Hunter*

## Adoration

O God, thou art our God, early will we seek thee. Blessed art thou, O Lord, Who gatheredst the water into the sea, and broughtest to sight the earth, and madest to sprout herbs and fruit trees. There are the depths and the sea as an heap, lakes, rivers, springs; earth, continent, and isles, mountains, hills, and valleys, glebe, meadows, glades, green pasture, corn, hay; herbs and flowers for food, enjoyment, medicine; fruit trees bearing fruits, wine, oil, and spices, and trees for timber; things under the earth, stones, metals, minerals, coals; blood, and fire, and vapour of smoke.

—*Lancelot Andrewes*

## Adventuring with God

LORD of life and death,
We thank thee for the great adventure of life,
With its untold possibilities,
Its uncalculable chances,
Its mighty opportunities.
We thank thee that—if we have thee with us—
There is no monotony or weariness in the world:
But we go on—for ever exploring and adventuring,
Across new seas where ship has never sailed before;
Over towering mountain-ranges,
Whence we look forth upon new expanses of wonder
Heretofore unseen by the eye of man.
We thank thee that, for those who dwell with thee,
Each day opens new a continent of vivid experience;
Each day shows new a world to conquer;
For thy love is new every morning,
And life with thee is daily born again from its beginning.

—*Anonymous*
(A Book of Prayers Written for Use in an Indian College)

## Aflame with God

O GOD, we thank thee for this universe, our great home; for its vastness and its riches, and for the manifoldness of the life which teems upon it and of which we are part. We praise thee for the arching sky and the blessed winds, for the driving clouds and the constellations on high. We praise thee for the salt sea and the running water, and for the everlasting hills, for the trees, and for the grass under our feet. We thank thee for our senses by which we can see the splendor of the morning, and hear the jubilant songs of love, and smell the breath of the springtime. We pray that we may have hearts wide open to all this joy and beauty and may keep our souls from being so steeped in care or so darkened by passion that we pass heedless and unseeing when even the thorn bush by the wayside is aflame with the glory of God.

—*Walter Rauschenbusch*
(Prayers of the Social Awakening)

## After Moving into a New House

OUR FATHER in Heaven, we are gathered round our table here in this new house today for the first time. In deep reverence and humility we pray that we may make thee the centre of our dwelling, Father of us all, thou Spirit of Eternal Love.

After years of planning and saving, our dream has come true and now we have at last complete, the house we have so long desired. We thank thee, our Father, for bringing to happy fulfilment these hopes and dreams.

We thank thee for all the good times we have had planning the house and garden. We thank thee for the little trees and flowers planted by loving hands. We thank thee for all the new things made by each one to add to the beauty and usefulness of the new house, the pot-holders, the rugs and curtains, the footstool and fireside seat and pictures.

We thank thee for all the workmen, the contractor, the carpenters and masons, the electricians and plumbers and painters who have done their work so carefully and well.

We thank thee for all those others who invented so many helpful machines for our comfort and health.

We thank thee for the beautiful wood that grew long years in the forest, to make our walls sturdy and give us joy to see.

Now that all preparations are completed, we have come to live here and make this building a home. May only love and kindness and helpfulness dwell within these walls, O God. May it be filled from the beginning with joy and happiness and good fellowship. May our warm love for each other keep it always an island of peace and harmony, in the midst of whatever conflict or struggle we may find without.

May all who enter find love and warm welcome.

May all who go out of its doors, go in peace, with increased courage and faith in mankind.

May no one leave our home hungry for bread or kindness.

With grateful hearts and sincere purpose we dedicate this house to all the uses and high ideals of a Christian home. Amen.

—*Lulu Snyder Hamilton*
(God Lives in Homes)

### Ahabak

WITH abounding love hast thou loved, O Lord our God. With great and overflowing pity hast thou had pity on us, our Father and our King. O our Father, merciful Father, ever compassionate, thou hast put into our hearts the power to discern and to understand; to hear, to learn and to teach; to observe and do and fulfil in love all the words of instruction in thy law. . . . We unite our hearts to love and to fear thy name that we may never be put to shame. Thou, O God, dost work our salvation. May we in love give thanks to thee and proclaim thy unity.

—*Anonymous*
(From the Jewish Shema)

### All Classes

OUR Father, we pray for all ministers of religion, and all who guide the thoughts of the people; for artists and authors, musicians and journalists; that our common life may be crowned with truth and beauty:

[ 275 ]

For all who heal the body, guard the health of the people, and tend the sick; that they may follow in the footsteps of Christ, the great physician:

For all on whose labor we depend for the necessaries of life; for those who carry on the commerce of the world, that they may seek no private gain which would hinder the good of all:

For parents and children; that purity, love, and honor may dwell in our homes, and duty and affection may be the bond of our family life:

For the weak in body and mind, that they may be restored to health; for those that are depressed and in pain, that they may be helped and comforted:

For all who draw nigh unto death, that they may know thy presence with them through the valley of the shadow, and may awake to behold thy face. Amen.

*—Anonymous*
*(New Every Morning)*

## All in Responsible Positions

O GOD, if they but respond to thee, thou dost guide all those who are bearing the burden of great responsibilities and wilt prosper their efforts for the welfare of the world. They who wait upon thee are inspired with wise judgment, that they may help to build a brotherhood of mankind in the fatherhood of God. And may we all be set free from the spirit which leads to strife, from the temper which refuses to forgive, and has no wish to forget; and from lack of faith in thee.

*—Anonymous*
*(New Every Morning)*

## All Nations Shall Worship Thee

LEADER: O worship the Lord in the beauty of holiness.
PEOPLE: Let the whole earth stand in awe of him.
L.: Whom have I in heaven but thee?
P.: And there is none upon earth that I desire in comparison of thee.
L.: Great and marvellous are thy works, Lord God Almighty.
P.: Just and true are thy ways, thou King of Saints.
L.: Who shall not fear thee, O Lord, and glorify thy name?
P.: For all nations shall come and worship before thee.
L.: The earth shall be full of the knowledge of God.
P.: As the waters cover the sea.[1]

*—Anonymous*
*(Westminster Abbey Prayer)*

## Anxieties and Fears

O MOST loving Father, who hast taught us to give thanks for all things, to dread nothing but the loss of thee, and to cast all our care on thee

[1] Used in World Church Service in the Abbey, Whitsunday, 1943

[ 276 ]

who carest for us: thou wilt preserve us from faithless fears and worldly anxieties, that no clouds of this mortal life may hide from us the light of that love which is immortal, and which thou hast shown to us in all the experiences of life. Amen.

*—Anonymous*
(New Every Morning)

## Artists and Craftsmen, Teachers and Writers

O GOD, thou dost lead men to desire thy perfection, to seek for truth, and to rejoice in beauty; and dost illumine and inspire all thinkers and writers, all artists and craftsmen; and all teachers and students in the schools and colleges of our land, who put their trust in thee. In whatsoever is true and pure and lovely may thy name be hallowed, and thy kingdom come on earth. Amen.

*—Anonymous*
(New Every Morning)

## Aspiration

O GOD of peace, we turn aside from an unquiet world, seeking rest for our spirits and light for our thoughts. We bring our work to be sanctified, our wounds to be healed, our hopes to be renewed and our better selves to be quickened, so that we may not sin but serve and walk humbly with thee. O thou in whom there is harmony, thou alone canst silence the discords of our lives. Thou whose greatness is beyond our utmost thought dost alone lift us above our common littleness and sendst visions of the beauty that is in thy world, of the love that is in thee, and of the good that may be in us. Amen.

*—Anonymous*

## At Twilight

Now as twilight enfolds us, we find safe shelter with all we love, and whom thou lovest more than we, beneath thy wings of mercy over-spread. May all thy children have rest and sleep, and if we awaken when the morrow dawns may we be still with thee to the glory of thy name. Amen.

*—Anonymous*
(The United Church Observer)

## Author of Life and Death

ETERNAL is thy power, O Lord, thou art mighty to save. In loving-kindness thou sustainest the living; in the multitude of thy mercies, thou preservest all. Thou upholdest the falling and healest the sick, freest the captives, and keepest faith with thy children in death as in life. Who

[ 277 ]

is like unto thee, Almighty God, Author of life and death, Source of salvation? Praised be thou, O Lord, who hast implanted within us eternal life!

—*Anonymous*
(The Union Prayerbook for Jewish Worship)

## A Beatitude

BLESSED are all bulbs and seeds, for they are promise of a spring to come, for they are symbols of a world to be, a promise of immortality, of life out of death and hope within despair, of whiter dawns on other days, of harvests, beautiful and brown, of plenty and of prophecy. Blessed are all bulbs and seeds.

—*William L. Stidger*

## Before Christmas

AT THE approach of the Christmas season, our Father, we seek thy presence, thankful beyond words for this beautiful time of the year, for all it means in happiness to little children and especially for the joy it brings to all. Thou hast been our Guide in years past when we created our traditions for this season. Every year they have taken on more meaning and become living symbols of our loyalty and love for each other and our devotion to Christ.

O God, thou wouldst have us explore new ways of adding meaning to these days when love is warmest in our hearts, and for expressing our love to thee especially through our concern for thy little ones. The great power of love which this season calls forth has never been given adequate expression. After we have done all the customary things, there seem to be great unused energies of good will left over, unexpressed. Thou wilt teach us how to direct it into channels of blessing for those who need it, for lives barren and hungry for affection. Let us not be selfish in keeping to ourselves alone. We would not be unaware of the lives about us that are hungry for love as some are for food, but neither would we burden others with sadness which would mar the perfect joy of these days.

We pray, our Father, for the peace and calmness that come from the indwelling of thy spirit. Let no business of preparations mar the serenity and evenness of our disposition. Let no attention to details of house or preparing of food keep us from being constantly aware of the supreme meaning of these days. May we be delivered from all temptation for elaborate externals or outward show. May we never depart from the beauty of simplicity. O God, may we have inexhaustible reserves of good humor and patience and understanding, that we may bring to a clearer, warmer glow the flame of family devotion and renew in the hearts of children and of all people the desire to make these blessings of home and family life available for all children of men.

—*Lulu Snyder Hamilton*
(God Lives in Homes)

## Benedictions

AND now unto the King eternal, immortal, invisible, the only wise God, be honor and glory for ever and ever. Amen.

*—I Timothy 1:17*

Now unto him that is able to do exceeding abundantly above all that we ask or think, according to the power that worketh in us; unto him be glory in the Church by Christ Jesus, throughout all ages, world without end. Amen.

*—Ephesians 3:20-21*

And now to God our Father be all honor, glory, thanksgiving and praise, this day and for ever more. Amen.

The blessing of God Almighty, Creator, Word, Eternal Spirit is upon all who truly seek him and abides with them forever. Amen.

The Lord bless thee and keep thee: The Lord make his face shine upon thee, and be gracious unto thee: The Lord lift up his countenance upon thee and give thee peace. Amen.

*—Numbers 6:24-26*

May the words of our mouths, and the meditations of our hearts and the whole influence of our lives be acceptable in thy sight, O God, our strength and our redeemer. Amen.

*—Based on Psalm 19:14*

Now may the God of hope fill you with all joy and peace in believing, that ye may abound in hope through the power of his spirit. Amen.

*—Romans 15:13*

Now the God of peace . . . make you perfect in every good work to do his will, working in you that which is well pleasing in his sight, through Jesus Christ; to whom be glory for ever and ever. Amen.

*—Hebrews 13:20-21*

Be perfect, be of good comfort, be of one mind, live in peace; and the God of love and peace shall be with you. Amen.

*—Corinthians 13:11*

Rejoice in the Lord alway: and again I say, Rejoice. Be careful for nothing; but in everything by prayer and supplication with thanksgiving let your requests be made known unto God. And the peace of God, which passeth all understanding, shall keep your hearts and minds through Jesus Christ. Amen.

*—Philistines 4:4, 6-7*

The grace of the Lord Jesus Christ, and the love of God and the communion of his spirit be with you all. Amen.

*—Corinthians 14:13*

## Bless Ye the Lord

O ALL ye works of the Lord, bless ye the Lord: praise him and magnify him for ever.

O ye heavens, bless ye the Lord: O ye sun and moon, bless ye the Lord.

O ye showers and dew, bless ye the Lord: O ye winds of God, bless ye the Lord.

O let the earth bless the Lord: praise him and magnify him for ever.

O ye mountains and hills, bless ye the Lord: O all ye green things upon the earth, bless ye the Lord.

O all ye fowls of the air, bless ye the Lord: O all ye beasts and cattle, bless ye the Lord.

O ye children of men, bless ye the Lord: praise him and magnify him for ever. Amen.

*—Based on Psalm 148*

## Blessed Are the Peacemakers

O GOD, who art Peace everlasting, whose chosen reward is the gift of peace, and who hast taught us that the peacemakers are thy children, may we so live that everything discordant may utterly vanish, and that all that makes for peace may be sought and cherished by us always. Amen.

*—Anonymous*
(Mozarabic and Ambrosian Rites)

## Blessed Art Thou, O Lord

BLESSED art thou, O Lord, Who broughtest forth the beasts of the earth, and cattle, and every thing that creepeth upon the earth, for food, clothing, help; and madest man after thine image, to rule the earth, and blessedst him.

The forecounsel, fashioning hand, breath of life, image of God, appointment over thy works, charge to the angels concerning him, paradise. Heart, reins, eyes, ears, tongue, hands, feet; life, sense, reason, spirit, free will, memory conscience; the revelation of God, writings of the law, oracles of prophets, melody of psalms, instruction of proverbs, experience of histories, service of sacrifices.

Blessed art thou, O Lord, for thy great and precious promises.

*—Lancelot Andrewes*

## Blessed Art Thou, O Lord God

BLESSED be thou, O Lord God, for ever and ever. Thine, O Lord, is the greatness, and the glory, and the victory, and the majesty: for all that is in the heaven and in the earth is thine: thine is the kingdom, O Lord, and thou art exalted as head above all: both riches and honour come of thee, and of thine own do we give unto thee. Amen.

*—Anonymous*

## Blessed Be Thou, O God

BLESSED be thou, Lord God of Israel our Father, for ever and ever. Thine, O Lord, is the greatness, and the power, and the glory, and the victory, and the majesty: for all that is in the heaven and in the earth is thine.

The nations tremble at thy presence, every king and every nation. Thine is the kingdom, O Lord, and thou art exalted as head above all. Both riches and honour come of thee, and thou reignest over all; and in thine hand is power and might; and in thine hand it is to make great, and to give strength unto all. Now therefore, our God, we thank thee, and praise thy glorious name.

*—Lancelot Andrewes*

## A Bride's Prayer

O FATHER, my heart is filled with a happiness so wonderful that I am almost afraid. This is my wedding day, and I pray thee that the beautiful joy of this morning may never grow dim with years of regret for the step I am about to take. Rather, may its memories become more sweet and tender with each passing anniversary.

Thou hast sent to me one who seems all worthy of my deepest regard. May I have the power to keep him ever true and loving as now and to prove indeed a helpmate, a sweetheart, a friend, a steadfast guiding star among all the temptations that beset the impulsive hearts of men. I pray that I may have skill to make home the best-loved place of all and to make its lights shine farther than any glow that would dim its radiance.

With thee I shall be able to meet the little misunderstandings and aches of my new life bravely. I know thou art with me as I start on my mission of womanhood, and will stay my path from failure all the way. May we walk with thee even to the end of our journey.

O Father, may our wedding day be blessed, and our marriage night hallowed. Sanctify my motherhood, if thou seest fit to grant me that privilege, and when all my youthful charms are faded, and the cares and lessons of life have left their touches, let physical fascination give way to the greater charm of companionship. And so may we walk hand-in-hand, down the highway of the Valley of Final Shadow, which we shall then be able to lighten with the sunshine of good and happy lives.

Our Father, this is my prayer. Amen.

*—Anonymous*

## A Bridegroom's Prayer

O GOD, my Father, the greatest joy has come to me—the unquestioning devotion of a true and noble life-companion. May I ever treasure this priceless gift. My love on this my wedding day is deep and strong, and my earnest prayer is that it may grow and ripen, and become ever more tender and understanding with each succeeding year.

[ 281 ]

I pray, O Lord, that I may never be untrue even in thought and may never give her cause to doubt, or bring pain to her pure spirit.

Thou hast made us with strong appetites, desires and passions. May these of mine be always restrained and hallowed by sensitive consideration and abiding love. May the physical ever be under the control of the spirit. And if our marriage is blessed with children, I pray that we may be consecrated to the high calling of fatherhood and motherhood and that we, together, may be worthy to teach, by word and life, the love of God to them.

And, my Father, may I so cherish my wife, that we will be lovers always, and hand in hand with each other, and with our hands in thine, face life and death with courage and dignity because we are bound up in the bundle of life with thee, our God and heavenly Father. Amen.

—*A. J. William Myers*

## Brotherly Love

OUR longing, O Lord, is to love thee with all our heart, with all our mind, and with all our soul, and our neighbor as ourselves: that the grace of brotherly love may dwell in us, and all envy, harshness and ill will die in us. May we rejoice in the happiness and good success of others, sympathize with them in their sorrows, and put away all harsh judgments and envious thoughts; and so follow thee, who thyself art true and perfect love. Amen.

—*Anonymous*
(New Every Morning)

## Calls to Worship

AND ye shall seek me and find me when ye shall search for me with all your heart.

—*Jeremiah 29:13*

The Lord is my strength and my song and he is become my salvation. I shall not die but live and declare the works of the Lord.
Worship the Lord in the beauty of holiness.

—*Psalm 96:9*

The Lord is nigh to all that call upon him, unto all that call upon him in truth.

—*Psalm 114:18*

Know thou the God of thy father, serve him with a whole heart, and with a willing mind; for the Lord searcheth the hearts and understandeth all the imaginings of the thoughts; if thou seek him he will be found by thee.

—*Chronicles 28:9*

[ 282 ]

Praised be he who by his creative word called the universe into being. Praised be he who sustains it by his might. Praised be he who orders it in his wisdom and establishes the world in righteousness.

Our help is in the Lord who made heaven and earth.

*—Psalm 124:8*

Let us with a gladsome mind
Praise the Lord, for he is kind.

*—John Milton*

Enter into his house with thanksgiving, and into his courts with praise: Be thankful unto him, and bless his name, for the Lord is good.

*—Psalm 100:4-5*

Walk slowly, be silent; for this is the place where loving kindness reminds us of God.

The sacrifices of God are a broken spirit; a broken and a contrite heart, O God, thou wilt not despise.

*—Psalm 2:17*

I will arise and go to my Father, and will say unto him, Father, I have sinned against heaven and before thee, and am no more worthy to be called thy son.

*—Luke 15:18-19*

Beloved, let us love one another: for love is of God; and everyone that loveth is born of God, and knoweth God.

*—John 4:7*

The Lord is my light and my salvation; whom shall I fear? The Lord is the strength of my life; of whom shall I be afraid?

*—Psalm 27:1*

Wait on the Lord: be of good courage, and he shall strengthen thine heart: wait, I say, on the Lord.

*—Psalm 27:14*

Let the wicked forsake his way, and the unrighteous man his thought, and let him return unto the Lord, and he will have mercy upon him, and to our God, and he will abundantly pardon.

*—Isaiah 55:7*

They that wait upon the Lord shall renew their strength; they shall mount up with wings as eagles; they shall run, and not be weary; and they shall walk, and not faint.

*—Isaiah 40:31*

[ 283 ]

O come, let us worship and bow down: let us kneel before the Lord our maker. For he is our God; and we are the people of his pasture, and the sheep of his hand.

*—Psalm 95:6-7*

Serve the Lord with gladness; come before his presence with singing. For the Lord is good; his mercy is everlasting; and his truth endureth to all generations.

*—Psalm 100:2, 5*

Let us search and try our ways and turn again unto the Lord. Let us lift our heart with our hands unto God.

*—Lamentations 3:40-41*

Rend your heart and not your garments, and turn unto the Lord your God; for he is gracious and merciful, slow to anger, and of great mercy.

*—Joel 2:13*

And the Spirit and the bride say, Come. And let him that heareth say, Come. And let him that is athirst come. And whosoever will, let him take the water of life freely.

*—Revelations 22:17*

O come, let us sing unto the Lord: let us heartily rejoice in the strength of our salvation. Let us come before his presence with thanksgiving: and show ourselves glad in him with psalms. For the Lord is a great God: and a great King above all gods.

*—Psalm 95:1-3*

Holy, holy, holy is the Lord of hosts: the whole earth is full of his glory.

*—Isaiah 6:3*

## Charity and Good Will

WE HUMBLY pray, O Father:

That we may be honest and true in all our dealings, and gentle and merciful to the faults of others, remembering of how much gentleness and mercy we stand in need ourselves;

That we may earnestly try to live in thy true faith, honor, and love, and in charity and good will with all our fellow creatures;

That we may worship thee in every beautiful and wonderful thing thou hast made, and sympathize with the whole world of thy glorious creation. Amen.

*—Charles Dickens*

[ 284 ]

## A Children's Litany of Praise

OUR Father,
For Jesus, teacher, physician and friend
We praise thee, O Lord.
For Pasteur and Lister and all the microbe hunters who gave their
lives in the attempt to control disease,
We praise thee, Lord.
For St. Francis and all like him who loved the birds and gave their
strength and their money to help people,
We praise thee, Lord.
For all who work with lepers and sick people in mission lands, and for
the privilege of sending money to help in this work,
We praise thee, O Lord.
For all who built and furnished this church and who made it a social
place of worship,
We praise thee, O Lord.
For all these and myriads of others who lived and worked in the spirit
of Jesus and who worshipped and served thee, the loving God and
Father,
We praise thee, O Lord.
For our boys and girls, who are the teachers, musicians, artists, re-
formers and the friendly folk in the better world that is to be,
We praise thee, O Lord our God and Father. Amen.
                            —*A. J. William Myers and Alma N. Schilling*
                                                    (Living Stone)


## Chippewa Indian Prayer

UPON the Mountain top alone I stand,
To Manitou, Great Spirit, I pray,
And in silence bring my daily wants to him. . . .
Abundance and happiness shall be in the teepee;
Manitou, the Great Spirit, hears.

                                                    —*Anonymous*


## Collects

O GOD, who art visible only to the pure in heart, and can be known
only by such as love the truth, we would in thy strength cleanse our
minds from all insincerity and self-deception, that there may be strengthened in us the appeal of all that is true and beautiful; that evil may lose
its power over us and that we ever more perfectly may do thy will. Amen.

O God, creator spirit, who hast made all men in thine own image,
thou hast commanded us to stir up this spirit within us that we may
attain something of its possibilities ourselves and may find thee in the
hearts of those with whom we dwell and whom we serve. Amen.

[ 285 ]

O God from whom all pure desires and holy aspirations come, we pray that we may be delivered from all coldness of heart and wanderings of mind, that with steadfast thoughts and kindled affections we may worship thee in spirit and in truth. Amen.

Almighty and everlasting God who dost enkindle the flame of love in the hearts of thy saints and dost grant to us the same faith and power of love; may we, as we rejoice in their triumphs, also follow their good example, in the spirit of Jesus Christ our master. Amen.

*—The Order of Divine Service*

Almighty and everlasting God, who adornest thy Church by the compassions of holy martyrs; we pray that, like them, we may glorify thee by our life and, in time of trial, prove faithful even unto death. Amen.

*—Common of Saints*[1]

## Daily Duties

WE PRAY, O God, that this day we may do whatever duty lies before us with cheerfulness and sincerity of heart and in all things fearlessly do what we know to be right. Thou alone canst save us from hypocrisy and pretence, and keep us truthful, unselfish and strong. And so we shall be brought to the ending of the day unashamed and with a quiet mind.

*—Anonymous*
(New Every Morning)

## The Day and the Night

PRAISED be thou, O Lord our God, ruler of the world, by whose law the shadows of evening fall and the gates of morn are opened. In wisdom thou hast established the changes of times and seasons and ordered the ways of the stars in their heavenly courses. Creator of heaven and earth, O living God, rule thou over us forever. Praised be thou, O Lord, for the day and its work and for the night and its rest.

*—Anonymous*

## The Day Returns

THE day returns and brings us the petty round of irritating concerns and duties. Help us to play the man. Help us to perform them with laughter and kind faces. Let cheerfulness abound with industry. Give us to go blithely on our business all this day, and bring us to our resting beds, weary and content and undishonored, and grant us in the end the gift of sleep. Amen.

*—Robert Louis Stevenson*

[1] Slightly altered.

## Dedication of a Home

OH GOD, we thank thee for the end of our labor, and for the finish of this new house we have built. By thy life in us we have had the wisdom and the strength for the work of building. All the material in the house is from thee. Before we began to build, behold thou didst go before us in the way, making for us what we would need to build our house. . . . Thy love is ever over us, as the roof of this house is over us; thy care is around us, as the walls of this house are around us. May we love one another in this house, and may we love thee. Then shall this house be blessed both in thy sight and before the eyes of the people in this town. Amen.

*—Jean MacKenzie*
(Listen)

## Dignity of Labor

THOU wilt show us, O God, the way of patient industry: that, honoring and praising thee in the work of our hands, and learning the dignity of honest labor, we may be faithful in small and humble tasks, good comrades with our fellows, and brave to fight against all that may hinder fulness of life. Amen.

*—Anonymous*
(New Every Morning)

## Dignity of Service

O GOD, who hast shewn us the dignity of service and dost teach us to be courteous and considerate to all who serve us in shops and offices, on our journeys, and in our homes; that so they may find joy and honour in their work, and may do it in praise of thee. Amen.

*—Anonymous*
(New Every Morning)

## Drivers of Cars

ALMIGHTY God, who dost sanctify the common ways of life we pray that all who use the roads may ever have the spirit of courtesy and good-will, of carefulness and self-control; that by our thought for others, we may all be preserved from needless danger and sudden death, and may live to glorify thee in our going out and our coming in. Amen.

*—Anonymous*
(New Every Morning)

## An Early Greek Prayer

MAY I be no one's enemy and may I be the friend of that which is eternal and abides. May I never quarrel with those nearest to me; and if I do, may I be reconciled quickly. May I never devise evil against any

[ 287 ]

one; if any devise evil against me, may I escape uninjured and without the need of hurting him. May I love, seek, and attain only that which is good. May I wish for all men's happiness and envy none. May I never rejoice in the ill-fortune of one who has wronged me. . . . When I have done or said what is wrong, may I never wait for the rebuke of others, but always rebuke myself until I make amends. . . . May I win no victory that harms either me or my opponent. . . . May I reconcile friends who are wroth with one another. May I, to the extent of my power, give all needful help to my friends and to all who are in want. May I never fail a friend in danger. When visiting those in grief may I be able by gentle and healing words to soften their pain. . . . May I respect myself. . . . May I always keep tame that which rages within me. . . . May I accustom myself to be gentle, and never be angry with people because of circumstances. May I never discuss who is wicked and what wicked things he has done, but know good men and follow in their footsteps.

*—Anonymous*[1]

## Entering a Church

FRIEND, you have come to this church: leave it not without earnest prayer.

Pray to God who loves you and bids you welcome and awaits your greeting.

Give thanks for those whose faith and vision and generous gifts have built this place to the glory of God and the service of mankind.

Praise God for his gifts of beauty in painting and architecture, handcraft and music.

Resolve that we who now live may help to build the spiritual fabric of the nation and of the world in truth, beauty, and goodness and that as we, in the spirit of Jesus, draw near to our Father in love and service, we may draw nearer one to another in perfect brotherhood.

The Lord preserve thy going out and thy coming in.

*—Anonymous*
(Church of St. John the Divine, New York)

## The Eucharist or Lord's Supper

IN THE service of thanksgiving, called the eucharist, give thanks thus. First, for the cup: "We thank thee, our Father, for the holy vine of David—thy child, which thou hast revealed to us through Jesus thy child. Thine is the glory for ever." Then, for the broken bread: "We thank thee, our Father, for the life and knowledge which thou hast revealed to us through Jesus thy child. Thine is the glory for ever. Even as

[1] Translated by Gilbert Murray in *Five Stages of Greek Religion*. He says the prayer is "from a certain Eusebius, a late Ionic Platonist of whom almost nothing is known, not even the date at which he lived."

this broken bread was scattered over the mountains and was brought together and made one, so may thy church be brought together from the ends of the earth into thy kingdom. For thine is the glory and the power through Jesus Christ for ever."

The after communion prayer:

After eating, thus give thanks: "We thank thee, holy Father, for thy holy name which thou hast sheltered in our hearts as in a tent. We thank thee for the knowledge, for the faith and for the immortality which thou hast revealed to us through Jesus thy child. Thine is the glory for ever. Thou, Lord and ruler of all, hast created all things for thy name's sake, and hast given food and drink to men for their enjoyment, that they might thank thee. To us thou hast vouchsafed spiritual food and drink and everlasting life through thy child. Above all things we thank thee that thou art mighty. Thine is the glory for ever. Remember, Lord, thy church, to ward off from it all evil and to make it perfect in thy love; bring it together from the four winds, made ready in holiness, into thy kingdom which thou hast prepared for it; for thine is the power and the glory for ever. Let grace come and let this world pass away. Hosanna to the God of David. Whoever is holy, let him come: whoever is not, let him repent. Maran atha, Amen.

*—The Didache[1]*

## Evening at Home

O LORD, our heavenly Father, we pray that we may live in thy spirit in our homes during the coming day. May we be loving and patient in our families, forgiving others as we remember how much we ourselves need to be forgiven. We pray that we may be kept from all hastiness of temper and all want of thoughtfulness for others in little things. We pray that in our homes the law of love may reign, bringing to us a foretaste of thy Kingdom, where thy love shall be the everlasting joy of thy people for ever.—Amen.

*—Anonymous*
(Now Every Morning)

## Everliving God

EVERLIVING God, thou abidest amidst the ceaseless tides of change which sweep away the generations of man! In the springtime of the year when field and forest reawaken from the seeming death of winter, when earth and sky resound with the song of life reborn, a renewed faith and confidence surge through our hearts. The clouds that darkened our spirits are dispelled by the miracle of reviving nature. The gloom of the valley of the shadow is pierced by the light of thy presence. Beyond the winter of death smiles thine eternal springtime. It cannot be that in a world of unending life, we, thy children, are given over to destruction; that fash-

[1] The oldest Christian Church manual, chapters IX and X. This is the earliest description of the Lord's Supper or Communion Service.

ioned in thine image we are doomed to annihilation. The spirit, implanted within us, cannot be only a passing breath. Thou art our dwelling place in life and in death.

—*Anonymous*
(The Union Prayerbook for Jewish Worship)

## The Fellowship of Suffering

ALMIGHTY God, who art afflicted in the afflictions of thy people, and art full of compassion and tender mercy: thou dost hear us as we pray for all who are in trouble; for those who have lost the health and strength that once was theirs; for those who are trying bravely to face illness and suffering:

For all who are handicapped in the race of life through no fault of their own; for the defective and delicate and the permanently injured:

For those who lie in pain; for any who have to undergo an operation; for the blind, the deaf, and the dumb; and for all who have to watch their loved ones suffer:

For those whose livelihood is insecure; for the hungry, the homeless, and the destitute; for those who have the will to work, but lack the opportunity of working:

For those who have to bear their burdens alone, and for all who have lost those whom they love:

For those who are in doubt or anguish of soul; for those who are victims of depression, anxiety, and fear; for those whose suffering is unrelieved by the knowledge of love.

And we thank thee, O Father, for all who hallow pain: for those whose thought is always for others; for those whose faith brings light to the dark places of life; for those whose patience inspires others to endure. We bless thee, O loving Father, that all who are bound in the mysterious fellowship of suffering, and have the sense of comradeship with others and the knowledge of thy love as revealed in Jesus, have the peace which passes all understanding. Amen.

—*Anonymous*
(New Every Morning)

## For All Animals

WE REJOICE, O God, that thy care embraces all animals, especially those in whose companionship and service we find joy and help. We entreat for them mercy and pity from those who deal with them, and hearts of compassion, gentle hands and kindly words. May we all be true friends of animals, and share with them the blessing of the merciful. Amen.

—*Anonymous*
(New Every Morning)

## For Animals

O GOD, who hast shown us that all the lower creation is thine, and that all birds and animals are under thy care, we praise thee for the love of all who have labored in the past to deliver animals from cruelty, neglect, ill treatment and needless pain.

We thank thee, Father, for all persons and all societies that minister to the wellbeing of domestic and wild animals and birds and household pets. May we fight valiantly for these our friends that cannot speak for themselves. And we pray that the hearts of all men and women may be gentle with love for all thy creation. Amen.

*—Anonymous*

## For Our Automobile

OUR Father, many times we come into thy presence to give thee thanks for thy manifold gifts to us, and to seek thy guidance as we venture in new ways. Daily we thank thee in our hearts for our home and each other, for health and food, for work and friends. Today we thank thee again for all these constant benefits which come to us so continuously from thy bountiful hands that we are likely to take them for granted.

Our special thanksgiving today is for our automobile and for inventors and workmen who made it possible. We want so to live with thee, our Father, that thou wilt strengthen us in our purpose to use this power worthily and to keep constantly in our mind the code we have made for ourselves:

To obey every traffic law, even when there seems to be no need of it;

To be courteous always to other drivers, even if they are in the wrong, or discourteous to us;

To be especially considerate of pedestrians;

To take no hazards at any time;

To consider the needs of other members of the family before our own pleasure; and

To be generous in using our car for others whenever possible.

It is our sincere purpose, our Father, to use this instrument and this power only for good. In thee we shall have strength of will to keep to our purpose, and self-control not to be tempted to show off before others, but to make our ways thy ways every day of our lives. Amen.

*—Lulu Snyder Hamilton*

## For This Realm

LORD, we pray for this realm, that religion and virtue may season all sorts of men; that there may be peace within our gates and prosperity in all our borders. In time of danger thou art our defence, and in peace thou dost preserve us from corruption. In our prosperity may we not forget thee; and, whether in plenty or in want, may all things be so ordered that we may seek thy kingdom and righteousness, the only full supply and sure foundation both of men and states; that we may continue a people to do thy service. Amen.

*—William Laud*

## Foreign Policy

Thou hast taught us, O God, to see every question of foreign policy in the light of our faith: that we may check in ourselves and in others every temper which makes for war, all ungenerous judgments, all promptings of self-assertion, all presumptuous claims; and, being every ready to recognize the needs and aspirations of other peoples, we would, with patience, do whatever in us lies to remove suspicions and misunderstandings; and to honour all men. Amen.

*—Anonymous*
(New Every Morning)

## Fountain of All Good

God is the source of life, the fountain of all good. He has given us dear ones and we rejoice in their love, grow strong through their care, and are ennobled by their influence. He has also fixed an end for life and earthly companionship. Ofttimes we cannot fathom his purpose, yet we trust in him. Though the longing within us seems more than we can bear, we know that our grief is according to our blessing. The sorrow of separation is the inevitable price of days and years of precious love; tears are the tender tribute of yearning affection for those who have passed away but cannot be forgotten.

Death is not the end; the earthly body vanishes, the immortal spirit lives on with God. In our hearts, also, our loved ones never die. Their love and memory abide as a lasting inspiration, moving us to noble deeds and blessing us evermore.

In humble gratitude for their life and love, and with steadfast faith, let us sanctify God's name.

*—Anonymous*
(The Union Prayerbook for Jewish Worship)

## From Ancient Service Books

We pray for the Church, O God, that it may be drawn from all evil and made perfect in thy love; and that from the four winds it may gather to thy Kingdom all that are hallowed by thy grace; for thine is the power and the glory forever. Amen.

*—Anonymous*
(The Didache, First and Second Centuries)

Eternal God, the light of the minds that know thee, the joy of the hearts that love thee, and the strength of the wills that serve thee; may we who know thee truly love thee, and so love that we may fully serve thee, to the honor and glory of thy name. Amen.

*—Anonymous*
(The Gelasian Service Book)

[ 292 ]

O God, to whom glory is sung in the highest, while on earth peace is proclaimed among men of good will; we pray for that same good will among us thy servants and cleansing from evil; through thy mercy, O blessed Lord God, who dost live and govern all things, world without end. Amen.

*—Anonymous*
(Mozarabic and Ambrosian Rites)

We rejoice heartily that thou dost receive us this day, and all our whole life from henceforth, into thy good keeping, ruling and governing us, that all manner of darkness and evil may be utterly chased and driven out of our hearts, and that we may walk in the light of thy truth, to thy glory and praise, and to the help and furtherance of our neighbor. Amen.

*—Anonymous*
(The Primer, 1545)

Thou, Lord, providest enough for all men with thy most bountiful hand. May we so live together that there may be meat for the hungry and drink for the thirsty; comfort for the sorrowful, cheer for the dismayed and strength for the weak; deliverance for the oppressed and hope and courage for them that are out of heart.

Thou hast taught us, O God, that we stand daily and wholly in need of one another. May we have grace of hand and mind to add our proper share to the common stock, and this we pray in the spirit of Christ. Amen.

*—Anonymous*
(An Elizabethan Prayer Book)

### The Fruits of Thy Spirit

WHOSOEVER will, O God, may be endued with the fruits of thy spirit, filled with love and joy and peace. So we shall live together in kindliness and generosity, in patience, gentleness, and good faith, shaping every power in the grace of self-control. Amen.

*—Anonymous*

### Fullness of Life

O GOD, we pray that in getting and spending we may not misuse thy gifts; that, in commerce and in sport, we may be saved from the greed that seeks gain without labor, and the thrill of excitement without care for its cost to others. We pray that those in the grip of gambling habits may break free to become masters of themselves, and that we may be enabled to curb the power of those who exploit the weakness of their fellows. We thank thee that the efforts of all who seek to lift the drabness from man's daily lot are greatly blessed, and that all may find their joy in thee, and fulness of life in thy service. Amen.

*—Anonymous*
(New Every Morning)

## Glorious Liberty

O GOD, who hast called us into the glorious liberty of the sons of God: we pray that we may not refuse from cowardice thy gifts of freedom, nor use them to hurt or maim the lives of others, or for our own selfish ends. In thy service we find our perfect freedom, O God, our Redeemer and our King. Amen.

—*Anonymous*
(New Every Morning)

## Godly Living

ALMIGHTY God, we do offer unto thee most high praise, and hearty thanks for all thy wonderful graces and virtues which thou hast manifested in all thy saints, and in all other good persons upon earth, who by their lights and labours have shined forth as lights in the several generations of the world; and for whom we praise and magnify thee, most humbly desiring that we may still continue in their communion and enjoy the comfort thereof, following with a glad will and mind their examples of godly living and steadfastness in thy faith. Amen.

—*Anonymous*
(The Scottish Liturgy, 1560)

## Good Workmanship

O GOD, thou dost ever inspire us with the love of good workmanship. When we are tempted to slovenly habits and to scamp work either on the farm or in the factory, in household duties or in the office, in store or in ships, in the study or in Christian service, may we remember the Master workman and the perfection of his craftsmanship. We greatly need the spirit that perseveres, and which alone, in the end, wins the reward of work well done. And if through the guilt of man or the injustice of society our labor is without profit or without joy, may we have that attitude which will keep us faithful and not embittered. But, O God, we need the sense of thy living presence to enable us to work with unflagging zeal to bring in speedily the new age where men's joy is their work, and of whom it can be said that "they maintain the fabric of the world, and in the handiwork of their craft is their prayer." We pray in the spirit of the Master workman. Amen.

—*A. J. William Myers*

## The Goodness of Mankind

THE heavens declare the glory of God and the earth showeth his handiwork. We have the ability to see thee in the stars, the birds, the flowers, the fruit and grain, and to see every common bush aflame with God.

But we marvel most of all, our Father, at the beauty and strength and goodness of mankind—the faith and courage, the fellowship and love—

[ 294 ]

that make common life almost divine. We would, O God, cherish these qualities with all our souls and incarnate them in our lives and in our society.

We remember today all those in our own and in other lands who have heavy burdens and live under grievous circumstances; the suffering and bereaved; those whose crops or business have failed; all whose hopes have been destroyed; for lands torn and distressed by war and under the iron heal of evil tyrants. May the nations rise above the law of the jungle and learn to live in amity and helpfulness.

By thy spirit we dedicate ourselves afresh to the noblest way of life as seen in Jesus Christ and to the great Creative Spirit of love. And to thee, O God, be all the praise and glory both now and evermore. Amen.

*—A. J. William Myers*

## Government and Electors

O GOD, Lord of lords and and King of kings, may our leaders and legislators and all in positions of trust in the nation ever seek thy guidance in all that they do as representatives of the Government. May they never lead the nation wrongly through love of power, the desire to please, or because of unworthy ideals. We pray that the love of righteousness and truth will ever be their inspiration and lodestar.

Lord, we pray also for the electors in this country. We would not be led astray by party passion or shallow sentiment, but exercise wise and calm judgment and choose those to represent us who are of good character, faithful and upright, and seek first the Kingdom of God. Amen.

*—Anonymous*

## Grace at Meals

CREATIVE spirit and eternal God, who gives us the fruits of the earth in their season, we thank thee for these great gifts, seeking ever to use them for thine honor and the relief of those in need. Amen.

Blessed art thou, O God, who causest food to grow from the ground and friendship and love in the heart of mankind. Amen.

Father of all goodness, we thank thee for thy gifts. Blessed be this bread and meat unto our bodies, and thy word to our souls. Amen.

*—Anonymous*

We thank thee, Father, for thy care
And for thy bounty everywhere.
For food and every other gift
Our grateful hearts to thee we lift.
*—Anonymous; tune: The Doxology*

[ 295 ]

Some hae meat and canna eat,
And some wad eat that want it;
But we hae meat, and we can eat,
And sae the Lord be thankit. Amen.

—*Robert Burns*

For our bodies, quick and strong,
Thee to serve the whole day long:
For the power to think and know,
For the will like thee to grow;
For the good by which we live,
Father, thanks to thee we give. Amen.

—*Anonymous*

We thank thee, O God, that thou dost prosper the husbandman and give us the fruits of the earth in due season so that, rejoicing in thy gifts, we may praise thee by living in the spirit of Jesus and ever doing thy gracious will. Amen.

—*Anonymous*

It's nice to bow the head before we start to eat;
It's like inviting in a guest sublime and sweet.
A blessing breathed at mealtime is old fashioned, some folks say,
But it is giving God a chance to share our day.

—*Margaret Sangster*

## Great and Simple Joys

LET us praise and thank God in gladness and humility for all great and simple joys:

For the gift of wonder and the joy of discovery, and for the constant newness of life:

For children and the joy of innocency; for the sanctities of family life, and for all that our friendships bring us:

For the fruits of sympathy and sorrow; for the gift of humor and gaiety of heart; and for the joy of work attempted and achieved:

For the gifts of science and invention; for singers and all musicians; for poets and craftsmen; for those who work in form and colour to increase the beauty of life; for the consecration of art in the service of God; and for all things that help us to see the beauty of holiness:

For the grace of Christ in common people; their forbearance and generosity, their good temper, their courage, and their kindness; and for all humble lives of service. Amen.

—*Anonymous*
(New Every Morning)

## Hallowed Be Thy Name

BLESSED, and praised, and celebrated, and magnified, and exalted, and glorified, and hallowed, be thy name, O Lord, its record, and its memory, and every memorial of it, for the most honourable patriarchs, the ever venerable band of the prophets, the glorious company of the apostles, the evangelists, the illustrious army of the martyrs, for youths and maidens, for infants the delight of the world, for their faith, their hope, their labours, their truth, their blood, their zeal, their diligence, their tears, their purity, their beauty, Glory to thee, O Lord, glory to thee, glory to thee who didst glorify them, among whom we too glorify thee. Great and marvellous are thy works, Lord God Almighty; just and true are thy ways, thou king of saints. Who shall not fear thee, O Lord, and glorify thy name? for thou only art holy: for all nations shall come and worship before thee; for thy judgments are made manifest. Praise our God, all ye his servants, and ye that fear him, both small and great. Alleluia: for the Lord God omnipotent reigneth; let us be glad and rejoice, and give honour to him.

Behold, the tabernacle of God is with men, and he will dwell with them, and they shall be his people, and God himself shall be with them, and shall wipe away all tears from their eyes; and there shall be no more death, neither sorrow, nor crying, neither shall there be any more pain: for the former things are passed away.

*—Lancelot Andrewes*

## Help and Refuge

O GOD, who are the help and refuge of all thy children: from everlasting to everlasting thou art God. In our weakness thou art strength. In our darkness thou art light. In our sorrow thou art comfort and peace. We cannot number thy blessings; we cannot fully declare thy love. For all thy goodness we bless thee and praise thee and would ever live as in thy presence, and love the things thou lovest, and serve thee with the service of our daily lives. Amen.

*—Anonymous*
(New Every Morning)

## The Horse's Prayer

TO THEE, my master, I offer my prayer: Feed me, water and care for me, and, when the day's work is done, provide me with shelter, a clean, dry bed, and a stall wide enough for me to lie down in comfort.

Always be kind to me. Talk to me. Your voice often means as much to me as the reins. Pet me sometimes, that I may serve you the more gladly, and learn to love you. Do not jerk the reins, and do not whip me when going up hill. Never strike, beat or kick me when I do not understand what you want, but give me a chance to understand you. Watch me, and if I fail to do your bidding see if something is not wrong with my harness or feet.

Do not check me so that I cannot have the free use of my head. If you insist that I wear blinders, so that I cannot see behind me as it was intended I should, I pray you be careful that the blinders stand well out from my eyes.

Do not overload me, or hitch me where water will drip on me. Keep me well shod. Examine my teeth when I do not eat; I may have an ulcerated tooth, and that, you know, is very painful. Do not tie my head in an unnatural position, or take away my best defence against flies and mosquitoes by cutting off my tail.

I cannot tell you when I am thirsty; so give me clean, cool water often. Save me, by all means in your power, from that fatal disease—the glanders. I cannot tell you in words when I am sick, so watch me, that by signs you may know my condition. Give me all possible shelter from the hot sun, and put a blanket on me, not when I am working, but when I am standing in the cold. Never put a frosty bit in my mouth; first warm it by holding it a moment in your hands.

I try to carry you and your burdens without a murmur, and wait patiently for you long hours of the day or night. Without the power to choose my shoes or path, I sometimes fall on the hard pavements which I have often prayed might not be of wood, but of such a nature as to give me a safe and sure footing. Remember that I must be ready at any moment to lose my life in your service.

And finally, O my master, when my useful strength is gone, do not turn me out to starve or freeze, or sell me to some cruel owner, to be slowly tortured and starved to death; but do thou, my master, take my life in the kindest way, and, by the grace of God, your own soul will be enriched. You will not consider me irreverent if I ask in the name of him who was born in a stable. Amen.

—*Anonymous*
(The Toronto Humane Society)


## Husband and Wife

OUR Father, we desire earnestly that we may have true family love, that we may belong more fully to those whom thou hast given us, understanding each other day by day more instinctively; forbearing each other day by day more patiently: growing day by day more closely into oneness with each other and with thee.

Our Father, Jesus has shown us that thou art love. Thou knowest the depth of pain and the height of glory which abide continually in love. We seek to be perfect in love for these our dear ones in the family circle, knowing that without them we can never be made perfect in thee.

Our Creator and our God, we can be brought to full fruit only in thine own nature, that nature of humble redemptive devotion, which,

out of two responsive souls, can create a new heaven and a new earth—
one eternal glory of divine self-sharing.

—*Anonymous*
(Prayers for Use in an Indian College)

## Ignatius de Loyola's Prayer

THOU art ever teaching us, good Lord, to serve thee as thou deservest;
to give and not to count the cost; to fight and not to heed the wounds;
to toil and not to seek for rest; to labor and to ask for no reward, save
that of knowing that we do thy will. Amen.

## Illumine Our Hearts

O GOD, who dost prefer before all temples the upright heart and pure,
and who dost instruct us in all truth: we know that if we walk with
thee what in us is dark thou wilt illumine; what is low, raise and support;
what is shallow, deepen; so that every chapter of our lives will witness to
thy power, and justify the ways of God to men.[1]

—*Anonymous*
(Westminster Abbey Prayer)

## Imagination and Courage

O GOD, from whom all goodness, truth, and beauty come, we pray for
a better spirit in ourselves and throughout the whole Church, because we
have been weak in thy service and blind to the vision of thy Kingdom;
praying that those who represent us may have imagination and courage,
wisdom and ability and charity among themselves. Amen.

—*Anonymous*

## In Church

GOD who invisible containest all things, and yet for the salvation of
mankind dost visibly show forth the tokens of thy power, thy presence
so lights up this sanctuary that all who come hither to pray, from whatsoever tribulation they cry unto thee, will obtain the blessing of thy
consolation; and for whatsoever praise and thanksgiving, the joy of thy
peace.[2]

—*Anonymous*

## In Difficult Times

WHEN we put our trust in thee, O Lord, thou dost support us all the
day long of this troublous life until the shadows lengthen and the

[1] Used in World Church Service in the Abbey, Whitsunday, 1943.
[2] Prayer on the wall of the Church of Scotland at the Empire Exhibition, Glas-
gow, July 4, 1938. Slightly altered and the last clause added.

evening comes, and the busy world is hushed and the fever of life is over and our work is done; and then by thy mercy, thou wilt grant us a quiet rest and a safe lodging and peace at the last.

*—Anonymous*
(Book of Common Prayer)

## In the Morning

OUR Father God, in the morning while the dew is fresh we call upon thee. Happy are they who seek thee early, and seeking find thee near. We would remember thee all through the hours, that we may abide in those true joys which can not be taken from us. As the flower lifts its open face to the sun from morn till eve, so may our faith be towards thee, the light of our life, that we may grow into thy likeness, even as reflected in the beauty of Christ. Amen.

*—Anonymous*
(The United Church Observer)

## In Thine Image

O GOD, who hast made all things, the flowers and trees and the green grass, the sea, the sky, the stars, the birds, and all living things: and hast made man in thine own image, that he might know who is the creator of all these things; we pray for the understanding heart that we may see thee everywhere and glorify thee in thy works. Amen.

*—Anonymous*
(New Every Morning)

## Infirmity and Trouble

WE THANK thee, O Father, that thou dost ever mercifully look upon our infirmities and that thy strength is sufficient in all our troubles if we put our whole trust and confidence in thee; and so evermore we shall serve thee in holiness and pureness of living, following the example of our lord, to thy honor and glory, world without end. Amen.

*—Anonymous*
(Based on the Book of Common Prayer)

## The Joy of This Day

ALMIGHTY God, we thank thee for the joy of this day: may we find gladness in all its toil and difficulty, in its pleasure and success, and even in its failure and sorrow. We would look always away from ourselves, and behold thy glory and the need of the world that we may have the will and the strength to bring the gift of thy gladness to others; that with them we may stand to bear the burden and heat of the day and offer thee the praise of work well done. Amen.

*—Charles Lewis Slattery*
(New Every Morning)

[ 300 ]

## Labor and Trust

O MOST dear and tender Father, our defender and nourisher, we long to be endued with thy grace and to cast off the blindness of our minds and carefulness of worldly things, and put our whole study and care in keeping of thy holy laws; and that we may labor and travail for our necessities in this life, like the birds of the air and the lilies of the field, without anxious care and worry, for thou art our Father and our God. Amen.

*—Anonymous*
(The Primer, 1545)

## Life More Abundant

THOU art ever seeking, O God, to inspire our minds and move our wills, and to deepen our love of the truth and our confidence in thyself; that being without fear and without rashness, impatient of wrong-doing yet patient under obstruction, we may boldly follow thee, with life more abundant and liberty to do thy work; who art, in all thy holiness and beauty, our God for ever and ever. Amen.

*—Anonymous*

## Life of Our Souls

ETERNAL Spirit, who seekest us even when we forget to seek thee, thou art ever inspiring and strengthening all waiting, worshipping spirits. We need thee, even though we neglect thee. We live inwardly restless and tortured lives in a violent world because we have closed our eyes to thy will, our minds to thy truth, and our hearts to thine obedience. Now we would put ourselves at thy disposal, our spirits open to thee, as the earth long bound by the cold of winter is open to the returning sun. Life of our souls, we need thy springtime there.

Our families are enfolded in thy care. For mothers and fathers, who were to us the first revealers of Divine love, for children who are to us life's best teachers, calling out in us the depths of selfless and sacrificial care, and for all the sacred and beautiful relationships of the home, we thank thee. We rejoice that in thy spirit we can make our homes worthy to stand in the great succession of holy families, like that from which the Lord Christ came.

O God we pray for this church: May her ministry be sustained here and among all peoples—especially in lands downtrodden and enslaved. By the courage and fidelity of thy servants who in daily jeopardy sustain unafraid their Christian testimony, shame us from our apathy and neglect. We would be worthy disciples of the Christ in this day of his appalling denial and of his great opportunity. May we so maintain our spiritual heritage and so establish those faiths and principles without which no life is healthy, no society secure, and no progress possible, that our children may rise up and call us blessed.

We pray in the spirit of Christ. Amen.

*—Harry Emerson Fosdick*

(The Church Monthly, Riverside Church, New York)

## Life of Those Who Love Thee

O GOD, light of the hearts that see thee, life of the souls that love thee, and strength of the thoughts that seek thee; from whom to be turned away is to fall, to whom to be turned is to rise, and in whom to abide is to stand fast forever; we would now accept thy grace and respond to thy love with all our hearts, and worship and serve thee with singleness of purpose, that thy will may be done in all the earth. Amen.

*—Anonymous*

## A Litany of Vocation and Ministry

O THOU who art the confidence of all the ends of the earth, and the refuge of thy children in all generations, and art ever eager to enlarge our faith and love; we desire to work for needs beyond our own, for our friends and brethren, for the church and for the world; for the lands from which we come and the land in which we live; for all rulers and lawmakers; for the cause of justice and brotherhood, that in the work of righteousness we may find peace, and that the effect of righteousness may be unto us quietness and assurance forever:

And to thee be all the praise and the glory.

For the Church throughout the world, that every member of the same in his vocation and ministry may truly and humbly serve thee:

We pray in thy name, O Lord.

For those who work with their hands, that they may serve thee in all things; for those who buy and sell and get gain, that they may be rich toward God; for the poor, that we may supply their needs; for the rich, that they may trust not in outward prosperity but only in thee, remembering that they are but stewards of thy bounty:

We pray in thy name, O God.

For all parents, that they may order their households in thy faith and service; for all children that they also may be thy faithful children and true disciples; for all who teach the young, that they may have faith and patience and be guided by thy spirit:

We pray in the spirit of our Master.

For all who are tried by passionate temptations, or cold ambitions, or mean suggestions, that thy love may be their salvation:

We pray in thy name, O God.

For all forgotten by us but dear to thee; for the whole family in heaven and on earth:

We pray in thy name, O Father of mankind.

O God our Father may we be channels of thine infinite pity and helpfulness, worthy to be co-workers with thee in bringing in a better day for all mankind:

And to thee be the praise and the glory, world without end. Amen.

—*Anonymous*

(Order of Service for Vespers, Tokyo Union Church)

## The Lord Reigns

MAY the time not be distant, O God, when thy name shall be worshiped in all the earth, when unbelief shall disappear and error be no more. We fervently pray that the day may come when all men shall invoke thy name, when corruption and evil shall give way to purity and goodness, when superstition shall no longer enslave the mind, nor idolatry blind the eye, when all who dwell on earth shall know that to thee alone every knee must bend and every tongue give homage. O may all, created in thine image, recognize that they are brethren, so that, one in spirit and one in fellowship, they may be forever united before thee. Then shall thy kingdom be established on earth and the word of thine ancient seer be fulfilled: the Lord will reign forever and ever.

—*Anonymous*

(The Union Prayerbook for Jewish Worship)

## Maker and Giver of All Things Beautiful

OUR Father we remember that Jesus was a lover of little boats, that his rest was to go out upon the lake and his teaching was, of choice, by the shore. We, here by the water where he loved to be, turn to thee for his secrets of rest and recreation.

We thank thee, O thou maker and giver of all things beautiful, for the glory and grace of the world; for the wonders of sea and sky; for the delight of the eye in color of marsh and wave of grass-stem and curl of breaker and leap of foam; for the gladness in the call of a song sparrow; for the scent of the sea; for the tonic touch of water and of air, O God, we turn to thee lest we forget in any hour whence these things come. May we have the gratitude that gives thanks, not in sentiment alone, but in living a life, large as the sea, open and pure as the sky, with grace in it and growth. Amen.

—*Anonymous*

## May We Achieve Peace

O LORD, since first the blood of Abel cried to thee from the ground that drank it, this earth of thine has been defiled with the blood of man shed by his brother's hand, and the centuries sob with the ceaseless horror of war. Ever the pride of governments and the covetousness of the strong have driven peaceful nations to slaughter. Ever the songs of the past and the pomp of armies have been used to inflame the passions of the people. Our spirit cries out to thee in revolt against it, and we know that our righteous anger is answered by thy holy wrath.

[ 303 ]

O God, we can break the spell of the enchantments that make the nations drunk with the lust of battle and draw them on as willing tools of death. In thee we may maintain a quiet and steadfast mind if our own nation clamors for vengeance or aggression. Thou wilt strengthen our sense of justice and our regard for equal worth of other peoples and races. We pray for the rulers of nations that they may have faith in the possibility of peace through justice, and for the common people a new and stern enthusiasm for the cause of peace. We thank thee for the willingness of all classes of men and women to answer the call of duty, and also for their hatred of war. May we never for the love of private glory or advancement provoke its coming. May our young men still rejoice to die for their country with the valor of their fathers, but O God, we pray that our age may find nobler methods of matching our strength and more effective ways of giving our life for the flag.

O strong Father of all nations, thou wouldst draw all thy great family together with an increasing sense of our common blood and destiny, that peace may come on earth at last, and thy sun shed its light rejoicing on a holy brotherhood of peoples.

—*Walter Rauschenbusch*
(Prayer of the Social Awakening)

## Meditation

WE HAVE meditated on thee, O Lord, in the night watches, for thou hast been our help. Blessed art thou, O Lord, who madest the two lights, sun and moon, greater and lesser, and the stars for light, for signs, for seasons, spring, summer, autumn, winter, days, weeks, months, years, to rule over day and night.

—*Lancelot Andrewes*

## A More Excellent Way

OUR heavenly Father, we thank thee for those who, out of the bitter memories of strife and loss are seeking a more excellent way for the nations of the world, whereby justice and order may be maintained and the differences of peoples be resolved in equity. We pray thee that their purpose may be based on the sure foundations of the teaching of Jesus— love to thee and to others—that thy will may be done throughout the whole earth. Amen.

—*Anonymous*
(New Every Morning)

## More Light and Truth

DEAR God, whose knowledge is beyond all human thought and whose understanding transcends man's search for truth, we kneel in darkness and are beset by doubts and fears. The exceeding wonder of thy works fills us with awe.

What is man that thou art mindful of him? Yet thou hast not withdrawn thyself from us, and thou comest to us in the ordinary experiences of our daily lives. The flower by the roadside, the clouds in the summer sky, the star of evening, awaken in us a sense of thy nearness. Beyond the miracles of every day thou hast revealed thyself as infinite love, through a child born in a manger.

O God may we never fail to wait on thee, seeking more light and fuller truth, for so we shall have courage to face the future and be able to stand steadfastly for those loyalties to which Jesus gave his life. Amen.

—S. *Ralph Harlow*
(Prayers for Times Like These)

## Morning

INTO thy hands, O Lord, we commit ourselves this day. We pray for a watchful, humble and diligent spirit, that we may seek in all things to know thy will; and when we know it may gladly perform it, to the honour and glory of thy name. Amen.

—*Anonymous*
(New Every Morning)

## The Nation

O GOD, who hast called our nation to a place of trust and responsibility throughout the world: we humbly thank thee for all the ways in which thou hast blessed and guided us unto this day. With thee in our hearts we will lose all false pride and greed and injustice, and will have the spirit of unselfish service which alone can make us great and glorify thee among all nations. Amen.

—*Anonymous*
(New Every Morning)

## Nation, Church and Self

ALMIGHTY and everlasting God, King of kings and Lord of lords, the only ruler in the kingdoms of men, we pray that all in positions of authority in the nations may be guided by that wisdom which is from thee; and in purity of life seek to work together for peace and goodwill among all peoples.

Our Father, giver of life and redeemer, the alone source of goodness, may the Church be so inspired by thy love that it will strive, with ever-increasing devotion and skill, to promote truth and justice, beauty and goodness, friendliness and true happiness in the hearts and lives of mankind.

O God in whom alone we have courage and hope, we would, like little children and like Jesus of Nazareth, trust and love and serve thee in purity, sincerity and true devotion all our lives. Amen.

—A. J. *William Myers*

[ 305 ]

## Navajo Youth

HEAR a young man's prayer!
Hear a prayer for cleanness;
Hear a prayer for wholeness;
Clear my feet of slothfulness.
Hear a prayer for straightness;
Hear a prayer for courage;
Hear a prayer for staunchness.

*—Anonymous*

## New Every Morning

FATHER, we thank thee for thy mercies which are new every morning; for the gift of sleep; for our measure of health and strength; for the promise of another day with its fresh opportunities of work and service; for all these and more than these we thank thee. Not without thee would we go forth to meet the duties and tasks of any day. Our prayer is that in all our work we may be faithful; amid trials, courageous; in suffering, patient; under disappointment, full of hope in thee. Amen.

*—Samuel McComb*

## Night Workers

OUR Father, in these hours of daylight we remember those who must wake that we may sleep. We thank thee for those who watch over us at night, the firemen and police, and all who carry on through the hours of darkness the restless commerce of men on land and sea. We thank thee for their faithfulness and sense of duty; we pray that we may not by our selfishness or luxury add to their nightly toil. We realize how dependent the safety of our loved ones and the comforts of life are on these our brothers and we think of them with love and gratitude. May the sense of our need and gratitude help to make their burden lighter. Amen.

*—Anonymous*
(New Every Morning)

## Of Him and Through Him and to Him

FROM thee, our God, we receive everything; through thee all is possible for us, and for thee we want to live.

From thee comes the joy of each day and the blessings that light our road; from thee the splendors of the earth and the friendships of men, from thee the flights of enthusiasm and the need of adoration, from thee the Christian family and the treasures it transmits, from thee the book which we would absorb, from thee the master who has conquered our heart. We thank thee, Lord, for all thou givest us.

And it is through thee that we accomplish each step of the way; through thee that we lift ourselves after a fall and set forth once more ever stronger; through thee that our indolence may be changed into life,

[ 306 ]

our doubt into faith, our despair into hope. Through thee we are each moment brought back, . . . understood, consoled. O God, we recognize everywhere the touch of thy hand.

And . . . it is for thee—in turning toward thee—that our life takes on meaning; for thee that it is worth while having arms, a heart and a brain, and for thee to seek, to suffer, to wait. For thee—since thou art our reward and the goal of our journey—there is no enemy that we dare not face, no peril that we would not wish to surmount, and no sacrifice for which we are not ready. O God, all we have, and the little that we are, we give . . . for thee![1]

—*Philippe Vernier*

## Of Thine Own We Give Thee

BLESSED be thou, O Lord God, for ever and ever. Thine, O Lord, is the greatness, and the glory and the victory, and the majesty: for all that is in the heaven and in the earth is thine: thine is the kingdom, O Lord, and thou art exalted as head above all: both riches and honour come of thee, and of thine own do we give unto thee.

—*Anonymous*
(The Scottish Liturgy)

## On Easter Morning

OUR Father, with deep joy and gladness we thank thee for the beauty of Easter morning, the beginning of the happiest time of the year, the season of up-springing life and freshness in all nature and in ourselves.

For, lo, the winter is past; the rain is over and gone; the flowers appear on the earth; the time of the singing of birds is come, and the voice of the turtle-dove is heard in our land.

Thou hast blessed us with great joys, Our Father, but with none more loved and anticipated than the return of spring after winter. So the disciples rejoiced when Jesus returned to them after his death, but with deeper joy, for he brought to them new life and new hope after the winter of their sorrow and despair. That hope still remains with us and we believe that after the winter and death of our bodies, we shall come again to a new spring of glad awakening in thy kingdom where we shall know eternal life.

We thank thee, our Father, for the happiness this hope brings us. We do not understand what eternal life means but we pray that thou wilt reveal something of its meaning to us as we grow older. We have learned a little of what love means from those who love us and whom we love. We know something about beauty from seeing and hearing beautiful things. We know, our Father, that thou wilt likewise teach us the meaning of eternal life as we live more and more in loving fellowship with each other and with all thy children. Amen.

—*Lulu Snyder Hamilton*
(God Lives in Homes)

[1] Translated by Edith Lovejoy Pierce.

[ 307 ]

## On Entering a Church

You enter this church not as a stranger, but as a guest of God. He is your heavenly Father. Come, then, with joy in your heart and thanks on your lips, offering him your love and service. Be grateful to the strong and loyal men and women and children who in the name of God builded this place of worship, and to all who have beautified it and hallowed it with their prayers and praises. May all who love this home of faith find the inspiration of their labor and rejoice in the power and love of God, that his blessing may rest on you both on your going out and on your coming in.

—*Anonymous*

(From a Twelfth-century Church, Boldre, Hampshire, England)

## On the Wedding Anniversary

OUR Father, we thank thee for the past _____ years, for the joy and fulfilment they have brought to all of us. That which was only a beautiful hope in the beginning is now a reality, precious and beautiful beyond anything we could have dreamed.

We thank thee that we have learned to know more about thee and thy law of life during these years, for thou hast been the centre of our living, revealing thyself to us in the profound sharing of the mutual experiences of our life. No trouble, or sorrow, or discouragement has been too great because we have had each other to rely upon. All our joys and successes have been enhanced because they have brought happiness to others.

As we look forward to the years to come, may the reality of thy love become ever more evident as each one of the younger members of our family chooses his mate and begins his own home.

May they always have thee in their minds so they may think clearly, and in their hearts that they may love truly, and may the community of loving fellowship we have created here in our home continue to grow in ever-widening circles, and in deeper reality as we go through the years to come. Amen.

—*Lulu Snyder Hamilton*
(God Lives in Homes)

## Our Air-Raid Shelter Prayer

WE KNOW, O God, that thy will is that the spirit of neighborliness may be increased among us, that in peril we may uphold one another, in calamity serve one another, in suffering tend one another, and in homelessness, loneliness or exile befriend one another. With brave and enduring hearts we would strengthen one another, as the Master taught, till the disciplines and testing of these days be ended, and thou dost give again peace in our time. Amen.[1]

—*Anonymous*

[1] This prayer was widely used in Hull, Birmingham, and Westminster.

[ 308 ]

## Our Country

ALMIGHTY God, our heavenly Father, may we as a nation so live and work that we shall be a blessing to the world; that our aspirations and ideals may be in accordance with thy will. We would be kept from all hypocrisy in feeling or in word or action and ever strive for sound government and just laws, good education and a clean press, simplicity and justice in our relations with one another, and a spirit of service and worship which will abolish pride of place, and prejudice and inequality of opportunity. Amen.

—*Anonymous*

## Our Guardian

EVERY living soul shall praise thee; the spirit of all flesh shall glorify thy name. Thou art God from everlasting to everlasting and besides thee there is no redeemer nor savior. Thou art the first and the last, the Lord of all generations. Thou rulest the world in kindness and all thy creatures in mercy. Thou art our guardian who sleepest not and slumberest not. To thee alone we give thanks. Yet though our lips overflow with song, and our tongues with joyous praise, we should still be unable to thank thee even for a thousandth part of the bounties which thou hast bestowed upon our fathers and upon us. Thou hast been our protector and our savior in every trial and peril. Thy mercy has watched over us, and thy lovingkindness has never failed us.

—*Anonymous*
(The Union Prayerbook for Jewish Worship)

## Our Homes

LET us think of our homes:

The room that is our room, the furniture that is our furniture, the favorite chair that is our chair, the home duties that are our duties, the home joys that are our joys, the home dreams that are our dreams, the home problems that are our problems, the selfishness that is our selfishness, the guests that are our guests, the enriching hospitality that could be our hospitality if we entertained "angels unawares" who are in particular need of the very atmosphere we could create for them: the lonely, the sorrowful, the newcomer, the foreign, the refugee, the orphan.

And to God who is our home we give the praise and the glory in the spirit of Jesus the Christ. Amen.

—*Anonymous*
(Bound in the Bundle of Life)

## The Out-of-Doors

DEAR Father, we thank thee for the things that are out-of-doors; for the fresh air and the open sky and the growing grass and the tiny flowers and the setting sun and the wooded hill and the brown earth beneath our feet. They are all good and they all speak the truth. We would be kept ever like thy good world, rugged and wholesome and true.

—*Anonymous*
(The Dartmouth College Club)

## A Pawnee Prayer

WE HEED as unto thee we call,
O thou who sendest thy potent aid:
Thou art our helper, Giver of breath:
We heed as unto thee we call.

We heed as unto thee we call:
Oh thou who sendest us thy potent aid.
Thou art our helper, Father of strength:
We heed as unto thee we call.

—*Anonymous*

## Perfect Freedom

ALMIGHTY and everlasting God: we seek purity of heart and strength of purpose, that no selfish passion may hinder us from knowing thy will, no weakness from doing it; but that in thy light we shall see light and in thy service find perfect freedom. Amen.

—*Anonymous*
(New Every Morning)

## A Prayer for Grace

THE day is gone and we give thee thanks, O Lord. Evening draws nigh; make it bright. As day has its evening, so also has life: the evening of life is age; and it may be bright with thee.

The day is fled and gone; life too is going, this lifeless life. Night cometh; and cometh death, the deathless death. As the end of the day is near, so too is the end of life; we then, also remembering it, beseech of thee, for the close of our life, for thou wilt guide it in peace to be Christian, acceptable, sinless, shameless, and, if it please thee, painless, Lord, O Lord, gathering us together under the feet of thy chosen, when thou wilt, and as thou wilt, only without shame and sin.

—*Lancelot Andrewes*

## The Prayer of Socrates

O GOD! we long to be beautiful in the inner man, and all we have of outer things to be at peace with those within. May we count the wise man only rich. And may our store of gold be such as none but the good can bear.[1]

—*Plato*
(Dialogues on Poetic Inspiration)

[1] His prayer is addressed to "beloved Pan, and all ye other gods who here abide." The prayer is changed into the plural.

[ 310 ]

## Prayer on Awaking

BLESSED art thou, O Lord, our God, the God of our fathers; who turnest the shadow of death into the morning, and renewest the face of the earth; who rollest away the darkness from before the light, banishest night, and bringest back the day; who lightenest our eyes, lest we sleep the sleep of death; who deliverest us from the terror by night, from the pestilence that walketh in darkness; who drivest sleep from our eyes, and slumber from our eyelids; who makest the outgoings of the morning and evening to rejoice; because we laid us down and slept and awaked, for the Lord sustained us: because we waked and beheld, and our sleep was sweet unto us. Thou teachest us thy loving kindness in the morning; for in thee do we trust: and to know the way wherein we should walk; for we lift up our souls unto thee. Thou art ever teaching us to do thy will; for thou art our God: thy spirit is good; lead us into the land of uprightness. Quicken us, O Lord, for thy name's sake.

*—Lancelot Andrewes*

## Prayers

THOU art ever inspiring us, O God, in our good resolutions, and in thy holy service: We resolve this day to make a good beginning. Amen.

O God, what shall we render unto thee for all these thy manifold mercies? O that we were able to serve thee all the days of our lives! O that even for one day we were enabled to do thee service worthy of thyself! For verily thou art worthy of all service, all honor, and praise without end. Amen.

Oh grateful and delightsome service of God, whereby man is made truly free and holy. We worship thee and seek ever to do thy will. Amen.

O God, excellent are thy works, true are thy judgments, and by thy providence are all things governed. Therefore praise and glory be unto thee, O Father. May all created things praise and bless thee forever. Amen.

We earnestly desire, O Lord, to know that which is worth knowing, to love that which is worth loving, to praise that which pleaseth thee best, to prize that which is precious to thee, and to hate all that is evil in thine eyes. We pray for wisdom and true judgment that we may search out and do what is well-pleasing unto thee. Amen.

*—Thomas à Kempis*
(Imitation of Christ)

## Public Worship

MAY we come intimately to thee, O God, whose will it is that not one of us should perish. Let the public worship of thy church include each of us as the love of a true family leaves no single child forgotten. Let the spoken prayer set free the secret cry of our hearts; let the united song release the private aspirations of our souls; let the public message be to us private and particular, meeting our inward needs. So thou wilt strengthen us in loneliness and bereavement, in temptation and sorrow, and recover us from the humiliation and guilt of our sin, and put strong foundations under our lives to meet the storms of these tempestuous days.

For those we love, far from us as we worship here, we pray with deep affection and desire. In camp and prison, on battlefield and in peril of the sea and air, our hearts go out to all the youths whose lives are put in jeopardy by the cruel necessities of war. Ours is the guilt who in the time of our opportunity, having sacrificed heavily for war, refused the requirements of peace; and now the burden of our sin's consequence falls on the lives of those we love better than ourselves. May our children be wiser than we have been, and so long as we, the older generation, still walk in the land of the living, let us, following our Lord and Master, count no sacrifice too great that will make the task of youth lighter or speed the day of a just and enduring peace for all nations. Amen.

—*Harry Emerson Fosdick*
(The Church Monthly, Riverside Church, New York)

## Rest and Sleep

THOU art present with us, O God, through the hours of the night as in the day. May all who are fatigued by work and illness, pain and the changes of this fleeting world have rest and sleep, reposing with the confidence of little children in thy unchanging love.

—*A. J. William Myers*

## Sailors and Fishermen

O GOD of our fathers, who art the protector of thy children everywhere, we commend to thy keeping sailors and fishermen and all who earn their livelihood upon the great waters. In thy strength they are able to face the perils of the sea and to ride its storms with brave hearts and simple trust; and, whether in life or in death, thou art able to bring them to the haven where they would be. Amen.

—*Anonymous*
(New Every Morning)

## A Shorter Litany

OUR heavenly Father we pray:

That all nations may so live in thee that they will attain unity, peace and concord:

And to thee be all the praise, O God.

That all who have erred and been deceived may be brought into the way of truth and love:
We pray in the spirit of Jesus our Master.

That we may put our trust in thee, O Lord, for thou wilt strengthen such as do stand, wilt comfort and help the weak-hearted, and wilt raise them that fall and enable us finally to beat down all evil under our feet:
And to thee be all the praise, O God.

That every care may be taken to preserve all that travel by land, on sea and in the air, all women in child-birth and all sick people, all prisoners and captives, and all children and youth.
We pray according to thy spirit, Our Father.

That all orphan children and widows, and all that are desolate and oppressed may be defended and supported by loyal friends:
We pray according to thy will, O God.

That we may have grace to forgive our enemies, persecutors and slanderers, and that their hearts may be turned to thee:
We pray according to thy will, O God.

That we all may have true repentance so that we can overcome our evil desires, negligence and ignorance and, trusting in thee, amend our lives according to thy holy will:
All this we pray, Our Father, in the spirit of Jesus and for thy praise. Amen.

—*Lionel James*
(School Prayers in War-Time, freely adapted)

## Snow Litany

WE CAN see the snow on the ground
It looks pretty when it is falling

(Response)
This is the doing of God,
We can but watch and wonder.

The snow sparkles when the sun shines,
It makes the trees and houses white,
And a blanket for the grass.
Each tiny snowflake has six points and yet no two are alike.

This is the doing of God,
We can but watch and wonder.

Icicles hang from the houses,
And Jack Frost paints pictures on the windows
And roses on our cheeks.

This is the doing of God,
We can but watch and wonder.

The birds go south when winter comes.
If they stay here they hide in trees and branches in the deep woods.

This is the doing of God,
We can but watch and wonder.

*—Anonymous*
(The Junior Church School, First Congregational Church, West Hartford, Conn.)


## Special Needs

O GOD, we pray
For all who are poor, and broken, and oppressed;
For all whose labor is without hope;
For all whose labor is without honor;
For all whose labor is without interest;
For all who have too little leisure;
For those who are underpaid;
For those who seek to oppress their employees;
For those who are unreasonable in their demands;
For all women workers;
For those who work in dangerous trades;
For those who cannot find work;
For those who will not work:
For those who have no home;
For prisoners and outcasts;
For all who are sick or hungry;
For all who are intemperate, luxurious and cruel;
The spirit of the Christ incarnating thy love alone can heal the hurt of all the people, and we pray that they will turn to thee to whom be the praise and the glory always. Amen.

*—Anonymous*
(Youth at Worship)


## Sunday

O GOD, who givest not only the day for labor and the night for rest, but also the peace of this blessed day; may we so use it that its quiet will be profitable to us in spiritual things, so that we shall be refreshed and strengthened to finish the work which thou hast given us to do. Amen.

*—James Martineau*


## Sursum Cordia

WE WOULD lift up our hearts and our spirits, O God, above the false shows of things, above fear and melancholy, above laziness and despair, above selfishness and covetousness, above custom and fashion, up to the everlasting truth and order. Amen.

[ 314 ]

We seek to lose, O God, all pride and vanity, boasting and forwardness; and to have the courage that shows itself by gentleness; the true wisdom that shows itself by simplicity; and the true power that shows itself by modesty. Amen.

*—Charles Kingsley*

## Thanksgiving

FATHER, we thank thee
For our church, school and friends,
For our fathers' and mothers' loving care,
For the friendly care of doctors and nurses in hospitals and homes,
For baby kittens and lambs and birds, and their parents.

Father we thank thee
For the beauty of the earth,
For the stars and moon that shine,
The bright sun and blue sky,
For the trees, the flowers, the birds that sing,
For every lovely thing.

Father we thank thee
For our food, the fruit upon the trees,
For the rain that helps to make things grow.

Father we thank thee
For lovingkindness all about us.

*—Anonymous*

(The Junior Church School, First Congregational Church, West Hartford, Conn.

## Thanksgiving

How truly meet, and right it is, and comely and due, in all, and for all things, in all times, places, manners, in every season, every spot, everywhere, always, altogether, to remember thee, to worship thee, to confess to thee, to praise thee, to bless thee, to hymn thee, to give thanks to thee, maker, nourisher, guardian, governor, healer, benefactor, perfecter of all, Lord and father, king and God, fountain of life and immortality, treasure of everlasting goods, whom the heavens hymn and the heaven of heavens, the angels and all the heavenly powers, one to other crying continually,—and we the while, weak and unworthy, under their feet,— holy, holy, holy, Lord God of hosts: full is the whole heaven, and the whole earth, of the majesty of thy glory. Blessed be the glory of the Lord out of his place, for his height, his sovereignty, his almightiness, his eternity, his providence. The Lord is our strength, our strong rock, our defence, our deliverer, our succour, our buckler, the horn of our salvation, our refuge.

*—Lancelot Andrewes*

## That We May Be Spiritually One

O GOD the Father, good beyond all that is good, fair beyond all that is fair, in whom is calmness, peace and concord; we seek to make up the dissensions which divide us from each other, and come into a unity of love, which may bear some likeness to thy divine nature. As thou art above all things, we may be one by the unanimity of a good mind; and through the embrace of charity and the bonds of affection, we may be spiritually one, as well in ourselves as in each other; through that peace of thine which maketh all things peaceful, and in likeness of the grace, mercy and tenderness of Jesus Christ, the pioneer of our faith. Amen.

—*St. Dionysius*

## They Labor in Vain

ALMIGHTY God, our heavenly Father, without whose help labor is useless, without whose light search is vain, thou wilt invigorate our studies and direct our enquiries, if we trust in thee, so that we may by due diligence and right discernment establish ourselves and others in thy holy faith. Amen.

—*Samuel Johnson*

## Those Who Form Public Opinion

O GOD, we pray for those who help form public opinion, that they may have the guidance of thy spirit, that this land may become more like the Kingdom of thy desire.

We pray, O God, for all kings and presidents; for all statesmen and persons in authority in every country; for the captains of industry and leaders of trade unions; for all journalists and leaders of the press and radio; for all writers of books and poetry, and plays and stories, and producers and actors of both the stage and screen; for all ministers and leaders in the churches; for all teachers and parents, and for ourselves. Remembering Jesus Christ, we would be kept from idle words and thoughtless acts and statements that do harm to others, and may all have greater wisdom in speech, greater courage in action, so we shall contribute to a better world because we have loved thee and our fellow-man. Amen.

—*Anonymous*
(Youth at Worship)

## Thou Art Always Near

ALMIGHTY God, we thank thee that thou art always showing us thy glory: in the universe around us, in the laws of nature, in the teachings of history and in the longings of our souls. We long to know more of thy fatherly goodness, through all that has been revealed to us by the experience of life and by the loving-kindness of men, and through all that our lord revealed in his life and teaching. O loving Father, we pray thee

[ 316 ]

that we may be strong in the faith that thou art always near, that thy love will never leave us nor forsake us, that thou art our refuge and underneath are thy everlasting arms. Amen.

*—Anonymous*
(New Every Morning)

## Thou Art Our God[1]

| Reader: | Congregation: |
|---|---|
| Thou art our God | in heaven and upon earth; |
| Mighty and powerful, | acclaimed by multitudes. |
| He spoke and it was; | He commanded and all was created. |
| His memorial is eternal; | He liveth for ever. |
| He is all seeing; | He dwelleth even in secret places. |
| His crown is salvation; | His garment is righteousness. |
| His robe is zeal; | He is girt with justice. |
| His secret is rectitude; | His counsel is faithfulness. |
| His work is truth; | He is righteous and just. |
| He is nigh unto them that call upon him in truth; | He is high and exalted. |
| He abideth in the heavens; | He suspendeth the earth in space. |

Living and enduring, revered, exalted and holy!

*—Eleazar Kalil*

## Thou Givest Liberally

O LORD our God, Almighty and Eternal Father, who givest to all thy children liberally and upbraidest not; we thank thee this day for thine infinite goodness to us and to all men. We thank thee for the world and all the good things which are therein; for the sky above us and the earth beneath our feet; for the changing seasons, the beauty of our homes, and for our friends. We bless thee for thy tender care which guards us, and for all thy good creatures by which we are enriched. We thank thee for Jesus, and for all the means of grace, and the hope of glory. In thy service we seek to live and in thy service may we die. Amen.

*—Anonymous*
(Daily Services)

## Thou Shalt Love the Lord Thy God

FATHER of all mankind we would remember, throughout this day and every day, that a very real portion of thy Kingdom is in our keeping.

May we love thee, O God, with all our mind that we may think thy thoughts after thee, making beautiful and significant each decision of our daily living; and putting away prejudice and small-mindedness, and keeping our minds renewed.

[1] Piyyut (hymn) composed in alphabetical acrostic (in Hebrew), translated by Rabbi Morris Silverman.

[ 317 ]

May we love thee, O God, with all our heart that we may love all whom thou lovest, feeling for even the most unlovable and difficult; and that we may learn to work with others, even if we disagree with them, in order that thy will may be done.

We would love thee, O God, with all our soul, and ever seek fresh ways in which we can be one in God our Father that thy divine powers may surge through the commonplace routine of our daily life. And in all the day's grind, O God, if we walk with thee we shall maintain the spiritual glow.

O GOD, we would love thee like the master, with all our heart and soul and mind and strength that we may work the works of him who sent us while it is day, seeking through every act the welfare of our neighbor and ourself. We worship and praise thee that we may be quickened and directed this day and all through our life by thy spirit. Amen.

*—Anonymous*
(A Call to Prayer, Congregational Church)

## Thy Strength Is Sufficient

MOST holy and most merciful God, the strength of the weak, the rest of the weary, the comfort of the sorrowful, the savior of the sinful, and the refuge of thy children in every time of need: thou dost ever help all to respond to thy loving will.

When our faith is growing weak, and our love cold; when we are losing our vision of thee, and the spiritual world is not real to us:

When we are tempted to mean and wicked ways, and sin grows less sinful in our sight; when duty is difficult, and work is hard, and our burdens are heavy:

When the unknown future troubles us, and in our fears and anxieties we forget thine eternal love and mercy; when the last darkness shall close around us, and heart and flesh fail, and vain is the help of man:

Heavenly Father, as Jesus taught, we know that thy strength is sufficient for every need. Amen.

*—Anonymous*
(New Every Morning)

## Thy Wisdom Is Our Guide

O GOD, who art from everlasting to everlasting, the creator and upholder of all things, the source of life and light: thy ways are not as our ways, nor thy thoughts as our thoughts; thy judgments are unsearchable, and thy ways past finding out.

Thou hast never left the world which thou hast made: day by day thou dost sustain it, bringing forth out of thy treasures things new and old. The seasons are thine with their changing beauty; the wealth of the earth is thine in its manifold splendour; all this thou hast given to man for him to use it and rejoice, seeing in it the bounty of thy love.

Throughout the ages thou hast led our race along the upward path,

[ 318 ]

encouraging us by thy many gifts, schooling us by the discipline of suffering. Thy wisdom has been our guide; thy love hast over-ruled our folly and sin. Thou hast raised up great leaders in time of need; thou hast inspired explorers in every realm of knowledge; and in every age thou hast made known thy law, that in the fear of thee is the beginning of wisdom, and that without righteousness no nation can be great.

—*Anonymous*

(New Every Morning)

## To Know Thee Is Eternal Life

O GOD above all, yet in all; holy beyond all imagination, yet friend of sinners; who inhabitest the realms of unfading light, yet leadest us through the shadows of mortal life; how solemn and uplifting it is even to think upon thee! Like sight of sea to wearied eyes, like a walled-in garden to the troubled mind, like home to wanderer, like a strong tower to a soul pursued; so to us is the sound of thy name.

But greater still to feel thee in our heart; like a river glorious, cleansing, healing, bringing life; like a song victorious, comforting our sadness, banishing our care; like a voice calling us to battle, urging us beyond ourselves.

But greater far to know thee as our Father, as dear as thou art near; and ourselves begotten of thy love, made in thy image, cared for through all our days, never beyond thy sight, never out of thy thought.

To think of thee is rest; to know thee is eternal life; to see thee is the end of all desire; to serve thee is perfect freedom and everlasting joy.

—*W. E. Orchard*

## The Triumph of Truth

O LORD, how can we know thee? Where can we find thee? Thou art as close to us as breathing and yet art farther than the farthermost star. Thou art as mysterious as the vast solitudes of the night and yet art as familiar to us as the light of the sun. To the seer of old thou didst say: thou canst not see my face, but I will make all my goodness pass before thee. Even so does thy goodness pass before us in the realm of nature and in the varied experiences of our lives. When justice burns like a flaming fire within us, when love evokes willing sacrifice from us, when, to the last full measure of selfless devotion, we proclaim our belief in the ultimate triumph of truth and righteousness, do we not bow down before the vision of thy goodness? Thou livest within our hearts, as thou dost pervade the world, and we through righteousness behold thy presence.

—*Anonymous*

(The Union Prayerbook for Jewish Worship)

## True Followers

WE THANK thee, O God, for thy many gifts. If we have been sullen and fretful, or mean and covetous, in the midst of them; if we have lived

[ 319 ]

ugly lives in thy beautiful world; we sincerely repent. We want above all, our heavenly Father, to be true followers of Jesus who dwelt among men. So we would learn to look with pure and reverent eyes upon all thy creation, and glorify thee daily in our bodies and our spirits, which are thine. Amen.

—*Anonymous*
(New Every Morning)

## Vision of Our Land

O God, sometimes we have a vision of our land, fair as she might be: a land of justice, where none shall prey on others; a land of plenty, where vice and poverty shall cease to fester; a land of brotherhood, where success shall be founded on service, and honour shall be given to worth alone; a land of peace, where order shall not rest on force, but on the love of all for their land, the great mother of the common life and welfare. This, O God, was the prayer of Jesus over Jerusalem and is the silent prayer of all our hearts as in city, town, and village, we pledge our time and strength and thought, to hasten the day of her coming beauty and righteousness. Amen.

—*Anonymous*
(New Every Morning)

## We Will Give Thanks

We will give thanks unto the Lord; with our whole heart will we praise thee, O God. We will show forth thy marvellous works. We will be glad and exult in thee. We will sing praise to thy name, O most high. For thou, O Lord, hast never forsaken any of the children of men. Amen.

—*An Anthem by Louis Campbell Tipton*

## The Weary and Heavy-Ladened

We bring before thee, O God, the cry of the prisoner, the distressed, the widow and orphan, the weak and helpless, the hunger and thirst of the starving, the weariness of the sick and aged, the temptations of the young and the miseries of all. Thou art ever working for the good of all and we seek in the spirit of Jesus to do what we can to right the wrong, to work and plan that all may have enough, to seek ever to bring in thy kingdom of grace and love, of righteousness and peace. Amen.

—*Anonymous*
(Morning Prayers)

## Welcome All Truth

O Lord, we pray that we may welcome all truth under whatsoever outward forms it may be uttered; that we may rise above all party strifes

[ 320 ]

and cries, to the contemplation of thy eternal truth and goodness, and grow in the likeness of Jesus, the pioneer of our faith. Amen.

*—Charles Kingsley*

## We Praise God for Light

WE PRAISE God for light, the waters and the firmament, the earth and the plants, the lights in the firmament of the heaven, the fishes and the fowls, the wild and tame beasts, the rest of the sabbath; for the making of man, after counsel held, with his own hands; for the breath of life, the image of God, the dominion over the creatures, for that which may be known of God, the work of the law written in the heart, the oracles of the prophets, the melody of the psalms, the wisdom of the proverbs, the experience of the histories; for our birth, bringing up, preservation, direction, instruction, civilised state, religion.

*—Lancelot Andrewes*

## Westminster Prayers

O THOU who art heroic love, may we keep in our hearts that adventurous spirit which scorns the way of safety, so long as thy will is done; and thus, Lord, we will be more worthy of those brave souls who in every age have ventured nobly in answer to thy call. Amen.

Heavenly Father, in whom we live and move and have our being, we humbly pray thee we may so be guided and governed by thee that in all the cares and occupations of our daily life we may never forget thee. We ask in the spirit of our master, Jesus Christ. Amen.

God, who art the living power of all things, within our being and beyond our thought, may we be pure in heart, that no false image hide thee from our sight, who art the goodness and the glory evermore. Amen.

Eternal God, in whose perfect kingdom no sword is drawn but the sword of righteousness, and no strength known but the strength of love, may all nations be gathered under the banner of the Prince of Peace, as children of one God and Father of all, to whom be dominion and glory, now and forever. Amen.

*—Anonymous*
(Westminster Prayers)

## We Thank Thee, O Lord

O LORD, our Lord, for our being, life, reason, for nurture, protection, guidance, for education, civil rights, religion, for thy gifts of grace, nature, worldly good, for redemption, regeneration, instruction, for our call, recall, yea, many calls besides; for thy forbearance, longsuffering, long long-suffering toward us, many seasons, many years; for all good things re-

[ 321 ]

ceived, successes granted us, good deeds done; for the use of things present, for thy promise, and our hope of the enjoyment of good things to come; for our parents honest and good, teachers kind, benefactors never to be forgotten, fellow-ministers who are of one mind, hearers thoughtful, friends sincere, domestics faithful; for all who have advantaged us by writings, sermons, conversations, prayers, examples, rebukes, injuries; for all these, and all others which we know, which we know not, open, hidden, remembered, forgotten, done when we wished, when we wished not, we confess to thee and will confess, we bless thee and will bless, we give thanks to thee and will give thanks all the days of our life. What shall we render unto the Lord for all his benefits toward us? for all things in which he hath spared and borne with us until now? Holy, holy, holy, thou art worthy, O Lord and our God, the holy one, to receive glory, honour, and power: for thou hast created all things, and for thy pleasure they are and were created.

—*Lancelot Andrewes*


## When Seeking Physical and Spiritual Renewal

OUT of the press of activities and the crowded days of life thou hast given us this day for rest and fellowship and worship. We have come from hours of exhaustion and weakness and emptiness, seeking refreshment and renewal. Days of ceaseless work and heavy responsibilities lie behind and ahead of us. Now we put from us all thoughts of things left undone or of things still to do. It is also for the sake of others that we would forget them now and seek only the restoration of thy presence, O God of Life and Love.

As the hart panteth after the water brooks, so panteth my soul after thee, O God. My soul thirsteth for God, for the living God.

With humble heart we truly seek thee, O God. Our spirit longs for the abundant life-giving power of thy eternal spirit. Our bodies are relaxed, at rest, quiet. Our eyes look only on the beauty of infinite spaces. We would be filled, O God, with thine infinite peace. Thou art strength, and life, and wisdom and love. As the wind of heaven blows over us we feel the peace and calmness of thy spirit, blowing away the weariness and strain and tenseness of our life. As the sun pours its life-giving rays upon us may we know the soul-healing beams of thine infinite love, pouring over our tired mind and spirit, and driving out all worries and fears and anxieties, all weakness and self-pity, and filling us with courage and strength.

O God of Life, eternal spirit of infinite Love, in these hours of rest and quiet we seek thee.

My soul waiteth in silence for God only; from him cometh my salvation. Amen.

—*Lulu Snyder Hamilton*
(God Lives in Homes)

## Women's Institute Prayer

MAY we be kept, O God, from pettiness. Let us be large in thought, in word, in deed.

Let us be done with fault-finding and leave off self-seeking.

May we put away all pretence and meet each other face to face— without self-pity and without prejudice.

May we never be hasty in judgment and always generous.

Let us take time for all things; that we may be calm, serene, gentle.

We would put into action our better impulses, straightforward and unafraid.

We recognize that it is the little things that usually create differences and that in the big things of life we are one.

And may we strive to touch and know the great, common human heart of us all, and, O Lord God, let us not forget to be kind.[1]

—*Mary Stewart*

## Workers in Industries

OUR Father, who hast sanctified labor to the welfare of mankind: thou wilt prosper the industries of this land, and all who are engaged therein, if they seek the common good. We pray that all workers, being shielded in their hardships and dangers, and receiving their due reward, will praise thee and live according to thy will. Amen.

—*Anonymous*
(New Every Morning)

## The World Is Full of Thy Glory

O GOD, who dost so fill the world with thy glory that everything we see can represent to us the presence, the excellency and the power of God, and our conversation with the creatures is able to lead us to the Creator. Amen.

—*Jeremy Taylor*

## A Zeal for Beauty

LEADER: God of all beauty and joy, we would this day share with thee the purity of thy divine passion for beauty, for beauty of form and sound.
GROUP: For beauty of thought and expression, for beauty of action and character, for beauty of life and beauty of soul.
L: Thou hast given us minds and hearts that we may see with divine joy all the radiant beauty of thy material world.
G: And thou hast given us the power of sight—eyes to see the disfigurement and sin, but also to see through them the divine possibilities of beauty which lie hidden beneath the loathsomeness.
L: Thou givest us the zeal for beauty enabling us to transform hideous

[1] This prayer has been used, especially by Women's Institutes, all over the world.

[ 323 ]

places, hideous lives and hideous souls into places fitted in beauty for thy habitation.

G: Into lives fitted in beauty for thy companionship, like Christ, into souls fitted in beauty for thine indwelling—ambassadors of thy Kingdom in which all things beautiful are forever preserved and perfected.

—*Anonymous*
(The Society Quarterly)

# BOOK V

# APHORISMS

•

The ways of God are as the number of the souls of the sons of men.
—*Persian Proverb*

A child will divine what we really worship and no teaching will avail with him if we teach in contradistinction to what we are.
—*Amiel*

The most regal gift we can give our fellowmen is aid in their own development. Other gifts are weakening and ephemeral, but this is creative and eternal.
—*The Wisdom of Wu Ming-fu*

Kneel always when you light a fire! Kneel reverently, and grateful be to God for his unfailing charity.
—*John Oxenham*

Keep a halo about life. Think glorious thoughts of God . . . and serve him with a quiet mind.
—*Anonymous*

Plato said that education should be a "turning of the eye of the soul toward light." . . . Education should be a magic casement. . . . It should be liberal like the dervish in the eastern tale who gave the prince an ointment which, rubbed upon his eyes, made him see all the hidden treasure and riches of the earth. It should fascinate the mind with the "fairy tale of science and the long result of time."
—*Ruth Perkins*

> In hearts too young for enmity
> There lies the way to make men free;
> When children's friendships are world-wide
> New ages will be glorified.
> Let child love child, and
> Strife will ease,
> Disarm the hearts, for that is peace.
> —*Ethel Blair Jordan*

A little thing this Church? Remove its roots
And Ossa upon Pelion would not fill the pit.
—*Edwin Ford Piper*

The madonnas I see are those that pass the house on the way to work, carrying little saviors in their arms.

—*Margaret T. Applegarth*

To have faith is to create;
To have hope is to call down blessing;
To have love is to work miracles.

—*Michael Fairless*

I had no shoes to my feet and I grumbled, until I met a man along the road who had no feet.

—*Proverb of India*

Home is a place that means something clean and decent and sweet.

—*Anonymous*

How far that little candle throws his beams!
So shines a good deed in a naughty world.

—*William Shakespeare*

Heaven doth with us as we with torches do,
Not light them for themselves; for if our virtues
Did not go forth of us, 'twere all alike
As if we had them not.

—*William Shakespeare*

O Lord, let me ever take one bite at every meal in memory of thee.

—*Maltbie Davenport Babcock*

He who hurts another harms himself; he who helps another helps himself; where love is, there God is also.

—*Russian Proverb*

When an old Negro woman tried to define homesickness she said: "It ain't so much the place where I is, as the place where I ain't."

—*Margaret T. Applegarth*

The mind is ever interested in novelties; but the heart ever seeks the permanent and unchangeable, and is assured that its quest is not vain, according to the song of our pilgrimage:

"His truth at all times firmly stood
And shall from age to age endure."

—*W. P. Patterson*

Music is love in search of a word.

—*Sidney Lanier*

[ 326 ]

Small kindnesses, small courtesies, small considerations habitually practiced in our social intercourse, give a greater charm to the character than the display of great talents and accomplishments.

—*M. A. Kelly*

The prodigal son "came to himself." All Buddhist schools agree that the "coming back to one's own heart," that is, to the original nature, is the great aim of life.

—*Karl L. Reichelt*

The church is not wood and stone and steel, but boys and girls, men and women, who live in the spirit of God. They are the Living Stone of the Living Church.

—*A. J. William Myers and Alma N. Schilling*

Hath man no second life? Pitch this one high!
Sits there no judge in heaven, our sin to see?
More strictly, then, the inward judge obey!
Was Christ a man like us? Ah! let us try
If we then, too, can be such men as he.

—*Matthew Arnold*

O thou Great Chief, light a candle in my heart that I may see what is therein and sweep the rubbish from thy dwelling place.

—*African Child's Prayer*

On the eve of Christmas
In the firelight's glow
Lie all the lovely unsaid things
That old friends know.

—*Anonymous*

Now, O Father,
Our thanks be unto thee,
Our thanks! Renew our plenty!
Our thanks!
Renew these thy gifts to us!

—*A Pawnee Prayer*

Kingsley said to Whittier, concerning the harsh and repellent theology of the time, that no words could describe his relief when he came to the conclusion that God is at least as good as the average church member. And Whittier wrote:

But nothing can be good in him
Which evil is in me.

[ 327 ]

The wrong that pains my soul below
I dare not throne above:
I know not of his hate—I know
His goodness and his love.
—*John Greenleaf Whittier*

I sometimes feel the thread of life is slender,
And soon with me the labor will be wrought;
Then grows my heart to other hearts more tender.
The time is short.
—*Dinah Moria Craik*

Never to tire; never to grow cold; to look for the budding flower and the opening heart; to hope always, like God; to love always—this is duty.
—*Amiel*

A kindly deed
Is a little seed
That groweth all unseen,
And lo, when none
Do look thereon,
Anew it springeth green.
—*Anonymous*

Make yourselves nests of pleasant thoughts. None of us yet know, for none of us have been taught in early youth, what fairy palaces we may build of beautiful thought—proof against all adversity. Bright fancies, satisfied memories, noble histories, faithful sayings, treasure-houses of precious and restful thoughts, which care cannot disturb, nor pain make gloomy, nor poverty take away from us—houses built without hands, for our souls to live in.
—*John Ruskin*

Rest is not quitting
The busy career;
Rest is the fitting
Of self to one's sphere.

'Tis loving and serving
The highest and best!
'Tis onward, unswerving—
And that is true rest.
—*J. S. Dwight*

Be not afraid of enthusiasm; you need it; you can do nothing effectually without it.
—*François Guizot*

[ 328 ]

True hope is swift, and flies with swallow's wings:
Kings it makes gods, and meaner creatures kings.
*—William Shakespeare*

To one who has been long in city pent,
　'Tis very sweet to look into the fair
And open face of heaven—to breathe a prayer
Full in the smile of the blue firmament.
*—John Keats*

　Every day is a fresh beginning,
　　Listen, my soul, to the glad refrain,
And, spite of old sorrow and older sinning,
　And puzzles forecasted and possible pain,
Take heart with the day, and begin again.
*—Susan Coolidge*

Gales may blow and frosts may come
　To silence the laughing rill,
But Christmas fires glow warm and bright,
　And holly is beautiful still.
*—Christina Rossetti*

　We saw the light shine out afar,
　On Christmas in the morning,
And straight we knew Christ's star it was,
　Bright beaming in the morning.
Then did we fall on bended knee,
　On Christmas in the morning,
And praised the Lord who let us see
His glory at its dawning.
*—Old English Carol*

For the glory of the morning,
For the starry rest of night,
For light, and life, and love, and mind,
　God's fulness of delight,
We would bring as our thanksgiving
　A true and open heart
And the wish that in God's beauty
　We too may be a part.
*—Anonymous*

Were half the power that fills the world with terror,
　Were half the wealth bestowed on camps and courts,
Given to redeem the human mind from error,
　There were no need of arsenals and forts.
*—Henry Wadsworth Longfellow*

They dwelt among the bravely dumb
Who did their deed and scorned
To blot it with a name.
—*Anonymous*

God speaks to me
In my mind.
He speaks and says,
"Be good, be kind."
—*Anonymous*

The witness in the souls of men,
The Spirit's ceaseless, brooding power,
In lands where shadows hide the light,
Await a new creative hour:
O mighty God, set us aflame
To show the glory of thy name.
—*Frank M. North*

Your son, my Lord, has paid a soldier's debt;
He only liv'd but till he was a man;
The which no sooner had his prowess confirm'd
In the unshrinking station where he fought,
But like a man he died!
—*William Shakespeare*

The spiritual interpretation of life teaches us that all human life is sacred; that we are members one of another; that the things which we have in common are greater than those which divide; that each is his brother's keeper.
—*W. L. Mackenzie King*

There cannot be much preaching worthy of the name where there is no thinking. Preaching is nothing but the bursting out of light, which has first burst in or up from where God is, among the soul's foundations.
—*Horace Bushnell*

God sleeps in a stone, dreams in a flower, moves in an animal, and wakes in man.
—*Irenæus*

When the heart is illuminated, then we shall perceive our real nature.
—*Chinese Saying*

I am a citizen, not of Athens or of Greece but of the world.
—*Socrates*

The foundation of every state is the education of its youth.
—*Diogenes*

[ 330 ]

All sunshine makes the desert.

—*Arabic Proverb*

Great hearts alone know how much glory there is in being good.

—*Pascal*

Talk does not cook rice.

—*Chinese Proverb*

There are two heavens,
Both made of love—one inconceivable
Ev'n by the other, so divine it is;
The other, far on this side of the stars,
By men called home.

—*Leigh Hunt*

Be like the bird who, halting in her flight,
Rests on a branch too slight,
And feeling it give way beneath her, sings,
Knowing that she hath wings.

—*Anonymous*

I dress the wound and God heals it.

—*On the walls of a French hospital*

"There is no God," the wicked saith,
"And truly it's a blessing,
For what he might have done with us
It's better only guessing."

—*Arthur Hugh Clough*

God's pampered people whom, debauch'd with ease,
No king could govern and no God could please.

—*John Dryden*

Whoever puts a beautiful thought into the world gives more than a
diamond of Golconda.

—*Proverb of India*

The good person increases the value of every other person whom he
influences in any way.

—*Anonymous*

He sings and plays
The songs which best thou lovest,
Who does and says
The things which thou approvest.

—*George Wither*

[ 331 ]

After all, man knows mighty little, and may some day learn enough of his own ignorance to fall down and pray.

—*Henry Adams*

God taught me to read. . . .
He lent me the world for a book
—*Jean Ingelow*

Sunshine is delicious, rain is refreshing, wind braces us, snow is exhilarating; there is really no such thing as bad weather, only different kinds of good weather.

—*John Ruskin*

If to do were as easy as to know what were good to do, chapels had been churches, and poor men's cottages princes' palaces.

—*William Shakespeare*

Just laws are no restraint upon the freedom of the good, for the good man desires nothing which a just law will interfere with.

—*James Anthony Froude*

Books are the food of youth and the solace of age;
They adorn prosperity, and are the comfort and refuge of adversity;
They amuse us at home and are no encumbrance abroad;
They accompany us at night, on our travels and in our rural retirement.

—*Cicero*

May the wee moosie ne'er leave your meal poke wi' a tear in its ee.

—*Scottish Proverb*

In Springtime a fair world of flowers and birds that sing.
In Summertime a green world—a very lovely thing.
In Autumntime a coloured world—all praise be there for him.

—*Anonymous*

To relieve men's calamities is ten times better than to worship Buddha.
To save men from danger is ten times better than to burn incense.

—*Chinese Proverb*

I would have you day by day fix your eyes upon the greatness of Athens, until you have become filled with the love of her. And when you are impressed with the spectacle of her glory, reflect that this empire has been acquired by men who knew their duty and had the courage to do it.

—*Pericles*

Physically speaking, a pile of stones in a quarry is infinitely more probable than the same stones built into a Taj Mahal, though both are

[ 332 ]

possible. Humanly speaking, it is the wishes of a king, the creative enthusiasm of an architect, and the skilful work of the artisans, all working within the limits of physical law, which determine that the stones must assume the forms of a beautiful building, a lasting monument to human love.

— *A. H. Canifton*

The contemplation of God is man's highest good and artistic creation is next to it in felicity.

—*Thomas Aquinas*

The archer hitteth the target, partly by pulling, partly by letting go; the boatman reacheth the landing, partly by pulling, partly by letting go.

—*Egyptian Proverb*

Nature is always calling to us, saying, "Wonder, enjoy, revere."

—*J. Arthur Thomson*

Slaves cannot breathe in England; if their lungs receive our air, that moment they are free; they touch our country and their shackles fall.

—*William Cowper*

Hats off to the past—
Coats off to the future.
—*Anonymous*

To this day this Galilean is too great for our small hearts.

—*H. G. Wells*

Let the following be your watchwords:
He who hurts another, harms himself;
He who helps another, helps himself.
—*Leo Tolstoy*

The tongue speaks wisdom when the soul is wise.

—*Homer*

Luck means the hardships and privations which you have not hesitated to endure; the long nights you have devoted to work. Luck means the appointments you have never failed to keep; the trains you have never failed to catch.

—*Max O'Rell*

A good book is the precious life-blood of a master spirit, imbalmed and treasured up on purpose to a life beyond life.

—*John Milton*

[ 333 ]

'Tis said that Galilee in Spring
Is one big bright bouquet,
And I am sure it must have been
The same in Jesus' day;
For in his words we well may trace
Fair flowers' fragrance and their grace.
—*Alice Crowell Hoffman*

"Why, I could make a better world than this myself," said the pessimist.

"That's exactly what you are here for," the optimist answered. "Let's go out and do it."

—*Margueritte H. Bro*

So that were man not by himself opprest, kings would not, tyrants could not, make him beast.

—*Fulke Grevelle*

A man lives by believing something; not by debating and arguing about many things.

—*Thomas Carlyle*

Money lost, little lost;
Health lost, much lost;
Heart lost, all lost.
—*Old English Proverb*

We shall defend our Island, whatever the cost may be; we shall fight on the beaches, we shall fight on the landing grounds, we shall fight in the fields and in the streets, we shall fight in the hills; we shall never surrender.

—*Winston Churchill*

Love's very pain is sweet.
But its reward is in the world divine
Which, if not here, it builds beyond the grave.
—*Percy Bysshe Shelley*

The omnipotence of God will mean neither the tawdry trappings of regal pomp nor the irresistible might of physical force. The divine omnipotence consists in the all-compelling power of goodness and love to enlighten the grossest darkness and to melt the hardest heart.

—*Seth Pringle-Pattison*

Not what we give, but what we share,
For the gift without the giver is bare;
Who gives himself with his alms feeds three,
Himself, his hungering neighbor and Me.
—*James Russell Lowell*

No Sunday, means no Church; no Church, means no worship; no worship means no religion; no religion, means no morals; no morals, means no society; no society, means no government; no government, means anarchy.

—*Charles Gore*

Time flies,
Suns rise
And shadows fall.
Let time go by.
Love is forever over all.
—*Old English Sundial*

If God is a mere spectator of it all, God must be something less than perfect love.

—*H. B. Streeter*

Let us not burden our remembrances
With a heaviness that's gone.
—*William Shakespeare*

Do not remove the fly from your friend's forehead with a hatchet.
—*Chinese Proverb*

Men at some times are masters of their fate:
The fault, dear Brutus, is not in our stars
But in ourselves, that we are underlings.
—*William Shakespeare*

A hundred men can build an encampment, but it takes a woman to make a home.

—*Chinese Proverb*

No wise man desires a soft life.

—*King Alfred*

To me every hour of the day and night is an unspeakably perfect miracle.

—*Walt Whitman*

It's good to have money and the things that money can buy, but it's good, too, to check up once in a while and make sure that you haven't lost the things that money can't buy.

—*George Horace Lorimer*

In the Spring a fuller crimson comes upon the robin's breast;
In the Spring the wanton lapwing gets himself another crest;
In the Spring a livelier iris changes on the burnished dove;
In the Spring a young man's fancy lightly turns to thoughts of love.
—*Alfred Tennyson*

Suffering passes away; to have suffered abides forever.
—*French Proverb*

What orthodox Christianity has always maintained is not that "God is a Person" but that there is personality in God, and that consequently it is possible for one to enter into a genuine personal relation with him.
—*A. E. Taylor*

Bring orchids, bring fox-glove spire,
The little speedwell's darling blue,
Deep tulips dashed with fiery dew,
Laburnums, drooping-wells of fire.
—*Alfred Tennyson*

A vague attachment to the whole human race is a poor substitute for the performance of a citizen.
—*Joseph Chamberlain*

The law of the upward urge (the attractive force of the Divine) is as universal in its application to humanity as the law of gravitation.
—*William C. Willoughby*

The will of God must be thought of as the embodiment of a single principle—the will of good.
—*H. B. Streeter*

In thy will is our peace.
—*Dante*

Earth's noblest thing—a woman perfected.
—*James Russell Lowell*

The liberty of each citizen ends where the liberty of another citizen commences.
—*French Revolution Convention*

Give all to love; obey thy heart;
Friends, kindred, days, estate, good-fame,
Plans, credit and the muse—
Nothing refuse.
—*Ralph Waldo Emerson*

Yet this I have learned from experience, that I am never less a prey to melancholy than when I am earnestly applying the feeble powers of my mind to some high and difficult object.
—*Philip Sidney*

Above revolutions Truth and Justice remain as the starry sky lies above and beyond tempests.
—*Victor Hugo*

[ 336 ]

Souninge in[2] moral virtue has his speche,
And gladly wold he lerne, and gladly teche.
—*Chaucer*

Friendship is a thing most necessary to life, since without friends no
one would choose to live, though possessed of all other advantages.
—*Aristotle*

Tea: Thou soft, thou sober, sage and venerable liquid. Thou female,
tongue-running, smile-soothing, heart-opening, wink-tippling cordial.
—*Colley Cibber*

There is one furnace that melts all hearts—love; there is one balm that
soothes all pain—patience; there is one medicine that cures all ills—time;
there is one light that illumines all darkness—hope.
—*Ivan Panin*

There is not the faintest trace that the shedding of our Lord's blood
on the cross was an expiatory sacrifice for the sin of the whole world.
—*W. O. E. Oesterley*

To win victory, much that was of great price has been given up, much
has been ravaged and destroyed by the hand of war. But the things that
have been saved are beyond price.
—*George VI of Great Britain*

The process of evolution is creative of reality. . . . It involves the
creative rise not only of new forms of groupings, but even of new
materials in the process of evolution.
—*Jan Christian Smuts*

It is to some a disquieting and to others a reassuring thought that
behind everything mind seems to have been at work from the beginning.
. . . No purely mechanistic interpretation of the world will ever satisfy
the human mind.
—*Walter Shepherd*

Loveliness needs not the foreign aid of ornament, but is, when un-
adorned, adorned the most.
—*James Thompson*

He is true to God who's true to man; wherever wrong is done
To the humblest and the weakest, 'neath the all-beholding sun,
That wrong is also done to us; and they are slaves most base,
Whose love of right is for themselves, and not for all the race.
—*James Russell Lowell*

[1] Clerk, teacher.
[2] Tending to.

The great use of life is to spend it for something that outlasts it.
—*William James*


I firmly believe that every enterprise which man undertakes, if it is to achieve any lasting success, must have a strong spiritual basis. If we attempt any great thing for solely material reasons, the results cannot be good.
—*Bernard Law Montgomery*


Free will—one's ability to move his hand at will—is much more directly and certainly known than are even the well tested laws of Newton.
—*Arthur H. Compton*


You better live your best and act your best and think your best today; for today is the sure preparation for tomorrow and all the other tomorrows that follow.
—*Harriet Martineau*


Know then thyself, presume not God to scan;
The proper study of mankind is man.
—*Alexander Pope*


The distinctive Christian teaching about God, if it can be compressed into a single phrase, is not that he is triune but that he is redemptive love.
—*John Baillie*


We have loved the stars too fondly
To be fearful of the night.
—*John Brashear's Epitaph to His Wife*


Take a compassionate view of the Bantu man, and you can hardly avoid the following conclusion: he is no exception to the rule that the deepest thing in the soul of man is . . . he feels that he is in some way related to the unseen and dependent upon it.
—*William C. Willoughby*


Give what you have. To some one it may be better than you dare to think.
—*Henry Wadsworth Longfellow*


The most important part of education is right training in the nursery. The soul of the child in his play should be guided to the love of that sort of excellence in which when he grows up to manhood he will have to be perfected.
—*Plato*

I do not believe there is a problem in this country or the world today which could not be settled if approached through the teaching of the sermon on the mount.

—*Harry S. Truman*

God prefers a loving sinner to a loveless saint.

—*Anonymous*

> Rest after toil, port after stormy seas,
> Peace after war, death after life;
> All these things do please.
> —*Anonymous*

Is death the last sleep? No, it is the last and final awakening.

—*Walter Scott*

The simple fact that we are compelled to pass judgment upon ourselves lies very near the centre of the religious field.

—*John Macmurray*

> True love is but a humble, low-born thing,
> And hath its food served up in earthen ware;
> It is a thing to walk with hand in hand,
> Through the every-dayness of this work-day world.
> —*James Russell Lowell*

A little philosophy inclineth a man's mind to atheism, but depth in philosophy bringeth men's minds about to religion.

—*Francis Bacon*

At all times and everywhere he gave his strength to the weak, his substance to the poor, his sympathy to the suffering and his heart to God.
—*On Chinese Gordon's Tomb in Westminster Abbey*

> I heard a bird sing in the dark of December
> A magical thing and sweet to remember:
> "We are nearer to Spring than we were in September"
> I heard a bird sing in the dark of December.
> —*Anonymous*

The statement that Jesus made the forgiveness of sin . . . dependent on his own death is to be placed among the most poverty-stricken of theological foundlings. He announced the full amnesty of the Father without bargaining or haggling.

—*Gustav A. Deissman*

> Marriage:
> The light of love shines over all,

[ 339 ]

Of love that says not mine and thine,
But ours, for ours is mine.
—*Henry Wadsworth Longfellow*

Would it not be a beautiful thing now if you were just coming instead
of going.
—*Celtic Farewell to a Guest*

Progress, man's distinctive mark alone,
Not God's and not the beasts':
God is, they are;
Man partly is, and wholly hopes to be.
—*Robert Browning*

I need not shout my faith. Thrice eloquent
Are the quiet trees and the green listening sod;
Hushed are the stars, whose power is never spent;
The hills are mute; yet how they speak of God.
—*Charles Hanson Towne*

Night is a good herdsman. He brings all creatures home.
—*Gaelic Proverb*

They are slaves who dare not be
In the right with two or three.
—*James Russell Lowell*

O wad some Power the giftie gie us
To see oursel's as ithers see us!
It wad frae monie a blunder free us,
An' foolish notion.
—*Robert Burns*

So frail the boat, so vast the sea.
—*Gaelic Proverb of the Individual Life*

Our country is the world—our countrymen are all mankind.
—*William Lloyd Garrison*

Whatsoever thy hand findeth to do, do it with thy might.
—*Ecclesiastes 9:10*

Whatsoever ye would that men should do to you, do ye even so to
them.
—*Matthew 7:12*

Where there is no vision the people perish.
—*Proverbs 28:19*

[ 340 ]

To know what you prefer instead of humbly saying Amen to what the world tells you you ought to prefer is to have kept your soul alive.
—*Robert Louis Stevenson*

Be inspired with the belief that life is a great and noble calling; not a mean and grovelling thing that we are to shuffle through as we can, but an elevated and lofty destiny.
—*William Ewart Gladstone*

Christmas: 'Tis the season for kindling the fire of hospitality in the hall, the genial fire of charity in the heart.
—*Washington Irving*

A propensity to hope and joy is real riches; one to fear and sorrow, real poverty.
—*David Hume*

No one could tell me what my soul might be.
I searched for God, and God eluded me.
I sought my brother out; and found all three—
My soul, my God, and all humanity.
—*Anonymous*

The best things are nearest; breath in your nostrils, light in your eyes, duties at your hand, the path of God just before you. Then do not grasp at the stars, but do life's plain, common work as it comes, certain that daily duties and daily bread are the sweetest things of life.
—*Robert Louis Stevenson*

That music is the usefulest which makes the best words most beautiful, which enhances them in our memory, each with its own glory of sound, and which applies them closest to the heart at the moment we need them.
—*John Ruskin*

If you look at men's faults you will have no friends.
—*Talmud*

There is more delight in hope than in enjoyment.
—*Japanese Proverb*

The measure of our sacrifice is the measure of our love.
—*Anonymous*

If you have two loaves of bread, sell one and buy a lily.
—*Chinese Proverb*

The most wasted of all days is the day when we have not laughed.
—*French Proverb*

[ 341 ]

If you know what hurts yourself you know what hurts others.

—*Malagasy Proverb*

Habits are at first cobwebs, at last cables.

—*Anonymous*

If you can't push, pull. If you can't pull, please get out of the way.

—*Anonymous*

A little too late is much too late.

—*Anonymous*

It is good to be children sometimes and never better than at Christmas when its mighty Founder was a child himself.

—*Charles Dickens*

It's the cleverest thing in the world to be merely happy, and the unhappiest to be merely clever.

—*Maarten Maartens*

Who is wise? He that learns from everyone. Who is powerful? He that governs himself. Who is rich? He that is content.

—*Benjamin Franklin*

Let us never forget that an act of goodness is of itself an act of happiness. No reward coming after the event can compare with the sweet reward that went with it.

—*Maurice Maeterlinck*

> Be good, sweet maid, and let who will be clever;
> Do noble things, not dream them all day long;
> And so make life, death, and that vast forever
> One grand, sweet song.
> —*Charles Kingsley*

Love is . . . a simple fire-side thing, whose quiet smile can warm earth's poorest hovel to a home.

—*James Russell Lowell*

> The trifles of our daily lives,
> The common things scarce worth recall
> Of which no visible trace remains—
> These are the mainsprings after all.
> —*Anonymous*

> Give love, and love to your heart will flow
> A strength in your utmost need.
> —*Anonymous*

He only is advancing in life whose heart is getting softer, whose blood is getting warmer, whose brain quicker, and whose spirit is entering into living peace.

*—John Ruskin*

The blue of heaven is larger than the cloud.

*—Elizabeth Barrett Browning*

> Were I so tall to reach the pole,
> Or grasp the ocean with my span
> I must be measured by my soul:
> The mind's the standard of the man.
>
> *—Isaac Watts*

I like not only to be loved, but to be told I am loved. The realm of silence is large enough beyond the grave.

*—George Eliot*

You are not responsible for the disposition you were born with, but you are responsible for the one you die with.

*—Maltbie Davenport Babcock*

I would rather be a poor man in a garret with plenty of books than a king who did not love reading.

*—Thomas Babington Macaulay*

> In men whom men condemn as ill
> I find so much of goodness still,
> In men whom men pronounce divine
> I find so much of sin and blot,
> I do not dare to draw a line
> Between the two, where God has not.
>
> *—Joaquin Miller*

I know that the Lord is always on the side of the right; but it is my constant anxiety and prayer that I and this nation should be on the Lord's side.

*—Abraham Lincoln*

Money is an article which may be used as a universal passport to everywhere except heaven, and a universal provider of everything except happiness.

*—Anonymous*

Applaud us when we run; console us when we fall; cheer us when we recover; but let us press on—for God's sake, let us press on.

*—Robert Louis Stevenson*

Every one truly lives so long as he . . . some way makes good the faculties of himself.

—*Thomas Brown*

I shall pass through this world but once. Any good therefore that I can do or any kindness that I can show to any human being, let me do it now. Let me not defer or neglect it, for I shall not pass this way again.

—*Anonymous*

If I were a cobbler, it should be my pride
The best of all cobblers to be;
If I were a tinker, no tinker beside
Should mend an old kettle like me.

—*Anonymous*

Except a living man there is nothing more wonderful than a book! a message to us from the dead—from human souls we never saw, who lived, perhaps thousands of miles away. And yet these, in those little sheets of paper, speak to us, arouse us, terrify us, teach us, comfort us, open their hearts to us as brothers.

—*Charles Kingsley*

A merry heart doeth good like a medicine.

—*Proverbs 17:22*

Christianity is not merely a creed, but an experience; not a restraint, but an inspiration; not merely an insurance for the next world, but also a program for the present world.

—*James Stalker*

Thou art welcome, whosoever thou art that enterest this Church; it is thy Father's house; come in the spirit of reverence; worship in the spirit of humility; and leave it not without a prayer to God for thyself, for those who minister, and for those who worship here.

—*Anonymous*

What we have somehow to do in the present age is to combine goodness and cleverness, to learn somehow to permeate those vast impersonal world organizations, which in this modern age we cannot do without, with the love of God and our neighbor. We have to learn to harness the scientific mind in the service of the merciful heart.

—*William Tucker Lindesay-Bethune*
(British Broadcasting Corporation Address)

The superior man cultivates himself not his appetite.

—*Chinese Proverb*

Righteousness exalteth a nation: but sin is a reproach to any people.

—*Proverbs 14:34*

That laughter costs too much which is purchased by the sacrifice of decency.

*—Quintilian*

He that findeth his life shall lose it: and he that loseth his life for my sake shall find it.

*—Matthew 10:39*

Whatsoever things are true, whatsoever things are honest, whatsoever things are just, whatsoever things are pure, whatsoever things are lovely, whatsoever things are of good report; if there be any virtue, and if there be any praise, think on these things.

*—Philippians 4:8*

Our growing thought makes growing revelation.

*—George Eliot*

He who findeth a good neighbor findeth a precious thing.

*—Hesiod*

Learning without thought is labor lost.

*—Confucius*

Above all wealth, honor or health is the attachment we form to noble souls, because to become one with the good, generous and true, is to become in a measure, good, generous and true ourselves.

*—Thomas Arnold*

Hospitality consists in a little fire, a little food, and an immense quiet.
*—Ralph Waldo Emerson*

God likes far better to help people from the inside than from the outside.

*—George Macdonald*

The foundation of domestic happiness is faith in the virtue of woman; the foundation of political happiness is confidence in the integrity of man; the foundation of happiness, temporal and eternal, is reliance on the goodness of God.

*—Walter Savage Landor*

Sweep first before your own door before you sweep the doorsteps of your neighbors.

*—Swedish Proverb*

How can we expect a harvest of thought who have not had a seed-time of character.

*—Henry David Thoreau*

An ounce of mirth, with some degree of grace, will serve God further than a pound of sadness.

—*T. Fuller*

I know indeed that wealth is good;
But lowly roof and simple food,
With love that hath no doubt,
Are more than gold without.

*James Greenleaf Whittier*

The human race is divided into two classes—those who go ahead and do something, and those who sit still and enquire, "Why wasn't it done the other way?"

—*Oliver Wendell Holmes*

A world without a Sabbath would be like a person without a smile, like a summer without flowers, and like a homestead without a garden. It is the joyous day of the whole week.

—*Henry Ward Beecher*

Utmost wisdom is not in self-denial, but in learning to find extreme pleasure in little things.

—*John Ruskin*

Virtue is a kind of health, beauty, and good habit of the soul.

—*Plato*

One must of necessity look into the face of his Father in the morning before he goes forth to look into the face of his brother.

—*J. H. Baily*

Worldly fame and pleasure are destructive to the virtue of the mind; anxious thoughts or apprehensions are injurious to the health of the body.

—*Chinese Proverb*

Of earthly goods the best is a good wife;
A bad, the bitterest curse of human life.

—*Simonides*

There are two freedoms—the false, where a man is free to do what he likes; and the true, where a man is free to do what is right.

—*Charles Kingsley*

It is the duty of all of you to be aristocrats. Of the aristocrat I know only one adequate definition. He is the man who gives to the world more than he takes from it.

—*John Buchan*

Performing miracles in a crisis—so much easier than loving God self-lessly every moment of the day! Which is why most crises arise—because people find it so hard to behave properly at ordinary times.

—*Aldous Huxley*

Only through love can we attain to communion with God.

—*Albert Schweitzer*

I am in God's presence night & day
And he never turns his face away.

—*William Blake*

Today is the tomorrow we dreaded yesterday, but God has not failed us yet.

—*Anonymous*

God hath not given us the spirit of fear; but of power, and of love, and of a sound mind.

—*II Timothy 1:7*

Human life is a voyage in which we can choose neither the vessel nor the weather, although much may be done in the management of the sails and the guidance of the helm.

—*Norman Macleod*

Beware of prejudice; light is good in whatever lamp it is burning. A rose is beautiful in whatsoever garden it may bloom. A star has the same radiance if it shines from the East or in the West.

—*Abdul Baba*

The true gentleman is God's servant. Virtue is his business, study his recreation, service his contentment and usefulness his reward.

—*Anonymous*

Do not pray for easy lives. Pray to be stronger. Do not pray for tasks equal to your powers. Pray for powers equal to your tasks. Then the doing of your work shall be no miracle. But you shall be a miracle. Every day you shall wonder . . . at the richness of life which has come to you by the grace of God.

—*Phillips Brooks*

Idleness is the glory of the sword and rust its honor.

—*Anonymous*

Gold and silver are tried in the fire but acceptable men in the furnace of humiliation.

—*Ecclesiasticus*

[ 347 ]

Love God, and you will throw off the love of self; love God and you will love all that he gives you to love for love of him.

*—François Fénelon*

God is greater than all our conceptions of him, and they one by one give way to make room for a fuller and better thought.

*—R. Whitwell*

He that believes dares trust God for the morrow, and is no more solicitous for the next year than he is for that which is past.

*—Anonymous*

Hope is like the sun, which, as we journey towards it, casts the shadow of our burden behind us.

*—Samuel Smiles*

The doing of evil to avoid an evil cannot be good.

*—Samuel Taylor Coleridge*

When you put on your clothes remember the labor of the weaver: when you eat your daily bread think of the hardships of the husbandmen.

*—Chinese Proverb*

The best means of destroying an enemy is to make him your friend.

*—Anonymous*

No one is so insignificant as to be sure his example can do no hurt— nor help.

*—Anonymous*

As there comes a warm sunbeam into every cottage window, so comes a love-beam of god's love and care for every separate need.

*—Nathaniel Hawthorne*

An education is good, when you get to the crossroads, to read the guide boards when you don't know which way to go.

*—A boy's definition of education. Anonymous*

Whether it be biography, introducing us to some humble life made great by duty done, or history opening vistas into the movements and destinies of nations that have passed away, or poetry, making music of all the common things around us and filling the fields and skies and the work of the city and the cottage with eternal meanings, whether it be these or story books or religious books or science, no one can become the friend even of one good book without being made wiser and better.

*—Henry Drummond*

For every child spiritual and moral training to help him stand firm under the pressure of life.
—*The Children's Charter, White House Conference on Child Health and Protection*

We hold that all children . . . are members of the Kingdom of God.
—*General Conference of The Methodist Church, 1856, and later incorporated in the Discipline*

Our law surely would say that it is best to keep as tranquil as possible in misfortune, and not to be vexed or resentful: for we cannot see what good or evil there is in such things, and impatience does not in any way help us forwards; also because nothing in human affairs deserves serious anxiety, and grief stands in the way to hinder the self-succor that our duty immediately requires of us.

—*Plato*

I find I never weary of great churches. It is my favorite kind of mountain scenery. Mankind was never so happily inspired as when it made a cathedral; a thing as single and as spacious as a statue at first sight and on examination as lively and interesting as a forest in detail.
—*Robert Louis Stevenson*

Make use of time if thou valuest eternity. Yesterday cannot be recalled; tomorrow cannot be assured; today only is thine, which, if thou procrastinatist, thou losest; which loss is loss forever.

—*Jeremy Taylor*

Words are the daughters of earth. Deeds are the sons of Heaven.
—*Ancient Proverb*

He is a happy man who enjoys his books, and to whom the day does not seem long enough for reading. For books are friends who never quarrel, never complain, are never false; who come from far ages and old lands to talk with us when we wish to hear them, and are silent when we are weary. Good books take us away from small troubles and petty vexations into a serene atmosphere of thought, nobleness, truth.
—*James Freeman Clarke*

There are six things that bring success: the first is will to work, and the other five are work.

—*Anonymous*

Never miss an opportunity of looking on beauty-fair sky, fair face, fair flower. Beauty is God's handwriting, a wayside sacrament. Rejoice in it and thank him for it—the Giver of all loveliness.

—*Anonymous*

A man looks upon God as his father and loves him in like measure.
—*Lao Tze*

The nearness of God is my good.

—*Psalm 73:28 (J. P. M. Smith)*

Be perfect, be of good comfort, be of one mind, live in peace; and the God of love and peace shall be with you.

—*II Corinthians 13:11*

Make no mistake about this, my beloved brothers: all we are given is good, and all our endowments are faultless, descending from above, from the Father of the heavenly lights, who knows no change of rising and setting, who casts no shadow on the earth.

—*James 1:16-17 (Moffatt)*

A diamond cannot be polished without friction, nor the man perfected without trials.

—*Chinese Proverb*

To be honest, to be kind, to earn a little and to spend a little less, to make a family happier for his presence—here is a task for all that a man has of fortitude and delicacy.

—*Robert Louis Stevenson*

Practice not deception even by mistake.

—*Sikh Religion*

Man must work with his hands at honest toil, so as to have something to share with those who are in need.

—*Ephessians 4:28 (An American Translation of the New Testament)*

God hath made of one blood all nations of men.

—*Acts 17:26*

His Kingdom is an everlasting Kingdom and his dominion is from generation to generation.

—*Daniel 4:3*

He becometh poor that worketh with a slack hand.

—*Proverbs 10:3*

Wise people falter not amidst praise and blame, as a rock is not shaken by the wind.

—*Buddha*

As a man thinketh in his heart, so is he.

—*Proverbs 23:7*

> So farewell hope, and with hope, farewell fear,
> Farewell remorse: all good to me is lost;
> Evil, be thou my good.

—*John Milton*

[ 350 ]

When the minaret of the mosque falls down and we put the factory chimney in its place; when the Hindu temple is deserted and the worshipers flock to the cinema they are no nearer to the Kingdom.

—*Basil Mathews*

Meaning thereby that a man cannot be taught. But though he cannot be taught, he can learn, meaning thereby that he can discover a self within himself.

—*George Moore*

Everywhere I go people thank me for saving their lives. I don't know why they do it. I didn't do anything. Nature makes penicillin. I just found it.

—*Sir Alexander Fleming*

> To love my crooked neighbor
> With all my crooked heart.
> —*Anonymous*

Leonidas with his thousand at Thermopylae stood against the vast armies of the Medes and Persians.

"The number of the barbarians is so great that when they shoot their arrows the sun will be darkened."

And Dienekes replied, "So much the better, we shall then fight in the shade."

—*Herodotus*

> The love of all
> Is but a small thing to the love of one.
> You bid a hungry child be satisfied
> With a heritage of many cornfields: Nay,
> He says he's hungry—he would rather have
> That little barley cake you keep from him
> While reckoning up his harvest.
> —*Elizabeth Barrett Browning*

Stand still, and consider the wonders of God.

—*Job 37:14*

Real statesmen are Artificers of Freedom.

—*Plato*

If it be life that waits I shall live forever. If death, I shall die at last strong in my pride and free.

—*Part of Inscription on War Memorial 1914-8, Edinburgh, Scotland*

If the spur of the scientist is the love of truth, the joy of the Christian is the truth of love. . . . If the satisfaction of the artist is the life of beauty, the joy of the Christian is the beauty of life, all life, man's life, the life of God.

—Van Ogden Vogt

Where song is, pause to listen.
Evil people have no song.

—Norwegian legend on decoration, Time and Life Building, Radio City, New York

Heroes have the whole earth for their tomb. Their bodies sleep in the earth, and their names are graven in stone, but their souls live on without visible symbol in other lands and in other years, woven into the stuff of other men's lives.

—Pericles

From our own selves our joys must flow,
And that dear hut, our home.

—Nathaniel Callon

Love is the inspiration of the poet, the wisdom of the philosopher, the courage of the warrior, the hope of the hero, the devotion of the mother. Without God's love humankind would perish.

—Anonymous

A man wrapped up in himself makes a very small parcel.

—Anonymous

It will never rain roses. If we want more roses we must plant more trees.

—Anonymous

Three things, I've heard tell, best support the world . . . the slender stream of milk from a cow's udder into the pail, the slender blade of green corn from the ground, and the slender thread over the hand of a skilled woman.

—Nora S. Unwin

To every hearth a little fire,
To every board a little feast,
To every heart a joy,
To every child a toy,
Shelter for bird and beast.

—Anonymous

"What," it will be Questioned, "when the sun rises, do you not see a round disk of fire somewhat like a Guinea." O no, no, I see an Innumerable company of the Heavenly host crying, "Holy, Holy, Holy is the Lord God Almighty."

—William Blake

[ 352 ]

We all want what peace makes but not what makes peace.

—*Anonymous*

That God, which ever lives and loves,
One God, one law, one element,
And one far-off divine event,
To which the whole creation moves.

—*Alfred Tennyson*

For books are more than books, they are the life,
The very heart and core of ages past;
The reason why men lived, and worked, and died
The essence and quintessence of their lives.

—*James Russell Lowell*

For why?—because the good old rule
Sufficeth them, the simple plan
That they should take who have the power,
And they should keep who can.

—*William Wordsworth*

The meat of the elephant is some good, some bad.

—*Bantu Proverb*

No heaven can come to us unless our hearts find rest in it today. Take Heaven. No peace lies in the future which is not hidden in this present instant. Take Peace. The gloom of the world is but a shadow; behind it, yet within our reach, is joy. Take Joy.

—*Fra Angelico*

Two things profoundly impress me: the starry heavens above me and the moral law within me.

—*Immanuel Kant*

Most people are bothered by those passages of Scripture they do not understand, but I have always noticed that the passages that bother me are those I do understand.

—*Mark Twain*

No, the heart that has loved never forgets,
But as truly loves on to the close;
As the sunflower turns to her god when he sets
The same look that she turned when he rose.

—*Thomas More*

In practice the great end is that the Love of God may become a habit of my soul, and particularly these things are to be sought: 1. The spirit of Love, 2. of self sacrifice, 3. of purity, 4. of mercy.

—*William Ewart Gladstone* (his Diary)

[ 353 ]

I am going out from Rome. Let those who wish to continue the war against the stranger come with me. I offer him neither pay, nor quarters, nor provisions: I offer hunger, thirst, forced marches, battle, and death. Let him who loves his country in his heart and not with his lips only, follow me.

—*Giuseppi Garibaldi* (*1849*)

God alone is Lord of the conscience, and hath left it free from the doctrines and commandments of men, which are in anything contrary to his word or beside it in matters of faith and worship.

—*Presbyterian Confession of Faith*

In War, Resolution. In Defeat, Defiance. In Victory, Magnanimity. In Peace, Good-will.

—*On a British War Memorial in France*

We hold these truths to be self evident,—that all men are created equal; that they are endowed by their Creator with certain unalienable rights; that among these are life, liberty and the pursuit of happiness.

—*United States of America Declaration of Independence*

I would not enter on my list of friends,
Though graced with manners and fine sense
(Yet wanting sensibility), the man
Who needlessly sets foot upon a worm.

—*William Cowper*

The High Priest of Science looks on a troubled world of Science misapplied to deeds of war, which are reprobated by the people they ruin.

—*On a Statue of Sir Isaac Newton, Grantham, England*

Solitude is as needful to the imagination as society is wholesome for character.

—*James Russell Lowell*

I believe in God the Father Almighty because whenever I have looked, through all that I see around me, I see the trace of an intelligent mind; and because in natural laws, and especially in the laws which govern the social relations of man, I see not merely the proof of intelligence but the proofs of beneficence.

—*Henry George*

Know how sublime a thing it is
To suffer and be strong.

—*Henry Wadsworth Longfellow*

We all need a certain stimulation which comes from immediate environment. We all seek obedience, compliments, courtesies, which are the vitamins of the spirit.

—*Pierre Janet*

[ 354 ]

Our earth is degenerate in these latter days; there are signs that the world is speedily coming to an end; bribery and corruption are common; children no longer obey their parents; every man wants to write a book, and the end of the world is evidently approaching.

—*Assyrian Tablet, Istanbul* (2800 B.C.)

Go with God.

—*Old Spanish Farewell*

The size of the deed is immaterial, the outward circumstances of life are immaterial. Marcus Aurelius was a great person in spite of his wealth, Epictetus was a great person in spite of his poverty and slavery.

—*Anonymous*

The doors of wisdom are never shut.

—*Benjamin Franklin*

As long as lynching goes on in America, she has very little brotherhood to export to the Orient.

—*Rabindranath Tagore*

These hath God married
And none shall them part
Dust on the Bible
And drought in the heart.
—*Anonymous*

When we consider this man's achievements, we shall be forced to admit that beside this little Jew of Tarsus [Saul], Alexander the Great is a phantom and Napoleon a puppet.

—*Lord Birkinhead*

Let knowledge grow from more to more,
But more of reverence in us dwell;
That mind and soul, according well,
May make one music as before.
—*Alfred Tennyson*

Like the beacon lights in the harbors, which, kindling a great blaze by means of a few fagots, afford sufficient aid to vessels that wander over the sea, so, also, a man of bright character in a storm-tossed city, himself content with little, effects great blessings for his fellow citizens.

—*Epictetus*

Be stirring as the time; be fire with fire;
Threaten the threatener and outface the brow
Of bragging horror; so shall inferior eyes,
That borrow their behavior from the great,

[ 355 ]

Grow great by your example and put on
The dauntless spirit of resolution.
—*William Shakespeare*

Nothing to fear in God: Nothing to feel in Death: . . . Good can be attained.
—*Diogenes*

Even a child is known by his doings.
—*Proverbs 20:11a*

Most of the evils you fear are false.
—*Epicurus*

Read not much at a time; but meditate on what you read as much as your time, capacity, and disposition will give you leave; ever remembering that little reading and much thinking, little speaking and much hearing, frequent and short prayers and great devotion, is the best way to be wise, to be holy, to be devout.
—*Jeremy Taylor*

Books we know
Are a substantial world, both pure and good.
Round these with tendrils strong as flesh and blood
Our pastime and our happiness will grow.
—*William Wordsworth*

Did I tell you that I have always made it a habit to pray before writing anything for publication, that there may be no self-seeking in it, and perfect candor, together with respect for the feelings of others.
—*Francis Galton*

Isaac Walton quotes the saying that doubtless the Almighty could have created a finer fruit than the strawberry, but that doubtless also he never did. Doubtless also he could have provided us with better fun than hard work, but I don't know what it is. To be born poor is probably the next best thing.
—*J. M. Barrie*

Our hands are guided by our hearts and poisoned hearts make violent hands.
—*Japanese Proverb*

And while I rejoice in the advance of science, I deplore the desuetude of regular religious services with their encouragement of worship and prayer for the good reason that personal experience and the study of history convince me that this absence of the religious habit leads to an ugly class in private and public morals and to a subtle lowering of the sense of beauty.

—*Beatrice Webb*

There is nothing like books. Of all things sold incomparably the cheapest, of all pleasures the least palling; they take up little room, keep quiet when they are not wanted, and when taken up bring us face to face with the choicest men who have ever lived, at their choicest moments.

—*Samuel Parker*

Sir Humphry Davy said, in reply to a question: "My greatest scientific discovery was Michael Faraday."

When you get into a tight place and everything goes against you, till it seems as if you couldn't hold on a minute longer, never give up then, for that's just the place and time that the tide'll turn.

—*Harriet Beecher Stowe*

We do not perfect character in our sleep. It comes to us like muscle, by doing things. It is the muscle of the soul.

—*Horace Bushnell*

The roof hides our stars but they are shining still, and the star of Bethlehem will never set.

—*A Christian Inscription in the Catacombs under the Appian Way*

He who rides a tiger dare not fall off.

—*Chinese Proverb*

Who taught mankind on that first Christmas Day
What 'twas to be a man: to give, not take;
To serve, not rule; to nourish, not devour;
To help, not crush; if need, to die, not live!

—*Charles Kingsley*

It is better to light one candle than to curse the darkness.

—*Chinese Proverb*

"God! Thou art love!" I build my faith on that.

—*Robert Browning*

For the morning will come. Brightly will it shine on the Brave and True. Kindly on all who suffer for the Cause. Gloriously upon the tombs of Heroes. Thus will shine the dawn.

—*Winston Churchill*

There is not enough darkness in all the world to put out the light of one small candle.

*Anonymous*

And silence like a poultice comes
To heel the blows of sound.
—*Oliver Wendell Holmes*

George Carver said that he thought of his laboratory as God's little workshop.
I fell into the habit of always talking with God on every occasion.
—*Horace Bushnell*

Practice the presence of God. . . . Let us think often that our only business in this life is to please God, and that all besides is but folly and vanity. . . . Let us think of him perpetually. Let us put all our trust in him. . . . We cannot have too much in so good and faithful a Friend, who will never fail us in this world nor in the next.
—*Brother Lawrence*

He that doeth live at home, and learns to know
God and himself, needeth no farther go.
—*Christopher Harvey*

A child should grow up a Christian and never know himself as otherwise.
—*Horace Bushnell*

Steadfastly do what ought to be done.
—*Buddha*

Study to show thyself approved unto God, a workman who needeth not to be ashamed.
—*II Timothy 2:15*

To see what is right and not to do it, is want of courage.
—*Confucius*

As thou dost desire, so shalt thou be.
—*Zoroaster*

Wisdom is better than strength.
—*Ecclesiastes 9:16*

God gave us not a spirit of fearfulness; but of power and love and discipline.
—*II Timothy 1:7*

In all thy ways acknowledge him and he shall direct thy paths.
—*Proverbs 3:6*

Jesus increased in wisdom and stature and in favor with God and men.
—*Luke 2:52*

[ 358 ]

God is no respector of persons.

*—Acts 10:34*

More things are wrought by prayer than this world dreams of.

*—Alfred Tennyson*

Blessed are the peacemakers for they shall be called the children of God.

*—Matthew 5:9*

Inasmuch as ye have done it unto one of the least of these my brethren ye have done it unto me.

*—Matthew 25:40*

We have nothing to fear but fear.

*—Franklin Delano Roosevelt*

Spirit, that's what God is, and they that worship him must worship him is spirit and in truth.

*—John 4:24*

Blessed are the pure in heart: for they shall see God.

*—Matthew 5:8*

# INDEXES

# INDEX OF POETRY BY AUTHORS

[ 364 ]

## INDEX OF POETRY BY TITLE

[ 367 ]

# INDEX OF POETRY BY FIRST LINE

Flower in the crannied wall—TENNY-SON, 50
For I dipt into the future, far as human eye could see—TENNYSON, 112

Give me a good digestion, Lord—ANONYMOUS, 118
Give me, O God, to sing that thought —WHITMAN, 12
Give me wide walls to build my house of life—ANONYMOUS, 102
Give thanks to God—KLEISER, 52
God created man for incorruption—APOCRYPHA, 93
God dwells among the lowliest of men —KAGAWA, 161
God, give me joy in the common things —T. C. CLARK, 53
God holdeth in his hand the measure of judgment—YANNAI, 54
God is at the organ—SANDFORD, 53
God is in his holy temple—MYERS, 54
God keep a clean wind blowing through my heart—CROWELL, 55
God of grave nights—WILKINSON, 21
God, though this life is but a wraith—UNTERMEYER, 45
God, we don't like to complain—UNTERMEYER, 17
Goddes love is unescapable as nature's environment, which if a man—ANONYMOUS, 57
Grow old along with me—R. BROWN-ING, 121

Happy the man, of mortals happiest he —GRANVILLE, 61
Hark to the sound of chiming bells—BROWN, 117
He built a house; time laid it in the dust—R. M. JOHNSON, 59
He leads us on—ANONYMOUS, 62
He prayeth best, who loveth best—COLERIDGE, 62
He saves the sheep, the goats he doth not save—M. ARNOLD, 59
He that is down needs fear no fall—BUNYAN, 132
Henceforward, listen as we will—WHITTIER, 87
Here, in this little Bay—PATMORE, 92
Here is a quiet room—COX, 21

Herself is not there, being Beauty Eternal, alive—MASEFIELD, 157
His magic was not far to seek—LOWELL, 65
How do I love thee? Let me count the ways—E. B. BROWNING, 6
How many of us ever stop to think—ANONYMOUS, 99
How old I am! I'm eighty years—NADAU, 18
How swift the summer goes—MASE-FIELD, 67

I bought a gay-roofed little house upon a sunny hill—DARROUGH, 143
I cannot say, and I will not say—RILEY, 9
I come in the little things—UNDER-HILL, 52
I crave, dear Lord—RILEY, 71
I dedicate myself to thee, O God—ANONYMOUS, 66
I have a friend whose stillness rests me so—V. JOHNSON, 51
I have a rendezvous with Death—SEEGER, 69
I have more food than I can eat—HENSEY, 102
"I have no faith in men," you say—ANONYMOUS, 103
I heard a bird at break of day—PERCY, 112
I heard the bells on Christmas Day—LONGFELLOW, 23
I hold with none who think not work a boon—ANONYMOUS, 30
I long for household voices gone—WHITTIER, 44
I love the Brooks which down their channels fret—WORDSWORTH, 145
"I love you, mother," said little John —ALLISON, 69
I make a pilgrimage to find the God —MARKHAM, 125
I never knew the earth had so much gold—UNTERMEYER, 42
I never saw a moor—DICKINSON, 22
I never think of God—W. MACDON-ALD, 72
I remember, I remember—HOOD, 70
I saw a stranger yestreen—ANONYMOUS, 126

Praise to the living God—Anonymous,
167
Praise we the Lord, who made all
beauty—Wilson, 19

Ring out, wild bells, to the wild sky—
Tennyson, 125

Say not, the struggle naught availeth—
Clough, 128
See! in the rocks of the world—M.
Arnold, 167
See the sole bliss Heaven could on all
bestow—Pope, 43
Seek not afar for beauty. Lo! it glows—
Savage, 38
She never touched with skillful brush
the canvas—Freer, 98
Shun delays, they breed remorse—
Southwell, 119
Sleep sweetly through the healing night
—Gates, 58
Slight those who say, amidst their
sickly healths—Herbert, 126
Snowflakes, falling, falling — Webb,
132
So I go on, not knowing—Brainard,
157
So live that when thy summons comes
to join—Bryant, 140
So long as there are homes to which
men turn—Crowell, 133
Sometimes I say an extra prayer—
McCullough, 47
Souls of men! Why will ye scatter—
Faber, 97
Speak, History! Who are Life's victors?
—Story, 164
Spring has now unwrapped the flowers
—Anonymous, 49
Sunset and evening star—Tennyson,
30

Teach me, Father, how to go—Mark-
ham, 138
That cause can neither be lost nor
stayed—Ostergaard, 11
The April winds are magical—Emer-
son, 7
The boy lay relaxed upon his back—
Myers, 73
The bravest battle that ever was fought
—Miller, 98

The cat stretched himself—Myers,
168
The cloud-capp'd towers, the gorgeous
palaces—Shakespeare, 158
The cry of men's anguish went up unto
God—Anonymous, 131
The curfew tolls the knell of parting
day—Gray, 41
The dark cat, Death—Brown, 32
The day becomes more solemn and
serene—Shelley, 68
The earth has grown old with its bur-
den of care—Brooks, 23
The groves were God's first temples,
Ere man learned—Bryant, 55
The heavens are declaring the Lord's
endless glory—Beethoven, 64
The kiss of the sun for pardon—
Gurney, 102
The Living God, The God that makes
the world—Gilman, 88
The night has a thousand eyes—
Bourdillon, 103
The night is beautiful—Anonymous,
11
The old order changeth, yielding place
to new—Tennyson, 109
The One bethought Him to make man
—Pai Ta-Shun, 108
The preparation of an evening meal—
Crowell, 44
The quality of mercy is not strain'd—
Shakespeare, 120
The radiant symbol of Easter is wings
—Morton, 164
The sea is mighty, but a mightier
sways—Bryant, 129
The shades of night were falling fast
—Longfellow, 46
The sumac has flamed in the uplands
—Anonymous, 123
The summer days are come again—S.
Longfellow, 136
The sun be warm and kind—Powers,
12
The sun, the moon, the stars, the seas,
the hills and the plains—Tennyson,
65
The toil-worn Cotter frae his labor goes
—Burns, 28
The very God! think Abib; dost thou
think—R. Browning, 2

[ 374 ]

The world stands out on either side—
MILLAY, 86
The year's at the spring—R. BROWN-
ING, 56
Then came the Autumne, all in yellow
clad—SPENSER, 8
There always will be gardens—LEVER-
IDGE, 141
There be who are afraid to fear—
THOMAS, 29
There is a beauty at the goal of life—
LAMPMAN, 83
There is a plan far greater than the plan
you know—ANONYMOUS, 142
There is a tale of Faustus—that one
day—LEE-HAMILTON, 47
There is a tide in the affairs of men—
SHAKESPEARE, 146
There is no death! The stars go down—
MCCREERY, 141
There is no flock, however watched and
tended—H. W. LONGFELLOW, 124
There is no unbelief—CASE, 153
There lies the port, the vessel puffs her
sail—TENNYSON, 26
There's a breathless hush in the close
to-night—NEWBOLT, 155
There's a part of the sun in the apple—
BAMBERGER, 111
There's but one gift that all our dead
desire—ANONYMOUS, 15
There they stand—MURDOCK, 132
There was a time when meadow, grove,
and stream—WORDSWORTH, 76
There where it is we do not need the
wall—FROST, 134
These are the gifts I ask of thee—
VAN DYKE, 8
These are the things I prize—ANONY-
MOUS, 143
They borrowed a bed to lay His head—
ANONYMOUS, 61
Thine are these orbs of light and shade
—TENNYSON, 74
This house is built of mortar and of
wood—CROWELL, 115
This is my prayer to Thee my Lord—
TAGORE, 52
This is the charge I keep as mine—
—HILL, 100
This is the church of my dreams—
MOORE, 24
This is the day of light—BERWALD, 144

Tho' growing with scarce a showing—
ROSSETTI, 115
Thou blossom bright with autumn dew
—BRYANT, 149
Thou hearest the nightingale begin
the song of spring—BLAKE, 13
Thou perfect master — ANONYMOUS,
145
Thou who sendest sun and rain—
CHADWICK, 145
Thus he dwells in all—R. BROWNING,
61
To be a girl, and see—ANONYMOUS,
148
To Mercy, Pity, Peace, and Love—
BLAKE, 35
True symbol of equality in worth— T.
WHITE, 150
Turn thou the key upon our thought,
dear Lord—SHEARD, 115
Two went to pray? Oh, rather say—
CRASHAW, 75

Under the wide and starry sky—
STEVENSON, 123
Up to me sweet childhood looketh—
ANONYMOUS, 112

We are the music-makers—O'SHAUGH-
NESSY, 99
We cannot kindle when we will—M.
ARNOLD, 96
We can only see a little of the ocean—
ANONYMOUS, 142
We die not at all, for our deeds re-
main—ANONYMOUS, 90
We get no good—E. B. BROWNING,
58
We live by Faith; but Faith is not the
slave—WHITTIER, 123
We thank thee, Lord, for eyes to see
—BROWN, 165
We will follow the upward road today
—EDGAR, 111
Welcome, wild North-easter—KINGS-
LEY, 107
Westward I chanced to look, ere yet
the night—LEPAGE, 15
What is death? A little broadening of a
ripple—ANONYMOUS, 160
What is more worth than rubies? Is it
wisdom—SALEEBY, 142

## INDEX OF PROSE BY AUTHOR

# INDEX OF PROSE BY TITLE

## INDEX OF PRAYERS BY AUTHOR

Harlow, S. Ralph, 304
Hunter, John, 273

James, Lionel, 312
Johnson, Samuel, 316

Kalil, Eleazar, 317
Kempis, Thomas à, 311
Kingsley, Charles, 314, 320

Laud, William, 291
Loyola, Ignatius de, 299

McComb, Samuel, 306
MacKenzie, Jean, 287
Martineau, James, 314
Milton, John, 283
Myers, A. J. William, 281, 294, 305, 312

Myers, A. J. William and Schilling, Alma N., 285

Orchard, W. E., 319

Plato, 310

Rauschenbusch, Walter, 274, 304

St. Dionysius, 316
Sangster, Margaret, 296
Slattery, Charles Lewis, 300
Stevenson, Robert Louis, 286
Stewart, Mary, 323
Stidger, William L., 278

Taylor, Jeremy, 323
Tipton, Louis Campbell, 320

Vernier, Philippe, 306

# INDEX OF PRAYERS BY TITLE

# INDEX OF APHORISMS BY AUTHOR

[ 382 ]

# INDEX OF APHORISMS BY FIRST LINE

An education is good—ANONYMOUS, 348

An ounce of mirth—FULLER, 346

And silence like a poultice comes— HOLMES, 358

And while I rejoice—WEBB, 356

Applaud us when we run—STEVENSON, 343

As a man thinketh—BIBLE, 350

As long as lynching goes on—TAGORE, 355

As there comes a warm sunbeam— HAWTHORNE, 348

As thou dost desire—ZOROASTER, 358

At all times and everywhere—ON CHINESE GORDON'S TOMB, 339

Be good, sweet maid—KINGSLEY, 342

Be inspired with the belief—GLADSTONE, 341

Be like the bird—ANONYMOUS, 331

Be not afraid of enthusiasm—GUIZOT, 328

Be perfect, be of good comfort— BIBLE, 350

Be stirring as the time—SHAKESPEARE, 355

Beware of prejudice—BABA, 347

Blessed are the peacemakers—BIBLE, 359

Blessed are the pure in heart—BIBLE, 359

Books are the food of youth—CICERO, 332

Books we know—WORDSWORTH, 356

Bring orchids, bring fox-glove spire— TENNYSON, 336

Christianity is not merely a creed— STALKER, 344

Christmas: 'Tis the season—IRVING, 341

Did I tell you that I have always—GALTON, 356

Do not pray for easy lives—BROOKS, 347

Do not remove the fly—CHINESE PROVERB, 335

Earth's noblest thing—LOWELL, 336

Even a child is known—BIBLE, 356

Every day is a fresh beginning— COOLIDGE, 329

Every one truly lives—BROWN, 344

Everywhere I go people thank me— FLEMING, 351

Except a living man—KINGSLEY, 344

For books are more than books— LOWELL, 353

For every child spiritual and moral training—THE CHILDREN'S CHARTER, 349

For the glory of the morning— ANONYMOUS, 329

For the morning will come—CHURCHILL, 357

For why?—because the good old rule— WORDSWORTH, 353

Free will—one's ability—COMPTON, 338

Friendship is a thing most necessary— ARISTOTLE, 337

From our own selves—CALLON, 352

Gales may blow and frosts may come —ROSSETTI, 329

George Carver said that he thought— BUSHNELL, 358

Give all to love—EMERSON, 336

Give love, and love to your heart will flow—ANONYMOUS, 342

Give what you have—LONGFELLOW, 338

Go with God—OLD SPANISH FAREWELL, 355

God alone is Lord of the Conscience —PRESBYTERIAN CONFESSION OF FAITH, 354

God gave us not a spirit—BIBLE, 358

God hath made of one blood—BIBLE, 350

God hath not given us—BIBLE, 347

God is greater than all our conceptions—WHITWELL, 348

God is no respector of persons— BIBLE, 359

God likes far better—G. MACDONALD, 345

God prefers a loving sinner—ANONYMOUS, 339

God sleeps in a stone—IRENÆUS, 330

God speaks to me—ANONYMOUS, 330

God taught me to read—INGELOW, 332

In practice the great end—GLADSTONE, 353

In Springtime a fair world of flowers— ANONYMOUS, 332

In the Spring a fuller crimson—TENNYSON, 335

In thy will is our peace—DANTE, 336

In War, Resolution—BRITISH WAR MEMORIAL, FRANCE, 354

Inasmuch as ye have done it—BIBLE, 359

Is death the last sleep—SCOTT, 339

Isaac Walton quotes the saying— BARRIE, 356

It is better to light—CHINESE PROVERB, 357

It is good to be children—DICKENS, 342

It is the duty of all—BUCHAN, 346

It is to some a disquieting—SHEPHERD, 337

It will never rain roses—ANONYMOUS, 352

It's good to have money—LORIMER, 335

It's the cleverest thing in the world— MAARTENS, 342

Jesus increased in wisdom—BIBLE, 358

Just laws are no restraint—FROUDE, 332

Keep a halo about life—ANONYMOUS, 325

Kingsley said to Whittier—WHITTIER, 327

Kneel always when you light—OXENHAM, 325

Know how sublime a thing it is— LONGFELLOW, 354

Know then thyself—POPE, 338

Learning without thought—CONFUCIUS, 345

Leonidas with his thousand—HERODOTUS, 351

Let knowledge grow from more to more—TENNYSON, 355

Let the following be your watchwords —TOLSTOY, 333

Let us never forget—MAETERLINCK, 342

Let us not burden our remembrances —SHAKESPEARE, 335

Like the beacon lights—EPICTETUS, 355

Love God, and you will throw off— FÉNELON, 348

Love is . . . a simple fire-side thing— LOWELL, 342

Love is the inspiration of the poet— ANONYMOUS, 352

Love's very pain is sweet—SHELLEY, 334

Loveliness needs not the foreign aid— THOMPSON, 337

Luck means the hardships—O'RELL, 333

Make no mistake about this—BIBLE, 350

Make use of time—TAYLOR, 349

Make yourselves nests—RUSKIN, 328

Man must work with his hands— BIBLE, 350

Marriage: The light of love—LONGFELLOW, 339

May the wee moosie—SCOTTISH PROVERB, 332

Meaning thereby that a man cannot be taught—MOORE, 351

Men at some times are masters— SHAKESPEARE, 335

Money is an article—ANONYMOUS, 343

Money lost, little lost—OLD ENGLISH PROVERB, 334

More things are wrought by prayer— TENNYSON, 359

Most of the evils you fear are false— EPICURUS, 356

Most people are bothered by those passages—TWAIN, 353

Music is love—LANIER, 326

Nature is always calling to us—THOMSON, 333

Never miss an opportunity—ANONYMOUS, 349

Never to tire—AMIEL, 328

Night is a good herdsman—GAELIC PROVERB, 340

No heaven can come to us—FRA ANGELICO, 353

No one could tell me—ANONYMOUS, 341

No one is so insignificant—ANONYMOUS, 348

[ 387 ]

The doing of evil—COLERIDGE, 348
The doors of wisdom are never shut—FRANKLIN, 355
The foundation of domestic happiness—LANDOR, 345
The foundation of every state—DIOGENES, 330
The good person increases—ANONYMOUS, 331
The great use of life—JAMES, 338
The High Priest of Science—STATUE OF SIR ISAAC NEWTON, 354
The human race is divided—HOLMES, 346
The law of the upward urge—WILLOUGHBY, 336
The liberty of each citizen—FRENCH REVOLUTION CONVENTION, 336
The love of all—E. B. BROWNING, 351
The madonnas I see—APPLEGARTH, 326
The measure of our sacrifice—ANONYMOUS, 341
The meat of the elephant—BANTU PROVERB, 353
The mind is ever interested—PATTERSON, 326
The most important part of education—PLATO, 338
The most regal gift—WU MING-FU, 325
The most wasted of all days—FRENCH PROVERB, 341
The nearness of God—BIBLE, 350
The omnipotence of God—PRINGLE-PATTISON, 334
The process of evolution—SMUTS, 337
The prodigal son—REICHELT, 327
The roof hides our stars—CHINESE INSCRIPTION, 357
The simple fact that we are compelled—MACMURRAY, 339
The size of the deed—ANONYMOUS, 355
The spiritual interpretation of life—KING, 330
The statement that Jesus—DEISSMAN, 339
The superior man cultivates himself—CHINESE PROVERB, 344
The tongue speaks wisdom—HOMER, 333

The trifles of our daily lives—ANONYMOUS, 342
The true gentleman is God's servant—ANONYMOUS, 347
The ways of God—PERSIAN PROVERB, 325
The will of God—STREETER, 336
The witness in the souls of men—NORTH, 330
There are six things that bring success—ANONYMOUS, 349
There are two freedoms—KINGSLEY, 346
There are two heavens—HUNT, 331
There cannot be much preaching—BUSHNELL, 330
There is more delight—JAPANESE PROVERB, 341
"There is no God"—CLOUGH, 331
There is not enough darkness—ANONYMOUS, 357
There is not the faintest trace—OESTERLEY, 337
There is nothing like books—PARKER, 357
There is one furnace—PANIN, 337
These hath God married—ANONYMOUS, 355
They are slaves who dare not be—LOWELL, 340
They dwelt among the bravely dumb—ANONYMOUS, 330
Thou art welcome—ANONYMOUS, 344
Three things, I've heard tell—UNWIN, 352
Time flies—OLD ENGLISH SUNDIAL, 335
'Tis said that Galilee in Spring—HOFFMAN, 334
To be honest, to be kind—STEVENSON, 350
To every hearth a little fire—ANONYMOUS, 352
To have faith is to create—FAIRLESS, 326
To know what you prefer—STEVENSON, 341
To love my crooked neighbor—ANONYMOUS, 351
To me every hour—WHITMAN, 335
To one who has been long in city pent—KEATS, 329

[ 389 ]

# ACKNOWLEDGMENTS

Acknowledgment is made on the copyright pages in the front of this volume to publishers and others for permission to reproduce in this anthology selections covered by copyright. Earnest efforts have been made to communicate with all copyright owners and to respect their rights. If any have been infringed upon, it is hoped that the editor may be informed of his unintentional oversight that proper credit may be given on the copyright pages of future editions.

Acknowledgment is also made to the following publishers, individuals and periodicals for permission to include the material indicated.

GEORGE ALLEN & UNWIN, Ltd. for "Spending Ourselves, Not Getting" from *Pillars of Security* by Lord Beveridge.

THOMAS BAKER for "The Most Certain Sign That We Love God" from *Interior Castle* by St. Teresa.

G. BELL & SONS, Ltd. for "Magna Est Veritas" from *Poems by Coventry Patmore*.

LORD BESSBOROUGH for "Satisfactions from Gardens."

A. & C. BLACK, Ltd. for "The Rune of Hospitality," an anonymous poem arranged by Kenneth MacLeod in *The Road to the Isles*.

WM. BLACKWOOD & SONS LTD. as the authorized publishers for "We Cannot Choose Happiness," "The Choir Invisible," "Making Life Worth While," and "Stradivarius" by George Eliot.

MRS. ROSALIE BOYLE for "Morning."

THE BRITISH BROADCASTING CORPORATION for the following anonymous selections from *New Every Morning*: "All Classes," "All in Responsible Positions," "Anxieties and Fears," "Artists and Craftsmen, Teachers and Writers," "Brotherly Love," "Build Us That Better World," "Daily Duties," "Dignity of Labor," "Dignity of Service," "Drivers of Cars," "Evening at Home," "Fellowship of Suffering," "For All Animals," "Foreign Policy," "Fullness of Life," "Glorious Liberty," "Great and Simple Joys," "Help and Refuge," "In Thine Image," "The Joy of This Day," "A More Excellent Way," "Morning," "The Nation," "Night Workers," "Perfect Freedom," "Sailors and Fishermen," "Thou Art Always Near," "Thy Strength Is Sufficient," "Thy Wisdom Is Our Guide," "True Followers," "Vision of Our Land," and "Workers in Industry."

THE BRITISH WEEKLY for "Thank You" by F. E. Christmas.

CHRISTY & MOORE, Ltd. for "At the Gate of the Year" by M. Louise Haskins.

THE CLARENDEN PRESS for "An Early Greek Prayer," anonymous, translated by Gilbert Murray in *Five Stages of Greek Religion*; "Beauty, Truth and Love Are One," "Love Thou Art Mine," and "Perfect Thy Kingdom" from *Poetical Works of Robert Bridges*.

W. B. CONKEY COMPANY for "To-day" and "The Winds of Fate" by Ella Wheeler Wilcox.

THE DALHOUSIE REVIEW for "The Nobility of 'Common' Men" from *Windjammers and Bluenose Sailors* by C. McKay.

THE DETROIT FREE PRESS for "There Is No Unbelief" by Lizzie York Case.

THE T. EATON CO., LTD. for "Peace at Last," anonymous.

RABBI LOUIS FINKELSTEIN for his translation of "Thou" by Isaac Levi ben Meir.

FIRST CONGREGATIONAL CHURCH, and the boys and girls of the First Grade Junior Church School, West Hartford, Conn., for "Snow Litany" and "Thanksgiving."

HARRY EMERSON FOSDICK for "Life of Our Souls" and "Public Worship."

THE GLOBE AND MAIL, Toronto, for "How Scrooge Spent Christmas," the condensed version of the last stave of A *Christmas Carol* by Charles Dickens; and Lilian Leveridge for "There Always Will Be Gardens"; and Terence Sheard for "Poems for Sleep" by Verna Sheard.

THE H. W. GRAY COMPANY, Inc. for "List to the Lark," anonymous (publishers of the complete edition, with music).

GREENBERG PUBLISHER for "The Petrified Fern" from *In a Valley Centuries Ago* by Mary L. B. Branch.

WILLIAM HEINEMANN, LTD. for "Love Is Stronger than Death" from *Dream Tales and Prose Poems* by Ivan Sergiewich Turgenev, translated by Constance Garnett.

JOHN O'LONDON'S WEEKLY for "Let Me Keep the Glow of Wonder," anonymous.

TOYOHIKO KAGAWA for "Tears" and "Where God Is."

GRENVILLE KLEISER for "Give Thanks," and "Waking Prayer"; "Carcassonne" by Gustave Nadau, quoted in *Humorous Hits* edited by Grenville Kleiser.

GLORIA LAURISTON and MACMILLAN & COMPANY OF CANADA LIMITED for "Let No Man Fear the Night" from *Voices of Victory* by Gloria Lauriston.

LONGMANS, GREEN & CO. LTD., London, for "Intellectual Death" (from "The Belfast Address") from *Fragments of Science* by John Tyndall.

MACMILLAN & CO., LTD., London, for "Endure Suffering" from *Francis of Assisi* by Margaret Oliphant; "Endure Trouble," "He Doeth Much Who Loveth Much," "Keep Thyself in Peace," "Sayings from Thomas à Kempis," and "The Wonderful Power of Love," by Thomas à Kempis from the W. Benham edition of the *Imitation of Christ*; and the author's trustees, for "My Garden" from *Collected Poems of Thomas Edward Brown*; and the author's representative, Mr. Owen Rolleston, for "The Earth and Man" (from "A Little Sun, a Little Rain") by Stopford Brooke, from *Poems of Youth* edited by Alice Cecilia Cooper.

THE REV. JOHN G. MAGEE for "High Flight" written by his late son, Pilot Officer John G. Magee, Jr.

THE MEDICI SOCIETY LTD. for "Jack Frost" and "The Snowflake Fairies" from *Christmas* by Marion St. John Webb.

METHUEN & CO., LTD. for "Having Eyes We See Not" and "The House of Beauty and Light" from *The World I Live In* by Helen Keller.

MRS. FRANCES M. MORTON for "Wings for Easter."

THE NATIONAL SUNDAY SCHOOL UNION, London, for "Pledge of the Seven Men of Preston" from *The Teaching of Temperance and Self-Control* by E. C. Urwin.

CAPTAIN FRANCIS NEWBOLT, executor, and JOHN MURRAY LTD. for "Vitae Lampada" from *Admirals All and Other Poems* by Sir Henry Newbolt.

OLIPHANTS, LTD. for "Adoration," "Blessed Art Thou, O Lord," "Blessed Be Thou, O God," "Hallowed Be Thy Name," "Meditation," "A Prayer for Grace," "Prayer on Awaking," "Thanksgiving," "We Praise God for Light," "We Thank Thee, O Lord" from *Lancelot Andrewes and His Private Devotions*.

MISS ERICA OXENHAM, The American Tract Society, and Methuen & Co., Ltd. for "All's Well," "The Pilgrim Way," and "Seeds" from *Bees in Amber* by John Oxenham.

OXFORD UNIVERSITY PRESS for "Man: Son of God" from *Discourses and Manual of Epictetus* translated by P. E. Matheson.

PUNCH for "Between Midnight and Morning" by Owen Seaman.

THE RIVERSIDE CHURCH, New York City, for "To the Worshipper" from the Church Calendar, June 9, 1946.

SATURDAY NIGHT, Toronto, for "The Dark Cat" by Audrey Alexandra Brown.

GEORGE BERNARD SHAW and CONSTABLE AND COMPANY, Ltd. for "Joan of Arc" from *Saint Joan* by George Bernard Shaw.

THE ROBERT SIMPSON COMPANY, Ltd. for "The White Road" by Bliss Carman.

WILLIAM L. STIDGER for "A Beatitude."

MRS. STEPHEN TALLENTS for "Roses in the Heart" from *Book about Roses* by S. R. Hole.

THE NEW YORK TIMES and ALICE FERRIN HENSEY for "The Needy"; and Lalia Mitchell Thornton for "Maple Sap."

CHARLES HANSON TOWNE for "An Easter Canticle."

MR. G. M. TREVELYAN for "Turning Grief into Loving Service" from *Life of John Bright*.

A. P. WATT & SON and the author's executors for "Where Did You Come From, Baby Dear?" from *Poetical Works of George MacDonald*.

MRS. G. P. WELLS and the author's executors for "Only with God" from *Mr. Britling Sees It Through* by H. G. Wells.

SIR THOMAS WHITE for "The Tomb of the Unknown Soldier."

YALE UNIVERSITY PRESS, London, for "The Great Way" by Li Ki, "Golden Sayings of Confucius" and "How to Treat People" by Confucius; "The Principle of Loving All" by Motse from *China's Spiritual Inheritance* by Warren Horton Stuart; "Carol of Beauty" by Steuart Wilson, "Flower Carol" and "Easter Carol," anonymous, translated by Percy Dearmer from *Oxford Book of Carols*; and the representatives of the late Mr. Aylmer Maude for "Where Love Is There God Is" by Leo Tolstoy from *Twenty-three Tales of Leo Tolstoy* translated by L. and A. Maude.

# PERSONAL INDEX

# PERSONAL INDEX

# PERSONAL INDEX

# PERSONAL INDEX